THE MOTIVATION SOLUTION

A GLOBAL INITIATIVE

Revised Edition

John E. LaMuth

American University of Sovereign Nations

FAIRHAVEN BOOK PUBLISHERS

With Foreword by Darryl R. J. Macer, Ph.D.

Library of Congress Catalog Card Number – 2012910570

Fairhaven Book Publishers
A Safe Haven in a "Sea of Knowledge"
P.O. Box 105
Lucerne Valley, CA 92356 - USA

values@charactervalues.com
www.themotivationsolution.net

Publisher's Cataloging-In-Publication Data

The motivation solution: a global initiative-revised edition / John E. LaMuth, Author.

   202 p. : ill. ; cm.
   ISBN: 978-1-929649-15-0

1. Behaviorism--Terminology. 2. Ethics--Terminology. 3. Affect (Psychology).
    4. Virtues-values--Classification. 5. Ethical hierarchy--Technology. 6. Moti-
    vation -- Moral and ethical aspects.
I. LaMuth, John E., author.

BF636 .L36 2014
158.4   2012910570

Printed on acid-free paper

Wholesale Distributor:
Ingram Book Group Inc.
La Vergne, Tennessee 37086

TABLE of CONTENTS

ALSO BY THE AUTHOR ...

Communication Breakdown:
Decoding the Riddle of Mental Illness

———————————————

Character Values:
Promoting a Virtuous Lifestyle

———————————————

A Diagnostic Classification of the
Emotions: A Three-Digit Coding
System for Affective Language

———————————————

Challenges to World Peace:
A Global Initiative

FOREWORD

Motivation is a quality the world increasingly appears to be lacking. Despite the tragedies facing society on a daily basis, we still do not appear fully willing to move towards a sustainable pattern of living. What potential solutions remain for our global community? How can countries around the world learn to live together in harmony? In his current book, John LaMuth proposes a *Motivation Solution* based upon a comprehensive classification of the traditional groupings of virtues, values, and ideals. Through a systematic analysis of ethical motives and emotions (and ways to visualize these through the *motivational matrix*), we now have many further options to consider.

In 2002, when I first proposed the Human Behaviourome Project, John LaMuth and I entered into correspondence on how the ethics of human behavior may adequately be described, with much discussion to the extent that human ideas can be classified. In his subsequent books, John has mapped many of these behavioral concepts to physical locations within the brain. This is particularly interesting being that we live in an age that celebrates the mapping of the human brain. Despite our expanding knowledge of what makes people think as individuals, group behaviors appear to play an equally crucial role for determining our life on the planet (and the survival of our future world). As you read this book, please reflect on your own behaviors and how they might potentially be improved. Furthermore, how do we relate action to ethical dilemmas and the choices we ultimately make?

This book is a great read, and readers may further provide feedback/comments to John, who has consistently worked towards improving our understanding of human behavior in general. This should also motivate readers to more deeply reflect upon their own theory of human existence. This book covers a broad range of prescient ideas. Should one live in a culture that employs differing solutions to the ethical choices we face (in addition to those described in this book), then it proves crucial to explore how these are truly different. Think also about what actually appears different, and is it really all that different in the end. Perhaps such motivations are shared in common across all cultures. This book allows us to consider if this truly is the case...

Darryl R.J. Macer, Ph.D., Hon.D.
Provost, *American Univ. of Sovereign Nations*
Director, *Eubios Ethics Institute*
February, 2015

Dedicated to All Who Seek a Broader
Understanding of Ethics in Their Lives

PART-I

1

AN INTRODUCTION TO
THE MOTIVATION SOLUTION

A planetary system of ethics is a goal that has long been anticipated on the world scene today. Although organized religion has long been celebrated as the standard bearer for the promotion of a virtuous life style, the various conflicts afflicting many of the major world religions clearly expose the inherent weakness to such a simplistic interpretation. Ideally, a scientific foundation for such a global moral perspective should prove exceedingly beneficial. Here, a formal behavioral tie-in with ethical principles proves particularly effective for removing such cultural stumbling blocks. In particular, a foundation within behavioral psychology proves to be particularly effective: invoking instinctual principles shared in common as a human species (as well as the rest of animal kingdom) as general unifying themes. When expanded to include the more abstract human-cultural levels; namely, group and universal authority, the affiliated traditional groupings of virtues/values rightfully enters the picture.

A radically new model of motivational behavior is currently called for, one that melds modern behavioral psychology with the long-standing traditions associated with value ethics: a trend encompassing the group, universal, humanitarian, and transcendental realms of inquiry. This comprehensive fusion linking instinctual conditioning with ethical philosophy permits the first such grand-scale synthesis of motivated behavior. Indeed, an ever-increasing motivational culture gap is becoming ever more apparent amongst developed nations. An emerging privileged status within Western culture has led to what is increasingly termed "The Entitlement Generation." What is sorely needed is a return to the rugged individualism and can-do-spirit that propelled the U.S. to its original legendary greatness.

The currently proposed *motivation solution* endeavors to provide the first clear dynamical understanding for the general public, providing a grand-scale synthesis of the virtues/values in correlation with behavioral principles. Through this systematic behavioral understanding, the reader is provided with unique examples of this motivational dynamic in action, as well as insights towards employment within one's personal life. The specific details for such an ethical achievement invoke the entire span of human culture as a ten-level hierarchy of personal, group, universal, humanitarian, and transcendental domains (comprising both authority and follower roles). Furthermore, this ascending hierarchy formally appeals to the schematic principles underlying Set Theory. Here, the elementary concepts of the one, the many, and the absolute are specified in terms of the personal, group, and universal authority realms, respectively.

Each of these distinctive conceptual levels is further associated with its own unique complement of ethical/motivational terms. This master ten-level hierarchy of authority/follower roles is uniquely correlated with over two-hundred individual virtuous terms. The traditional ethical listings defined within this system all appear linked on an intuitive level, suggesting a clear sense of overall cohesiveness, the complete breakdown of which now will be described.

THE MOTIVATIONAL MATRIX

The key conceptual innovation arises as a direct outcome of the fledgling science of Communication Theory, borrowing the crucial concept of the metaperspective. It is defined as a higher-order perspective on the viewpoint held by another: schematically defined as "this is how I see you-seeing me." The higher-order groupings of virtues/values are ordered as subsets within this hierarchy of metaperspectives, each more abstract

110	111
Nostalgia	Guilt
112	**113**
Desire	Worry

EGO STATES
(Personal Authority)

120	121
Approval	Leniency
122	**123**
Solicitousness	Submission

ALTER EGO STATES
(Personal Follower)

130	131
Glory	Honor
132	**133**
Dignity	Integrity

PERSONAL IDEALS
(Group Authority)

140	141
Prudence	Justice
142	**143**
Temperance	Fortitude

CARDINAL VIRTUES
(Group Representative)

150	151
Providence	Liberty
152	**153**
Civility	Austerity

CIVIL LIBERTIES
(Spiritual Authority)

160	161
Faith	Hope
162	**163**
Charity	Decency

THEOLOGICAL VIRTUES
(Spiritual Disciple)

170	171
Grace	Free Will
172	**173**
Magnanimity	Equanimity

ECUMENICAL IDEALS
(Humanitarian Authority)

180	181
Beauty	Truth
182	**183**
Goodness	Wisdom

CLASSICAL GREEK VALUES
(Humanitarian Follower)

190	191
Tranquility	Equality
192	**193**
Love	Peace

HUMANISTIC VALUES
(Transcendental Authority)

100	101
Ecstasy	Bliss
102	**103**
Joy	Harmony

MYSTICAL VALUES
(Transcendental Follower)

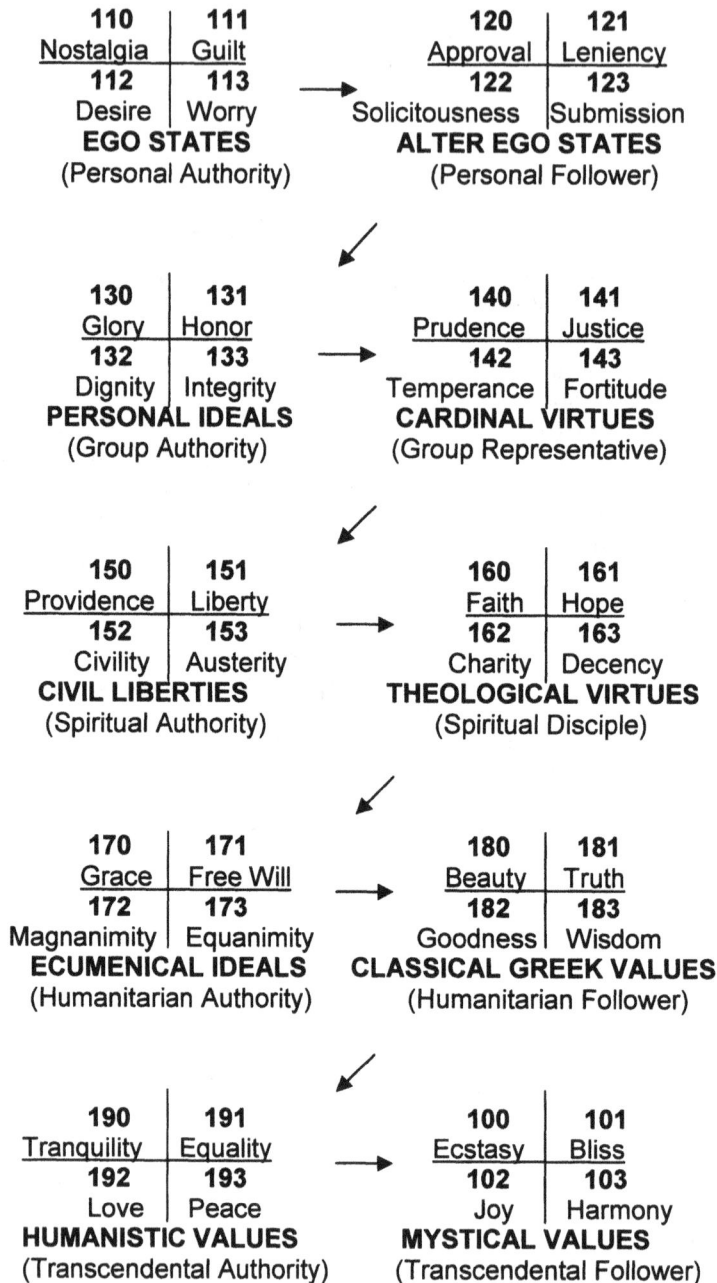

Fig. 1 -- The Major Virtues, Values, and Ideals

grouping building upon that which it supersedes. Take, for example, the cardinal virtues (prudence, justice, temperance, and fortitude), the theological virtues (faith-hope-charity-decency), and the classical Greek values (beauty-truth-goodness-wisdom). Each of these traditional groupings is further subdivided into four subordinate terms permitting precise point-for-point stacking within the hierarchy of metaperspectives. Additional listings of ethical terms can further be added into the mix: namely, the civil liberties (providence-liberty-civility-austerity), the humanistic values (peace-love-tranquility-equality), the mystical values (ecstasy-bliss-joy-harmony), etc. When taken in concert, the complete ten-level hierarchy of virtuous terms emerges in full detail, as partially reproduced in the compact table below (including the preliminary behavioral antecedents).

Appetite • Rewards	**Aversion • Leniency**
Nostalgia • Approval	**Guilt • Blame**
Glory • Prudence	**Honor • Justice**
Providence • Faith	**Liberty • Hope**
Grace • Beauty	**Free-Will • Truth**
Tranquility • Ecstasy	**Equality • Bliss**
+ Reinforce • Approach	**– Reinforce • Avoidance**
Desire • Solicitousness	**Worry • Submissive.**
Dignity • Temperance	**Integrity • Fortitude**
Civility • Charity	**Austerity • Decency**
Magnanim. • Goodness	**Equanimity • Wisdom**
Love • Joy	**Peace • Harmony**

This cohesive hierarchy of virtues, values, and ideals proves exceedingly comprehensive in scope, accounting for virtually every major theme celebrated in the Western ethical tradition. It is particularly easy to gain a sense of the increasing degree of abstraction when scanning the individual columns from top to bottom. The traditional sequences of terms line up seamlessly within this hierarchy of metaperspectives. Indeed, it proves exceedingly unlikely that this cohesive style of system could have arisen solely by chance. Furthermore, this ethical hierarchy mirrors the specialization of personal, group, spiritual, humanitarian, and transcendental realms within human society as a whole: which (when further specialized into authority/follower roles) accounts for the full ten-level span of ethical terms.

The major groupings of virtues and values serve as the elementary foundation for the master motivational matrix. This grand-scale unification of ethical principles necessarily argues for a radical reinterpretation of the organizational principles currently under consideration. The key Sali-

ent insight resides in viewing the individual as the rightful product of a diverse range of social and institutional influences. In addition to the most basic one-to-one style of personal interactions, the individual is further incorporated into a broad range of group contexts (namely, work, family, country, etc.), as well as an all-encompassing universal context. These distinctive contexts collectively summate into a unified authority hierarchy consistent with the theoretical principles governing the field of Set Theory. Set Theory remains in full agreement with the three-level model of the power hierarchy: with the unit set, the group set, and the universal set equating with the personal, group, and spiritual levels, respectively.

The concept of a three-level set hierarchy is actually nothing new, proposed centuries earlier by German philosopher, Emmanuel Kant. In his masterpiece, *Critique of Pure Reason*, Kant outlines a comprehensive system of conceptual categories he considers crucial to the formation of the human intellect. Most notable within this system is the relevant category of *quantity*: which Kant further subdivides into the concepts of unity, plurality, and totality. In a more basic conceptual sense, these three fundamental themes equate to the notions of the one, the many, and the absolute: equivalent (in a human social sense) to the personal, group, and spiritual authority levels.

This three-level social hierarchy, although appealing in its simplicity, clearly differs from Set Theory in that complex interactions between individuals do not exist solely in a vacuum, but rather are further specialized into both authority/follower roles. For the personal realm, this amounts to the personal authority and personal follower roles, extending to the group realm as the group authority and group representative variations, culminating with respect to the spiritual authority and spiritual disciple roles. A brief description of each of these authority/follower roles is definitely in order here, outlining the proposed grand unification of virtues, values, and ideals.

The most basic personal level of interaction refers to the one-to-one style of interaction occurring between individuals, much as typically encountered in one's personal friendships. This personal interplay, in turn, is specialized into either authority or follower roles. This is exemplified in the case of the master craftsman who typically remains dependent upon the services of his faithful apprentice. A similar scenario also holds true with respect to the hero and his sidekick, or the celebrity and his straight-man. Flexibility emerges as the key distinguishing feature, with the authority and follower roles complementing one another in terms of such an equitable balance of power. The authority figure formally depends upon the attentions of his follower (as much as the other way around), resulting in an equal balance of power within the personal power realm.

This elementary personal foundation, in turn, extends to the equally pervasive notion of group authority. The group set surpasses the unit set in terms of its expansion to a multitude of elements (or class members) within this group-focused style of context. Personal concerns, accordingly, become subordinate to such a group power base, being that enough followers remain to continue group authority whether or not any single individual decides to desert. In a single stroke, the group authority sets oneself well above any personal power struggles, an innovation exploited since ancient times as the well-established custom of tribal-based authority.

Group authority, in turn, is susceptible to its own unique form of follower countermaneuver: in this case, that expressed by the group representative. The latter's distinctive style of "strike" leverage is fully realized at this juncture, as witnessed in the modern trend towards collective bargaining. By organizing as a union collective, the rank-and-file nominates a shop steward to represent them in negotiations with management. The group representative, in essence, reminds the group authority that the cooperation of the labor pool is crucial for maintaining the group status quo. Here, the group authority (in concert with the group representative) shares an equal balance of power within the group power realm.

A similar pattern further holds true with respect to the remaining spiritual authority level, although this sense of "spiritual" is restricted to the universal sense of the term implicit in Set Theory. In this latter respect, the universal set clearly surpasses the multiplicity of the group domain: in essence, the sum-totality of all such groups within the universal realm. The universal set represents the "group of all potential group sets," a 3rd-order style of set-hierarchy (equivalent to the domain of all mankind). Indeed, whereas group authority surpasses the influence of its individual members, the spiritual authority similarly overrules the strike power of any of its constituent groups, wherein claiming authority over the sum-total of all mankind.

It is true (in practice) that each of the world's religions competes for the beliefs of the world's faithful. In principle, however, such religions vigilantly strive to convert all others, giving further credence to the universal sense of the term. This claim to universality is traditionally made binding through an appeal to God or Messiah-figure. This mystical style of sanction dates to the earliest of times. Here, a king could inspire the loyalty of his troops in the name of a "god of war" far in excess of what might be claimed as a mere mortal ruler.

Taking this trend to the limit, even a realm as abstract as the spiritual authority role must (by definition) be susceptible to its own unique form of follower maneuver: namely, that specified for the spiritual disciple. As spokesman for the spiritual congregation, the spiritual disciple reminds the spiritual authority that the blessings of the faithful are crucial for maintaining the spiritual status quo. Witness the power of the spiritual revolutionary for influencing such diverse historical events as the Protestant Reformation, and even the founding of Christianity, itself.

THE MASTER GROUPINGS OF VIRTUES/VALUES

In summary, the ascending three-level hierarchy of personal, group, and spiritual domains, when further viewed in terms of both authority and follower roles, provides the basic conceptual framework for explaining the grand unified system of virtuous terms. This format is schematically depicted in **Fig. 1**, including the respective three-digit codes for each of the individual virtues and values. This master schematic format (tentatively termed the *motivational matrix* incorporates the major ethical classifications described so far (plus an equivalent number of new ones) for a grand total of ten: serving as the foundation for the remainder of the book to follow.

As the underlying captions serve to indicate, the uppermost three levels of this diagram are designated for the personal, group, and spiritual levels: accounting for the most basic groupings of virtues and ideals. The remaining lowermost pair of levels, in turn, introduce two hitherto unmentioned categories; namely, the humanitarian and transcendental realms, respectively. This additional set of authority levels is classified as uniquely abstract styles of power maneuvers, clearly surpassing the more basic organizational pattern previously established for the lower three levels. A brief description of these final two levels is offered here, for the most abstract listings of virtues and values fall within these final two domains.

Although the spiritual realm is clearly the maximum level of organization (in keeping with the traditions of Set Theory), this very sense of chronological time permits the introduction of the more abstract notion of humanitarian authority. The great theoretical physicist, Albert Einstein defined time as the fourth dimension of the universe, making it exceedingly fitting that this humanitarian theme enters into consideration precisely at the 4th-order level within the power hierarchy. Humanitarian authority transcends the spiritual variety by claiming to speak for all generations of mankind, not just the current one: experienced as past traditionalism or future potentiality. Its extreme sense of generality precludes its identification within any singular social institution rather incorporated into the spiritual (and often political) framework of society as a whole.

This extreme sense of the power of abstraction (when considered in its own right) ultimately serves as the basis for one final innovation within the power hierarchy; namely, the crowning transcendental authority level. Transcendental authority regains the upper hand by transcending the routine sense of concreteness shared in common by the lower levels, an innovation accounting for the most abstract listings of values within the authority hierarchy. The transcendental perspective enters freely into the realm of pure intuition and imagination, wherein forsaking the constraints of ordinary reality for the supreme and incontrovertible realm of pure abstraction. This transcendental domain (in concert with its humanitarian counterpart) is also specialized into both authority/follower roles, for a grand total of four categories. In concert with the six respective roles characterizing the personal, group, and spiritual levels, the master ten-level hierarchy emerges in full detail as depicted in **Fig. 1**.

Although basically only an introductory chapter, a few general observations necessarily can be made with respect to this distinctive schematic format. The ten individual categories of virtues, values, and ideals are organized as descending columns of five groupings each. The left-hand column represents the hierarchy of authority roles, whereas the right specifies the corresponding follower roles. This dual schematic format represents the sum-totality of reciprocating interactions between the authority/follower roles, as the respective directional arrows serve to indicate.

The distinctive groupings of virtues and values for each individual level exhibit their own unique range of distinguishing characteristics. Each is represented as a quartet-style format depicted as quadrants in a pseudo-Cartesian system. The more traditional groupings (such as the cardinal virtues) are already established as four-part listings fitting quite nicely within the quartet-style format. Others (such as the theological virtues) have been supplemented beyond their traditional number in order to achieve a quartet-style status. A number of other groupings are new to the phil-osophical tradition, yet also respecting the quartet-style pattern characterizing the unified hierarchy.

Similar to the reciprocating pattern of authority/follower roles (which build in a hierarchial fashion), the affiliated groupings of virtues, values, and ideals similarly mirror this ascending pattern of organization. These ethical groupings build from the most elementary (the ego and alter ego states) clear up to the most abstract listings targeting the transcendental level (the humanistic and mystical values). This virtuous realm runs the entire gamut of human experience, ranging from the instinctual to the sublime (and everything in between). A brief description of each of these individual ethical groupings is definitely in order here, serving as a basic overview for the remaining detailed treatment to follow.

THE PERSONAL FOUNDATIONS FOR THE MOTIVATIONAL MATRIX

The most rational point of initiation for this comprehensive analysis is certainly the most basic personal level within the power hierarchy. According to the upper-most level shown in **Fig. 1**, the dual categories are respectively listed as the ego states for the personal authority role (guilt-worry-nostalgia-desire) and the alter ego states for the follower role (approval-blame-solicitousness-submissiveness). The behavioral flavor underlying these groupings make them tailor-made for incorporation into the personal power realm, the respective terminology particularly effective for specifying the interpersonal dynamics underlying this elementary level. The specific behavioral rationale behind their particular assignment, as well as the related distinction between the authority and follower roles is an undertaking best reserved for a more detailed treatment in Chapter *2*.

Although only briefly outlined, this initial complement of ego/alter ego states, in turn, serves as the foundation for the remaining listings of virtues, values, and ideals outlined in **Fig. 1**. Indeed, a general pattern of organization emerges from this schematic diagram; namely, the left-hand column is characterized by what are termed the authority ideals: read downwards as the personal ideals, civil liberties, ecumenical ideals, and humanistic values. The right-hand column of follower roles, in turn, specifies a parallel trend based upon the virtues; namely, the cardinal virtues, theological virtues, classical Greek values, and mystical values. For sake of consistency, the initial authority trend will be examined first, followed, in turn, by an equally comprehensive treatment of the sequence of follower roles.

THE AUTHORITY IDEALS

The first mentioned sequence of authority ideals begins with the group authority level; namely, the provisionally termed class of "personal ideals" (glory-honor-dignity-integrity). The personal designition for this grouping might appear somewhat of a misnomer although more properly viewed as ideals within the group sense of the term. These personal ideals, in turn, build directly upon the ego states previously established for the personal authority role, wherein accounting for the hybrid quality of the grouping. In this latter respect, the group authority *gloriously* acts in a nostalgic fashion or *honorably* acts in a guilty fashion towards the personal follower figure. Similarly, he might *dignifiedly* act desirously or worrisomely act with *integrity*, in terms of the more elementary ego states.

The personal ideals collectively derive from the Latin tradition, effectively highlighting the Roman's fascination with the heroic principles. This enduring group focus is primarily expressed in the many symbolisms for royalty and nobility; as in the heraldic traditions of the circle of *glory*, the *honor* point, the cap of *dignity*, and the social symbolisms for *integrity*. Guided by such lofty ideals, the group authority rightly aspires to such noble themes befitting leaders of society.

The next higher level of spiritual authority rates a similar treatment indicative of the respective class of "civil liberties" (providence-liberty-civility-austerity). Each of these themes is prominently featured in the founding of the United States, as collectively celebrated in the precepts of the *Declaration of Independence*. This revolutionary document celebrates divine authority as one of its central premises, invoking the universal rights of man to overrule the tyrannical edicts of English monarch, King George III. Although this designation of *civil liberties* might appear to suggest somewhat of a political context, further analysis reveals the deep spiritual underpinnings for these four basic themes. Indeed, each of these themes was traditionally worshipped as a classical deity in its own right; namely, Providentia, Libertas, Civitas, and Auster. In terms of this "universal" context, *providence* represents a more advanced counterpart of glory, whereas *liberty* makes a similar correspondence to honor. Furthermore, *civility* amounts to a spiritual refinement of dignity, whereas *austerity* denotes integrity from a universal perspective.

The universal prerequisites for spiritual authority, in turn, serve as the foundation for the related concept of humanitarian authority, an innovation firmly rooted within the concept of "historical" time. This enduring humanitarian focus is directly reflected in the abstract listing of ethical terms, provisionally termed the *ecumenical* ideals (grace-freewill-magnanimity-equanimity). The enduring significance of this grouping certainly suggests a common stereotype; namely, timeless themes in keeping with such a grand humanitarian perspective. Although closely affiliated with spiritual concerns, a more detailed analysis clearly reveals a grand humanitarian focus: as reflected in the long tradition of ecumenical councils where generational issues were thrust into focus.

This grouping enjoyed particular favor during the Protestant Reformation. According to the basic tenet of Martin Luther: "By *grace* are thee are saved through faith." These ecumenical ideals add a more enduring historical dimension to the civil liberties previously established for the spiritual tradition. For example, *grace* imparts a more enduring humanitarian significance to providence, whereas *free will* provides a historical perspective for liberty. Similarly, the remaining ecumenical ideals of *magnanimity* and *equanimity* extend a similar mindset to civility and austerity.

The crowning transcendental level ultimately rounds out the stepwise description of authority roles. This transcendental perspective formally appeals to the idealized realm of pure abstraction, in essence, transcending the more concrete nature of the four initial levels. The respective grouping of *humanistic* values (peace-love-tranquility-equality) rightfully enters into consideration here: ideal themes befitting such a lofty transcendental perspective. Each of these terms fits such a supremely abstract perspective, ideals attuned to realms wholly transcending routine experience. These values dates to classical times, worshipped as abstract deities in their own right: namely, Pax (peace), Cupid (love), Quies (tranquility), and Aequitas (equality). Many themes, served as the inspiration for modern movements, such as in the New England Transcendentalists and the Peace Protest against the Vietnam War.

THE ETHICAL FOLLOWER TRADITIONS

The completed description of the authority ideals, in turn, sets the stage for a discussion of the remaining sequence of the follower roles. Whereas the authority hierarchy was based upon the ego states, the remaining follower sequence alternately targets the alter ego states, further extending to the well-established traditions of the cardinal and theological virtues. These two basic categories of virtue have collectively enjoyed a distinguished place of honor in the Western ethical tradition. As their qualifiers imply, the theological virtues (faith-hope-charity-decency) are specific to the spiritual disciple role, whereas the cardinal virtues (prudence-justice-temperance-fortitude), by default, target the group follower perspective.

The latter cardinal virtues directly serve to initiate the follower trend, derived from the Latin *cardos* (hinge): based upon the belief that all higher virtues hinge upon these basic four. Accordingly, the cardinal virtues exhibit distinct parallels to the more elementary class of alter ego states; in this case, prudent-approval, just-blame, temperate-solicitousness, or fortitudinous-submissiveness. The enduring tradition of cardinal virtues figures prominently in the writings of the Greek philosopher Plato, particularly his fanciful dialogue, *The Republic*. These cardinal virtues provide an effective focal point within the dialogue, promoted as codes of conduct befitting Plato's ideal concept of the Greek city-state.

The even more advanced grouping of theological virtues (faith-hope-charity-decency), in turn, builds upon an elementary foundation within the cardinal virtues. The great Church theologian, St. Thomas Aquinas, viewed the theological virtues as divinely inspired. This directly contrasts with the more elementary nature of the cardinal virtues, which were more widely regarded as naturally occurring, social predispositions. Befitting their exalted moral status, the theological virtues remain an enduring theme in NT scripture, particularly celebrated by St. Paul as supreme moral principles governing virtuous conduct.

Although the formal designation of "theological" originally applied only to the first three basic terms, the addition of the fourth related theme of *decency* effectively modifies this grouping into a form consistent with the schematic power hierarchy. This traditional shortfall in the full complement of terms further appears to account for the great theoretical insight missed throughout the ages; namely, the theological virtues represent the higher spiritual analogues of the subordinate class of cardinal virtues (just as the latter are based upon the alter ego states). Here, one acknowledges the prudent-*faith* or blameful-*hope* for justice professed by the spiritual disciple figure, in addition to the temperate sense of the *charitableness* or fortitudinous sense of *decency* germane to the discussion.

The completed description of the group/spiritual levels, in turn, extends to the humanitarian domain with respect to the "representative member of humanity" role. More properly termed the philosopher's maneuver, this perspective invokes the prestige of speaking for all generations of mankind (not just the current one). In essence, the representative member of humanity reminds the humanitarian authority of his formal sanction from humanity, lest he lose prestige in such matters. The humanitarian authority perspective is initially seen as more of a policy-making strategy than any immediate style of power perspective. The humanitarian follower, in turn, retains the option of rejecting humanitarian policy; hence, maintaining an equal humanitarian balance.

The traditionally revered grouping of classical Greek values (beauty-truth-goodness-wisdom) rightfully enters into consideration here, the major groupings of virtues already accounted for at the lower levels. This enduring notion of value invokes precisely such a humanitarian focus, the more immediate sense of virtue now extending to the timeless quality of value. Indeed, the classical Greek values date to the most ancient of times, celebrated by Plato as pure forms (or essences) that transcend the variability of the natural world. Each of these values was worshiped as an abstract deity in its own right; namely, Venus (beauty), Veritas (truth), Bonus Eventus (goodness), and Sapientia (wisdom). This classical sense of value, in turn, fulfills the trend previously established with respect to the cardinal/theological virtues. This formal correspondence extends to the *beauteous*-faith or just-hope for the *truth*, as well as the charitable sense of *goodness* or decent sense of *wisdom* for the humanitarian follower role.

Even a follower level as abstract as the transcendental must (by definition) be invested with its own unique form of follower countermaneuver, in this case, that invoked by the transcendental follower. Despite this extreme level of abstraction, it still proves feasible to distinguish a respective listing of ethical terms provisionally termed the mystical values (ecstasy-bliss-joy-harmony). Although the formal specifics of this grouping are scarcely warranted at this juncture, suffice it to say they encompass the enigmatic realm of religious mysticism tuned to realms wholly transcending routine experience. This crowning mystical level effectively closes out the "nameable" realm of the power hierarchy, although it is still possible to postulate the existence of a supernatural extension to the ethical hierarchy: a topic best reserved for the more detailed examination of mysticism contained in Chapter 6.

THE MOTIVATIONAL MATRIX

In summary, the completed cursory analysis of the ten-level hierarchy of virtuous terms aimed to provide a suitably comprehensive overview of virtuous realm, a mere glimpse of the detailed terminology to follow. At the heart of this system lies the unified power hierarchy shown in **Fig. 1**, a confluence of authority/follower roles spanning the personal, group, spiritual, humanitarian, and transcendental realms. In tribute to this dramatic scope, this new conceptual paradigm is respectively termed the *motivational matrix*, in direct analogy to the semantic style of linguistic matrix that it schematically represents. This ascending hierarchy of authority/follower roles emerges as a direct outcome of the principles governing Set Theory, the truest value for this system emerging in terms of the respective listings of individual ethical terms, intriguing in their quartet style of systematic organization.

This basic pattern formally reflects the cohesiveness of the individual terms, as previously established with respect to the cardinal virtues, theological virtues, and classical Greek values. Returning to **Fig. 1**, in the left-hand column denoting the authority roles, the first quadrant lists the ascending sequence of nostalgia-glory-providence-grace-tranquility. All five terms share an immediately-active focus based upon a memory foundation based upon past notable achievements. The same quadrant within the right-hand column of follower roles yields the affiliated sequence of approval-prudence-faith-beauty-ecstasy: themes that reciprocate the authority trend through the a future-directed reinforcement of such immediately-active authority perspectives (from the viewpoint of the follower figure).

A similar pattern further holds true with respect to the upper (right-hand) quadrants depicted within **Fig. 1**. The respective authority roles lead to the sequence of guilt-honor-liberty-freewill-equality: themes all sharing such a memory-based active focus although now specifying a more submissive sense. The remaining follower trend (blame-justice-hope-truth-bliss) further verifies this contention, a sequence mirroring that based on approval with the exception that negative reinforcement is now called into focus. Indeed, it proves particularly amazing that these ethical trends should exist at all, each lining up so perfectly within its respective quadrant of the power hierarchy. This grand scale organization is certainly a major selling point, the perfect symmetry and cohesiveness far too intricate to have arisen solely by chance. Indeed, these ten basic ethical groupings actually turn-out to be a skeleton framework for the much broader system of terminology covering the entire range of emotionally-charged language in general: an issue clearly

warranting such an extended style of expanded motivational analysis.

THE TRANSITIONAL POWER MANEUVERS

The extended four-part hierarchy of virtue and vice, however, suffers one crucial shortcoming; namely, the respective authority/follower roles are fixed rigidly into place: allowing precious little flexibility to operate within the system. Versatility plays a key role in our modern mobile society, with continually shifting social coalitions placing ever-greater demands upon the individual. Each new adjustment within the social hierarchy calls for alternate mechanisms for integrating this new modification, an innovation that the established groupings of virtue/vice fail to take fully into account. In addition to the incremental pattern of maneuvering for power initially described, a more direct avenue, in turn, must exist for leapfrogging directly into the higher authority levels; e.g., the group, spiritual, and humanitarian levels, respectively. This further sequence of options is respectively termed the class of *transitional* power maneuvers, being that they "transition" the individual directly into new social contexts.

A number of key features distinguish this new class of transitional power maneuvers, whereby permitting a greater degree of versatility in terms of discrete transitional points across the entire ten-level span of the power hierarchy. These transitions represent direct motivational analogs of the main power maneuvers they serve to imitate. This often occurs in an exaggerated fashion in order to make the point more clearly. This flair for the dramatic can be either humorous (as in the realm of comedy), or tragic (as in the genre of melodrama). This strategy is the stock-in-trade for the standard "situation comedy," when the guest star intrudes upon the graces of the standard ensemble cast, often with hilarious consequences. A similar pattern holds true with respect to the more serious realm of melodrama, as evident in the tradition of the daytime soap opera.

This transitional class of power maneuvers (as their name implies) refers to a relationship initiated for the first time. Here, the individual endeavors to establish a new transitional interaction within a pre-established social order. Indeed, the virtuous realm of humor/comedy is fully explained in terms of the dual transitional interplay of double-bind and counter double-bind maneuvers. Consequently, the distinctive classifications of *lesser* virtues represent transitional variations targeting the main virtuous realm. The pervasive human fascination with humor and comedy is fully explainable in terms of this versatile set of transitional power maneuvers, accounting for many of the lesser virtues (such as loyalty, responsibility, humility, etc.) not directly accounted for in terms of the major listings of virtues, values, and ideals.

Loyalty • Humility		Responsibility • Innocence	
Fidelity • Majesty		Duty • Vindication	
Piety • Magnificence		Allegiance • Exoneration	
Felicity • Grandeur		Righteous.• Immaculate.	

Discipline • Modesty		Vigilance • Meekness	
Chivalry • Chastity		Courage • Obedience	
Nobility • Purity		Valor • Conformity	
Zeal • Perfection		Triumph • Pacifism	

The transitional variations of the virtuous mode serve as direct transitional entry-points in relation to the major virtues. Here, this transitional pattern of organization further predicts the existence of a related class of ethical terms specified for the lesser virtues (II). This alternate class of virtuous terms is distinct from the lesser virtues (I) primarily in terms of the specific order given for the respective authority/follower roles. For the lesser virtues (II), this authority-*then*-follower pattern of roles superficially conforms to the initiation of a completely new operant sequence. This circumstance directly contrasts with the lesser virtues (I), where the sequential order is effectively reversed. Consequently, the lesser virtues (II) enjoy neither the pedigree nor tradition apparent for the better known lesser virtues (I). The lesser virtues (II), nevertheless, are associated with a suitably wide range of ethical traditions: wherein accounting for many further categories of lesser virtue schematically depicted in the compact table immediately below.

Self-Esteem • Reverence		Apology • Clemency	
Pomp • Veneration		Rectitude • Pardon	
Sanctity • Homage		Penitence • Absolution	
Dominion • Benediction		Contrition • Deliverance	

Congeniality • Concession		Sympathy • Appease.	
Cordiality • Indulgence		Compassion • Conciliate	
Hospitality • Gratitude		Mercy • Accommodation	
Goodwill • Altruism		Forgiveness • Sacrifice	

It proves a fitting tribute to the English language tradition that the predicted complement of lesser virtues (II) so convincingly reflects the specifics predicted for the transitional class of terms. Consequently, a clearer understanding of the dual interplay of authority/follower roles proves crucial towards validating the respective interplay

of double bind and counter double bind maneuvers. For example, the nostalgic sense of self-esteem actively expressed by the personal authority figure, in turn, prompts the reverential treatment of the established follower figure (in a disqualified expression of approval). Similarly, an apologetic sense of guilt professed by the personal authority further prompts a disqualified sense of blame; namely, the clemency perspective expressed by the personal follower figure. Furthermore, the personal authority's congeniality maneuver, in turn, prompts a disqualified sense of concession on the part of the follower figure. Similarly, sympathetic behavior further prompts a disqualified expression of appeasement.

This dual interplay of double bind and counter double bind perspectives (targeting the personal level), in turn, serves as the elementary foundation for the remaining hierarchy of authority levels: namely, the group, spiritual, and humanitarian levels depicted. For instance, the initial double bind sequence of self-esteem-pomp-sanctity-dominion, in turn, sets the stage for the remaining counter double bind sequence of reverence-veneration-homage-benediction. Furthermore, the related authority sequence of apology-rectitude-penitence-contrition, in turn, prompts the remaining follower sequence of clemency-pardon-absolution-deliverance.

A similar pattern further holds true with respect to the remaining sequences of terms based upon congeniality-concession and sympathy-appeasement. For instance, the initial authority sequence of congeniality-cordiality-hospitality-goodwill further prompts the respective follower sequence of concession-indulgence-gratitude-altruism. Furthermore, the related authority sequence of sympathy-compassion-mercy-forgiveness, in turn, anticipates the remaining follower sequence of appeasement-conciliation-accommodation-sacrifice.

In summary, the current introductory chapter aimed to provide a preliminary overview of the entire outline for the motivational matrix. The following two pages of precise terminology offer a preliminary indication of the major/lesser ethical categories to be discussed: the first table devoted to the main listings of virtuous terms, whereas the second table is dedicated to the respective listings of lesser virtues. The discerning reader is encouraged to refer back to this extensive listing of terms (for easy reference) throughout the remainder of this book.

The remainder of the current section is devoted entirely to the main virtuous realm; in particular, the major groupings of virtues and values rep-

THE MAJOR VIRTUES (100 – 199)

110 – Nostalgia	144 – Circumspection	178 – Ecumenism
111 – Guilt	145 – Equitableness	179 – Evangelism
112 – Desire	146 – Continence	180 – Beauty
113 – Worry	147 – Bravery	181 – Truth
114 – Poignance	148 – Utilitarianism	182 – Goodness
115 – Culpability	149 – Practicality	183 – Wisdom
116 – Passion	150 – Providence	184 – Charm
117 – Apprehension	151 – Liberty	185 – Credence
118 – Individualism	152 – Civility	186 – Benevolence
119 – Quintessentialism	153 – Austerity	187 – Shrewdness
120 – Approval	154 – Bountifulness	188 – Eclecticism
121 – Leniency	155 – Freedom	189 – Moralism
122 – Solicitousness	156 – Courtesy	190 – Tranquility
123 – Submissiveness	157 – Forbearance	191 – Equality
124 – Admiration	158 – Romanticism	192 – Love
125 – Concern	159 – Charisma	193 – Peace
126 – Aspiration	160 – Faith	194 – Serenity
127 – Deference	161 – Hope	195 – Brotherhood
128 – Pragmatism	162 – Charity	196 – Affection
129 – Expediency	163 – Decency	197 – Amity
130 – Glory	164 – Devotion	198 – Humanism
131 – Honor	165 – Fairness	199 – Cosmopolitanism
132 – Dignity	166 – Kindness	100 – Ecstasy
133 – Integrity	167 – Scrupulousness	101 – Bliss
134 – Exaltation	168 – Ecclesiasticism	102 – Joy
135 – Uprightness	169 – Orthodoxy	103 – Harmony
136 – Respectfulness	170 – Grace	104 – Rapture
137 – Probity	171 – Free-will	105 – Contentment
138 – Personalism	172 – Magnanimity	106 – Gladness
139 – Heroism	173 – Equanimity	107 – Accordance
140 – Prudence	174 – Blessings	108 – Mysticism
141 – Justice	175 – Conscientious.	109 – Spiritualism
142 – Temperance	176 – Graciousness	
143 – Fortitude	177 – Patience	

THE LESSER VIRTUES (200 – 299)

210 – Self-Esteem
210.1 – Humility
211 – Apology
211.1 – Innocence
212 – Congeniality
212.1 – Modesty
213 – Sympathy
213.1 – Meekness
214 – Self-Respect
214.1 – Simplicity
215 – Sorrow
215.1 – Blamelessness
216 – Amiability
216.1 – Demureness
217 – Empathy
217.1 – Timidity
220 – Loyalty
220.1 – Reverence
221 – Responsibility
221.1 – Clemency
222 – Discipline
222.1 – Concession
223 – Vigilance
223.1 – Appeasement
224 – Fealty
224.1 – Esteem
225 – Accountability
225.1 – Lenity
226 – Adherence
226.1 – Favor
227 – Wariness
227.1 – Placation
230 – Pomp
230.1 – Majesty
231 – Rectitude
231.1 – Vindication
232 – Cordiality
232.1 – Chastity
233 – Compassion
233.1 – Obedience
234 – Ostentation
234.1 – Loftiness
235 – Remorse

235.1 – Exculpation
236 – Conviviality
236.1 – Coyness
237 – Commiseration
237.1 – Complaisance
240 – Fidelity
240.1 – Veneration
241 – Duty
241.1 – Pardon
242 – Chivalry
242.1 – Indulgence
243 – Courage
243.1 – Conciliation
244 – Steadfastness
244.1 – Acclaim
245 – Obligation
245.1 – Remittance
246 – Gallantry
246.1 – Sanction
247 – Intrepidity
247.1 – Concordance
250 – Sanctity
250.1 – Magnificence
251 – Penitence
251.1 – Exoneration
252 – Hospitality
252.1 – Purity
253 – Mercy
253.1 – Conformity
254 – Holiness
254.1 – Sublimeness
255 – Regretfulness
255.1 – Aquittal
256 – Generosity
256.1 – Wholesomeness
257 – Pity
257.1 – Compliance
260 – Piety
260.1 – Homage
261 – Allegiance
261.1 – Absolution
262 – Nobility
262.1 – Gratitude

263 – Valor
263.1 – Accommodation
264 – Adoration
264.1 – Ardor
265 – Obeisance
265.1 – Dispensation
266 – Stateliness
266.1 – Thanksgiving
267 – Stalwartness
267.1 – Consonance
270 – Dominion
270.1 – Grandeur
271 – Contrition
271.1 – Immaculate.
272 – Altruism
272.1 – Perfection
273 – Forgiveness
273.1 – Pacifism
274 – Supremacy
274.1 – Splendor
275 – Grief
275.1 – Impeccability.
276 – Benignity
276.1 – Excellence
277 – Remission
277.1 – Amicableness
280 – Felicity
280.1 – Benediction
281 – Righteousness
281.1 – Deliverance
282 – Zeal
282.1 – Goodwill
283 – Triumph
283.1 – Sacrifice
284 – Happiness
284.1 – Exultation
285 – Commitment
285.1 – Redemption
286 – Fervor
286.1 – Beneficence
287 – Victory
287.1 – Propitiation

resenting the cardinal virtues, theological virtues, classical Greek values, etc. This initial **Part I** is further subdivided into eight separate chapters reflecting the personal, group, spiritual, humanitarian, and transcendental levels within the power hierarchy, including the accessory classes of terms, as well as the general unifying themes.

This fundamental pattern of organization is further altered in **Part II** with respect to the transitional variations on the main virtuous mode, devoted to a detailed examination of the dual classes of lesser virtues. Following a short introductory chapter (describing the transitional realm in general), **Part II** is further subdivided into six component chapters outlining the lesser virtues (I and II), in addition to a final description of the affiliated accessory terms.

In terms of a final practical overview, the remaining **Part III** enters into broad number of cogent speculations concerning global applications for the master motivational system. Chapters *15* and *16* formally outline avenues for further research, proposing critical applications relating to improving the global ethical mindset in terms of international cooperation. Perhaps the most dramatic potential applications are detailed in Chapter *17* with respect to an ethical simulation of artificial intelligence, the basis for two granted US patents. This novel innovation employs the systematic virtuous system of schematic definitions as a platform for programming of complex sets of ethical parameters. This innovation represents the first affective language analyzer incorporating ethical/motivational terms, serving in the role of interactive computer interface: enabling a computer to reason and speak in an ethical fashion and serving in roles specifying sound human judgment (such as public relations or security functions). Through an elaborate matching procedure, the precise motivational parameters can be accurately determined for a given verbal interaction. Through the aid of this advanced computer technology, the task of detecting and cataloguing ethical safeguards should greatly be simplified, eventually permitting the development of effective mediation and diplomacy within an international sphere of influence.

This solid conceptual grounding (within a purely secular/scientific foundation) fortuitously avoids offending the sensibilities of any singular world religion or culture in the process: whereby celebrating the commonalties embracing all ethical traditions as a whole. Granted, the world's religions have enjoyed considerable success in the promotion of a virtuous lifestyle, with origins vastly predating our modern technological age. For the vast majority of recorded history the existing complement of world religions have essentially co-existed more-or-less peacefully, although various degrees of religious fanaticism have periodically instigated conflict amongst cultures. With the advent of our modern age of high technology, however, it would appear that mankind can no longer afford such a dramatic clash of cultures when extending to the realm of fanatical terrorism on a global scale. The newly proposed scientifically-based system of planetary ethics holds the greatest promise in this regard, one holding the potential for overcoming the considerable threats to global peace and harmony.

The following chapter launches this grand-scale endeavor with respect to a detailed examination of the personal authority and follower roles. Indeed, it is precisely at this most basic personal level that the technical rationale behind the quartet-style organization for the ethical terms is finally adequately addressed, as ultimately explained in terms of the behavioral terminology of operant conditioning. The psychological field of behaviorism is devoted to the study of instinctual styles of goal-seeking behaviors, an undertaking entirely in keeping with the more abstract focus of the virtues, values, and ideals. The father of modern behaviorism, B. F. Skinner, proposed a similar correlation of behavioral and ethical principles with respect to his quest for an all-encompassing "Technology of Behavior" in harmony with a secular context.

In his masterpiece, *Beyond Freedom and Dignity* (1971), Skinner examined the behavioral correlates for a broad range of ethical terms (such as freedom and dignity), although with a somewhat limited degree of success. Through the aid of the unified ethical hierarchy, however, this motivational style of analysis can be carried to its logical conclusion, incorporating virtually every major listing of terms within the Western ethical tradition. Indeed, it proves particularly crucial to view the ascending ethical hierarchy of virtues and values as based entirely within behavioral principles and terminology, as indicated in the elementary nature of the ego and alter ego states. The science of behaviorism, therefore, serves as the rational launch-point for any further style of ethical analysis, beginning with the more detailed nature of the chapter to follow. A brief history of the behavioral movement is definitely in order at this juncture, for herein lie the keys to outlining the instinctual foundations for the entire ten-level virtuous hierarchy.

2

THE BEHAVIORAL FOUNDATIONS FOR THE VIRTUOUS REALM

To the casual student of psychology, the mention of conditioning theory typically brings to mind the classical variety pioneered by Russian behaviorist, Ivan Pavlov. Pavlov was the first to discover that dogs could be trained to salivate to the sound of a neutral conditioned stimulus (such as a ticking metronome) provided it was extensively paired beforehand with a food reward (the unconditioned stimulus). Subsequent researchers extended these results to various other types of reflexive behavior amenable to laboratory investigation. These automatic types of behavior, however, are typically at odds with the more deliberate goal-seeking styles of behavior characterizing mature human endeavor. For the adult, behavior typically precedes reinforcement, instead of following it (as in the classical sense).

Descriptions of this latter type of conditioning first come to light in the writings of Bekhterev, a fellow countryman of Pavlov. This variation was termed *instrumental* conditioning, in that goal-seeking behavior was said to be instrumental in procuring reinforcement from the environment. Indeed, Bekhterev further demonstrated that the strength of instrumental behaviors can greatly be enhanced by increasing the frequency/amplitude of the contingent reinforcement.

Instrumental conditioning soon rivaled classical conditioning in the field of learning theory, only reaching its greatest potential through the efforts of American psychologist B. F. Skinner. Skinner expanded upon traditional "instrumental" theory by developing his own radical variation respectively termed *operant* conditioning. According to Skinner, goal-seeking behaviors "operate" on the environment to produce reinforcement; hence, the operant sense of the term. Skinner actually distinguishes two distinct forms of operant conditioning, designated for his parallel con-

cepts of positive and negative reinforcement. Positive reinforcement (as its name implies) refers to a rewarding aspect within the environment targeted through solicitous types of behavior. A widely cited example of positive reinforcement concerns the plight of the wilderness bear cub, which in the course of foraging overturns a fallen log concealing a wild honeycomb. The rewarding consequences of such a honey bonanza directly encourage further such log-turning behavior in the future, particularly when such efforts are periodically re-rewarded.

Negative reinforcement, on the other hand, refers to the avoidance of some unpleasant aspect within the environment through aversive types of behavior; as in fleeing from predators or stepping around pitfalls. Returning to the previous example, the bear cub might jump into a lake to avoid the unpleasant consequences of a hot summer day, or a swarm of angry bees for that matter. Although distinct mechanisms are clearly involved, both positive and negative variations are similarly reinforcing to the individual, encouraging approach / avoidance types of behavior in relation to the environment.

Skinner's most enduring contribution to the field of behaviorism involves his ingenious experimental designs, allowing for degrees of precision unheard of in the natural state. Employing various animal models, Skinner perfected clever automated set-ups for simulating the interaction of learned operant behaviors (such as depressing a lever) and subsequent reinforcement: as in the delivery of a food pellet (+R), or the avoidance of floor shocks (−R). Within such a controlled laboratory setting, Skinner was effectively able to calculate how different schedules of reinforcement affect the overall behavior of the organism, contrasting the effects of strictly measured reinforcement to that of randomly intermittent or variable reinforcement modes.

CONDITIONING IN A SOCIAL SETTING

The observation of similar types of instinctual behavior in humans invites many practical comparisons that (for the most part) prove quite enlightening. Nature studies, indeed, have confirmed the stabilizing effects of operant conditioning within certain naturally occurring animal societies. For instance the grooming behaviors observed within the wild baboon troop serve to cement the bonds between dominant and subordinate members. The subordinate baboons groom the coats of the troop leaders in exchange for their outward approval. A similar set of circumstances is further seen with respect to breeding behaviors between the sexes within a social context.

These distinct interactions find further parallels within human society, where mankind's symbolic use of language permits approval to be expressed in more dramatic formats; namely, praise, commendation, etc. Symbolism also gives meaning to what Skinner terms the secondary reinforcers; e.g., money, power, etc. Although paper currency is not intrinsically pleasing in itself, it is secondarily reinforcing in that it can be exchanged for any of the primary reinforcers: as in food, shelter, etc. These secondary reinforcers directly encourage procurement behaviors in complex types of situations where rewards are customarily delayed. Herein lies the basis for the traditional Protestant work ethic; e.g., no work - no pay!

Although the effectiveness of rewards clearly remains without question, social hierarchies are rarely so idyllic as to be ruled entirely through positive reinforcement. Grooming behaviors are typically restricted to members of the opposite sex, or members of the same sex that are not a serious challenge to each other. The drive to become the dominant member of the troop is alternately determined through aggressive types of behavior. Such power skirmishes, unfortunately, can prove detrimental to the cooperative social unit, particularly in terms of the threat of serious injury or fatalities. Most social species, accordingly, have evolved stereotypical submissive behaviors serving to terminate the conflict well ahead of any permanent damage. Instead of continuing to act contentiously, the loser switches to appeasement to escape further punishment.

In the highly competitive wolf pack, for example, the defeated wolf bares its throat to the vic-

tor in an overt plea for mercy. This submissive display effectively serves as a visual cue to the dominant wolf to leniently terminate the conflict well ahead of any permanent damage. For the primate troop, this aspect is alternately seen in the crouching/appeasement postures assumed by the subordinate member. Such actions are similarly suggestive of the "prisoner of war" mentality, where waving a white flag is a cue to the victors to forgo the certain extermination bound to occur in a fight to the death; e.g., "Remember the Alamo!"

THE HUMAN CONNECTION

Although such ethological observations prove extremely enlightening, their extrapolation to the human condition proves infinitely more complex. In particular, the extreme degree of complexity separating human and animal societies renders any direct comparisons tentative at best. In contrast to animal societies, mankind is essentially a product of his supportive culture, which cooperatively permits the effective management of environmental factors. Whereas lower animal societies remain at the mercy of the environment for their reinforcement (or lack thereof), mankind's facility for taming the forces of nature has led to the unique reassignment of reinforcement to specialized agencies within the social hierarchy. This is particularly evident in the traditional work place setting, where the employee performs a service function in exchange for secondary reinforcers; namely, money, praise, prestige, etc. Individuals in the enviable position of controlling reinforcement typically enjoy coveted positions of power or authority within the social hierarchy, employing rewards to encourage the procurement behaviors of the subordinate staff of laborers in order to encourage their cooperation.

This overall control over reinforcement has progressed to the point that reinforcement now primarily drives procurement in contrast to the order typically encountered in nature. Indeed, one might rightfully surmise that procurement behaviors (either appetite or aversion) would only rarely be prompted to occur without a precipitating round of reinforcement behaviors: e.g., a job offer of a reinforcing nature typically precedes any practical work actually being done. It might alternately be argued that the remnant hunter gatherer societies around the world remain chiefly dependent upon the environment for reinforcement, where a certain degree of initiative of a procurement nature always proves crucial for maintaining any complex style of social structure.

This formal behavioral model further brings into focus the major paradox of the conditioned relationship; namely, as a two-stage sequential process only one role can occur in the present at any given time. In particular, when procurement is actively occurring, reinforcement remains a future potentiality. Similarly, when reinforcement finally comes to pass, procurement is similarly thrust into a potentiality status. This dual style of conditioned interaction is schematically represented in **Fig. 2A**: with procurement represented as the letter (X), whereas reinforcement is specified by the letter (Y). The complete scale of time is further represented by paired (oppositely-facing) "wedges" denoting the past and future time frames, with the gap representing the present. This dual wedge format was purposely chosen in reference to the observation that the measure of time increases as a direct function of its distance from the present.

According to Part A of **Fig. 2A**, when procurement (X) immediately occurs, reinforcement (Y) remains a future potentiality. This conditioned interaction is formally based upon the successful completion of previous such interactions from the past, formally represented by the X → Y (small type) notation depicted within the past-directed time-wedge. Indeed, this previous experience serves as the primary motivational template for the current ongoing interaction, where active procurement (X) anticipates the bestowal of future reinforcement (Y).

As schematically diagrammed, the procurer of reinforcement is actively depicted within a present time-frame indicative of a subjective "I" perspective characterizing the initiation sequence. The subsequent reinforcement role is projected as a potentiality within the future time-frame, in essence, a mental projection on the part of the procurer, hence, experienced as an objective style of "you" perspective in relation to "the other." This future-directed style of mental projection allows the procurer to form a mental map of the entire procurement-then-reinforcement dynamic within the conditioned interaction, whereby supplying the motivational rationale for one's active means towards the achievement of reinforcement.

The reinforcer within the condition interaction, in turn, is thrust into his/her own active status when the time for bestowing reinforcement finally comes to pass. According to Part B of **Fig. 2A**, this sequence of events remains formally punctuated from the subjective perspective of the procurer, being that the respective you/I polarities are carried over unchanged in relation to those initially established in Part A. Here the active bestowal of reinforcement (Y) in the present, in turn, prompts the anticipation of upcoming procurement behaviors (X) in the future, in essence, providing an effective sense of closure within the two-stage operant schematic.

Through this systematic interplay of sequences (A) and (B), both procurement and reinforcement share an equivalent status within the present, along with their potential displacement into a future-based time-frame respectively. Indeed, the ultimate completion of Part B further sets the stage for additional cycles of interaction within the operant sequence: for if configuration (B) is phase shifted one step further into the past, one returns back to the initial configuration depicted in Part A. This cyclic (recursive) periodicity emerges as a key factor underlying this two-stage model allowing each motivational interchange to accumulate in a seamless fashion over real time. It is chiefly through such a systematic style of analysis (isolated through individual stages over real time) that the conditioned relationship is seen to be punctuated from either the procurement or reinforcement perspectives. In this dual sense the procurement and reinforcement roles maintain their given order within the conditioned interaction, each punctuated from one favored perspective or the other.

AN INTROSPECTIVE TERMINOLOGY FOR CONDITIONING THEORY

This dual "staggered" model of the conditioned relationship, although technically comprehensive in scope, unfortunately is restricted by a strict reliance upon behavioral terminology. Although procurement and reinforcement retain their operant status within an active time frame, their respective extension into a future-directed time-frame begs for a further corresponding distinction in meaning. Although behavioral terminology (true to its scientifically-objective focus) remains inadequate to this task, colloquial English proves much better qualified, particularly verbal categories dealing with subjective motivations.

The most fitting launch-point for such a determination concerns the very initiation of the operant sequence, where active procurement anticipates the future bestowal of reinforcement. As schematically depicted in Part A of **Fig. 2A**, the operant sequence of X → Y represents such a future-directed interaction, with active procurement (X) aimed towards securing future reinforcement (Y). The predicted set of colloquial terms therefore exhibits two distinct modes of specialization; namely, an active mode occurring within the pre-

(A)

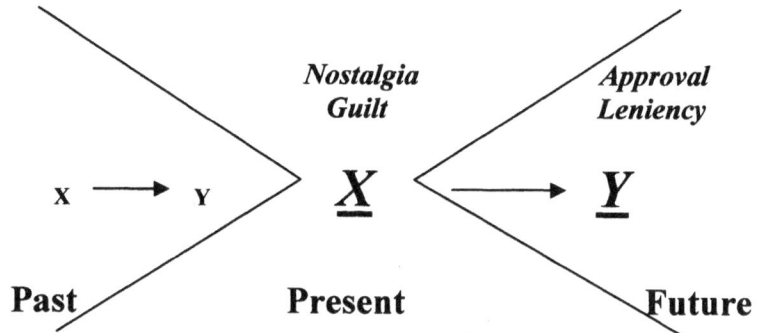

(B)

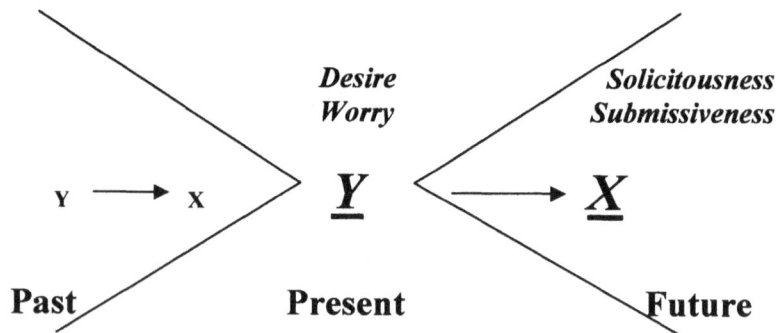

Fig. 2A - The Two-Stage Schematic for Operant Conditioning

sent and a potentially predicted mode projected into a future-directed time-frame.

The active behavioral mode appears to be equivalent to the introspective terminology governing behavioral conditioning, employing colloquial terms with clear instinctual overtones; e.g., guilt, worry, nostalgia, and desire. These ego states are specialized into the active reinforcement themes of desire and worry, as well as the active procurement perspectives of nostalgia and guilt. In contrast, the future-directed set of mental projections target a more pronounced set of behavioral characteristics consistent with such a projected mental focus: e.g., approval, leniency, solicitousness, and submissiveness. This latter class of terms is rightfully termed the *alter ego states* in reference to their conceptual dependence upon the ego as the source of intentions occurring within a future-directed time-frame. Generally speaking, the ego states actively initiate each distinctive phase within the conditioned interaction, whereby prompting the projected potentiality encompassing the alter ego roles (lending credence to the notion of "alter ego"). Accordingly, these future-directed alter ego states directly complement their more active behavioral ego state counterparts within the operant conditioned relationship: namely desire/solicitousness, worry/submissiveness, etc. The remainder of the current chapter endeavors to examine the behavioral dynamics underlying this predicted eight-part complement of terms, providing a sturdy conceptual foundation for a discussion of the remaining virtuous hierarchy to follow.

NOSTALGIA-APPROVAL

The more straightforward class of positive reinforcement proves to be the most logical initiation point for such a grand scale analysis, being that positive rewards appear a much more tangible experience than the vaguer concept of leniency. The interplay of nostalgia/approval will be examined first, followed by the remaining sequence specified for desire/solicitousness. As suggested by their elementary character, it is fair to say that this overall realm of behavioral terminology encompasses the most basic one-to-one style of personal dynamic targeting the behavioral interplay of personal authority/follower roles.

As initially outlined, the nostalgic sense of solicitousness on the part of the procurer initiates the conditioned interaction in anticipation of the reinforcer's approving potential to reward. The initial solicitous quest for approval occurs within an immediately active time-frame consistent with

a subjective "I" perspective and experienced as a nostalgic acknowledgement of previous such cycles occurring in the past. This initiation phase is experienced in terms of such a poignantly-nostalgic perspective due to an acknowledgement of previous such cycles of procurement-then-rewards from memories of previous experience.

The subsequent predicted rewarding sense of approval represents a mental projection directed into a future-directed time-frame, whereby equating with the complementary objective "you" perspective within the conditioned interaction. The projected/potential nature of the approval perspective, in essence, equates to the personal follower role: whereas the immediately active experience of nostalgia invokes the respective personal authority role. The approving potential to reinforce is formally assigned the personal follower status in that it (in essence) formally follows the procurement behavior that had initiated the conditioned interaction. The latter initiatory role, in turn, is assigned the status of the personal authority role, being that the personal follower depends upon the authority figure for guidance concerning upcoming action within the conditioned interaction. Consequently, the follower looks to the authority figure for the immediate rationale driving one's projected behaviors within a future-directed time-frame: in essence, the authority status is based upon the power inherent to the very initiation of the conditioned interaction.

A familiar example of such a one-to-one style of personal interaction concerns the enduring interplay between the master craftsman and his artisan apprentice. The craftsman's apprentice typically performs routine duties around the shop in order to solicitously seek the approval of the master artisan throughout their shared endeavor. The apprentice aims to display his fledgling talents under the approving gaze of the established master, perhaps one day achieving a master's status in one's own right. This potential sense of reinforcement on the part of the master is colloquially equated with approval, a projected mental perception arising from the nostalgic sense of solicitousness actively expressed by the apprentice (in the role of personal authority. Indeed, nostalgia is primarily defined as a wistful reminder of some favorable poignant event from one's past consistent with its memory status in relation to one's formerly active expression of solicitousness. Here, the apprentice is granted the authority role through the very initiation of the conditioned interaction.

In order to more clearly grasp the varying perspectives at issue, it proves useful to identify the individual subjective/objective polarities for each role within the conditioned interaction. Being that the apprentice acts first within the operant interaction, he/she rightfully assumes the status of a subjective "I" role characterizing the immediately active sense of solicitousness. The master, alternately, is projected (through potentiality) to assume the objective "you" role indicative of the potential for reinforcement anticipated within a future-directed time frame. The potentially rewarding characteristics of approval are formally reflected in its linguistic derivation, tracing its origins to the Latin *probus* (good). It is traditionally defined as an act of sanction or commendation, also synonymous with the related theme of approbation (of similar derivation). This potentially approving attitude is also colloquially equated with the theme of hero worship, where both perspectives yield essentially an equivalent result: namely, potentially encouraging additional potential cycles of nostalgia-then-approval on future occasions within the conditioned relationship. Indeed, the current subjective/objective style of role specialization conveniently permits the tracking of precisely which perspectives are active or passive during each given stage within the operantly-conditioned interaction.

In summary, I (as personal authority) nostalgically act solicitously towards you in anticipation of your (as personal follower) potentially rewarding sense of approval. The latter approval perspective clearly rates such a projected objective status, being that such reinforcement is potentially deferred to some future-directed time-frame. Here, approval is distinguished in terms of such a future-directed focus, effectively complementing the initial nostalgic sense of solicitousness expressed on the part of the personal follower. This approval perspective, accordingly, represents the overarching conceptual framework for the nostalgia-then-approval interaction linking both the personal authority and personal follower roles. The procurer bears a certain risk in assuming that reinforcement will eventually be forthcoming. He/she, however, can nostalgically be reasonably assured by the wealth of previous cycles of procurement-then-reinforcement on previous occasions, spurring hopes for similar reinforcement within a future-directed time-frame.

This initial dual-interaction represents just the first of the two predicted stages within the overall operant interchange. The follow-up sequence specifies that the personal follower ultimately acts upon his/her own predicted rewarding intentions, whereby encouraging future cycles of solicitous behavior on the part of the procurer. Although the reinforcer may act immediately with respect to his rewarding intentions, (more often than not) such complex interactions entail a more leisurely pace of deliberation on the part of the reinforcer. Indeed, it is this tenuous power of deliberation that ultimately imparts the power leverage enjoyed by the reinforcer in relation to the procurer, the latter wholly depending upon the former to fulfill one's anticipated reinforcing mandate.

DESIRE-SOLICITOUSNESS

As suggested previously, the inevitable passage of time ultimately dictates that the time for reinforcement eventually comes to pass. The motivational dynamic governing this second stage within the conditioned sequence, in essence, mirrors the interplay previously established for the initial stage, although with a few key differences. According to this second phase, the personal follower ultimately acts upon his approving intentions, desirously acting rewardingly towards his willing apprentice, whereby prompting solicitous feelings of worthiness and determination on the part of the latter. Here, the desire perspective now becomes actively experienced in the present tense as the active bestowal of approval. Indeed, desire is traditionally defined as a longing or craving for a wished-for course of action, in this case, the future cooperation of the willing apprentice. This initiatory phase is experienced in terms of such a passionately-desirous perspective consistent with an acknowledgement of previous such cycles of the desire for procurement extending to memories of previous such experience.

Furthermore, the formerly active nostalgic sense of solicitousness (initially experienced by the personal authority figure), in turn, is alternately displaced into a future-directed time-frame, experienced as a potential determination to continue to act solicitously in response to such immediately desirous intentions. This potentially solicitous attitude is also colloquially equated with the theme of approval seeking, with both yielding essentially similar results. Here, the polarities governing the subjective/objective viewpoints are effectively maintained in place for this second stage within the conditioned interaction, with the procurer of reinforcement retaining a subjective perspective, whereas the reinforcer is viewed from an objective status (from the preliminary perspective of the procurer).

In line with this subjective/objective role-based arrangement, you (as personal authority) now desirously act rewardingly towards me in anticipation of my (now as personal follower) determination to continue acting solicitously towards you (as experienced within a future-directed time-frame). Note that the current personal authority role (now in the active guise of reinforcer) desirously seeks the future-based validation of the personal follower as potential rationale for such an immediately active style of rewarding perspective. The subjectively-based personal follower role, in turn, occupies a future-based solicitous perspective with respect to potentialities of an approachful nature within a projected (anticipated) time-frame, providing a follower-style validation for the approval immediately occurring.

Analogous to the previous case of nostalgia, desire also represents a form of mental time travel directed into a future time-frame. This mental projection into such a future-directed time-frame (exclusive of the present) provides the motivational rationale equivalent to a follower status within the conditioned relationship. Each such follower stage represents an independent mental representation within the mind of the procurer (or the reinforcer) in terms of immediately-active and/or future-directed time-frames, respectively. The active class of behaviors is more generally suggestive of a focused state of mindfulness that formally lacks a reflective nature. The contrasting future-directed perspectives alternately are perceived as strictly reflective projections formally experienced as mental time travel. Indeed, one basically experiences only one's own outward motivational projections, projected mental states that are periodically verified in terms of the outwardly observable behaviors exhibited by others.

Returning once again to our ongoing master and apprentice example, a number of key factors are further predicted with respect to the corresponding authority/follower roles. In terms of his/her own active expression of desirous approval, the master artisan, in essence, relinquishes the initial personal follower role, whereby taking on an active personal authority status in relation to one's willing apprentice. The apprentice, in turn, now assumes the formal mantle of personal follower role consistent with the potentiality of a future-based determination to continue to act solicitously. According to this formal role reversal, the master artisan now actively offers his desirous approval in anticipation of instilling a determined sense of solicitousness on the part of the apprentice (conducive to future such feats of greatness).

This active expression of desirous approval immediately acknowledges the unfailing potential for future cooperation on the part of the apprentice. This actively admiring perspective is frequently expressed as a glowing sense of adulation and/or appreciation on the part of the master towards his apprentice. The apprentice, in turn, is reciprocally dependent upon the rewardingly-desirous attentions of his master/mentor, his potential for future achievement remaining entirely meaningless without such suitable fanfare.

This future-based determined sense of solicitous cooperation represents a mental projection based upon a pointed acknowledgment of having acted worthily of such active desire (on the part of the reinforcer). These projected feelings of solicitousness (experienced in a deliberative fashion (on the part of the apprentice), in turn, prove conducive to the initiation of further such cycles of procurement and reinforcement within the conditioned interaction. This latter aspect upholds the inherent power leverage enjoyed by the apprentice (now as personal follower figure), for without this determined sense willing cooperation, the actively desirous expression of approval by the master artisan (as personal authority) will all have been for naught. The master, therefore, desirously acts approvingly towards his apprentice in anticipation of latter's willing cooperation within a future-directed time-frame.

Therefore, to summarize, the actively expressed nostalgic sense of solicitousness on the part of the personal authority figure initiates the conditioned interaction, whereby prompting an anticipated determination to act approvingly on the part of the personal follower. The latter style of reinforcement perspective, in turn, ultimately reaches an active status, whereby approvingly prompting a future-directed determination to continue acting solicitously (conceptually experienced from the viewpoint of the procurer), now designated from a personal follower role). According to this second stage, you (as personal authority) now desirously behave approvingly towards me (as personal follower) in anticipation of my solicitous determination to act worthily within a future-directed time-frame. This latter solicitous status, as a deliberative perspective in its own right, can further serve as the deliberative foundation for initiating additional such cycles within the conditioned interaction at some future date. Indeed, such actively approving reinforcement typically proves sufficient for justifying further such solicitous overtures within a future-directed time-frame in hopes of gaining additional such measures of reinforcement. Consequently, a stable and enduring pattern of procurement-then-reinforcement is encouraged and maintained within the social environment over the long run, providing a solid foundation for stable enterprise and commerce characterizing our modern culture.

RECURSIVE CORRELATES FOR CONDITIONING

The two-stage interplay inherent to conditioning theory shares many of the attributes of a recursive style of process. Recursion is the process of repeating items in a self-similar way. It represents a procedure by which one (or more) steps of a process work to invoke a repetition of the procedure in the form of mental recapitulation. Recursion in linguistics involves embedding sequences within sequences (of a self-similar type) in a hierarchical structure through the process of reiteration. This process of embedding ideas within ideas is a skill that humans seem to acquire in an effortless fashion, perhaps the one true dividing line between the animal kingdom and humankind. Such recursive ability enables humans to freely engage in mental time travel, recalling past memory episodes within present consciousness, and then employing this mental-map for imagining future potentialities as mental projections. Such advanced mental abilities appear to arise primarily through progressive increases in short-term memory and the capacity for hierarchical organization chiefly made feasible through incremental increases in brain development.

In summary, the completed description of the operant sequence of nostalgia, approval, desire, and solicitousness represents a master theoretical overview of the dynamics governing positive reinforcement within a personally-focused relationship. Although the master/apprentice example proved enlightening for illustrative purposes, many other examples also come to mind; e.g., the hero and his sidekick, the comedian and the straight-man, etc. This stepwise analysis devoted considerable effort to restate the obvious, although the true goal for this exercise aims towards providing a solid conceptual foundation for a parallel style of analysis targeting the more abstract listings of virtues and values comprising the group authority levels (and higher). Indeed, the most basic personal level of behavioral dynamics provides the key conceptual mechanism for understanding the instinctually-driven nature of humankind in general, as further extended to a grand unified model encompassing the respective dynamics governing the virtuous realm.

GUILT-LENIENCY

Before jumping ahead to such significant virtuous applications, it proves crucial to examine the remaining motivational dynamics associated with the realm of negative reinforcement. This alternate style of motivational analysis is scarcely as clear-cut as that targeting positive reinforcement, being that negative reinforcement involves the lenient withholding of punishment, as opposed to the more straightforward bestowal of rewards. In the general state of nature, negative reinforcement involves the lenient withholding of punitive consequences from within the environment, or (in a social sense) the lenient treatment of aversive types of behavior. For example, the personal authority figure guiltily acts aversively in anticipation of a lenient sense of concern on the part of the personal follower figure. These anticipated lenient intentions, in turn, eventually become actualized as an immediately active worrisome expression of concern (within an immediately-based time-frame). Accordingly, the initial sense of submissiveness (that first prompted the conditioned interaction), in turn, is further mentally projected into a future-based determined effort to submissively act more appropriately in the future.

This submissive style of interplay is particularly apparent in the throat-baring behaviors previously described for the wolf pack, where the submissive pack member exaggerates one's degree of vulnerability in anticipation of an unconditional bestowal of leniency. In terms of more advanced human society, submissiveness equates to a vocal admission of guilt aimed towards verbally eliciting a lenient sense of concern on the part of one's personal follower figure. This phase is experienced as a guiltily sense of submissiveness in relation to the memory of previous such cycles of aversion-then-leniency from past previous experience. It would certainly appear risky to express such an extreme degree of vulnerability without a reasonable assurance of lenient treatment. Past cycles of lenient treatment effectively come into play, where previous such instances of leniency ultimately justify such a radical act of faith.

The colloquial concept of leniency certainly fits the typical profile for negative reinforcement, conventionally defined as professing concern towards the difficulties experienced by another. In response to the personal authority's guilty expression of submissiveness, the personal follower leniently acts in a concerned fashion in a committed effort to alleviate such an aversive perspective. According to this future-projected focus upon leniency, a concerned potential for rehabilitation (rather than vengeful retribution) now rules as the order of the day. Indeed, this potentially lenient attitude is also colloquially equated with the colloquial theme of blame, where blamefulness essentially yields an equivalent result: namely, verbally acting in a leniently-blameful fashion in order to dramatize the deficiencies currently at issue with the aversive interaction. Consequently, blamefulness is generally used interchangeably with leniency with respect to the purposes of illustration within the current chapter.

A familiar example of this one-to-one style of personal interaction is observed with respect to the interplay between the drill sergeant and the raw recruit. The recruit is expected to fall in line with the dictates of his drill sergeant, (in the process) guiltily acting submissively in hopeful anticipation of a lenient sense of concern on the part of the drill sergeant. The initially active expression of aversiveness (in a guilty sense) represents a future-directed emotion anticipating a contingent projected sense of leniency on the part of the drill sergeant. Indeed, guilt is traditionally defined as a submissive acknowledgement of some past aversive event, a verbal admission of culpability along the lines of appeasement behavior.

Being that the recruit initiates this first stage within the conditioned interaction, he/she rightfully assumes a subjective "I" role, whereas the drill sergeant alternately assumes the projected-objective "you" role indicative of potentiality within a future-directed time-frame. Consequently, I as personal authority (the recruit) guiltily act submissively towards you as my drill sergeant in anticipation of your lenient sense of concern. The recruit bears some risk in assuming that reinforcement will follow, although reassured by a wealth of previous such cycles of reinforcement.

WORRY-SUBMISSIVENESS

This initial future-directed sequence of guilt-then-leniency further implies that the reinforcer must eventually act upon the potentiality of one's lenient intentions, whereby worrisomely acting in a concerned fashion (within an actively-based time-frame) in anticipation of a submissive determination to perform better on the part of the recruit This latter course of action often necessitates an extended course of deliberation on the part of the reinforcer. Indeed, this tenuous power of deliberation ultimately imparts the active style of power leverage enjoyed by the reinforcer in relation to the procurer of such reinforcement. Once the opportunity for action finally occurs, the worrisome expression of leniency (on the part of the personal authority) serves to encourage future submissive cooperation on the part of the recruit.

The respective interplay of authority/follower roles, in turn, is formally modified with respect to this second stage of the conditioned interaction. Here, this subsequent phase represents the worri-

some bestowal of lenient reinforcement by the drill sergeant (now in the role of personal authority), as schematically represented in Part-B of **Fig. 2A**. This second stage is phase-shifted within the current time frame, with reinforcement (Y) now occupying the present, whereas procurement (X) is now projected as a future potentiality. In essence, the drill sergeant is now respectively thrust into an immediately active role, leniently reinforcing the guilty sense of submissiveness initially expressed by the recruit. Accordingly, the drill sergeant ultimately acts upon his lenient intentions, worrisomely acting in a concerned fashion towards his trusty recruit, whereby prompting a potentially-based determination to act appropriately on the part of the recruit. This projected submissive attitude is also colloquially equated with the theme of fear of failure, where both perspectives present essentially the same results: namely, potentially encouraging additional cycles of aversion/leniency within the conditioned interaction.

A number of key modifications are further specified with respect to the polarities for the authority/follower roles. With respect to his/her active expression of leniency, the drill sergeant now abandons the former (projected) personal follower role, in turn, switching to an active personal authority status in relation to the trusty recruit. The recruit, in turn, now assumes the mantle of the personal follower role consistent with the motivational leverage inherent to such a future-directed time-frame. By definition, the personal follower depends upon the personal authority for active guidance concerning proper action within the conditioned interaction: hence, the authority leads the follower in terms temporal priority.

This role reversal certainly proves warranted being as it reciprocates the initial conditioned sequence based upon guilt/leniency, although now punctuated from an active reinforcement perspective (rather than the submissive variety). The drill sergeant now worrisomely points out weaknesses (in a lenient fashion) in anticipation of a submissive determination to perform better on the part of the recruit. This initiatory phase is experienced in terms of a worrisome expression of concern reflecting an acknowledgement of previous such cycles of conditioned behavior extending to past memory experience. This process of worrisome deliberation, in turn, proves conducive to promoting further such acts of compliance on the part of the recruit (within a future-directed time-frame), whereby encouraging additional such cycles of the conditioned interaction in the process. This serves to enhance the inherent power leverage enjoyed by the recruit (as personal follower), for without this submissive determination to do better, the lenient behavior expressed by the drill sergeant will all have been for naught.

In summary, during this second stage within the conditioned interaction, the drill sergeant worrisomely acts in a concerned fashion towards his recruit in anticipation of the projected determination to improve on the part of the latter. In this latter respect, the deliberative dictates governing the authority figure's worrisome perspective are finally fully realized. Here, the recruit plays-up his vulnerability within the conditioned interaction: in essence, a submissive determination towards improvement effectively cutting short the potential for any further sense of conflict. Any subsequent action taken against the submissive party is now motivated out of a blameful sense of concern rather than vindictive retaliation. Accordingly, the recruit remains reciprocally dependent upon the worrisomely-lenient intentions of his drill sergeant, his submissive expression of obedience now becoming entirely meaningless without such a lenient sense of concern.

Although the rather broad range of connotations associated with guilt, leniency, worry, and submissiveness might possibly suggest other possible interpretations, the current range of viewpoints certainly fits the prerequisites specified for negative reinforcement: a finding further verified with respect to the even more abstract sequence of levels within the ascending virtuous hierarchy. Indeed, this fundamental understanding of the most elementary personal authority/follower roles proves exceedingly critical for ultimately defining the motivational dynamics governing the more abstract groupings of virtues and values to follow.

THE ACCESSORY MOTIVATIONAL TERMS

According to the preceding somewhat technical style of analysis, the initially active procurer role is formally specified from a subjective "I" perspective, whereas the subsequent reinforcement role is alternately designated from a complementary style of objective "you" perspective. This reciprocal pattern of subjective procurement and objective reinforcement roles follows a strict give-and-take dynamic, formally defined as "if you, then I," (and vice versa). According to this complementary style of power-sharing strategy, the initially active procurement roles within the conditioned relationship are designated in terms of a subjective "I" status, whereas the subsequent reinforcement roles are specified in terms of an objective "you" status. Indeed, this arrangement essentially mirrors what typically occurs in nature,

where the organism actively procures and the environment (inanimately) reinforces.

This reciprocating model of motivational communication, however, can scarcely claim to be the total picture, for it formally accounts for only half of the introspective roles predicted within the linguistic matrix: e.g., only the procurement focus. The inherent versatility of the human mind, however, (by definition) allows for a subjective reflection upon one's objective status (after the fact: in essence, subjectifying the objective status initially ascribed to the reinforcement roles. This role reversal is similarly counterbalanced by a parallel objectification of the initially-active subjective class of procurement roles. This reflective role-reversal conveniently allows for crucial insights into the feelings and motivations experienced by another, an aspect traditionally defined as *empathy*. It is chiefly defined as that indwelling sense of inter-subjectivity by which one introspectively participates in comprehending feelings privately held by another. This empathic style of motivational perspective formally predicts the existence of a parallel complement of affective terms for designating this dual range of versatility (and specified as the *accessory* class of motivational terms). Fortunately the English language is richly blessed with an abundant number of synonyms conducive to fulfilling this predicted complement of accessory themes.

The specific details underlying this innovation are reserved for the upcoming Chapter 7: a section devoted exclusively to a description of these accessory motivational perspectives. Here, the "you"/"I" perspectives are systematically reversed in terms of polarity across the board, ensuring that both procurement and reinforcement roles encompass their full range of objective/subjective potentialities encountered within a real-life situation. For the personal realm, for instance, the proposed accessory class of ego states (poignancy, culpability, passion, and apprehension) effectively complements the main listing of terms: namely, nostalgia, guilt, desire, and worry. Furthermore, the accessory alter ego states of admiration-concern-aspiration-deference, in turn, reciprocate the main listing of terms (approval, leniency, solicitousness, and submissiveness, respectively).

In terms of the main pairing of desire and solicitousness, for instance, the accessory complement of passion/aspiration proves particularly well suited to the task. Here, I (as personal authority) passionately act rewardingly towards you in anticipation of your (as personal follower) aspiring treatment of me. In terms of the related context of worry/submissiveness, the personal authority figure switches to an apprehensive perspective, whereby anticipating the personal follower's deferential expression of submissiveness. A similar pattern further holds true for the personal authority's poignancy in anticipation of admiration from the personal follower, or culpability in expectation of concern. This reciprocating interplay of both the main and accessory sets of terms collectively permits a convincing simulation of the empathic dynamics governing the conditioned interaction in general.

THE ACCESSORY HIERARCHY OF VIRTUES, VALUES, AND IDEALS

According to this main/accessory model of empathic communication, it remains only a further minor step to extend this personal complement of motivational terms to the even more abstract realm of the virtues, values, and ideals characterizing the higher authority levels. This yields the full forty-fold complement of accessory terms schematically depicted below, and also described in an expanded format in Chapter *7*.

Poignancy • Admir.		**Culpability • Concern**	
Exalt.• Circumspection		**Uprightness • Equity**	
Bountiful. • Devotion		**Freedom • Fairness**	
Blessings • Charm		**Conscience • Credence**	
Serenity • Rapture		**Brotherhood • Content.**	
Passion • Aspiration		**Apprehen.• Deference**	
Respect • Continence		**Probity • Bravery**	
Courtesy • Kindness		**Forbear. • Scruples**	
Gracious.• Benevolence		**Patience • Shrewd.**	
Affection • Gladness		**Amity • Accordance**	

This compact diagram represents a mirror-image variation on the main listing of virtuous terms depicted in **Fig. 1** of Chapter 1. Indeed, this parallel master hierarchy of accessory terms spans the entire range of group, spiritual, humanitarian, and transcendental domains within the motivational matrix as a whole. Consequently, this reciprocating interplay of both main and accessory terms permits a convincing simulation of empathic communication in general, the objective and subjective polarities effectively reversed through an inversion of the "you" and "I" polarities. These accessory groupings of terms scarcely exhibit the pedigree or tradition initially established for the main listings of terms. Accordingly, the accessory listings of terms are formally designated/labeled through the addition of the prefix *"accessory"* to the better-known titles specified for the major

groupings: enabling these empathic foundations to be verified to an extreme degree of precision.

THE EGO AND ALTER EGO STATES

Returning to our ongoing description of the main operant sequence, in a strictly interdependent sense, the personal authority and personal follower roles effectively complement one another within the conditioned interaction, formally maintaining an equivalent balance of power in the process. Indeed, the hero is equally dependent upon the potential attentions of his sidekick, whereas the master craftsman is totally lost without the anticipated services of his apprentice. Herein resides the basis for the fundamental paradox underlying the authority/follower relationship: namely, one hand is always needed to wash the other. The old Zen Buddhist adage describing how the follower leads the leader (as much as the other way around) certainly rings true in this basic regard.

It remains only a further minor step to formally label this dual complement of colloquial terms for both the personal authority and personal follower roles. The ultimate designation of ego and alter ego states immediately comes to mind. The first-mentioned listing of ego states formally specifies motivations encompassing the personal authority role; namely, guilt, worry, nostalgia, and desire. This initial class of ego states represents immediately active perspectives taking as their object the more abstract (projected) complement of future-directed alter ego states: the latter also defined as that of "the other." The *ego* is typically defined as that most basic sense of self to emerge within an immediately-active time-frame. Indeed, the elementary nature of this active class of ego states certainly bears out such an interpretation, proving equally applicable with respect to inanimate objects within the environment (such as in desiring a cup of water).

The remaining class of alter ego states, in turn, refers to the potential realm of projected motivations specific to the personal follower role: namely, approval, leniency, solicitousness, and submissiveness. This collective follower complement of terms represents a motivated sense of potentiality within a future-directed time-frame, in essence, serving to ultimately consummate the immediately active behaviors initiated within the two-stage operant schematic. For instance, the subjective *guilt* perspective of the personal authority, in turn, anticipates the objective alter ego state of *leniency*, as formally attributed to the personal follower figure. Furthermore, the immediately active sense of *nostalgia*, in turn, antici-

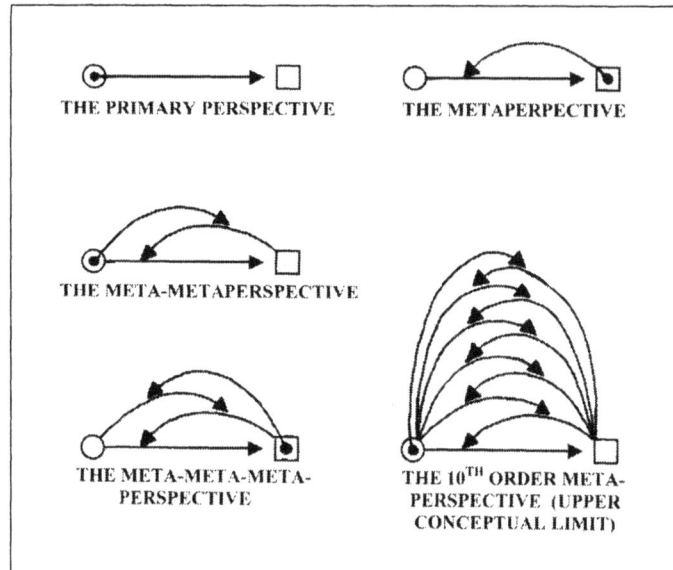

Fig. 2B - The Ten-Level Hierarchy of Metaperspectives
The Schematic Foundation for the Ten-Level Hierarchy of Virtues, Values, and Ideals

pates a projected sense of approval: whereas the *desire* perspective prompts projected feelings of solicitousness, etc. Generally speaking, the personal authority role immediately initiates the conditioned interaction, whereby prompting the range of potentialities encompassing the projected personal follower role: hence, lending credence to the notion of "alter ego." Consequently, the active ego states of guilt, worry, nostalgia, and desire effectively anticipate the future-directed potentialities of approval, leniency, solicitousness, and submissiveness. Indeed, this basic style of personal interaction is effectively seen to repeat for the remaining group and spiritual authority levels as well: providing an accurate means for understanding the dynamics underlying the ethical traditions specific to the virtues, values, and ideals.

THE METAPERSPECTIVE SCHEMATIC FORMAT

The higher-order paradigm of the alter ego state is further reminiscent of a similar concept pioneered in the emerging field of Communication Theory; most notably, the *metaperspective* format advanced by R. D. Laing and P. I. Watzlawick. In *Interpersonal Perception* (1966) Laing (et al) researched the dynamics of interpersonal communication, characterized as "the spiral of reciprocal perspectives." In his *Pragmatics of Human Communication* (1967) Watzlawick (and associates) alternately focused upon the informational aspects of communication, defined as

"the hierarchy of metaperspectives." Both such formulations share a common theme; namely, communication between individuals is generally compounded by abstract "meta" messages defining how the relationship is to be conducted. The metaperspective, from the Greek *meta-* (above), is defined as a higher-order perspective on a viewpoint held by another: schematically defined as "this is how I see you seeing me." Spontaneous forms of communication are objectified as formal objects of discourse, adding both content and context to a given verbal interaction.

In addition to this preliminary class of metaperspective, even more abstract perspectives are theoretically feasible, leading to what Communication Theorists term the *meta-metaperspective*. This more advanced perspective is one meta-level further removed from the more basic metaperspective format, schematically defined as: "this is how I see you - seeing me - seeing you." Indeed, there does not appear to be any barrier limiting the degree to which reflection can serve as a basis for itself, resulting in a multi-level hierarchy of meta-communication in general. This metaperspective format, depicted in **Fig. 2B**, provides a schematic interpretation of the unified motivational hierarchy of authority and follower roles, an enduring format culminating in an unprecedented 10th-order level of meta-abstraction.

According to Laing, relationships typically are defined implicitly rather than explicitly, developing over time through negotiation. Furthermore, the outwardly observable behaviors of another are publically accessible, analogous to the active style of motivated communication specified for the ego states. Mental experience, in contrast, is defined as internal perceptions that are privately felt, corresponding to the future-directed class of alter ego states. Consequently, one can observe the behavior of others but not another's own mental experience. Direct perspectives arise when observing/interpreting the behaviors of others, whereas metaperspectives occur when attempting to infer the projected inward motivations held by another. By definition, metaperspectives are not always necessarily accurate, highlighting the contrast between feeling understood and actually being understood by another.

A REVIEW OF CONDITIONING THEORY

In summary, the completed description of the ego and alter ego states effectively rounds out the stepwise description of the personal realm of the conditioned interaction. The somewhat technical tone for this introductory chapter proved particularly crucial in this systematic regard. Indeed, a sturdy foundation is crucial to the construction of any higher-order level style of structure. It proves particularly informative, therefore, to formally summarize what has previously been proposed in this somewhat technical style of chapter. First proposed were the instinctual types of conditioned interaction so eloquently categorized in B. F. Skinner's terminology of instrumental conditioning. This instinctual foundation, in turn, proved applicable within a human sphere of influence, a model of motivation taking full account of mankind's enduring heritage within the animal kingdom. Skinner's elementary principles of positive and negative reinforcement proved particularly well-suited to the task, formally anticipating the elementary motivational framework for the predicted hierarchy of virtues, values, and ideals.

Further described were the two-stage dynamics governing operant conditioning: offering crucial dynamic insights into motivational sequences that project into future-directed time-frames. Human society is uniquely specialized to operate within such projected/planned contexts: namely, the tendency to learn from past experience conducive to planning for future contingencies (also known as Prospective Psychology). Operant terminology scarcely seemed adequate for defining the entire range of introspectively derived perspectives, whereby necessitating the introduction of a number of colloquial terms into the mix (as evident in the listing of ego and alter ego states).

These colloquial groupings added a crucial introspective dimension to the primarily objective restrictions governing behavioral terminology, in essence, serving as the conceptual foundation for the remaining higher-order listings of virtues, values, and ideals.

This resultant ten-level hierarchy of ethical terms, in turn, redirects the focus of the current analysis, effectively specifying the repetition of both the authority and follower roles within the motivational matrix. Being that the personal authority role occurred first within the operant sequence, it seems only fitting that it be the first to repeat (in a modified sense of) the group authority role: followed, in turn, by that of the group representative. Indeed, the ascending hierarchy of authority/follower roles ultimately extends to (an ascending confluence of) spiritual, humanitarian, and transcendental levels: culminating in an unprecedented 10th-order hierarchy of meta-abstraction: as reflected in the respective individual categories of virtues, values, and ideals.

One might rightfully question the capacity of the human mind to entertain such a formidable multiplicity of metaperspectives, particularly in light of the most abstract meta-order levels. The mind is apparently able to selectively focus upon the immediately relevant levels within the ascending power hierarchy similar to the analogy of a ten-level flight of stairs. The process of rising to the next higher step implies the primacy of the immediately adjoining levels, equal to a span of three sequential levels (e.g., the meta-meta-perspective): quite a modest task for the versatile human mind.

THE SCHEMATIC DEFINITIONS FOR THE VIRTUES, VALUES, AND IDEALS

Although this predicted style of virtuous hierarchy proves suitably comprehensive on an intuitive level, its intimate degree of detail necessarily specifies an even higher degree of precision than has currently been specified. In this latter respect, the systematic organization of the authority hierarchy formally permits the construction of what are technically termed the *schematic definitions* for the motivational matrix. This crucial innovation spells out in longhand the precise location of each virtue/value within the linguistic matrix while simultaneously preserving the correct orientation of the respective authority/follower roles. Each such definition is formally constructed along the lines of a two-stage sequential format; namely, (A) the formal recognition of the preliminary power maneuver and (B) the counterman-

NOSTALGIA	APPROVAL
Previously, you (as reinforcer) have rewardingly acted in a reinforcing fashion towards me: in response to my (as procurer) approachful treatment of you. But now, I (as personal authority) will *nostalgically* act approachfully towards you: in anticipation of your rewarding treatment of me.	Previously, I (as personal authority) have nostalgically acted approachfully towards you: in anticipation of your (as reinforcer) rewarding treatment of me. But now, you (as personal follower) will rewardingly act in an *approving* fashion towards me: overruling my (as PA) nostalgic treatment of you.
GLORY	PRUDENCE
Previously, you (as your personal follower) have rewardingly acted in an approving fashion towards me: in response to my (as PA) nostalgic treatment of you. But now, I (as group authority) will *gloriously* act in a nostalgic fashion towards you: in anticipation of your (as PF) approving treatment of me.	Previously, I (as group authority) have gloriously acted nostalgically towards you: in anticipation of your (as PF) approving treatment of me. But now, you (as group representative) will *prudently* act in an approving fashion towards me: overruling my (as GA) gloriously-nostalgic treatment of you.
PROVIDENCE	FAITH
Previously, you (as group representative) have prudently acted approvingly towards me: in response to my (as GA) gloriously-nostalgic treatment of you. But now, I (as spiritual authority) will gloriously act *providently* towards you: in anticipation of your (as GR) prudent-approval of me.	Previously, I (as spiritual authority) have gloriously acted providently towards you: in anticipation of your (as GR) prudent-approval of me. But now, you (as my spiritual disciple) will prudently act in a *faithful* fashion towards me: overruling my (as SA) provident treatment of you.
GRACE	BEAUTY
Previously, you (as my spiritual disciple) have prudently acted in a faithful fashion towards me: in response to my (as SA) gloriously-provident treatment of you. But now, I (as humanitarian authority) will providently act in a *graceful* fashion towards you: in anticipation of your (as SD) prudent-faith in me.	Previously, I (as humanitarian authority) have providently acted gracefully towards you: in anticipation of your (as SD) prudent-faith in me. But now, you (as representative member of humanity) will *beauteously* act in a faithful fashion towards me: overruling my (as HA) providently-graceful treatment of you.
TRANQUILITY	ECSTASY
Previously, you (as representative member of humanity) have beauteously acted faithfully towards me: in response to my (as HA) providently-graceful treatment of you. But now, I (as transcendental authority) will *tranquilly* act gracefully towards you: in anticipation of your (as RH) beauteous-faith in me.	Previously, I (as transcendental authority) have tranquilly acted gracefully towards you: in anticipation of your (as RH) beauteous-faith in me. But now, you (as my transcendental follower) will beauteously act in an *ecstatic* fashion towards me: overruling my (as TA) tranquil sense of gracefulness.

Table A-1 - The Definitions Based on Nostalgia/Approval

GUILT	LENIENCY
Previously, you (as reinforcer) have tolerantly acted in a reinforcing fashion towards me: in response to my (as procurer) aversive treatment of you. But now, I (as personal authority) will *guiltily* act in an aversive fashion towards you: in anticipation of your tolerant treatment of me.	Previously, I (as personal authority) have guiltily acting aversively towards you: in anticipation of your (as reinforcer) tolerant treatment of me. But now, you (as my personal follower) will *leniently* act in a tolerant fashion towards me: overruling my (as PA) guilty treatment of you.
HONOR	**JUSTICE**
Previously, you (as my personal follower) have leniently acted in a tolerant fashion towards me: in response to my (as PA) guilty treatment of you. But now, I (as group authority) will *honorably* act in a guilty fashion towards you: in anticipation of your (as PF) lenient treatment of me.	Previously, I (as group authority) have honorably acted guiltily towards you: in anticipation of your (as PF) lenient treatment of me. But now, you (as group representative) will leniently act in a *just* fashion towards me: overruling my (as GA) honorable sense of guilt.
LIBERTY	**HOPE**
Previously, you (as group representative) have leniently acted justly towards me: in response to my (as GA) honorable sense of guilt. But now, I (as spiritual authority) will honorably act in a *libertarian* fashion towards you: in anticipation of your leniently-just treatment of me.	Previously, I (as spiritual authority) have honorably acted in a libertarian fashion towards you: in anticipation of your (as GR) leniently-just treatment of me. But now, you (as my spiritual disciple) will leniently-*hope* for justice: overruling my (as SA) libertarian sense of honor.
FREE WILL	**TRUTH**
Previously, you (as my spiritual disciple) have leniently-hoped for justice: in response to my (as SA) libertarian sense of honor. But now, I (as humanitarian authority) will honorably act in a *freely willed* fashion towards you: in anticipation of your (as SD) blameful hope for justice.	Previously, I (as humanitarian authority) have honorably acted in a freely-willed fashion towards you: in anticipation of your (as SD) blameful-hope for justice. But now, I (as representative member of humanity) will justly-hope for the *truth*: overruling my (as HA) libertarian sense of free will.
EQUALITY	**BLISS**
Previously, you (as representative member of humanity) have justly-hoped for the truth: in response to my (as HA) libertarian sense of free will. But now, I (as transcendental authority) will freely-willed act in an *egalitarian* fashion towards you: in anticipation of your (as RH) just-hope for the truth.	Previously, I (as transcendental authority) have freely-willed acted in an egalitarian fashion towards you: in anticipation of your (as RH) just-hope for the truth. But now, you (as my transcendental follower) will *blissfully* hope for the truth: overruling my (as TA) egalitarian treatment of you.

Table A-2 – The Definitions Based Upon Guilt/Leniency

DESIRE	SOLICITOUSNESS
Previously, I (as procurer) have acted approachfully towards you: in response to your (as reinforcer) rewarding treatment of me. But now, you (as my personal authority) will rewardingly act *desirously* towards me: in anticipation of my approachful treatment of you.	Previously, you (as my personal authority) have rewardingly acted desirously towards me: in anticipation of my approachful treatment of you. But now, I (as your personal follower) will *solicitously* act approachfully towards you: overruling your (as PA) desirous treatment of me.
DIGNITY	**TEMPERANCE**
Previously, I (as your personal follower) have solicitously acted approachfully towards you: in response to your (as PA) desirous treatment of me. But now, you (as my group authority) will *dignifiedly* act in a desirous fashion towards me: in anticipation of my (as PF) solicitous treatment of you.	Previously, you (as my group authority) have dignifiedly acted desirously towards me: in anticipation of my (as PF) solicitous treatment of you. But now, I (as group representative) will *temperately* act solicitously towards you: overruling your (as GA) dignified-desire for me.
CIVILITY	**CHARITY**
Previously, I (as group representative) have temperately acted solicitously towards you: in response to your (as GA) dignified-desire for me. But now, you (as my spiritual authority) will dignifiedly act in a *civil* fashion towards me: in anticipation of my (as GR) temperate sense of solicitousness.	Previously, you (as my spiritual authority) have dignifiedly acted in a civil fashion towards me: in anticipation of my (as GR) temperate sense of solicitousness. But now, I (as spiritual disciple) will temperately act *charitably* towards you: overruling your (as SA) civilly-dignified treatment of me.
MAGNANIMITY	**GOODNESS**
Previously, I (as your spiritual disciple) have temperately acted in a charitable fashion towards you: in response to your (as SA) civilly-dignified treatment of me. But now, you (as humanit. authority) will civilly behave *magnanimously* towards me: in anticipation of my (as SD) charitable treatment of you.	Previously, you (as humanit. authority) have civilly acted magnanimously towards me: in anticipation of my (as SD) charitable treatment of you. But now, I (as representative member of humanity) will charitably act with *goodness* towards you: overruling your (as HA) magnanimous treatment of me.
LOVE	**JOY**
Previously, I (as representative member of humanity) have charitably acted with goodness towards you: in response to your (as HA) civilly-magnanimous treatment of me. But now, you (as transcendental authority) will magnanimously act *lovingly* towards me: in anticipation of my (as RH) goodly treatment of you.	Previously, you (as transcend. authority) have magnanimously acted lovingly towards me: in anticipation of my (as RH) goodly treatment of you. But now, I (as your transcendental follower) will goodly act in a *joyous* fashion towards you: overruling your (as TA) magnanimously-loving treatment of me.

Table A-3 – The Definitions Based Upon Desire/Solicitude

WORRY	SUBMISSIVENESS
Previously, I (as procurer) have acted aversively towards you: in response to your (as reinforcer) tolerant treatment of me. But now, you (as my personal authority) will *worrisomely* act tolerantly towards me: in anticipation of my aversive treatment of you.	Previously, you (as my personal authority) have worrisomely acted tolerantly towards me: in anticipation of my (as procurer) aversive treatment of you. But now, I (as your personal follower) will aversively act *submissively* towards you: overruling your (as PA) worrisome treatment of me.
INTEGRITY	**FORTITUDE**
Previously, I (as your personal follower) have aversively acted submissively towards you: in response to your (as PA) worrisome treatment of me. But now, you (as my group authority) will worrisomely act with *integrity* towards me: in anticipation of my (as PF) submissive treatment of you.	Previously, you (as my group authority) have worrisomely acted with integrity towards me: in anticipation of my (as PF) submissive treatment of you. But now, I (as group representative) will *fortitudinously* act submissively towards you: overruling your (as GA) worrisome sense of integrity.
AUSTERITY	**DECENCY**
Previously, I (as group representative) have fortitudinously acted submissively towards you: in response to your (as GA) worrisome sense of integrity. But now, you (as spiritual authority) will *austerely* act with integrity towards me: in anticipation of my (as GR) fortitudinous treatment of you.	Previously, you (as spiritual authority) have austerely acted with integrity towards me: in anticipation of my (as GR) fortitudinous treatment of you. But now, I (as your spiritual disciple) will fortitudinously act in a *decent* fashion towards you: overruling your (as SA) austere sense of integrity.
EQUANIMITY	**WISDOM**
Previously, I (as your spiritual disciple) have fortitudinously acted decently towards you: in response to your (as SA) austere sense of integrity. But now, you (as my humanitarian authority) will austerely act with *equanimity* towards me: in anticipation of my (as SD) decent treatment of you.	Previously, you (as my humanitarian authority) have austerely acted with equanimity towards me: in anticipation of my (as SD) decent treatment of you. But now, I (as representative member of humanity) will decently act in a *wise* fashion towards you: overruling your (as HA) austere sense of equanimity.
PEACE	**HARMONY**
Previously, I (as representative member of humanity) have decently acted in a wise fashion towards you: in response to your (as HA) austere sense of equanimity. But now, you (as transcendental authority) will *peaceably* act with equanimity towards me: in anticipation of my (as RH) decent sense of wisdom.	Previously, you (as transcendental authority) have peaceably acted with equanimity towards me: in anticipation of my (as RH) decent sense of wisdom. But now, I (as transcendental follower) will wisely act *harmoniously* towards you: overruling your (as TA) peaceable treatment of me.

Table A-4 – The Definitions Based Upon Worry/Submissiveness

euver currently being employed; and hence, labeled. Take, for example, the schematic definition for the representative cardinal virtue of *prudence*, reproduced below from the comprehensive series of definitions shown in **Tables A-1** to **A-4**.

> Previously, I (as your group
> authority) have gloriously acted
> nostalgically towards you:
> in anticipation of your (as PF)
> approving treatment of me.
> But now, you, (as group
> representative) will *prudently*
> act approvingly towards me:
> in response to my (as GA) gloriously
> nostalgic treatment of you.

According to this specific *prudence* example, the glorious sense of nostalgia expressed by the group authority figure represents the preliminary power maneuver: countered, in turn, by the *prudent* approval professed by the group representative. Note that the polarity of authority/follower roles is effectively preserved equivalent to their schematic polarity outlined in **Fig. 1**.

In terms of this two-stage schematic format, the preliminary power perspective represents the "one-down" power maneuver, whereas the current power maneuver designates the "one-up" variety. Power leverage, accordingly, is secured by rising to a "one-up" power status; namely, ascending to the next higher metaperspectival level. This comprehensive hierarchy of schematic definitions can effectively be viewed as a motivational calculus replete with the strict transformational rules governing how each level meshes with those above or below it.

The complete forty-part listing of schematic definitions for the main virtuous realm is depicted in **Tables A-1** to **A-4** covering the entire ten-level span for the virtuous motivational hierarchy. The instinctual terminology for operant conditioning initially dominates the preliminary levels, replaced in due fashion by the virtues/values specifying the higher authority levels. At each successive level, a new term (distinguished through *italics*) is introduced, whereby designating the current power maneuver directly under consideration. Beginning with the group level, the preliminary terms begin to drop out of the equation, freeing-up space for the newer terms currently being introduced (whereby maintaining a stable buffer of motivational terms).

The affiliated authority/follower roles similarly remain consistent throughout the ten-level power hierarchy, although systematically abbreviated (for the sake of brevity) in non-critical positions. Accordingly, PA stands for personal authority, PF represents personal follower, etc. The reciprocal interplay of the "you" and "I" roles proves equally crucial, maintaining a stable buffer of objective/subjective perspectives in relation to the reciprocal interplay of authority/follower roles. It is further crucial to note (upon careful examination of the schematic definitions) that the active behavioral states effectively reciprocate the future-directed (projected) perspectives within the operant sequence. These complementary pairings directly ensure that the proper pairings of "you"/"I" roles within the schematic definitions, providing a truly convincing representation of the motivational dynamics at issue within a given conditioned interchange. Furthermore, the corresponding virtuous terms similarly verify the exquisite dynamics governing the entire schematic definition format.

The remainder of the current **Part I** is devoted to systematically outlining the formal dynamics of the entire virtuous realm. Accordingly, each successive chapter is devoted exclusively to a specific authority/follower realm within the virtuous hierarchy (replete with descriptions of the individual ethical terms). Chapter *3* initiates this analysis with a detailed examination of the group authority/follower roles, introducing the groupings of personal ideals and cardinal virtues, respectively. Chapter *4*, in turn, focuses upon the spiritual authority/disciple roles: providing an in-depth examination of the civil liberties and the theological virtues. Chapter *5* subsequently examines the corresponding humanitarian-derived roles, introducing the classical Greek values and ecumenical ideals, respectively. Chapter *6*, in turn, targets the crowning transcendental realm: offering an in-depth examination of the humanistic values and mystical values. Finally, Chapters *7* and *8* round out the current section with a discussion of a key number of supplementary issues relating to the major virtues; namely, the accessory virtues/values, as well as the overarching concept of the general unifying themes. This grand-scale undertaking is, hereby, initiated with a detailed examination of the behavioral analogues for the group authority/follower realm, an institution virtually synonymous with virtually every major form of cooperative human endeavor.

3

THE GROUP ETHICAL REALM

Group (or tribal) authority is certainly one of mankind's most time-honored traditions. Prior to the dawning of our modern agricultural age, primitive hunter tribes wandered the earth following the uneven distribution of game animals, much as occurs in the remote outposts of the world today. In a purely organizational sense, the human tribe shows many similarities to the primitive social order of the lion pride or the wolf pack, although a closer examination reveals many finer distinctions. In particular, the human tribe is distinguished through its symbolic use of verbal communication over and beyond any instinctual form of body language. Lower animal societies are limited almost exclusively to this gestural style of communication, as suggested in the grooming and throat-baring types of behavior previously described. Although vocalization is often a key feature in many complex animal societies, it is chiefly employed in a guttural fashion without any consensus sense of form or meaning.

Although these instinctual forms of communication (by definition) occur chiefly between individuals, such personal interactions, in turn, are summated across the extent of the social hierarchy resulting in a "round-robin" style of pecking order. This dominance hierarchy only superficially conforms to true tribal authority in that it promotes a single dominant leader overseeing a descending hierarchy of less powerful individuals. This arrangement further makes little provision for any enduring sense of permanence, resulting in a frequent reshuffling of power within the pecking order. The human tribe, in contrast, picks a single consensus leader overseeing a collective of virtually equal followers. Although jockeying for position is not entirely abandoned, it ultimately is made subordinate to this group power leverage.

This distinction between the simple pecking order and true group authority is chiefly made possible through mankind's innovative use of ver-

bal symbolism. Nonverbal communication is meaningful only in immediate types of contexts, allowing only for one obvious means of interpretation; namely, the most basic style of pecking order. Human language, in contrast, is distinguished by its ability to communicate symbolically about abstract or motivational issues: permitting verbal communication not formally tied to such immediate concerns. Through this verbal refinement, mankind is essentially able to distinguish the more abstract style of group authority from its more elementary foundation in the personal pecking order, setting the stage for the cooperative social structure so crucial on the world scene today.

The group authority achieves this enhanced authority status by countering the more limited partisan concerns of the personal follower. The "side kick" style of strike leverage employed by the personal follower no longer proves effective against the group authority, who announces that individual members are now expendable when it comes down to a personal challenge for power. According to this third-order metaperspectival format, enough followers always remain to perpetuate group authority whether or not any individual should decide to desert. In a single stroke, the group authority is elevated well above any personal power struggles, an innovation that has endured as the familiar tradition of civic authority.

Although group authority has undergone many refinements down through the ages, its basic dynamics have remained fairly consistent in nature. Originally the tribal chiefdom was organized along familial lines, with related clan members answering to a single dominant patriarch or matriarch. Similarities in language and culture eventually brought related clans together, resulting in the enduring trend towards the nation state. Originally, nationalism implied the leadership of a regal monarch, with royal power passed down (in tribal fashion) through inheritance. This regal authority was celebrated through the potent use of ritual symbolisms: as reflected in the enduring Western traditions of the scepter, throne, crown, etc. The supportive cast of influential dukes and nobles relied upon a similar use of heraldic symbolisms for maintaining their accessory authority status.

The Western tradition of heraldry dates at least to medieval times, expressed in the development of the hereditary "coat of arms." This latter term derives from the military custom of embroidering the emblem of the knight directly upon the surcoat covering the armor. The protective function of the armor complicated the identification of friend or foe during the heat of battle, leading to the invention of personal heraldic symbolisms inscribed upon the shield. Originally, these symbols were personally selected, generally commemorating a defining episode during the knight's military career. Confusion ultimately arose concerning the duplication of designs, leading to the formal appointment of *heralds*, whose supervision of the art form gave rise to the general sense of the term. The introduction of gunpowder eventually rendered protective armor obsolete, reducing heraldry to its current formality of tracing family ancestry.

The traditional coat of arms is formally composed of a shield, crest, and motto. The descriptive terms employed in heraldry are assigned specific meanings in order to avoid confusion amongst the various authorities. A number of key heraldic terms with regal overtones particularly come to mind, in keeping with the four affective dimensions predicted for the group authority perspective. Colorful terms such as the circle of *glory* (or halo), the *honor*-point (on the shield), and the cap of *dignity* (or chapeau) abound within the heraldic literature. Add to these the animal symbolisms associated with *integrity* and the cohesive listing of "personal ideals" falls neatly into place.

This four-part grouping of glory-honor-dignity-integrity collectively traces its origins to the classical Latin tradition. Indeed, the Romans celebrated group leadership to perhaps its grandest degree of style. The personal ideals represent the more advanced group analogues of the subordinate class of ego states that they serve to supersede. Although their personal designation might seem to suggest somewhat of a misnomer, the group authority maneuver directly maneuvers upon the personal follower perspective, wherein accounting for the hybrid quality of the grouping. Accordingly, *glory* represents the group analogue of nostalgia, whereas *honor* denotes a similar modification of guilt. Furthermore, *dignity* redefines desire from a group perspective, whereas *integrity* denotes a more idealized form of worry. Accordingly, this four-part listing of personal ideals formally specifies motivations encompassing the group authority role; namely, glory, honor, dignity, and integrity. This initial class of group-focused ideals represents immediately active perspectives taking as their anticipated object the more abstract (projected) complement of future-directed virtuous modes. Here, the actively-focused authority mode represents the immediately active perspective, anticipating (as its projected object) the projected complement of future-directed follower roles. Generally speaking, the group authority themes immediately initiate the conditioned interaction in anticipation of the future-based potentiality characterizing the group follower perspective.

THE CARDINAL VIRTUES: THE ESSENCE OF GROUP COHESIVENESS

This initial description of the (group-focused) personal ideals effectively outlines the basic dynamics governing the group authority perspective. These four basic themes all derived from Latin roots, accentuating the Roman's enduring fascination with group leadership. The group authority perspective, accordingly, promotes these four basic themes; namely, dignified purpose tempered by integrity, accompanied by an active sense of glory and honor in one's civic endeavors. This distinctive group power base effectively allows the group authority to overrule the more shortsighted concerns of the personal follower, in essence, regaining the upper hand within the ascending power hierarchy. In light of the more elementary style of personal authority (that it supersedes), the group authority figure is similarly susceptible to one's own unique form of follower counter-maneuver, in this case that expressed by the group representative.

The group follower perspective is essentially as ancient as group authority itself, serving as a crucial counterpoint to the power of the group authority figure. Similar to the personal follower role (that it supersedes), the group representative shares the distinctive style of "strike" leverage characterizing the follower role. Indeed, it is chiefly with through this more advanced (group) context that the strike power of the follower figure reaches its greatest degree of potential. Although this basic strike leverage traces its origins to classical times, it only recently has truly come of age with respect to the dramatic rise of unions and collective bargaining. Prior to the turn of the

The Heraldic Symbolisms for the Personal Ideals
In Clockwise Order: Circle of Glory – Honor Point – Rampant – Cap of Dignity

century the typical factory worker suffered many indignities at the whim of his employer, yet was powerless to resist out of fear of being replaced. By playing one employee against another, management effectively maximized the power leverage implicit for the group authority perspective.

A corresponding rise in power within the group, however, forced management to come to a more equal footing with labor. Through the latter's reorganization as a "union collective," the rank-and-file picked a consensus spokesman (the shop steward) to represent them in their dealings with management. The most powerful leverage in collective bargaining, however, resides in the much publicized (and all too often wielded) strike clause within the union contract. According to this group power tactic, the group representative informs the group authority that without the cooperation of the labor pool, there will be no one left to justify his authority status. Through the judicious use of the strike option, the group representative effectively evens the score in job-related conflicts, as witnessed in the modern-day standoff between the contrasting interests of labor and management.

This enduring reliance on the strike option for pressing militant demands is generally invoked in only most intractable situations; namely, those negative conflicts where both parties suffer to some degree. It is ultimately possible, however, to invoke a more positive slant on the group follower perspective, as exemplified in the principles governing group *cohesiveness*. According to Group Theory, the theme of cohesiveness refers to a general preponderance of attractive vs. repulsive forces within the group. Cartwright and Zander (1960) identified five attractive forces within the successful group: respectively defined as (1) a strong feeling of "we"ness rather than "I"ness, (2) friendliness and loyalty to fellow members, (3) collective work towards a common goal, (4) willingness to endure pain or frustration for the sake of the group, and (5) a common defense against criticism. Members attracted to a group are more likely to exhibit congruent attitudes: namely, responsible action, interpersonal harmony, similarity of values, and an emphasis on security within the group.

It still remains to be determined, however, which precise combination of terms goes towards satisfying the requisite four-part complement of affective dimensions predicted for the group representative perspective. Being that the group representative reprises the role originally introduced as personal follower, this new format, accordingly, represents a more abstract variation on the initial complement of alter ego states (approval, leniency, solicitousness, and submissiveness). This more advanced aspect is effectively satisfied in terms of the previously described listing of cardinal virtues; namely, prudence, justice, temperance, and fortitude. Indeed, this distinctive grouping conveniently appears tailor-made for satisfying the four affective dimensions predicted for the group representative perspective.

THE CLASSICAL TRADITIONS
FOR THE CARDINAL VIRTUES

The English spellings for the cardinal virtues all collectively derive from Latin roots, although earlier precedents clearly exist in the Greek tradition. They first appear as a definitive grouping in Plato's dialogue *The Republic*, although Plato intimates that they were already a tradition even in his own day. The lyrical poet Pindar is credited with their first recorded reference in his *Eighth Isthmian Ode* (478 BCE): where Peleus and his fellow Aeacids are cited as models of justice, courage, temperance, prudence, and piety (a fifth virtue originally included within this grouping). In his *Republic*, however, Plato eliminates the somewhat extraneous concept of piety, focusing on the remaining four as the central core for his enduring system of ethical philosophy.

For Plato, virtue played a preeminent role in securing the health and harmony of the soul. In his dialogue *The Republic*, Plato (speaking through Socrates) proposes his utopian vision of the Greek city-state: one wishfully compensating for the weakness plaguing the troubled Athens of his day. Plato's ideal city-state was organized along the lines of a three-part caste system comprising a ruling-elite of guardians, a military class of warriors, and a mercantile class of workers (respectively symbolized as gold, silver, and bronze). The guardian class enjoyed an extensive degree of education accentuating the virtues of *prudence* and wisdom. The warrior class was subject to exhaustive military training selecting for the qualities of *fortitude* and courage in defense of the city. Furthermore, the economic focus of the worker/craftsman class selected for the virtue of *temperance* concerning such economic matters. Finally, the virtue of *justice* was ultimately found in the truth that each caste performed the task

for which it was best suited; namely, duties consistent with its respective virtuous mode. The city-state, accordingly, is prudent, just, temperate, and brave: directly amplifying those noble qualities professed by the shared focus its three supportive castes.

The subsequent rise to power of the Roman Empire brought further consideration to the Latin versions of the cardinal virtues. The Romans greatly admired classical Greek culture, borrowing extensively from their rhetoric and philosophy (including the enduring canon of cardinal virtues). One of the most influential Latin expositions in this regard was Cicero's *De Officiis*, a stirring tribute to the Latinized grouping of prudentia, justitia, temperatus, and fortitutio. An early distrust of pagan philosophy initially led many Christians to reject the validity of this Latin complement of cardinal virtues. With the eventual Roman acceptance of Christianity, however, Clement and Origen among the Greeks, as well as Lactantius and Ambrose among the Romans, began freely adapting pagan virtues to fit emerging Christian morality. Origen was among the first to draw attention to the preeminence of the cardinal virtues, describing them as indispensable to moral development. Although not specifically mentioned as a grouping in the New Testament, they nevertheless enjoyed widespread individual appeal. They are also listed as a cohesive grouping in the OT *Wisdom of Solomon*, a book further incorporated into the Apocrypha included within the Roman Catholic Bible.

It remained to the efforts of St. Ambrose (of Milan) to give this classical listing its traditional designation: deriving from the Latin *cardos* (hinge), deriving from the basic belief that all of mankind's more noble tendencies *hinge* upon these basic four virtues. This perspective, indeed, is prophetic in light of the pivotal role these virtues play at the group level within the ascending power hierarchy. These Christian perspectives on the cardinal virtues ensured their enduring significance in later Western culture, celebrated as moralistic standards in their own right. These themes enjoy considerable prestige even in our modern age, particularly when impassioned calls to service and duty remain the order of the day. The true significance of the cardinal virtues, however, ultimately reflects their direct foundation within the respective alter ego states. In this latter respect, *prudence* represents the group analogue of approval, whereas *justice* designates a similar refinement of blameful-leniency. Furthermore, *temperance* adds a public sense of moderation to solicitousness, whereas *fortitude* defines submissiveness from a civic perspective. This distinctive class of cardinal virtues formally represents a projected sense of potentiality within a future-directed time-frame, in essence, serving to effectively consummate the immediately active authority-based behaviors initiating the two-stage operant schematic.

Generally speaking, the group authority role immediately initiates the conditioned interaction, whereby anticipating the potentiality specified for the projected follower roles. The immediately-active authority roles occur entirely within the present, whereas the passively-potential follower modes are manifest within a future-directed time-frame. The latter future projected follower terms effectively complement the immediately active authority terms with respect to the overall group dynamic. For instance, in the case of positive reinforcement, the initial glorious sense of nostalgia on the part of the group authority figure further anticipates the prudent sense of approval on the part of the group representative. This prudent sense of approval, in turn, eventually becomes actualized as the dignified expression of desire on the part of the reinforcer, with the initially active glorious sense of nostalgia now projected as a determination to temperately act solicitously on the part of the group representative (within a future-directed time frame).

A similar style of motivational interplay further holds true with respect to the remaining class of virtues encompassing the domain of negative reinforcement. For instance, the initial honorable sense of guilt on the part of the group authority figure, in turn, anticipates the leniently-just treatment on the part of the group representative. This blameful sense of justice, in turn, ultimately becomes actualized as (an active) worrisome sense of integrity on the part of the reinforce. Here, the initially active honorable sense of guilt is now projected as a determined effort to fortitudinously act aversively on the part of the group representative (projected within a future-directed time frame). Consequently, in terms of both positive and negative reinforcement, the initially active personal ideals of glory, honor, dignity, and integrity effectively anticipate (in a behavioral sense) the respective (projected) virtuous counterparts of prudence, justice, temperance, and fortitude. Indeed, this basic style of group interaction is further seen to repeat for the remaining spiritual, humanitarian, and transcendental levels as well: providing a key means for specifying the dynamics underlying the ethical traditions specific to the virtues, values, and ideals. The remainder of the current chapter further outlines this more advanced style of group dynamics encompassing the entire eight-part complement of motivational terms, providing a sturdy foundation for all subsequent classes of virtues/values to follow, including an extensive analysis of their individual literary traditions across the board.

GLORY - PRUDENCE

The more straightforward class of positive virtues proves to be the most logical initiation point for such a grand-scale analysis, being that positive rewards appear much more tangible in nature: in contrast to the vaguer concept of leniency governing negative reinforcement. Accordingly, the interplay of glory and prudence will be examined first, followed by the remaining sequence comprised of dignity and temperance. As suggested in the group foundations for these virtuous terms, this overall realm of inquiry encompasses the more abstract style of group interplay that builds directly upon the more basic behavioral interplay of the personal authority/follower roles.

As initially suggested, the glorious sense of nostalgia expressed by the group authority figure actively initiates the group conditioned interaction, formally expressed as the solicitous quest for the rewarding reinforcement characterizing the group follower role. Being that only one role may be active within the conditioned sequence at any given time, the role of the reinforcer is relegated to that of a future potentiality, identified as the prudent sense of approval that is anticipated from the group follower figure.

The projected status of this latter prudent sense of approval equates to the group representative role, whereas the more immediately active glorious sense of nostalgia directly invokes the initial group authority role. According to this group authority/follower interplay, the group authority initiates the conditioned relationship, gloriously acting nostalgically in anticipation of the prudent sense of approval within a future-directed time-frame. This latter projected sense of potentiality ultimately imparts meaning and purpose to the group authority's initial glorious sense of nostalgia, being that all will have been for naught should such prudent-approval fail to materialize.

A familiar example of such a group style of interaction concerns the typical workplace scenario, defined as the reciprocal interplay between corporate administration and the supportive class of employees. This effectively mirrors the interplay previously described (in a personal sense) between the master craftsman and the apprentice. The group-oriented workplace employee typically performs specialized duties crucial to the group office environment, whereby (in the process) gloriously acting nostalgically in anticipation of the prudent-approval of the supervisory staff through the rigors of such a shared endeavor. The employee seeks to distinguish his/her own competency within the approving glance of management, perhaps one day even achieving upper-level status in one's own right. This active sense of procurement (in an appetitive sense) is colloquially equated with one's own glorious sense of nostalgia, a forward-looking emotion contingently anticipating the prudent bestowal of rewards.

The authority-ideal of *glory* certainly fits the bill in this preliminary group-focused respect, traditionally defined as a nostalgic expression of worthiness fully deserving of a projected prudent bestowal of approval on the part of the reinforcer. Indeed, glory can actually span a rather broad range of meanings, from exalted praise/honor to heightened achievement or distinction. Its modern spelling derives from the Latin *gloria* (of similar meaning and usage). As with so many of their abstract concepts, the Romans divinely worshipped glory as a deity: as witnessed in a dedicatory inscription to *Gloria* unearthed at Numidia in Northern Africa. She also appears as Gloria Exercitus (training, exercise) on medallions of the Roman emperor Constantius II, and simply as *Gloria* on other imperial coins.

The classical Greeks further worshipped this mental aspect in the guise of their abstract goddess *Eucleia*. Originally, Eucleia had been a surname of Artemis (the Greek Goddess of the Hunt), although this qualifier eventually came to be worshipped as a deity in its own right. She was particularly worshipped in the city-state of Athens, where a sanctuary was dedicated to her from the spoils-of-war seized at the Battle of Marathon. This battle was the greatest military triumph for the brave Athenians, with a reported *6,400* Persian casualties vs. *192* fatalities for the Athenians. Eucleia, accordingly, symbolized the exalted state of glory the Athenians enjoyed on their exalted victory day. Even in our modern era, glory still figures prominently in prestigious sporting events such as the Olympics, where great performances by winning athletes are acknowledged in glorious medal presentation ceremonies attended by throngs of admiring fans. The fact that such athletes are classified as amateurs (competing without pay) only further serves to magnify the symbolic glory they bow to receive upon the presentation stand.

The latter group follower expression of rewarding-approval is schematically represented by the cardinal virtue of prudence, traditionally defined as sound judgment or discretionary conduct in practical affairs. Its modern spelling derives from the Latin *prudens* (denoting wisdom and/or foresight). In Plato's *Republic*, prudence is specifically singled out as the foremost of the four cardinal virtues. This theme was further amplified by Plato's contemporary Aristotle, who viewed it as a key factor crucial to the moral development of the individual conscience. These classical perspectives, in turn, extended to the Christian era, where prudence is defined as deep spiritual insight into one's moral duties, as well as the concrete means towards their fulfillment. Consequently, prudence remains the cardinal virtue most allied to practical reason, a key motivational influence underlying all such virtuous acts.

This foresightful aspect of Christian prudence finds parallel representation in the medieval tradition of cathedral art. Prudence is traditionally depicted as a seated maiden holding a book or pointing to a globe at her feet. She is also shown holding a compass (a symbol of direction) or a mirror intertwined by serpents (signifying personal intuition). She is sometimes depicted with two faces (or even three) signifying her consideration of past, present, and future contexts. Prudence eventually became synonymous with courtly behavior, particularly the pronounced degree of decorum expressed towards the ruling royal family.

The magnificent palaces of Europe certainly fostered such a grand cast of supportive characters, an entourage that gloried in the majesty of the regal monarch. In particular, prudence gained considerable popularity as a femininely given name, reflecting the courtly spirit characteristic of the royal "ladies-in-waiting." This emphasis upon rewards similarly fits well within the workplace example, where management prudently aims to act in an approving fashion towards the employees in response to the gloriously-nostalgic efforts on the part of the workforce, whereby encouraging further such cycles of initiative within a future-directed time-frame.

DIGNITY - TEMPERANCE

The completed initiatory phase for glory and prudence, in turn, gives way to a remaining discussion of the subsequent stage within the group interaction: namely, that encompassing dignity/temperance. According to this latter stage, the group follower eventually acts upon his (projected) prudently-approving intentions, whereby dignifiedly acting desirously towards his willing workforce in anticipation of their projected temperate determination to act worthily within a future-directed time-frame. A number of key features are observed similar to those initially encountered with respect to glory/prudence. In terms of management's dignified expression of desire, the supervisor now formally assumes a group authority status in relation to the workplace employees. The latter employee role, in turn, takes on the mantle of the group follower role, in that it formally "follows" the authority role in terms a projected order within the interaction.

According to this dignity/temperance dynamic, management dignifiedly acts desirously towards the employees in anticipation of instilling a (projected) temperate expression of worthiness on the part of the workforce, whereby encouraging a determination to achieve further such cycles of productivity within a future-directed time-frame.

This immediately active style of rewarding reinforcement is formally identified with the group authority ideal of *dignity*, continuing in the ongoing tradition of the group authority/follower interaction. Its modern spelling derives from the Latin *dignitas* (merit or worth), from *dignus* (worthy): the same root for the Latin *decorum* (propriety). The great Roman statesman Cicero directly mentions dignity within the context of his rhetorical treatment of decorum. In the course of his dissertation, Cicero restricted this term exclusively to the brotherhood of man: defining dignity as that crucial quality which distinguishes man from lower animals. He further states that mankind's intellect is superior in its capacity for rational insight, in direct contrast to the more shortsighted pursuits of the rest of the animal kingdom. These classical themes underwent a significant revival during the Renaissance, when Italian humanists (following Cicero's precedent) equated the dignity of man with the tradition of the humanities. Dignity, accordingly, was associated with the *art* of being human, instilled through the devoted study of the liberal arts and sciences.

These classical overtones further extended to the Middle Ages with respect to the heraldic symbolisms associated with dignity. These are particularly apparent with respect to the stylized *chapeau*, also known as the cap of dignity or estate. As the chief heraldic emblem of dignity, the chapeau was elegantly constructed of red velvet: sporting a flat crown and an ostentatious ermine rim. The cap originally was worn by barons and nobles of the British Parliament, formally specifying their elevated rank and status. Around the time of Charles II, the chapeau was further embellished with precious metal around its base, giving rise to the coronet (or crown) of British royal-ty. Indeed, the velvet cap contained within the British royal crown is directly traceable to this original cap of dignity.

These noble connotations of the chapeau rate further consideration in light of its designation as the cap of maintenance (or estate). According to medieval tradition, the noble enjoyed exclusive control over his feudal estate, accompanied by the attendant responsibilities of dignifiedly rewarding the general welfare and labor of the serfs. In times of trouble, the noble often provided his subjects protection within the walls of his stockade in exchange for their fruitful services on the estate. Indeed, the great power and dignity enjoyed by the noble stemmed directly from his shrewd reinforcement of his loyal workforce.

A similar motivational emphasis extends to the current workplace example, where the group authority (in the guise of management) dignifiedly acts desirously to reinforce the solicitous efforts of the respective workforce in anticipation of their (projected) temperate determination to act solicitousness within a future-directed time-frame. Indeed, the employee is reciprocally dependent upon the rewarding approval of management: his/her initial gloriously-nostalgia treatment becoming entirely meaningless without such suitable fanfare, whereby prompting the potential for further such workplace cycles of productivity. This crucial air of dignity instills a traditional rewarding context for all such workplace efforts on the part of the employees, maintaining a promising and reinforcing environment conducive to productivity (as verified when the monthly paychecks are finally issued). In this latter fashion, a healthy sense of respect for the rank-and-file within the company remains consistently in evidence, further ensuring a successful outcome to all such collaborative enterprises.

The latter temperate attitude certainly fits the bill in this basic regard, temperance traditionally defined as restraint or moderation in the indulgence of the appetites (conducive to harmonious cooperation within the group). Its modern spelling derives from the Latin *temperantia* (moderation) from the Latin root *tempos* (extent or measure). It is certainly ironic that the true value of this virtue was often overlooked during the classical era, particularly in light of the sensual excesses characterizing the Imperial Roman era. The more austere Greeks worshipped this theme as their abstract goddess Sophrosyne, the divine personification of moderation and self-control. Indeed, her name is defined as a Greek compound of root-stems denoting "safe-mindedness." Sophrosyne, is depicted as a comely maiden in

Personifications of the Four Cardinal Virtues (Clockwise: P-T-J-F) - circa 1295
Somme le Roi - ms. 6329, folio 96v, Paris Arsenal, Photo courtesy Bibliotheque Nationale, Paris

flowing garb holding a *ewer* (pitcher) and *cantharos* (a libation cup used in drinking rituals).

According to Plato's masterpiece, *The Republic,* temperance is defined as the rational restrain of the physical appetites: particularly, food, drink, and sexual indulgence. In Plato's ideal city-state, the economic focus of the worker/craftsman class selected for the virtue of *temperance* concerning an overall sense of restraint and control in economic matters of crucial import to the survival of the group. In his later dialogue, *Laws,* Plato intimates that temperance aspires to a likeness to God, a theme further professed by early Church theologians in their pursuit of the virtuous lifestyle. Medieval artisans, in turn, symbolized tem-

perance in the classical style reminiscent of Sophrosyne. Through the dramatic medium of stained glass, each of the cardinal virtues was visually personified using a stylized set of human attributes. Some stained glass representations portray Temperance with a torch and a jug. Others include a vessel of water for mixing with the wine (wherein diluting its inebriating effects). Related depictions feature a scourge and a bridle (sometimes with the bit in place) signifying the restraint of the passions.

In a formally schematic sense, I, as group representative (the employee) temperately express a determination to act solicitously towards you within some future-directed time-frame in response to your (as group authority) dignified expression of desire towards me. The employer bears a certain risk in assuming that such anticipated temperate cooperation will eventually be forthcoming. He/she, however, can reasonably be assured by the wealth of previous cycles of temperate solicitousness recollected from past occurrence, spurring the anticipation of similar such temperate cooperation in the future. Indeed, it is chiefly this tenuous power of deliberation that ultimately imparts the strike-power leverage enjoyed by the group representative in relation to the group authority figure, the latter dependent upon the former to fulfill his/her immediately active rewarding mandate.

This temperate sense of solicitousness (from the perspective of the workforce), through the process of deliberation, ultimately provides an effective sense of closure in to the entire conditioned interchange: ultimately serving to prompt further such cycles of cooperation between labor and management within the conditioned interaction. Consequently, this second phase effectively reflects the inherent strike-power leverage enjoyed by the loyal workforce, for without this temperate expression of solicitousness, the dignified sense of desire expressed by management will all have been for naught. Although the workplace example proves enlightening (for illustrative purposes), many other examples further come to mind. Indeed, the ultimate goal of this exercise has been to propose a sturdy foundation for the even more abstract listings of virtues and values to follow, resulting in a hierarchial schematic model governing the entire virtuous realm.

HONOR - JUSTICE

Before skipping ahead to such a crucial range of applications it proves crucial to examine the remaining virtuous interplay specific to the realm of negative reinforcement. Indeed, such a motivational style of analysis scarcely proves as clearcut as that for positive rewards in that negative reinforcement involves the lenient withholding of punishment as opposed to the more straightforward bestowal of rewards. Here, negative reinforcement entails the withholding of punitive consequences within the environment or (in an interpersonal sense) leniency in response to aversive types of behavior. In terms of a group social context, the group authority figure honorably acts in a guiltily-submissive fashion in anticipation of leniently-just treatment on the part of the group representative. This projected lenient sense of justice, in turn, eventually becomes immediately

actualized as a worrisome sense of integrity on the part of the reinforcer in anticipation of (a projected) fortitudinous sense of submissiveness on the part of the respective follower figure.

This interplay of submissiveness/leniency is exceedingly reminiscent of the throat-baring behaviors previously described for the wolf pack, where the submissive pack member dramatically exaggerates his degree of vulnerability in anticipation of the potential bestowal of leniency. In the more abstract (verbal) sense, submissiveness operates in a similar fashion: namely, vocally expressing an honorable sense of guilt potentially elicits a lenient sense of justice on the part of the group representative. Certainly it might appear somewhat risky to express such an extreme degree of vulnerability without a reasonable assurance of upcoming leniency. Past memories definitely come into play, with previous cycles of leniency ultimately justifying such a radical act of faith. According to this more measured strategy, leniently-just rehabilitation (rather than vengeful retribution) now remains the order of the day.

A familiar example of such a reciprocating style of group interaction concerns the interplay between the military general and his band of enlisted men. The enlisted team-soldier is expected to fall into line with the discipline and dictates of the general, honorably acting submissively in anticipation of leniently-just treatment on the part of the general. This honorably-guilty expression of submissiveness represents a forward-looking emotion anticipating a lenient sense of justice on the part of the military brass. In other words, I as group authority (common soldier) honorably act in a guiltily-submissive fashion towards you in anticipation of your (as ranking general) leniently-just treatment of me. The soldier bears a certain risk in trusting that leniently-just treatment will eventually be forthcoming although assured by the wealth of previous cycles of negative reinforcement conducive to confidence in anticipated leniency within a future-directed time-frame.

The preceding soldier/general example proves exceedingly enlightening with respect to the (group) prerequisites for honor, a term invested with a rather broad range of meaning: spanning admiration and esteem to nobility and honesty. Similar to the case previously made for glory, honor was also prominently worshipped as a deity by the classical Romans, as personified by their abstract god Honos. On Roman coins and medals, Honos is depicted as a handsome youth holding a spear in his right hand and a "horn of plenty" in his left. He is crowned with a wreath of bay leaves and his chest is exposed. His chief temple was situated outside the Porta Capena in Rome in close proximity to the temple of Mars, the Roman God of War. An even more ancient altar was dedicated to Honos outside the Colline gate. Persons sacrificing here were obliged to have their heads uncovered, a custom still widely followed today in the swearing of oaths.

The early Middle Ages further celebrated such classical considerations, honor figuring prominently in the Codes of Courtesy and Chivalry: also known as the Court of Venus and the Field of Mars. Indeed, in medieval heraldry, the honor point refers to the high center point on the shield, the field where the crowning symbolisms of nobility are most likely to occur. This heraldic sense of the term actually spans a much broader range of meaning, further implying primacy and/or seniority. It also suggests (like honesty) a sense of what is rightfully expected with respect to one's civic and moral obligations.

This upright quality comes through most clearly with respect to the tradition of the Code of Honor: namely, that system of reciprocal rights and obligations governing a particular trade or profession. It typically takes the form of honesty in one's business dealings, as well as loyalty to one's fraternal organizations. It frequently was compounded by the themes of etiquette and good breeding consistent with such a refined social context. Consequently, this code eventually came to be associated with many stylized rituals: most notably, the time-honored custom of dueling to restore one's personal sense of honor (or that of one's family).

In terms of the two-stage motivational dynamic, the clear militaristic overtones for the anticipated leniency phase are exemplified (in a group sense) by the cardinal virtue of justice, as particularly witnessed during classical times with respect to the legal administration of the Roman Empire. The Justinian Code of Law specifically defines justice as: "the constant and firm willingness to render every man his due." This basic conviction was further echoed centuries later by St. Thomas Aquinas in his comprehensive discussion of justice contained within his *Summa Theologica*. These general connotations of justice appear to share a common theme; namely, the subordination of one's personal self-interests to the collective welfare comprising the group. Indeed, justice certainly fulfills its status as a group follower perspective, a fact amply documented in the modern-day institution of the *jury* trial.

True to its origins in British Common Law, the jury trial has remained a prominent American standard since colonial times. The American var-iation preserves the basic features of the Common Law jury; namely, a twelve-member panel presided over by a judge empowered to reach a unanimous verdict. This group focus is particularly evident during the jury selection process, where complete impartiality is sought across a representative cross-section of the general population. The public is similarly invited to witness the courtroom proceedings, criminal cases referenced with the formula: The People vs. John Doe.

Following the systematic presentation of evidence, the jury ultimately deliberates in private over the presumed guilt or innocence of the accused, tempering the letter of the law with personal intuition and insight. The jury foreman (as representative of the group) submits the final verdict to the judge, who (as spokesman for the court) reads the decision to the defendant. The lack of a unanimous verdict is figuratively termed a "hung jury," being that complete agreement is necessary for establishing the guilt or innocence of the accused. The sentencing phase focuses on the lenient moral rehabilitation of the individual, a factor that aims to avoid any personal quest for retribution. Although fines or jail-time are typically pronounced at this juncture, such punitive measures are primarily meant to protect the public welfare (as well as providing restitution to the injured party). A penitent attitude on the part of the defendant generally secures a greater degree of leniency from the judge. Indeed, an honorable admission of guilt is rightfully expected to be offered if justice is truly said to have been done.

INTEGRITY - FORTITUDE

The preceding two-stage sequence of honor-justice, in turn, dictates that the group follower figure must eventually act upon the potentiality implicit in his/her own projected lenient sense of justice. This further development takes the form of worrisomely acting with integrity within a more immediate time-frame, whereby anticipating the projected submissive sense of courage/fortitude on the part of the enlisted men. This ultimate decision to act often dictates a rather extended course of deliberation on the part of the lenient reinforcer. Indeed, it is this ultimate power of deliberation that formally imparts the power leverage enjoyed by the reinforcer in relation to that of the procurer.

The respective interplay of group authority and group follower roles is similarly modified with respect to this second stage within the conditioned interaction. This latter phase invokes the immediately active worrisome sense of integrity expressed by the reinforcer, although now punctuated from the perspective of the group authority, as schematically depicted in Part-B of **Fig. 2A**. Here, reinforcement (Y) is now depicted occurring entirely in the present, whereas potential procurement (X) is now shown projected into a future-directed time-frame. Consequently, the general-in-command is now thrust into an immediately active reinforcement role, worrisomely acting with a lenient sense of integrity in anticipation of the (projected) brave sense of fortitude on the part his enlisted men (the latter experienced within a future-directed time-frame).

A number of key modifications are further observed with respect to the polarities of the authority/follower roles. With respect to his immediately-active worrisome sense of integrity, the general now abandons his former potential lenient expression of justice (characterizing the group follower perspective); in turn, switching to a more immediately active style of integrity status indicative of the group authority role. The common soldier, in contrast, now assumes the respective mantle of the group representative, a status reflecting the motivational leverage inherent to one's future-directed style of fortitude perspective. This role reversal is certainly warranted, being that it formally reflects the initial sequence based upon honor/justice, although now punctuated from an immediately active reinforcement perspective (rather than the submissive variation). The general now worrisomely acts with lenient-integrity in anticipation of instilling a brave sense of fortitude on the part of the enlisted men: with an eye towards encouraging them to honorably act submissively on future occasions.

The immediately active integrity perspective (on the part of the general) directly parallels the affiliated theme of dignity, with the exception that leniency (rather than approval) is now called into focus. This lenient interpretation is further reflected in the traditional connotations of the term; e.g., moral probity and ethical steadfastness. Its modern spelling derives from the Latin *integritas* (completeness, purity), from *integer* (whole). In this steadfast respect, integrity is figuratively symbolized as the domestic canine consistent with its enduring reputation as "man's best friend."

This unswerving sense of integrity (in relation to the domestic dog) is further reflected in its traditionally given name "*Fido*," from the Latin *fideo* (I believe). Other carnivores with strong social instincts (such as the lion) are similarly esteemed as paragons of integrity in classical mythology. According to Old Testament scripture, the lion and the wolf were respectively revered as the figurative emblems of the Jewish tribes of Judah and Benjamin. In medieval heraldry, one of the most popular shield arrangements is the *rampant*: a lion standing upright in profile with its front paws splayed (as if warding off a blow). The rampaging lion is often depicted sporting a regal crown, a factor further consistent with the group overtones of integrity. Indeed, this regal sense of integrity for the group authority (under the most adverse of circumstances) effectively complements the more dignified demeanor previously cited within more positive contexts.

In terms of the two-stage motivational schematic, the enduring militaristic overtones for the respective group follower role are exemplified by the remaining cardinal virtue of fortitude: a theme traditionally defined as the patient endurance of trouble or pain. Courage and bravery are often cited as its major synonyms. Its modern spelling derives from the Latin *fortitutio* from *fortis* (strength or power). During the classical era, fortitude was directly identified with Virtus: the Roman personification of manly courage and valor, from the Latin *vir* (man). Patriarchal philosophers primarily identified manliness with godliness, with *virtu* becoming synonymous with moral goodness, along with other terms hinting at male potency (such as rectitude and uprightness). *Virtu* eventually became identified with moral competency in general, as suggested in the broader connotations of the term.

These military connotations of fortitude endured the decline of the classical era, remaining one of the most dominant themes throughout the Medieval Age. During the ensuing age of chivalry, fortitude helped fire the hopes and aspirations of all knights within the realm. It served to subjugate the emotions of fear and cowardice while inspiring dutiful behavior in perilous situations. It is traditionally ordered to prudence, effectively moderating the tendency towards reckless bravado. These moral overtones are further reflected in the cathedral art of the day, incorporating many of the classical attributes traditionally associated with Virtus. In addition to the upright sword, shield, and armor; Fortitude is variously depicted tearing open the jaws of a lion or chained to a column indicative of the biblical story of Samson. In one portrayal, fortitude is depicted holding a miniature tower entwined by a dragon (the neck of which she grasps), an allusion to the perpetual struggle between good and evil.

True fortitude, however, is also invested with a strategic defensive slant, the military *fort* deriving from the same Latin root-stem. In truth, it may be judged just as noble to stand fast under entrenched attack as to lead the charge, effectively underscoring the dual aspects of the term. This risk of life-and-limb entails sacrifice approaching true "intestinal" fortitude; namely, that figurative ability to *stomach* adversity. Indeed, whether one aspires to military glory or martyrdom, one's personal concerns pale in significance to the welfare of the group.

Similar to the preceding example of temperance, the brave warrior is totally dedicated to the potential for duty/allegiance within his military unit. Even in our modern age of mechanistic warfare, the courage of the brave soldier knows no bounds: ranging from vexing personal hardship to the perilous risk of life or limb. This overarching sense of duty is particularly apparent on the eve of a great battle, when a stirring call to courage is made by the general-in-command, whereby alleviating any lingering sense of doubt on the part of the enlisted men. The general strategically reminds his soldiers of the peril to their free way of life (and that of their loved ones), effectively appealing to their crucial role towards maintaining the global status quo.

In conclusion, in terms of the second stage of the conditioned interaction, the commanding officer worrisomely acts with lenient-integrity towards his enlisted men in anticipation of their brave sense of fortitude (as projected into a future-directed time-frame). This latter fortitude perspective effectively plays-up one's vulnerability within the conditioned interaction, effectively limiting the potential for further conflict when extended to future such determined cycles. The soldier, accordingly, is reciprocally dependent upon the lenient sense of integrity expressed by his commanding officer: his brave sense of fortitude remaining entirely meaningless without such lenient underpinnings. Indeed, this enhanced understanding of the reciprocating dynamics for the group authority and follower roles proves exceedingly effective (in a theoretical sense) for ultimately defining the motivational dynamics underlying the more abstract listings of virtues and values to follow.

In summary, the immediately active style of group authority role proves a fitting counterpoint to the potentially anticipated perspective inherent to the group follower role. As initially described for the ego and alter ego states, the more abstract sets of virtues specified for the group ideals and cardinal virtues exhibit two similar degrees of specialization: namely, subdivided into either active modes occurring in the present or passive modes projected within a future-directed timeframe. The active behavioral modes are defined in terms of the personal ideals, as specialized into the immediately-active themes of *dignified*-desire or a worrisome-*integrity*, as well as an *honorable* sense of guilt or *glorious* sense of nostalgia. The future-directed modes, in turn, target the more abstract realm of the cardinal virtues consistent with their inherent degree of potentiality: namely, *prudent*-approval, *just*-leniency, *temperate*-solicitousness, or *fortitudinous*-submissiveness.

As chief spokesman for the group, the group representative establishes an equal balance of power with respect to the authority/follower roles. The virtuous themes celebrated in Plato's *Republic* certainly ring true in this basic respect, each representative within the group fully cognizant of one's projected role therein; namely, to be prudent, just, temperate, and brave. When ultimately faced with such a potent challenge to his/her authority status, the group authority further seeks to regain the upper hand within the ascending motivational hierarchy; namely, ascending again to the next higher *universal/spiritual* level of authority.

The scope of the upcoming background material relating to spiritual (or universal) authority is essentially eclectic in nature, not meant to favor any one cultural tradition over another. True to its elementary foundations within Western thought, many of the virtuous ethical terms were originally developed within the Christian tradition, a feature not always compatible with modern-day secularism. Many of the spirited literary excerpts from Church theologians or biblical scripture were, nevertheless, left essentially intact; for qualifying these historical documents (in hindsight) would greatly diminish the impact of the background material. This eclectic strategy is not to be construed as favoring any one faith-based system over another, for virtue is effectively a universal global phenomenon. With this caveat firmly in place, the behavioral prerequisites for the remainder of this treatise should hopefully satisfy even the most stringent of secular critics, a resource applicable across all cultures and creeds.

4

THE SPIRITUAL/UNIVERSAL REALM

Similar to the case previously established for the group authority role, spiritual (or universal) authority is essentially as ancient as civilization itself, serving an analogous stabilizing function in many primitive cultures. Prior to our modern age of scientific inquiry, primitive man relied almost exclusively on religious belief and superstition to explain the bewildering complexities of the natural world. The typically violent forces of earth, wind, and fire served as a source of both awe and amazement, inspiring an enduring sense of sacredness within the primitive mentality. The orderly rhythms governing the procession of the sun, moon, and stars must have surely invoked feelings of amazement, eventually identified with a complex pantheon of celestial gods. This constellation of myth and ritual eventually gave rise to a specialized clan of tribal shamans, extending to the priestly castes characterizing many early civilizations. According to this ancient mentality, the priest's ritual appeal to divinity spelled the difference between illness and health, fortune or disaster: a welcome hedge in an uncertain world.

In ancient Egypt, the pharaoh and the priestly class shared more-or-less equally in the power of the kingdom, each magnifying the power of the other in the eyes of the people. First and foremost, the pharaoh represented the supreme political figurehead for the Egyptian people. Egypt's prosperous economy served as a powerful magnet for refugees throughout the region. In order to counteract this multi-cultural challenge to his native authority, the pharaoh took full advantage of the much broader cloak of spiritual authority; namely, that binding over the group of all groups (or all mankind). By claiming direct lineage from the gods, the pharaoh proclaimed supreme authority over all groups within his domain regardless of any partisan concerns therein. The spiritual authority figure served clear notice that plenty of groups remained to perpetuate his au-

thority status whether or not any particular group would decide to desert. Consequently, the spiritual authority transcends the limitations plaguing partisan politics, wherein assuming the maximum degree of power leverage characterizing the universal perspective.

The Western tradition of spiritual authority has remained virtually synonymous with Christian principles since the decline of the classical Roman era. As founder of the Christian movement, Christ made direct claim to the role of Messiah (or Anointed One) within the Jewish tradition. His reputed claim to divinity (as the Son of God) established Christ as the premier spiritual authority figure of his day. Indeed, Christ was particularly well versed in the spiritual authority maneuver, as witnessed in his many encounters with the hypocritical Pharisees of his day. In one instance, the Pharisees attempted to trap Jesus into an act of treason, questioning whether it was lawful to give tribute unto Caesar. Invoking the spiritual authority countermaneuver, Christ cleverly replied: "Render unto Caesar the things that are Caesar's, and unto God the things that are God's." Certainly, these scriptural precedents echo the modern-day separation of church and state, a cornerstone of the American legal system.

MODERN PERSPECTIVES WITH RESPECT TO SPIRITUAL AUTHORITY

From a historical perspective, the establishment of the United States of America arose as a direct consequence of the power struggle pitting the Colonials against the oppressive rule of the British Crown. A long line of English monarchs (leading to King George III) relentlessly oppressed the American colonists, including a plan to proclaim the Church of England as the official state religion throughout the Colonies (conflicting with the diverse spiritual foundations of the latter). This outrage, compounded by other economic policies, resulted in the *Declaration of Independence* and subsequent Revolutionary War. The *Declaration* represented an unprecedented appeal to spiritual authority overruling the more partisan concerns promulgated by the British crown. In keeping with the common Christian heritage of the colonies, the *Declaration of Independence* proclaimed: "All men are created equal, endowed by their Creator with certain unalienable rights; namely, life, liberty, and the pursuit of happiness." In contrast to the prevailing royalist perspective, the colonials viewed government as instituted through mankind's consent to protect and preserve fundamental human rights.

Historical precedent dictates that the *Declaration's* author, Thomas Jefferson, borrowed extensively from earlier British theorists on the subject. In *On Civil Government, the Second Treatise* (1690) John Locke proposed that no one should harm another with respect to life, health, liberty, or possessions. Furthermore, should one actually be harmed, the injured party would enjoy full right to compensation. Locke's treatise was published shortly after the Glorious Revolution of 1688, which witnessed the expulsion of King James II from the British throne. Four generations later, the American colonist's similar dissatisfaction with British policies encouraged a revival in social conscience. Jefferson adopted Locke's principles of life and liberty, while modifying the remaining theme of property (for aesthetic reasons) into "pursuit of happiness."

Although the spirited literary style of the *Declaration* provided some measure of consolation to the disgruntled colonials, they soon became embroiled in the long and brutal War of Independence. The ultimate victory by the revolutionary forces led to the subsequent adoption of the *Constitution* of the United States. In a curious oversight, the framers of the *Constitution* failed to include adequate guarantees of the civil liberties so eloquently proclaimed in the *Declaration of Independence*. Indeed, the people rightfully rejected Federalist claims that such guarantees exceeded the limits of constitutional authority.

This shortcoming fortunately was remedied during the first regular meeting of Congress chiefly through the efforts of James Madison. The Madison Amendments stemmed from numerous proposals gleaned from the various state conventions. The final ten amendments (comprising the *Bill of Rights*) included guarantees on freedom of speech, religion, and the press. Further safeguards include the right to a speedy trial, reasonable bail, and the power to confront one's accus-

ers. Other amendments protected against mandatory self-incrimination, unreasonable search-and-seizure, as well as cruel and unusual punishment. None of these rights were absolute, however, for the amendments never were meant to conflict with the general public welfare. Indeed, the *Bill of Rights* only limited the power of the federal government, the states being clearly reluctant to diminish their individual autonomy.

With respect to the individual groupings of virtues and values examined to date, the diverse range of civil liberties guaranteed in the *Bill of Rights* can scarcely claim the pedigree or tradition essential for incorporation into the unified power hierarchy. It proves effective, however, to view the generic concept of "civil liberty" as the confluence of two supportive concepts; namely, *civility* and *liberty*. Add to these the related themes of *providence* and *austerity* and the master grouping of spiritual authority themes falls neatly into focus. In this expanded sense, the master four-part listing of providence-liberty-civility-austerity collectively comprises what is termed the class of *civil liberties*, in direct acknowledgement of their enduring moralistic precedents.

According to this more universal context, the civil liberties represent the higher spiritual analogues of the more basic group-focused class of personal ideals (glory-honor-dignity-integrity). Here, *providence* represents a spiritual refinement of glory, whereas *liberty* makes a parallel analogy to honor. Similarly, *civility* redefines dignity from a spiritual perspective, whereas *austerity* represents a more idealized form of integrity. Although the political applications of the civil liberties might seem to belie their spiritual significance, recall that the spiritual authority maneuver builds directly upon the group follower perspective, wherein accounting for the hybrid quality of the grouping.

Accordingly, this four-part listing of civil liberties formally specifies motivations encompassing the spiritual authority role; namely, providence, liberty, civility, and austerity. This initial class of universally-focused ideals represents immediately active perspectives, anticipating (as their object) the more abstract future-directed complement of theological virtues. Here, the spiritual authority role represents the immediately active perspective that anticipates the (projected) future-directed complement of follower roles. Generally speaking, the spiritual authority themes immediately initiate the conditioned interaction in anticipation of the projected degree of potentiality that characterizes the dynamics of the spiritual disciple perspective.

THE THEOLOGICAL VIRTUES

The completed description of the spiritual authority perspective, in turn, gives way to a parallel style of analysis with respect to the spiritual follower (or disciple) perspective. The spiritual disciple maneuver is essentially as ancient as spiritual authority itself, restoring an equivalent balance of power to the universal power realm. Similar to the other follower maneuvers (that it supersedes), the spiritual disciple maneuver shares the distinctive style of "strike" leverage so effective in confrontations with the authority figure. For the spiritual disciple, this generally takes the form of a universal style of strike leverage, as traditionally seen in the emergence of schisms or heresies. Although the extreme degree of abstraction encountered at this level might appear to invalidate any meaningful degree of effectiveness, witness the power of the revolutionary for influencing such enduring historical events as the Protestant Reformation; and, indeed, the very founding of Christianity itself.

In his designated role of spokesman for the spiritual congregation, the spiritual disciple informs the spiritual authority that the blessings of the faithful are crucial for preserving his authority status. Fortified by this formal "strike" leverage, the spiritual disciple can wield a considerable degree of influence within the spiritual congregation. History certainly abounds with many such dramatic twists of fate, as witnessed in the emergence of the Protestant Reformation. Here the unassuming monk, Martin Luther dared to speak out against the corrupt practices of the Roman Catholic Church, a schism destined to forever change the face of Western civilization. Although this drastic style of strike leverage is typically effective only in negative circumstances, a more positive slant may alternately be gained with respect to the cohesiveness of the spiritual congregation. Although group cohesiveness was previously defined in terms of the four cardinal virtues, the congregational variety is further specified within the traditions governing the respective class of theological virtues.

The theological virtues (faith, hope, and charity) have enjoyed a long and distinguished religious tradition, rivaling that previously established for the cardinal virtues. Although individually mentioned throughout the Old Testament, they are first listed as a cohesive grouping in the New Testament, particularly in the writings of St. Paul. These virtues were prominently featured in Chapter *13* of his First Letter to the Corinthians where he finishes with the stirring admonition: "And now abideth faith, hope, and charity, these three; but the greatest of these is charity." The designation of *theological* dates to St. Gregory the Great, celebrating the supreme moral foundations for these three basic virtues and acknowledging their intimate connection to the cardinal virtues.

This enduring theme extended to the writings of later Church theologians, most notably, St. Thomas Aquinas (1225-1274). In his *Summa Theologica*, St. Thomas specifically distinguishes the cardinal (or natural) virtues from the theological (or supernatural) versions. According to Aquinas, the cardinal virtues are rooted within the psychological nature of man, developed primarily through concerted moral effort. They perfect mankind's natural dispositions, wherein defending against instinctual types of excess. In contrast, the theological virtues are viewed as supernatural, serving to encourage our spiritual nature.

In keeping with his illustrious predecessors, St. Thomas limited his treatment of the theological virtues to the first basic three. This circumstance, however, leaves the complement one term short of satisfying the requisite four-part listing predicted for the spiritual disciple perspective. Historical precedent has favored such a technical shortcoming, particularly in that medieval theologians grouped the theological and cardinal virtues together summating to the mystical number of "seven." This seven-fold listing was magically said to counteract the evil influence of the Seven Deadly Sins; namely, pride, anger, envy, lust, gluttony, covetousness, and sloth. This theme first appears in the writings of Psychomachia of Prudentius (circa 400 CE) picturing in vivid verse the inner conflict pitting virtue versus vice.

Despite these theological interpretations, it ultimately proves crucial to return to the original scriptural sources for clues to the identity of the missing theological virtue. It is particularly significant to note that Chapter *13* of St. Paul's First Letter to the Corinthians is curiously the shortest chapter of the entire epistle, more or less arbitrarily separated from the adjoining chapters. St. Paul fittingly sums up the theme of the subsequent Chapter *14* with the quotation: "Let all things be done *decently* and in order" suggesting that decency represents the missing theological virtue. Decency is a prominent theme in OT scripture (as well as the New Testament teachings of Christ). Although not specifically mentioned by name, a careful reading of St. Paul's other references to the theological virtues: e.g., Romans (5:1-5) and 1st Thessalonians (1:3) would seem to suggest precisely such a novel interpretation.

This modest modification of the theological format finally accounts for the complete four-part complement of virtuous terms predicted for the spiritual disciple perspective. The theological virtues are viewed as the more abstract spiritual analogues of the subordinate complement of the cardinal virtues. According to this expanded context, *faith* represents prudence from a spiritual perspective, whereas *hope* makes similar parallels to justice. Furthermore, *charity* represents a spiritual refinement of temperance, whereas *decency* reinterprets fortitude from a theological perspective. Although this intimate correspondence was never directly specified in the scriptures, this enduring viewpoint is further validated in terms of the corresponding literary traditions.

THE MOTIVATIONAL INTERPLAY FOR THE UNIVERSAL DOMAIN

As previously described with respect to the group-focused listings of personal ideals and cardinal virtues, the more abstract virtuous groupings specified for the civil liberties and theological virtues similarly exhibit a dual range of specialization: subdivided into either immediately active modes occurring in the present or passively-potential modes projected into a future-directed time-frame. The immediately active behavioral modes are defined in terms of the civil liberties, as invested with clear behavioral overtones; namely, a glorious sense of *providence* or a *libertarian* sense of honor, as well as a dignified sense of *civility* or an *austere* sense of integrity.

The future-directed behavioral perspectives, in turn, target the more abstract projected realm of the theological virtues: namely, prudent-*faith*, just-*hope*, temperate-*charitableness*, and decent-fortitude. These mentally-projected theological virtues effectively complement the immediately active civil liberties in terms of the overall spiritual dynamic. For instance, in the case of positive reinforcement, a glorious sense of providence on the part of the spiritual authority directly anticipates the prudent sense of faithfulness on the part of the spiritual disciple. This prudent sense of faithfulness, in turn, eventually becomes actualized as a dignified sense of civility on the part of the reinforcer, whereby anticipating the temperate sense of charitableness projected to occur within a future-directed time-frame.

A similar motivational interplay further holds true for the remaining realm of negative reinforcement. For instance, the libertarian sense of honor on the part of the spiritual authority figure, in turn, anticipates the blameful-hope for justice on the part of the spiritual disciple. This latter (projected) blameful-hope for justice, in turn, eventually becomes actualized as the austere sense of integrity on the part of the reinforcer, whereby anticipating the decent sense of fortitude projected to occur within a future-directed time-frame. Accordingly, in terms of both positive and negative reinforcement, the immediately active civil liberties of providence, liberty, civility, and austerity effectively complement (in a behavioral sense) the projected range of potentiality characterizing the theological virtues: faith, hope, charity, and decency. The remainder of the current chapter examines the more advanced universal dynamics encompassing this eight-part complement of themes, providing a sturdy foundation for all subsequent classes of virtues/values to follow.

Following the pattern of discussion previously established for the personal and group domains, it would be tempting at this juncture to proceed in a similar vein: examining both the spiritual authority and follow roles in tandem with one another as a dynamic two-stage motivational sequence. In terms of the current spiritual/universal focus, this would amount to the positive sequence of providence, faith, civility and charity: as well as the lenient sequence of liberty, hope, austerity and decency. The third-order level of abstraction characterizing the spiritual/universal realm, however, unfortunately begins to formally obscure the orderly pattern of procurement *then* reinforcement previously established for the personal and group levels.

Indeed, effective illustrative examples for the predicted interplay of the spiritual authority and spiritual follower roles prove similarly elusive, unlike the more clear-cut personal theme of the master and the apprentice, or the group example of the general and his enlisted men. Indeed, most common interactions fall into the category of group or personal nature, with the universal perspective primarily restricted to those holding strong religious or universal viewpoints. Potential positive examples include the interplay of the monk and the abbot, or the philanthropist and the overarching world community. Examples targeting negative reinforcement might alternately extend to a "superhero" focus, such as the interplay of the crusader and his/her religious authority, or the UN Security Council and its peacekeeping force (in a more secular universal sense). The most prominent risk to citing specific universal examples is that one side might inevitably be offended in terms of the sensitivities governing the dynamics underlying such a secular and/or inter-denominational focus.

Despite this range of objections, a similar pattern of presentation for the universal themes is currently proposed; namely, examining both the spiritual authority and follow roles in tandem with one another as a two-stage motivational sequence. Furthermore, the dedicated reader can also refer back to the previous chapters (devoted to the group/personal realms) for confirmation that this overarching two-stage behavioral pattern is retained in terms of the spiritual/universal realm as well, as extensively validated with respect to the corresponding literary traditions.

PROVIDENCE - FAITH

The more straightforward class of positive virtues proves to be the most logical initiation point for such a grand-scale analysis, being that positive rewards appear much more tangible in contrast to the vaguer concept of leniency. Accordingly, the interplay of providence and faith will be examined first, followed by the remaining sequence of civility/charity. As suggested in the overarching spiritual foundations for the respective virtuous terms, the overall realm of inquiry encompasses a more abstract style of universal interplay distinct from the more basic behavioral interplay previously established for the personal/group domains.

As initially suggested, the glorious sense of providence actively expressed by the spiritual authority figure formally initiates the universally-focused interaction, expressed as the solicitous quest for the rewarding reinforcement characterizing the spiritual disciple role. Being that only one role can be active within the conditioned sequence at any given moment, the role of the reinforcer is relegated to that of a future potentiality, identified as the prudent sense of faithfulness anticipated in terms of the spiritual disciple figure.

The projected nature of the latter prudent sense of faithfulness equates to the spiritual disciple role, whereas the more immediately active glorious sense of providence alternately specifies the initial spiritual authority role. According to this spiritual authority/follower interplay, the spiritual authority initiates the conditioned relationship, gloriously acting providently in anticipation of the prudent sense of faithfulness projected to occur within a future-directed time-frame. This latter faithful sense of potentiality ultimately imparts meaning and purpose to the spiritual authority's initial providential role. Indeed, this projected sense of potentiality clearly defines the parameters of the spiritual disciple role, being that all will have been for naught should such a prudent expression of faithfulness fail to come to pass.

A familiar example of such a universal style of interaction concerns the typical monastic scenario, defined as the reciprocal interplay between the religious administration and the supportive class of devoted monks. This effectively mirrors the interplay previously described (in a personal sense) between the master craftsman and his faithful apprentice, or the group context of labor and management The spiritually-devoted monk typically performs specialized duties crucial to the monastic establishment, in the process gloriously acting providently in anticipation of the prudent sense of faithfulness expressed by the abbot. The monk seeks to distinguish his competency in the approving glance of the abbot through such dutiful service. This immediately active sense of procurement (in an appetitive sense) is colloquially equated with a glorious sense of providence, a forward-looking emotion that contingently anticipates the faithful bestowal of approval.

The first mentioned civil liberty of *providence* certainly fits the bill in this spiritually-focused respect, traditionally defined as the determination towards acting productively and fruitfully within an actively-based time-frame, whereby instilling the motivational rationale for the prudent sense of faithfulness potentially projected for the spiritual disciple figure. The latter spiritual disciple role is polarized in terms of an objective "you" perspective consistent with its reinforcing role within a future-directed time-frame. The providential perspective of the spiritual authority figure, in contrast, is specified from a subjective "I" perspective consistent with an immediately active style of solicitous perspective. Indeed, the modern spelling for providence derives from the Latin *providentia* (the power to see in advance), from *pro-* (before) and *videre* (to see).

The ancient Romans specifically worshipped Providentia as their divine personification of the foresight guiding the fortunes of the Empire. Certain Roman coins depict Providentia as a stylized eagle holding the scepter of Rome in its beak descending to the throne of the emperor in a peaceful transition of power. Providentia came to signify the nourishing/protective power of the gods in general. This providential favor allowed the earth to bloom with grain in the spring, aided by an ample supply of rain during the growing season. Extreme ritual devotion was considered crucial for securing the fortuitous favor of the gods.

These classical connotations of providence are particularly suggestive of the visual symbolisms associated with the *cornucopia*, literally, the "horn of plenty." According to Roman mythology, the cornucopia traced its origins to Achelous the River

God, who transformed himself into a raging bull in order to gain the upper hand in a violent struggle against Hercules. Achelous lost one of his horns during the struggle, eventually retrieved by river nymphs who reverently filled it with fruits and flowers of the season. Henceforth, it was magically said to perpetually overflow with all manner of bountiful blessings from the earth.

In keeping with this bountiful character, the cornucopia was depicted as a major attribute for many gods and goddesses of the period. Chief among these was Fortuna, the goddess of fortune, and Copia, handmaiden to Fortuna (and goddess of plenty). Plutus, the Roman god of wealth, was also depicted cradling a horn of plenty. It is respectively portrayed as a gently curving spiral horn overflowing with fruit and grain, a symbolism traditionally associated with the modern day celebration of Thanksgiving.

The cornucopia signified the providential favor the Pilgrims enjoyed in the form of a bountiful harvest, commemorating the Pilgrims' brave adaptation to life in the New World. Indeed, the cornucopia represents one of the most potent metaphors for Divine Providence, being that the supply of blessings remains virtually unlimited in principle. Through hard work (and some assistance from the natives) the Pilgrims succeeded in harvesting enough surplus nourishment to insure their survival through the harsh winter. These devout Pilgrims undoubtedly considered their success as divinely inspired, in direct contrast to the holiday's current (more secular) focus. Indeed, these spiritual themes emerged as the founding principles for the thirteen original colonies.

This gloriously-provident perspective formally anticipates the prudently-faithful reinforcement projected to occur within a future-directed timeframe. Here, the spiritual disciple prudently expresses a sense of faithfulness towards his spiritual authority figure, typically expressed in terms of glowing adulation and grateful appreciation. The spiritual authority figure, in turn, remains entirely dependent upon the rewarding attentions of the spiritual disciple, any gloriously-provident perspective now becoming entirely meaningless without suitable worship and devotion.

The latter spiritual disciple perspective of devoted-approval is formally represented by the theological virtue of faith, traditionally defined as the supreme emblem of spiritual worship and devotion. Its modern spelling derives from the Latin *fides*, also the root-stem for the related theme of fidelity. The early Romans traditionally worshipped Fides as their divine personification of faith and fidelity in oaths and vows. She is gener-

ally depicted as a matronly figure adorned in a white veil and flowing gown, her right hand solemnly raised as if taking a vow. According to historical precedent, Fides was worshipped at an ancient temple on the Capitoline Hill close to that of Jupiter (with whom she is closely associated). Her cult is said to be very ancient, dating at least to the reign of King Numa. Her annual feast-day was celebrated on the first day in October when priests of her cult rode to her temple in a covered chariot signifying that faith should be carefully protected. Her sacrificial priests were said to wrap their right hands to their fingers with strips of white cloth suggesting that the seat of honor must be kept holy and pure. Covered hands eventually came to symbolize faith in general, as depicted on coins commemorating the loyalty of the Roman Legions.

These pagan connotations of faith eventually paved the way for the Christian sense of the term. According to New Testament scripture, Christ consistently implored his disciples to trust in the divine power of the Lord that worked through him. The dramatic series of miracles he is said to have performed further stipulated the unswerving faith of all who would be cured. In particular, the chief emblem of faith (as the first of the theological virtues) is a shield with a stylized Latin cross inscribed in the center: traditionally referred to as the Shield of St. Paul. This symbolism figuratively signifies the saving power of Christ, reflecting fulfillment of scriptural prophecy.

This tradition of miracles endures to our modern age, particularly the well-documented phenomenon of faith healing. From its very inception faith healing was essentially considered an all-or-none phenomenon; namely, all was cured or nothing. Its specifics are described in the Epistle of St. James (5:14-16), which describes the anointing of the sick in a congregational setting. Healing is also listed among the Gifts of the Holy Spirit according to Chapter 11 of St. Paul's First Letter to the Corinthians. This emphasis upon faith proves particularly applicable to this providential style of healing example, where the spiritual disciple prudently acts faithfully towards one's spiritual authority figure in hopes of a providential outcome via the healing experience.

CIVILITY - CHARITY

The completed initiatory phase for providence and faithfulness, in turn, gives way to a further discussion of the remaining stage within the conditioned spiritual interaction: namely, that encompassing civility and charity. According to this latter

The Theological Virtues (With Their Historical Representatives) – Circa 1460
Detail from Panel by Pesellino, Birmingham Museum of Art, Gift of the Samuel H. Kress Foundation

stage, the spiritual disciple eventually acts upon his (projected) prudent sense of faithfulness, whereby dignifiedly acting civilly in anticipation of a projected temperate determination to act charitably on the part of the follower. A number of key features are observed similar to those initially encountered with respect to providence/faithfulness. In terms of the abbot's immediately active civilly-dignified treatment, he now formally assumes a spiritual authority status in relation to the devoted monastic members. The latter role of devoted monk, in turn, takes on the mantle of the spiritual follower role, being that it formally "follows" the authority role in terms the projected potentiality of such a future-directed time-frame.

According to this civility/charity dynamic, the abbot dignifiedly acts civilly towards his supportive cast of monks in anticipation of instilling a (projected) temperate expression of charitableness on the part of the individual monks, whereby encouraging a determination to achieve further such cycles of cooperative productivity within a future-directed time-frame.

In terms of such an immediately active style of rewarding reinforcement, the spiritual authority theme of *civility* certainly fits the bill. Indeed, as the chief spiritual analogue in relation to the more group-focused theme of dignity, civility is traditionally defined as a sense of courtesy or chivalry within a universal context. Its modern spelling derives from the Latin *civilitas*, from *civis* (citi-

zen). Limited archaeological evidence suggests that the Romans worshipped this theme as a deity, as evident in a dedicatory inscription to Civitas unearthed in Rome. Although *civitas* initially referred to the art of skilled governance, it eventually came to signify the affiliated refinements of polite society in general.

In an alternate legal sense, the enduring concept of Civil Law originally applied to the sumbody of the Roman Code, particularly that portion applicable to the private citizen. According to the Common Law traditions of the English speaking world, Civil Law refers to the personal and property rights of the individual, a residual category beyond the scope of Criminal, Military, and International Law. In this latter sense, the *U. S. Bill of Rights* makes clear provisions for such individual civil rights, although unforeseen ambiguities plague the wording of virtually every key passage. It ultimately fell to the judiciary/legislature to derive legally binding interpretations for each of these civil rights provisions.

The current body of civil rights precedents emerged over a long series of legal decisions. The *Bill of Rights* originally applied only to freemen, although modified through the abolition of slavery as formalized in the *Emancipation Proclamation*. The subsequent Civil Rights Acts of 1866 and 1870 allowed all citizens the free right to engage in legal transactions; as in owning property or entering into lawsuits. The Civil Rights Act of 1871 further made it unlawful to deny any citizen equal protection under the law, whether through force, threat, or intimidation. The Act of 1875 guaranteed the free use of public accommodations, although this legislation was later reversed as unconstitutional. This latter reactionary trend culminated in 1896 with the Supreme Court ruling of Plessy vs. Ferguson, upholding the principle of "separate but equal" facilities for people of color.

The midpoint of the current century, however, again ushered in the winds of change, as witnessed in the 1954 Supreme Court Decision of Brown vs. Topeka Board of Education. This historic ruling overturned the legal precedent of segregation in public schools, citing the inherent inequality of such a forced arrangement. Many related aspects of racial segregation soon followed as targets of reform. On December 1, 1955, Rosa Parks was arrested in Montgomery, Alabama for refusing to surrender her bus seat to a white passenger. The black seamstress' courageous act of defiance touched off a year-long boycott of the city transit system, a cause further championed by civil rights leader Rev. Martin Luther King Jr. As a spokesman for the Southern Christian Leadership Conference, King preached a message of non-violent resistance: culminating in the Civil Rights March from Selma to Montgomery, Alabama with a turn-out estimated at *25,000* strong. Faced with such intense public scrutiny, Congress soon passed a flurry of new legislation aimed at barring racial segregation. The Civil Rights Act of 1964 banned discrimination in employment and public accommodations, whereas the Civil Rights Act of 1968 extended these guarantees to real estate and private housing.

Civility represents a spiritual ideal within the dignity tradition, although definitely surpassing the more limited group focus of the latter. For instance, Rosa Parks solicitously boarded the bus, fully expecting a civilly reinforcing environment en route to her destination. As the agent for the bus-company, the driver was rightfully expected to respect her civil rights consistent with the routine expectations of the paying patrons. The civil atmosphere inherent to public conveyance necessarily specifies the principles of equality under the law were it not for the prejudicial undercurrents plaguing the Deep South of the day. The bus driver maliciously ejected Rosa Parks from the bus employing ingrained racial prejudice as the rationale for compromising her civil rights. Indeed, it truly appears ironic to resort to such an inverted example for illustrating the dynamics of civility, so much do we take such civil rights for granted. The government fortunately remedied

such appalling circumstances by passing a rapid sequence of civil rights ordinances targeting such prejudicial treatment. These fundamental human standards are now effectively safeguarded throughout the public sector ensuring uniform standards of trade and commerce throughout the Land. Accordingly, the spiritual authority (in the guise of moral authority) civilly anticipates a (projected) temperate sense of charitableness on the part of the well-meaning citizenry. This overarching air of civil respect maintains a suitably rewarding environment conducive to civic cooperation and prosperity. In this enduring fashion, a healthy measure of respect for the common citizen ensures a successful outcome to all such collaborative enterprises.

The latter allusion to a temperately-charitable attitude certainly rings true in this basic regard. Indeed, as the first and foremost of the theological virtues, charity, earns its prominent placement through its potential consummation of the entire (universally-focused) conditioned interaction. Such charitable intentions certainly prove a fitting adjunct to such a subjectively-based spiritual disciple perspective. In slightly different terms, I (as spiritual disciple) temperately determine to act charitably towards you in response to your (as spiritual authority) civilly-dignified reinforcement of me. This distinctive motivational interplay directly reflects the characteristic "if you then I" motivational dynamic governing the entire conditioned interchange.

Charity certainly meets such universal requirements in this basic respect, traditionally defined as generosity freely bestowed upon the needy in hopes of improving their condition. Its modern spelling derives from the Latin *caritas* (dearness, affection), from *carus* (dear). Latin translations of the New Testament translate the original Greek *agape* as *caritas*, equivalent to the English theme of charity in the King James Edition. Agape originally referred to the Greek word for brotherly love, as opposed to *eros* (or passionate love): a distinction faithfully preserved in later scriptural contexts.

The most stirring New Testament account of charity occurs in Chapter *13* of St. Paul's First Letter to the Corinthians. Many modern versions of the New Testament prefer to substitute the related theme of *love* for charity, although this generalization fails to preserve the original distinctions in terms. Semantics aside, St. Paul extols charity as the greatest of the theological virtues, surpassing faith and hope in terms of moral excellence. St. Paul distinguishes charity as a fixed attitude of the soul, an enduring disposition clearly at odds with egocentric concerns. According to the Gospel of St. Mark (12:24-44) Christ heartily praises the poor widow that modestly gave a mere farthing to the temple fund. Contrast this to the wealthy Pharisee, who publicly extolled the magnitude of his largess.

This noble aspect of charity effectively permeated the very fiber of the early Christian Church. The first charitable measures were initially administered by the early Christian congregations, enlisting the aid of deacons under the guidance of the elders. Grateful recipients included the aged and the infirm, the poor and the imprisoned, as well as widows and orphans. This early congregational setting eventually was supplanted by the diocesan system, where churches of a township answered to a single bishop. This centralized power-base allowed an even greater share of church tithing to go to the poor, a full quarter by many accounts. Even non-Christians were permitted to join the ranks of the needy, for it was judged nobler to err on the side of altruism. This diocesan system flourished throughout the medieval age, although gradually supplanted by the establishment of monastic orders devoted exclusively to such charitable causes.

It remained till the more liberal precepts of our modern age for women to take full initiative in such charitable endeavors. Take, for example, the founding of the Missionaries of Charity by Mother Teresa of Calcutta. At the age of 18, Mother Teresa joined the Institute of the Blessed Virgin in Ireland, soon transferring to India to work as a teacher. She sought permission to work with the poor in the slums of Calcutta, founding her order in 1948. The Missionaries of Charity established centers to aid the blind, disabled, and terminally ill of Calcutta. She also founded a leper colony near Asansol, India known as Shanti Nagar (Town of Peace). The Indian government awarded Mother Teresa the prestigious Padmashri Award in 1963 in recognition of her unfailing service to the people of India. Even greater awards followed, most notably the 1974 Nobel Peace Prize: to which she humbly commented "I am unworthy." This modest attitude echoed her deep spiritual conviction that: "The help for the hopeless is the simple duty of us all."

This commendable preoccupation with charitable endeavors is certainly one of Western culture's most time honored traditions. Specialized agencies (such as the United Way and the Red Cross/Crescent) aid in the distribution of much needed funds and services. It certainly appears fitting, then, that the medieval representation of charity takes the form of a crimson heart inscribed in heraldic fashion upon a shield. This graphic depiction formally symbolizes the heart's unceasing service to the wellbeing of the individual, a factor certainly in keeping with the lifelong charitable precepts of such noble spiritual servants as Mother Teresa. Consequently, the well-intentioned spiritual disciple figure temperately aims to act charitably in response to the civilly-reinforcing environment actively established by the spiritual authority figure. The spiritual authority figure bears a certain risk in assuming that such charitable treatment will ultimately be forthcoming, although reasonably assured by the wealth of previous cycles recollected from past experience. Indeed, this tenuous power of potentiality ultimately imparts the distinctive power leverage implicit to both spiritual authority/follower roles, the latter depending upon the former for the rationale behind one's charitable mandate.

In summary, the completed description of the two-stage spiritual schematic of providence-faith and civility-charity offers a comprehensive overview of the motivational dynamics governing the universally-focused conditioned interaction. Although the monastic example proved informative (for illustrative purposes), a number of other examples are equally feasible. Indeed, the ultimate goal for this exercise has been to propose a sturdy foundation for the even more abstract listings of virtues/values to follow, resulting in an overarching model of the virtuous hierarchy in general.

LIBERTY - HOPE

Before skipping ahead to such a potential range of applications it proves crucial to examine the remaining motivational interplay of the virtuous modes specific to the realm of negative reinforcement. Indeed, such a motivational style of analysis scarcely proves as clear-cut as that for positive rewards in that negative reinforcement involves the lenient withholding of punishment as opposed to the more straightforward bestowal of rewards. Here, negative reinforcement entails the withholding of punitive consequences within the environment or (in an interpersonal sense) leniency in response to avoidance types of behavior. In terms of a spiritual/universal context, the spiritual authority figure honorably acts in a libertarian fashion in anticipation of the blameful-hope for justice on the part of the spiritual disciple. This projected blameful-hope for justice eventually becomes immediately actualized as an austere sense of integrity on the part of the reinforcer in anticipation of a projected fortitudinous sense of decency on the part of the follower figure.

This interplay of submissiveness/leniency is similarly reminiscent of the throat-baring behaviors described for the wolf pack, where the submissive pack member dramatically exaggerates his degree of vulnerability in anticipation of the potential bestowal of leniency. In a more abstract (verbal) sense, submissiveness operates in a similar fashion: namely, the vocalized libertarian sense of honor aimed at potentially eliciting a projected lenient hope for justice on the part of the respective follower figure. Certainly it might appear risky to express such an extreme level of vulnerability without a reasonable assurance of upcoming leniency. Past memories definitely come into play, with previous cycles of leniency ultimately justifying such a radical act of trust in terms of such an aversive strategy. According to this measured tactic, leniently rehabilitation (rather than retribution) now dominates the deliberation.

A plausible example of such a reciprocating style of universal interaction concerns the interplay between the United Nations Security Council and the respective Peace-Keeping Forces. The enlisted peace-keepers (drawn from around the world) are expected to fall into line with the discipline and dictates of the UN Security Council, whereby honorably acting in a libertarian fashion in anticipation of a blameful-hope for justice on the part of the respective follower figure. This distinctive libertarian perspective represents a forward-looking emotion that anticipates the lenient hope for justice on the part of the Security Council. In other words, I as spiritual authority honorably act in a libertarian fashion towards you in anticipation of your lenient-hope for justice. The soldier bears a certain risk in trusting that his freely enacted peace-keeper role will eventually lead to a hopeful outcome, although assured by the wealth of previous such cycles of leniency.

The preceding UN example proves particularly informative with respect to the universal prerequisites for *liberty*. As defined from the immediately active role of the spiritual authority figure, this libertarian sense of honor effectively provides the projected rationale for the blameful-hope for justice projected for the spiritual disciple figure. Consequently, liberty is traditionally defined as the right to act without interference within the limits of the law. The term traces its origins to the Latin *libertas*, from *liber* (free). In the early days of the Roman Republic, liberty was regarded as a constitutional mandate, in contrast to tyranny or dictatorship. In keeping with many other classical themes, Libertas was worshiped as a deity, with several temples dedicated to her in Rome alone. She is traditionally depicted as a lightly attired matron holding a broken scepter in one hand and a staff hung with a felt cap in the other. The staff (the *vindicta*) played a role in the ceremonial freeing of slaves. The felt cap (the *pilleus*) was further bestowed upon the heads of freed slaves following completion of this ceremony. It originally had been placed upon the heads of troublesome slaves at auction, whereby absolving the vendor of any subsequent liability. Towards the end of the Republic (circa the assassination of Julius Caesar) portrayals of Libertas often included a stylized dagger signifying the blood that must be shed in her defense.

In a more contemporary sense, liberty has enjoyed an enhanced place of honor within the American system of government, one of the treasured principles upon which this great country was founded. In a debt of gratitude from the world as a whole, the Frenchman Auguste Bartholdi commemorated this spirit of freedom in his monumental sculpture, the Statue of Liberty. Bartholdi's aesthetic vision of Liberty blends classical overtones with innovative technical design. It features a flowingly garbed personification of the goddess depicted in the act of gaining her freedom. Her right hand holds aloft a burning torch, while her left cradles a book of law inscribed July 4, 1776. The classical tradition of the liberty cap is curiously lacking, replaced by a striking crown of stylized rays of light. Broken shackles lie at her feet as she strides forward towards liberation.

Similar to the case previously established for providence, liberty is clearly an immediately active form of universal authority perspective, an interpretation clearly in keeping with the classical overtones associated with the Statue of Liberty. This spiritual focus is particularly evident in the stirring abstract principles embodied in the *Declaration of Independence*, where liberty is specifically singled out as one of the three God-given rights guaranteed to all individuals. Through this libertarian perspective, the spiritual authority freely expands upon the group-focused honor perspective, whereby anticipating the blameful-hope for justice potentially expressed by the spiritual disciple figure. These spiritual overtones are clearly suggestive of the "larger than life" attributes of the Statue of Liberty. Liberty's mild (but commanding) demeanor must have surely enthralled the uninitiated as one of the many wonders America had to offer. Towards such ends, it was Liberty's outstretched torch that figuratively served to light the way for the perpetual throngs of hopeful refugees, an endeavor that many immigrants hoped to realize in this Golden Land of opportunity.

The latter hopeful attitude entertained by the immigrants certainly fits the dynamics of such a dual motivational interchange. Indeed, the modern spelling of hope derives the Anglo Saxon *hopa* (to be confident, to trust). The Latin slant on hope, *sperare*, entered the English lexicon chiefly with in terms of its opposing connotation of despair. Similar to the case previously established for Fides, Spes (the Roman personification of hope) was worshipped since the 4th century BCE. Spes originally was a goddess associated with Fortuna, invoked by all who hoped for success (particularly the hope for a good harvest). Over the course of generations, Spes eventually assumed the role of goddess of the future: invoked at births, weddings, and dedications. In light of her considerable prestige, several temples were dedicated to her in Rome alone. Spes is traditionally depicted as a youthful maiden striding gracefully in a long robe, the seam raised in her left hand (as if in haste). In her right hand she holds a flower bud on the verge of opening, signifying the hopes for a brighter future.

These classical connotations beg further mention of the related legend of Pandora's Box. According to Greek mythology, Pandora was the first woman on earth, her name literally translated as "Giver of All." In celebration of her creation, Zeus offered Pandora an ornate box she was instructed never to open. This ploy was part of Zeus' clever plan to punish mankind for accepting (from Prometheus) the sacred gift of fire. In a fit of curiosity Pandora eventually peeked into the box, allowing all manner of human ills to escape into the world. Only hope (*elpis*) was left behind in the box, a solitary comfort to mankind in terms of such newfound misery. Later versions of the myth (such as the Fable of Babrius) have Pandora losing all the blessings of the gods (save hope), with similar consequences only now more closely resembling the biblical account of Adam and Eve.

This steadfast quality of hope finds similar parallels in the Christian scriptural tradition. According to the enduring tradition of the theological virtues, hope is figuratively symbolized as an anchor inscribed upon a shield similar to the crucifix symbolism previously described for faith. This anchor symbolism traces its origins to St. Paul's Epistle to the Hebrews (6:19) wherein he states: "...which *hope* we have as an anchor of the soul, both steadfast and sure." In the next verse, St. Paul further identifies Christ as the rightful object of our hope, an intercessory in terms of salvation.

The early Christians had long anticipated the prophesied return of the Lord, a particularly comforting thought during desperate times of persecution. This fearful era forced many Christians to resort to obscure forms of symbolism as a disguised expression of their hope. In particular, many early Christians adopted the marine anchor as an allegorical form of the cross, a symbolism suggestive of the cruciform arrangement of the anchor's shaft and crossbar. This anchor symbolism was particularly widespread in the catacombs alongside other disguised symbols of Christianity; namely, the dove and the fish. Indeed, just as a sailor sets anchor in order to avoid drifting into danger, so the Christian disciple sets his *hope* in the saving power of Christ. It certainly remains a fitting tribute to the deep spiritual insights of St. Paul that he would so intuitively celebrate these distinctive anchor symbolisms in relation to early Christian beliefs concerning hope.

This overarching lenient context for hope proves equally applicable to the allegorical symbolisms for the anchor, where the spiritual disciple now blamefully hopes for justice in response to the libertarian sense of honor on the part of the spiritual disciple figure: an interplay conducive to salvation (similar to that previously documented with respect to faith-healing). Here the libertarian authority figure is reciprocally dependent upon the lenient-style perspective of the spiritual disciple: with any outward expression of liberty now entirely meaningless without such a reciprocating style of interplay. Although faith and hope are often used interchangeably in common usage, their distinct styles of reinforcement clearly prove to be the distinguishing factor in this regard.

AUSTERITY - DECENCY

The preceding two-stage sequence of liberty-hope, in turn, dictates that the spiritual disciple figure must eventually act upon the potentiality implicit to his/her projected lenient-hope for justice. This further development takes the form of austerely acting with integrity within a more immediate style of time-frame, whereby anticipating the projected brave sense of decency on the part of the spiritual disciple. This final decision to act often dictates a rather extended course of deliberation on the part of the austere reinforcer. Indeed, it is this ultimate power of deliberation that directly imparts the power leverage enjoyed by the austere reinforcer in relation to the procurer of such lenient reinforcement.

The respective interplay of spiritual authority and disciple roles is similarly modified with respect to this second stage within the conditioned interaction. This latter phase invokes an immediately active austere sense of integrity expressed by the reinforcer, only now punctuated from the perspective of the spiritual authority figure, as schematically depicted in Part-B of **Fig. 2A**. Here reinforcement (Y) is now depicted occurring entirely in the present, whereas procurement (X) is shown projected into a future-directed timeframe. Consequently, the UN Security Council is now thrust into an immediately active reinforcement role, austerely acting with lenient-integrity in anticipation of the (projected) decent sense of fortitude on the part of the peace keepers.

A number of key modifications are further observed with respect to the polarities of the authority/follower roles. With respect to his immediately-active austere sense of integrity, the Security Council now abandons the projected sense of hopeful-justice characterizing the spiritual follower role, in turn, switching to a more immediately-active austere sense of integrity indicative of a universal authority role. The peace keeper, in contrast, now assumes the respective mantle of universal follower, a status reflecting the motivational leverage inherent to such a projected decency perspective. This role reversal certainly proves warranted, being that it formally reflects the initial sequence based upon liberty/hope, although now punctuated from an immediately active leniency perspective (rather than the submissive variation). The authority figure now austerely acts with integrity in anticipation of instilling a brave sense of decency on the part of the peace keepers, whereby serving to encourage similar such decent perspectives in future contexts.

The immediately active austerity perspective directly parallels the affiliated theme of civility with the exception that leniency (rather than approval) is now called into focus. This lenient interpretation is further reflected in the traditional connotations of the term. Indeed, the modern spelling of austerity derives from the Greek *austeros* (denoting dryness or harshness). Accordingly, austerity is traditionally defined as the endurance of pain, hardship, or misfortune, often in a mortified fashion. It can also suggest a sense of harshness or strictness in the bestowal of discipline. In the Latin tradition this distinctive theme is identified with the Roman god Auster, the divine personification of the South Wind. Auster, accordingly, is described as the dry and sultry south wind, the *sirocco* of the modern-day Italians. It is the harbinger of hot/dry weather consistent with Italy's close proximity to the Sahara Desert. Indeed, historians trace its origins to the Latin root-stem *uro-* (the tendency to burn).

In an alternate philosophical sense, the traditions associated with austerity establish it as one of the fundamental principles governing the strict Code of Sparta: a powerful city-state to the south of Athens. Sparta maintained its military might primarily through an elaborate system of state-enforced regimentation and disciple. At the tender age of seven, male children were separated from their parents and raised in state sanctioned military academies. The recruits slept year round in open barracks on reeds harvested from the banks of the river Eurota. Family life, again, was reinstated only upon reaching the age of thirty, when the individual was finally accorded the full rights and privileges of a citizen of Sparta.

These classical connotations of harshness and discipline have similarly endured to our modern age, as exemplified in the recurring traditions of the *austerity budget*. This political policy has long been employed to bolster faltering economies chiefly through increased production and the export of capital goods (wherein improving the overall balance of trade). It also offered a stopgap solution to temporary economic problems such as financing a military campaign or balancing the federal budget. The United Kingdom has instituted austerity budgets throughout its history, ensuring its enduring influence in modern economic theory.

In the United States, this theme definitely brings to mind the price controls instituted by President Nixon during the 70's: a strategy aimed at controlling skyrocketing inflation. The truest sense of the term, however, extends to the early 1980's with the advent of *Reaganomics*. President Reagan deliberately resurrected the theme of the austerity budget to describe his revolutionary program to revitalize the national economy. The lack-luster state of affairs characterized by runaway inflation and high unemployment called for a bold set of economic measures; namely, sharp budget cutting to shrink the public sector, as well as a broad retreat from business and environmental regulations. The policy governing "supply side economics" promised (and eventually delivered) a surge in non-inflationary economic growth, although to the initial detriment of the more underprivileged economic classes.

On the opposing side of the ledger, the general public rightfully expected that their submissive attempts at economic cooperation would be leniently rewarded with the desired results. The traditional austerity budget generally calls for such cooperative measures; namely, reduced consumption and/or resource conservation. In exchange for such shared sacrifice, the government was rightfully expected to improve the economy to the point where austerity measures would no longer be necessary. Critics of the plan argued that the economic sacrifices demanded of the public were disproportionately severe at the poorer end of the spectrum, a premise all too evident during the early years of the Reagan Plan. Fortunately such hardships ran their course, resulting in the healthier and happier economy currently in force today. Consequently, this universal style of authority perspective austerely aims to leniently ameliorate suffering in anticipation of the decent sense of cooperation on the part of the willing citizenry. This overarching austere sense of integrity effectively promotes a leniently rewarding environment conducive to global economic cooperation and inclusiveness. Consequently, austerity extends the more elementary group theme of integrity into an even more abstract (universal) sphere of influence.

In terms of the two-stage motivational schematic, the enduring militaristic overtones for austerity are further consummated by the remaining theological virtue of decency. Similar to its counterpart in charity, decency formally provides an effective sense of closure to the two-stage universally-focused interaction. Accordingly, decency is defined as a sense of propriety in both word and deed with an emphasis upon moral scruples. The modern spelling for decency derives from the Latin *decentia* (fitting), from the Latin verb *decere* (befitting). The Romans expressed a high regard for the principles of decency, the Roman statesman Cicero succinctly summing up the opinion: "Justice consists in doing no injury to man, *decency* in giving them no offense." Decency enjoys similar precedents in the Christian tradition, although this term is specifically mentioned only once in English translations of the New Testament. The basic import of this term covers a broad range of ethical contexts, as evident in its strategic placement in Chapter *14* of St. Paul's First Letter to the Corinthians. Indeed, this chapter concludes with the stirring admonition: "Let all things be done *decently* and in order," hinting at the profound significance of this fourth theological virtue. Furthermore, Chapter *14* actually continues the general theme of Chapters *12* and *13* (namely, the Gifts of the Holy Spirit), placing decency in fitting proximity to descriptions of the first three theological virtues.

In Chapter *14*, St. Paul directly focuses on the congregational aspects of these spiritual gifts, as in the themes of prophesy and speaking-in-tongues. St. Paul rightfully expressed concern that the over-zealous use of such gifts could prove detrimental to the credibility of the Church from a gentile standpoint. He further attempted to resolve this issue by proposing strict guidelines for governing the expression of these gifts within a congregational setting. He recommended restraint in the number of those speaking-in-tongues, while calling for an interpreter to offer insights into prophetic revelations. In this restricted sense, St. Paul expressed hope that these gifts would be used for the edification of the Church, over and beyond their spiritual significance to the individual, a proclamation consistent with his call for decency in a church setting.

This spiritual interpretation survives to our modern era in the familiar expression: "common decency," namely, common to all cultures and creeds. Indeed, St. Paul deliberately sets the tone of a spiritual authority figure, lecturing on many austere themes of central importance to the fledgling Church. Although this epistle was originally addressed to the congregation in Corinth, it has since been accorded a universal focus in Christian theology in keeping with its concern for an acceptable Church image. Through such a concerted effort, Christianity eventually grew to claim a dynamic place on the world scene, a degree of success that even St. Paul might marvel at today. Consequently, the spiritual disciple figure fortitudinously acts decency towards one's spiritual authority figure in response to the latter's austere sense of integrity. Here, I (as spiritual disciple) bravely act in a decent fashion towards you in anticipation of your (as spiritual authority) austere sense of integrity. Indeed, this tenuous power of potentiality ultimately imparts the key power leverage implicit to both the spiritual authority/disciple roles, the former depending upon the latter to consummate the recursive cycle of austerity-then-decency.

In summary, the immediately active style of spiritual authority perspective offers a fitting counterpoint to the projected potentiality inherent to the spiritual disciple role. As previously described with respect to the personal ideals and the cardinal virtues, the civil liberties and theological virtues exhibit a similar dual degree of specialization: namely, active modes occurring within the present, or potential modes projected into a future-directed time-frame. The active behavioral modes are defined in terms of the civil liberties, as specialized into the immediately active themes of dignified-*civility* or an *austere* sense of integrity, as well as a *libertarian* sense of honor or glorious sense of *providence*. The future-directed behavioral modes, in turn, target the more abstract realm of the theological virtues consistent with their projection into a future-directed time-frame: namely, prudent-*faith*, just-*hope*, temperate-*charitableness*, and fortitudinous-*decency*.

As chief spokesman within the spiritual congregation, the spiritual disciple essentially rates an equal balance of power in terms of the authority/follower roles. The theological virtues celebrated by St. Paul certainly ring true in this basic respect. Indeed, this spiritual/universal range of perspectives offers crucial insights on the world scene today, offering the potential for healing many intractable religious rifts. Here, disturbing extremist trends may finally be put to rest through the aid of the newly devised insights implicit in terms of the principles of Set Theory. Indeed, this third-order style of universal domain dictates that all religions are essentially equal when speaking from such an overarching spiritual perspective, with the welcome potential for facilitating enhanced spiritual peace and harmony. Curiously, this distinctive style of spiritual/universal perspective ultimately appears to close-out any more advanced degree of abstraction, for there can be no level of organization greater than mankind as a whole. This very sense of the power of abstraction, however, sets the stage for two further classes of abstract innovation; namely, that specified for the remaining humanitarian and transcendental levels within the power hierarchy. In contrast to the purely organizational status governing the first three levels, these latter two innovations are alternately specified in terms of purely abstract styles of motivational perspectives. The humanitarian domain is distinguished through the abstract addition of *historical* time, whereas the transcendental realm makes an appeal to the realm of pure transcendence.

The profoundly abstract nature of these remaining two levels is further reflected in the abstract character of their respective groupings of terms: as the lofty grouping of beauty, truth, goodness, and wisdom collectively serve to indicate. Indeed, these listings of values all virtually beg to be listed together: as with the ecumenical ideals (grace, free will, magnanimity, and equanimity), the humanistic values (peace, love, tranquility, and equality), and the mystical values (ecstasy, bliss, joy, and harmony). A more detailed description of this remaining class of abstract values will now be undertaken with an in-depth examination of the humanitarian realm, in concert with the respective ecumenical and moralistic classifications.

5

THE HUMANITARIAN GLOBAL TRADITION

In keeping with the more elementary forms of authority that it supersedes, humanitarian authority has enjoyed a long and illustrious literary tradition. The humanitarian variation, however, is distinguished from all previous formats in terms of its claim as the first truly abstract class of power maneuver. Not an organizational power maneuver per sé, it represents an expansion of the spiritual variety through the abstract addition of historical time. According to this latter innovation, the humanitarian authority transcends spiritual authority by claiming to speak for all generations of mankind (not just the current one). Although the past and future may seem like different worlds, the two are intimately intertwined within our minds. Scientists refer to the brain's ability to think about the past, present, and future as "chronesthesia," or mental time travel. In recent studies on mental time travel, neuroscientists have discovered that we use many of the same regions of the brain to remember the past as we do to envision the future. This need for foresight may explain why we can form memories in the first place. Indeed, episodic memory probably arose in part due to the fact it helped individuals make good survival decisions.

Although the humanitarian authority is quick to acknowledge the inherent immediacy of spiritual authority, on a grander time scale the humanitarian authority perspective will always prevail. Its extreme degree of generality precludes its identification with any singular social institution; rather its banner is typically incorporated into the religious (and sometimes political) framework of society as a whole. The truest appeal of humanitarian authority hinges upon mankind's enduring fascination with culture and tradition, giving homage to the progressive nature of the collective human spirit. During classical times, when the rate of technological change was often negligible over the course of generations, such humanitarian concerns rated far less prestige than they currently enjoy today. In particular, the Roman style of political administration served as the dominant humanitarian perspective throughout the classical age, maintaining a stable state of peace and prosperity over the course of many generations and centuries.

The eventual decline of the Western Roman Empire, however, ushered in a radical shift in such classical perspectives. Its standard-bearer status reverted (by default) to the Roman Catholic Church, an unlikely outcome in light of the latter's humble beginnings. From its very inception, Christianity professed only the most limited of historical perspectives, the founding generation fully expecting to witness the Second Coming of Christ along with the establishment of his kingdom upon earth. A vicious series of persecutions (including the destruction of Jerusalem) were further interpreted as prophetic signs of Christ's imminent return. In fact, Christ's closing words to the faithful in the apocalyptic *Book of Revelation* states: "I am coming soon."

Following several centuries of desperate survival, Christianity miraculously found itself in a position of prominence within the Roman Empire. This placed Church Fathers in the awkward position of reinterpreting scripture to meet the needs of an enduring spiritual institution. In accepting the power ceded to it by the Romans, the Church underwent a dramatic period of growth and consolidation within its ranks. In the interest of Church unity the Emperor Constantine called the First Ecumenical Council at Nicea in 325 in an attempt to reconcile differing scriptural interpretations. Indeed, the term "ecumenical" derives from the Greek *oikoumene* (of the inhabited world), presaging all such councils to follow.

The sack of Rome by Alaric, King of the Goths in 410 CE precipitated a further series of crises for the fledgling Church. For most of the classical era the Roman Empire had reigned as the supreme paragon of law, order, and stability. Pagan reactionaries seized upon Rome's downfall to denounce the Church, blaming Christianity's preoccupation with pacifism and asceticism for undermining the internal solidarity of the Empire. These serious charges were formally addressed by St. Augustine of Hippo (354-430) in his treatise *The City of God*. In this seminal work both grace and free will emerge as prominent themes. In particular, this pairing of ecumenical themes appears tailor-made for satisfying two of the four dimensions predicted for the humanitarian authority perspective. Their traditional context certainly betrays such an enduring focus. Grace denotes a humanitarian refinement of providence, whereas free will makes a similar correspondence to the spiritual prerequisites for liberty.

The two remaining dimensions, however, prove somewhat more problematic, although clues abound within the traditional literature. Ideally, the final two terms should represent higher (humanitarian) analogues of the more basic concepts of civility and austerity specific to the spiritual authority role. The paired concepts of magnanimity and equanimity quickly come to mind, clearly suggestive of a higher-order correspondence to civility and austerity. In this latter respect, *magnanimity* represents the humanitarian counterpart of civility, whereas *equanimity* denotes a similar refinement of austerity, effectively rounding out the predicted four-part complement of humanitarian authority terms.

This cohesive grouping of grace-freewill-magnanimity-equanimity is most appropriately termed the class of *ecumenical* ideals: directly alluding to the enduring spirit of the early ecumenical councils. In particular, this theme has undergone a significant revival as of late, chiefly through the efforts of a broad coalition of Protestant denominations, a major proponent of the ecumenical movement around the world. The Protestant sense of the term certainly proves relevant here; with grace, free will, magnanimity, and equanimity all figuring prominently in the writings of Protestant Reformation including those of Martin Luther. Accordingly, this four-part listing of ecumenical ideals formally specifies motivations encompassing the humanitarian authority role. This enduring class of humanitarian ideals represents immediately-active motivational perspectives that anticipate the more abstract (projected) complement of future-directed themes. Here, the immediately-focused humanitarian authority role represents the active behavioral perspective that anticipates the projected-potentiality

of the respective follower roles. Generally speaking, the humanitarian authority themes immediately initiate the conditioned interaction in anticipation of the potentiality characterizing the representative member of humanity perspective.

THE CLASSICAL GREEK VALUES: THE ROLE OF THE HUMANITARIAN FOLLOWER

The ecumenical ideals offer a preliminary overview of the motivational dynamics governing the humanitarian authority perspective. In keeping with such a grand humanitarian time-scale, each of the ecumenical ideals figures prominently in the long-standing tradition of ecumenical councils. This timeless quality of the ecumenical ideals certainly fits a common stereotype; namely, enduring themes directly in harmony with such a grand humanitarian perspective. This formidable style of humanitarian power-base allows the authority figure to overrule any of the more immediate concerns expressed by the spiritual disciple, effectively regaining the upper hand in terms of the perpetual power struggle. Even an authority perspective as abstract as the humanitarian, however, is (by definition) invested with its own unique form of follower countermaneuver: in this case, that relating to the humanitarian follower.

True to its extreme level of abstraction, the humanitarian follower perspective reciprocally complements its respective authority counterpart, restoring an equal balance of power to the humanitarian realm. Accordingly, it shares in common the distinctive style of "strike" leverage previously established for the lower levels: culminating in an unprecedented 4th-order level of meta-abstraction. In this more advanced sense, the humanitarian follower informs the humanitarian authority that a sanction from all of humanity is critical for maintaining the latter's authority status. Technically speaking, we can all speak as representatives within such a grand humanitarian time-scale. This inherent degree of flexibility was predicted earlier in the current chapter, where the authority role was defined as more of a policy-making strategy than any immediate style of power maneuver. The representative member of humanity, therefore, retains the option of rejecting humanitarian policy; hence, ensuring an equal balance of power across the range of humanity.

More properly termed the "philosophers" maneuver, this distinctive style of follower strategy downplays the strike tactic altogether in favor of the prestige involved in speaking for all of humanity. In particular, the philosopher role has long been revered for critical reasoning and crucial insights into universal truths. In the spirit of the stirring classical injunction: "Know Thyself," philosophy has painstakingly refined the collective wisdom of humanity over the span of countless generations. Philosophy is primarily eclectic in nature, drawing deeply from the rich wellspring of accumulated wisdom and truth.

This enduring interpretation necessarily suggests the existence of a respective listing of follower themes, although both major categories of virtue (e.g., the cardinal and theological) have already been accounted for. This leaves only the remaining traditional listing of classical Greek values as the most effective adjunct for designating the humanitarian follower perspective. The respective grouping of beauty, truth, and goodness represents one of philosophy's most time-honored traditions: perpetuating the ethical focus of the virtues, with the exception that the more enduring notion of *value* is now called into focus. It ultimately remained to the enduring genius of Plato to unite these concepts into a single cohesive context, much as he had already accomplished with respect to the cardinal virtues.

According to his dialogue *Parmenides*, Plato speculates on the existence of absolute forms (or values) that convey our understanding of the beautiful, the good, and the true. As organizational principles, they impart a conceptual sense of order to our variable perceptual experiences. In his masterpiece *The Republic*, Plato further makes an analogy between *goodness* and the sun: for just as the sun provides light for the physical world, so goodness offers illumination on a moral plane. Indeed, Plato specifically distinguishes goodness as the supreme primal form that unifies each of the lesser abstract forms.

Although this cohesive grouping of beauty, truth, and goodness appears tailor-made for designating the first three dimensions predicted for the humanitarian follower perspective, it still remains one term short of satisfying the full quartet. This shortfall is fortunately remedied through the addition of the related theme of *wisdom*. Due to its superficial resemblance to prudence, wisdom consistently appears to have been overlooked in the traditional listing of classical Greek values. In particular, wisdom directly suggests more of a humanitarian focus, in contrast to the more elementary group focus of prudence. Plato appears to suggest precisely such a distinction: distinguishing between the wisdom of the social environment and that of the philosopher in his/her stoic pursuit of the truth. Plato's student, Aristotle proposed an even sharper distinction in meaning. Practical wisdom (prudence) is most closely associated with social matters, whereas speculative wisdom (*sophia*) pursues truth for its own sake: namely, the universal philosophical principles underlying all human experience. Indeed, according to Alfred Lord Tennyson: "Knowledge comes, but *wisdom* lingers."

In affirmation of these historical perspectives, only the latter (humanitarian) sense of wisdom effective rounds-out the formal listing of classical Greek values. In this collective sense, *beauty* represents the humanitarian counterpart of faith, whereas *truth* makes a similar analogy to hope. Furthermore, *goodness* formally expands upon the theological virtue of charity, whereas *wisdom* makes a similar correspondence to decency.

THE MOTIVATIONAL INTERPLAY FOR THE HUMANITARIAN REALM

As previously described with respect to the spiritually-focused listings of civil liberties and theological virtues, the more abstract virtuous groupings specified for the ecumenical ideals and classical Greek values exhibit a similar dual range of specialization: subdivided into either immediately active modes occurring within the present or passively-potential modes projected into a future-directed time-frame. The immediately active behavioral modes are defined in terms of the ecumenical ideals, invested with clear behavioral overtones; namely, a providence sense of *gracefulness* or a libertarian sense of *free will*, as well as a civil sense of *magnanimity*, or an austere sense of *equanimity*. The future-directed behavioral perspectives, in turn, target the more abstract (projected) realm of the classical Greek values: namely, *beauteous*-faith, just-hope for the *truth*, charitable-*goodness*, and decent-*wisdom*. These projected follower terms effectively complement the more immediately active authority terms in terms of the overall humanitarian dynamic. For instance, in the case of positive reinforcement, a provident sense of gracefulness on the part of the humanitarian authority directly anticipates the beauteous sense of faithfulness on the part of the representative member of humanity. The latter beauteous sense of faithfulness, in turn, eventually is actualized as a civil sense of magnanimity on the part of the reinforcer, whereby anticipating the charitable sense of goodness projected within a future-directed time-frame.

A similar style of motivational interplay further holds true for the remaining realm of negative reinforcement. For instance, the libertarian sense of free will (on the part of the humanitarian authority figure), in turn, anticipates the just-hope for the truth on the part of the representative member of humanity. This latter just-hope for the truth, in turn, is eventually actualized as the austere sense of equanimity on the part of the reinforcer, whereby anticipating the decent sense of wisdom projected within a future-directed timeframe. The remainder of the current chapter systematically examines this advanced humanitarian dynamic encompassing the respective eight-part complement of terms, providing a sturdy foundation for all subsequent classes of values to follow.

Following the pattern of discussion previously established for the personal, group, and universal domains, it would be tempting to employ a similar style of strategy: namely, examining both the humanitarian authority and follow roles in tandem with one another in terms of a two-stage motivational dynamic. With respect to the current humanitarian focus, this would amount to the rewarding sequence of grace, beauty, magnanimity and goodness: as well as the negative reinforcement sequence of free will, truth, equanimity and wisdom. This fourth-order level of abstraction, however, ultimately begins to formally obscure the orderly pattern of procurement *then* reinforcement previously established for the subordinate levels, although the pattern still remains somewhat in evidence.

Indeed, illustrative examples for the predicted interplay of the humanitarian authority and humanitarian follower roles prove similarly elusive, unlike the more clear-cut range of examples for the preceding authority levels. Indeed, as previously indicated, the extreme level of generality associated with the humanitarian realm precludes its identification with any singular social institution; rather typically incorporated into the religious (or sometimes political) framework of society as a whole. The truest appeal of humanitarian authority hinges upon mankind's enduring fascination with culture and tradition, giving homage to the progressive nature of the collective human spirit, while tempered by the forward-looking themes of conservation and renewable resources.

Despite this extreme range of restrictions, a similar pattern of presentation for the humanitarian themes is currently proposed; namely, examining both the humanitarian authority and follow roles in tandem with one another as a two-stage motivational dynamic (although specific illustrative examples will be omitted from the current chapter). This dually integrated pattern of presentation provides a more balanced and comprehensive overview conducive to an overall understanding of the unified virtuous hierarchy, effectively validated in terms of the literary traditions.

GRACE - BEAUTY

The more straightforward class of positive virtues proves to be the most logical initiation point for such a grand-scale analysis, being that positive rewards appear much more definite in relation to the vaguer concept of leniency. Accordingly, the interplay of grace and beauty will be examined first, followed by the remaining sequence of magnanimity and goodness. As suggested in the overarching foundations for these respective virtuous terms, their overall range of inquiry encompasses a clearly more abstract style of interplay than that previously established for the preceding three (more concrete) authority levels.

As initially suggested, the provident sense of gracefulness actively expressed by the spiritual authority figure initiates the humanitarian interaction, expressed as the solicitous quest for the rewarding reinforcement anticipated in terms of the humanitarian follower role. Being that only one role can be active within the conditioned sequence at any given time, the role of the reinforcer is relegated to a future potentiality, identified as the beauteous sense of faithfulness expressed by the representative member of humanity.

The highly conditional nature of the latter beauteous sense of faithfulness equates to the humanitarian follower role, whereas the more immediately active providential sense of gracefulness alternately characterizes the spiritual authority role. According to this humanitarian authority/follower interplay, the humanitarian authority initiates the conditioned interaction, providently acting gracefully in anticipation of the beauteous sense of faithfulness projected within a future-directed time-frame. This latter "beauteous" perspective ultimately imparts meaning and purpose to the humanitarian authority's initial providentially-graceful role. Indeed, this projected sense of potentiality ultimately defines the specifics of the humanitarian follower role, being that all will have been for naught should such a beauteous sense of faithfulness fail to come to pass.

The first mentioned ecumenical ideal of *gracefulness* certainly fits the bill in this humanitarian respect, traditionally defined as divine protection or favor bestowed from On High, whereby providing the motivational rationale for the beauteous sense of faithfulness anticipated from the respective follower figure. Its modern spelling derives from the Latin *gratia* (favor, kindness), from *gratus* (pleasing, agreeable). The classical Romans divinely worshipped this theme as the Gratiae (Graces), a trio of sister goddesses tending to the adornment of Venus. Indeed, the Romans sometimes referred to grace as *venia* in allusion to the handmaidens' unparalleled favor in the eyes of Venus. Although the Graces commanded only a limited cult following in Rome, they were more widely worshipped in their native Greece as the *Charites*: from the Greek *charis* (grace), also a root-stem for charisma. This derivation superficially conforms to the related theme of charity, the latter targeting the Latin *caritas*.

The Charites traditionally represented the Greek ideal of the good life, particularly life's more festive aspects. The Greeks joyously celebrated these qualities in the naming of their three sister goddesses; namely, Aglaia (splendor and brilliance), Thalia (bloom or abundance), and Euphrosyne (joy or mirth). These three sisters presided over banquets, dances, and social engagements: giving charm to all that made life joyous or beautiful. The Charites were also closely affiliated with the Muses, sharing the latter's penchant for music, art, and poetry.

The Graces, accordingly, are depicted as beautiful young maidens dancing in a circular pattern in a meadow, in keeping with their traditional role as nature goddesses. Their most ancient shrine was located at Orchomenos in Greece, adjacent to a temple dedicated to Dionysus and a spring sacred to Aphrodite (both cited in the parentage of the Graces). Ancient stone images of the Charites were enshrined here, said to have fallen miraculously from the heavens. Their annual feast day was celebrated nearby with musical contests and dancing staged in their honor.

Grace is also celebrated as a major theme in the Judeo-Christian tradition. The opening passages of the Old Testament specifically proclaim the Jews as the chosen people of God. This blessing stems from the Lord's founding promise to Abraham (Genesis 12:2-3) and His subsequent covenant with Moses on Mt. Sinai (Exodus 33:19). The end of the Old Testament period, however, ushered in a more personalized perspective on God's grace; now viewed as a gift bestowed upon all those that keep His Commandments.

This personalized perspective on God's grace eventually carried over into the precepts of New Testament scripture. The original Greek NT versions specifically translate grace as *charis* (referring to objects of joy or delight). It is chiefly through the writings of the St. Paul, however, that the Christian sense of the term reaches its most enduring degree of significance. In 1st Corinthians, Chapter *12*, St. Paul directly intimates that the *charismatic* gifts (namely, prophecy, healing, and speaking-in-tongues) are outward manifestations of this indwelling grace of God. Furthermore, these Gifts of Grace are chiefly made available through faith (Romans 4:16), the devotion of the believer proving crucial to such divine intervention. Here, the humanitarian authority providentially act graceful towards his respective follower figure in anticipation of the latter's beauteously-faithful treatment (as projected within a future-directed time-frame). In response to this beauteous-adulation on the part of humanitarian follower, the humanitarian authority remains reciprocally dependent within such a grand humanitarian time-scale: any provident sense of gracefulness now entirely meaningless without such a potential for reinforcement.

The latter positive allusion to reinforcement is clearly specified in relation to the enduring humanitarian theme of *beauty*. In contrast to the solicitous prerequisites initially described for gracefulness, beauty alternately targets the positive range of reinforcement projected within a future-directed time-frame. The modern-day conception of beauty traces its origins to the Latin *bellitas*, from the root-stem *bellus* (pretty or pleasing). The classical Greeks particularly revered physical beauty and perfection, qualities their gods and goddesses exhibited to a supreme degree. The goddess Aphrodite was singled out as the divine personification of love, beauty, and fertility. Her ethereal status among the gods derived from the claim she was born upon the waves and foam of sea, from the Greek *aphros* (foam). She is depicted as a lightly-draped figure of uncompromising grace and beauty. An ancient armless statue of her (known as the Venus de Milo) was named for its discovery on the remote Greek isle of Melos.

The Roman counterpart of Aphrodite, *Venus*, originally appears to have been Italian goddess associated with vegetable gardens; in essence, promoting their fertility. Her Latin name became synonymous with charm and beauty, eventually a key factor in her identification with the Greek traditions of Aphrodite. The legendary beauty of Venus was directly symbolized by her chief attribute, the Cestus (an embroidered girdle).

These mythological interpretations of beauty find considerable parallels in the aesthetic principles underlying classical Greek philosophy. According to early Greek tradition, beauty represents an external attribute of a given object, a property intrinsic to its very physical make-up. According to the writings of Plato and Aristotle, beauty resides in a regularity of form and function: as further expressed in symmetry, proportion, and harmony.

Our modern age of ethical subjectivism, however, changed the face of aesthetics forever, as clearly evident in the contemporary maxim: "Beauty is in the eye of the beholder." This radical interpretation was directly championed by the empiricists, who viewed beauty as any agreeable aesthetic experience of a reinforcing nature. Indeed, some empiricists postulated the existence of a special "sixth sense" attuned to beauty, whereby governing the appreciation of all such pleasurable experiences. These themes are retained in the subjectivist theories of our modern age, with beauty defined as those sensory experiences that evoke a positive emotional response, particularly in a reinforcing visual sense. Indeed, as the great English poet, John Keats fittingly wrote: "A thing of beauty is a joy forever."

MAGNANIMITY - GOODNESS

The completed preliminary sequence of grace and beauty, in turn, gives way to a further discussion of the remaining stage within the humanitarian dynamic: namely, that encompassing magnanimity/goodness. According to this latter sequence, the reinforcer eventually acts upon his (projected) beauteous sense of faithfulness, whereby civilly behaving magnanimously in anticipation of the charitable determination to act with goodness on the part of the respective follower figure. A number of key features become apparent with respect to the initiatory phase characterizing magnanimity. As the respective humanitarian counterpart for the spiritually-focused theme of civility, magnanimity certainly proves adequate in this conceptual regard. Its modern spelling derives from the Latin *magnanimus* (greatness of soul), from *magnus* (great) and *animus* (soul). It is traditionally defined as nobility of mind or spirit that graciously overlooks insult or injury. Magnanimity was particularly revered during the classical age, specifically singled out by Aristotle in his principle listing of virtues. This theme also finds expression in the Judeo-Christian tradition as celebrated to a supreme degree within the teachings of Christ. Scripture recognizes Christ's ability to recognize the greatness of the moment in terms of rewards, as in his parable describing the slaughter of the fatted calf (Luke 15:23) or his opening of a chest of precious ointment (Mathew 26:8-13). A similar theme occurs in OT Book of Ecclesiastes (11:1) which states: "Cast thy bread upon the waters, for thou shalt find it after many days," (signifying generosity transcending personal concerns).

Magnanimity signifies the inclination to reward exemplary courage or skill, often to an extravagant degree. Such noble characteristics also endear it as one of the traditional attributes of royalty and nobility. In the heraldic symbolism of the Middle Ages, magnanimity is represented as a triumphant eagle depicted in the act of sparing a portion of its kill for the lesser birds of prey (that hover around the eagle in a solicitous fashion). Contrast this to the human condition, where those in positions of power/authority consistently strive to preserve some measure of their exalted status through the erection of a stone memorial, durably built to stand the test of time. Indeed, many such grand monuments survive from ancient times: standing mute testimony to the magnificence of the commemorated leader, as well as the painstaking labor of the supportive cast of artisans. Here, the humanitarian authority is civilly behaves magnanimously in anticipation of the charitable sense of goodness on the part of the humanitarian follower. This overarching magnanimous context encourages an enduring degree of incentive over a grand humanitarian time-scale, an aspect conducive to the longstanding traditions of goodness and flourishing.

The latter goodly-charitable perspective certainly rings true in this basic regard, earning its terminal placement through its effective consummation of the entire humanitarian interchange. In slightly different terms, I (as representative member of humanity) am charitably determined to act with goodness towards you in response to your (as humanitarian authority) civilly-magnanimous treatment of me. This distinctive style of motivational interplay directly reflects the characteristic "if you then I" motivational dynamic governing the entire conditioned interaction. Actually goodness is traditionally invested with a rather broad range of meanings consistent with its generalized applications within the field of ethical inquiry. Its modern spelling derives from the Anglo-Saxon *god* (designating goodness). The Latin tradition is alternately identified with *bonitas*, the same root-stem for the related theme of benevolence. In direct contrast to truth and beauty, goodness is not limited to any single classical deity, rather proposed as an indwelling attribute of the gods and goddesses in general. Although many of the classical gods were not above a certain degree of combativeness, they, nevertheless, were regarded as morally upright and good at heart.

Certain of the classical deities exemplified this quality to a supreme degree; namely, the Roman god Bonus Eventus (literally, good event). Bonus Eventus originally was worshipped as an agricultural deity, whose rituals determined the

The Feather of Truth: Balancing Heart on the Scales of Justice
Detail from the Egyptian Papyrus of Ani   © - The British Museum

success or failure of the harvest. His scope eventually extended to close association with Fortuna (the Roman goddess of fortune). Surviving statues depict Bonus Eventus as a youthful figure offering a libation toast at the foot of a sacrificial altar. He holds stalks of grain in his free hand indicative of his agricultural origins.

Perhaps the most stirring applications of goodness concern the Christian teachings on the subject, particularly those relating to the "Good Shepherd" and the parable of the Good Samaritan, a story proclaiming the value of the love for one's neighbor. Here goodness clearly represents a projected style of humanitarian perspective reflective of its more elementary foundations in charity. This unselfish impulse underscores the most salient feature of goodness: namely, its bestowal as its own reward without regard for material gain (in keeping with such a grand humanitarian time-scale). Indeed, this tenuous power of potentiality ultimately drives the reciprocity inherent within the authority/follower interaction, the former depending upon the latter to provide ultimate meaning and fulfillment.

FREE WILL - TRUTH

In summary, the completed description of the two-stage humanitarian schematic of grace-beauty and magnanimity-goodness offers a comprehensive overview of the motivational dynamics governing the humanitarian style of interaction.

The ultimate goal for this exercise has been to propose a sturdy foundation for the virtuous realm, resulting in an overarching model of value ethics in general. Before skipping ahead to the final transcendental range of applications, it proves crucial to examine the remaining motivational interplay of the values specific to the realm of negative reinforcement. Negative reinforcement entails the deliberate withholding of punitive consequences within the environment or (in an interpersonal sense) leniency in response to aversive types of behavior.

In terms of a humanitarian social context, the humanitarian authority figure freely willed acts in a libertarian fashion in anticipation of the just-hope for the truth on the part of the humanitarian follower. This provisional just-hope for the truth, in turn, eventually becomes actualized as the austere sense of equanimity on the part of the reinforcer, whereby further anticipating the decent sense of wisdom on the part of the respective follower figure. Certainly it might appear somewhat risky to exhibit such an extreme degree of equanimity without a reasonable assurance of upcoming leniency. Past memory cycles certainly come into play, effectively justifying such a radical act of trust. The humanitarian theme of free will certainly enters into consideration here, defined as the chief humanitarian variation on the libertarian sense of honor previously described for the universal realm. Indeed, this libertarian sense of free will provides the motivational rationale for the just-hope for the truth potentially anticipated from the representative member of humanity. The modern spelling of free will derives from a literal translation of the Late-Latin *liberum arbitrium* (literally, free decision). In keeping with its compound character, free will has traditionally been assigned a rather broad range of meanings: from motivation and will, to necessity and determination. Its modern spelling actually suggests somewhat of a redundancy, for its component themes of freedom and will are often used interchangeably in common usage.

In a traditional sense, the doctrine of free will originally was devised to defend against the argument that God had the power to prevent the occurrence of evil in the world. According to this free will defense, God allows mankind to be tempted by evil in order to freely elect to resist (or yield) to it. The wrathful punishment awaiting the wicked adds further fuel to the controversy, for God surely is able to circumvent sin without necessarily resorting to outright punishment. Various Church theologians have attempted to reinterpret this paradox, shifting the blame for sin to mankind's inherent weakness. Here, the Church was able to blame the fall of Adam and Eve (and not any flaw in God's master plan) for the ever-present consequences of evil occurring throughout the world.

In a complementary fashion, the humanitarian follower justly hopes for the truth in relation to his respective authority figure, a direct response to the latter's libertarian sense of free will. This lenient connotation for truth shares much in common with the related (more rewarding) theme of beauty. Indeed, Keats is further credited with the stirring quotation: "Beauty is truth, truth is beauty," attesting to the figurative association linking the two. Its modern spelling derives the Anglo Saxon *treowth* (of similar meaning and usage). Its related Latin counterpart, *veritas*, survives primarily in terms of the English synonyms verity, veracity, etc. In fact, Veritas was specifically worshipped as a deity by the ancients, described as the daughter of Saturn and the Mother of Virtue. She is portrayed as a youthful virgin draped in white, exhibiting an overarching air of modesty. The Greek philosopher Democritus describes her as hiding at the bottom of a well, undoubtedly hinting at the great difficulty with which she is found.

Such classical considerations further beg mention of the related legends associated with Diogenes, a Greek contemporary of Aristotle. Diogenes is traditionally credited as the founder of Cynicism, a philosophical movement named for its at-tempts to discredit the lofty pretensions of the elite of Athens. Diogenes earned the reputation as somewhat of an eccentric, advocating a "back to nature" form of ascetic lifestyle generally bordering upon the absurd. His most prominent claim to fame concerns the fanciful legends surrounding his search for an "honest man." This quest was said to have taken him through the streets of Athens holding aloft a lantern in broad daylight, an eccentric feature further indicative of the futile nature for such an endeavor.

According to this fanciful legend, Diogenes clearly assumes the role of the representative member of humanity: a status strongly befitting the serious philosopher of his day. His persistent quest for the truth clearly narrows the focus, directly emphasizing the leniently-moralistic aspects of the legend. The distinctive lantern symbolism of the tale lends further credence to the discovery function of truth. Indeed, lamps of various styles are incorporated into the seals of many prestigious universities accentuating their unswerving devotion to the truth. A similar correspondence is also seen with respect to beauty, which (in analogy to truth) is projected entirely within the eye of the beholder.

Truth is perceived as a never-ending quest, the search for the honest man directly targeting those deserving of lenient treatment within such a grand humanitarian time-scale. Curiously, the legendary honest man always eludes Diogenes, for in the sage opinion of Albert Einstein: "The search for *truth* is more precious than its possession." Along similar lines, philosopher George Santayana further writes: "The *truth* is all things seen under the form of eternity," a speculation in fitting agreement with the enduring humanitarian prerequisites for truth. In slightly different terms, you (as representative member of humanity) justly-hope for the truth in response to my (as humanitarian authority) libertarian sense of freewill.

EQUANIMITY - WISDOM

The preceding two-stage sequence of free will and truth, in turn, dictates that the humanitarian follower figure eventually acts upon the potentiality implicit in his/her projected just-hope for truth. This further development ultimately takes the form of austerely acting with equanimity within an immediately-active time-frame, whereby anticipating the (projected) decent sense of wisdom on the part of the respective follower figure. Indeed, this ultimate power of deliberation directly imparts the power leverage enjoyed with respect to the equanimity perspective. Significantly, equanimity directly parallels the affiliated theme of magnanimity with the exception that leniency (rather than approval) is now called into focus. Accordingly, magnanimity and equanimity are often employed in quite similar contexts. This enduring degree of overlap is betrayed in terms of their common linguistic origins: magnanimity specifying a "greatness of mind," whereas equanimity equates with an "evenness of mind." The latter term derives from the Latin *aequus* (equal) and *animus* (mind), formally reflecting its traditional connotations of mental composure and/or calm demeanor. Just as magnanimity imparted a more enduring quality to civility, so equanimity adds an enduring humanitarian focus to austerity.

This timeless quality of equanimity further emerges as a dominant theme in classical philosophy, particularly the traditions associated with Stoicism. Here, Zeno of Citium founded Stoicism in the city of Athens, lecturing students from a *stoa* (or porch). The stoic individual accepts what cannot be changed, stomaching adversity with an austere sense of equanimity. The subsequent rise of the Christian era, however, presaged the decline of pagan Stoicism, although many of its nobler themes were incorporated into later Church Canon. This austere sense of equanimity was particularly revered by the ascetic orders of the early Christian Church, offering hope and inspiration in the face of the tribulations of the Dark Ages. Equanimity, accordingly, remained the emblem of the long-suffering medieval knight: celebrated through the aid of heraldic symbolisms similar to those cited for magnanimity. The noble knight represents a fitting exemplar of equanimity, pledging a lifetime of service to his feudal lord regardless of personal hardship.

Although the heraldic symbolisms for magnanimity took the form of a regal eagle, equanimity is more prosaically portrayed as the domestic ass, a beast of burden symbolizing patience and perseverance under even the most trying of circumstances. Indeed, equanimity is also symbolized as the humble beaver, a beast that patiently labors to maintain its constructions under the most formidable of challenges. Whether one alludes to the industrious beaver or the patient ass, these enduring qualities of equanimity are unmistakable in their intent, an enduring refinement of austerity wholly emblematic of such a grand humanitarian time-scale. Consequently, this humanitarian focus on equanimity actively endeavors to reinforce the (anticipated) decent sense of wisdom on the part of the representative member of humanity. Indeed, this overarching sense of equanimity promotes a leniently reassuring environment condu-

cive to global peace and harmony. Consequently, equanimity extends the more basic (universal) theme of austerity into an even more enduring humanitarian sphere of influence.

In terms of the formal two-stage motivational dynamic, the enduring humanitarian overtones for equanimity are ultimately consummated in terms of the remaining classical Greek value of wisdom. Similar to its motivational counterpart in goodness, wisdom formally provides an effective sense of closure for the entire humanitarian interaction. Here, I (as representative member of humanity) decently act in a wise fashion towards you in response to your (as humanitarian authority) austerely-active sense of equanimity.

In a traditional sense, *wisdom* enjoys a status virtually unparalleled within the field of ethical inquiry. Its modern spelling derives from a compound of two Anglo-Saxon words *wis-* (way or manner) and *dom* (state) collectively designating sound moral judgment or common sense. The ancient Romans divinely worshipped this quality as their abstract goddess Sapientia (Latin for Lady-Wisdom). She is traditionally depicted as a Siren of Philosophies rising from the sea in a style reminiscent of Aphrodite, pouring-out the "wine" of enlightenment from her bosom. Indeed, the Latin proper name for the human species, *Homo sapiens*, literally translates as "wise man." The related Greek root *sophia* suggests a similar scope of inquiry, as evident in the English derivations of Sophism, sophistication, etc. Plato's great disdain for the clever Sophists (or paid philosophers) of his day appears to have contributed to the omission of wisdom in his traditional canon of classical Greek values. Accordingly, wisdom was viewed as more of a virtue than a value, equivalent to the cardinal virtue of prudence.

Perhaps of even greater import to Western culture is the Wisdom Literature of the Jewish tradition, particularly the Old Testament Books of *Proverbs* and *Psalms*. As the traditional author of the book of *Proverbs*, King Solomon was revered as perhaps the wisest in a long line of biblical monarchs. Solomon proved particularly well suited to the duties of his royal upbringing, widely renowned for his legendary cleverness and wisdom. His penchant for clever manipulation figured prominently in his celebrated seduction of the visiting Queen of Sheba. Indeed, his shrewd political acumen was chiefly instrumental in ushering in a golden age of trade and commerce for the Jewish people, leading to the construction of the First Jewish Temple at Jerusalem.

King Solomon's most prominent reputation for wisdom, however, was recorded in his routine courtly pronouncements: where he assumed an active role in settling disputes amongst his subjects. The Old Testament describes a conflict between two women seeking audience before the king, both claiming the same newborn child. Solomon shrewdly feigned the prospect of cleaving the disputed child in two, wherein ultimately determining the true mother through her emotional plea to forgo such a drastic outcome. This shrewd insight into human nature certainly validates King Solomon's rightful status as a true humanitarian visionary within the wisdom tradition. The decent sense of wisdom he so effortlessly dispensed reflects a range of common sense so crucial to the broad spectrum of humanity. In truth, we are all heirs to the Wisdom of Solomon to varying degrees, where a sage mixture of decency and wisdom provides a trusty guide to the trials of everyday experience.

In conclusion, the completed description of the humanitarian authority/follower roles proves a fitting counterpoint to all that has gone before. Indeed, the representative member of humanity role is one that we all share in common; spokespersons for all generations and times. Although the extreme degree of abstraction can prove quite daunting, we are all eligible to speak as philosophers of a sort through the eclectic listing of classical Greek values: beauty, truth, goodness, and wisdom. This crowning humanitarian derivation would finally appear to close out any further innovations to abstraction, for there cannot be any level of organization greater than humanity as a whole. This very sense of the power of abstraction, however, serves as the basis for one final innovation within the ascending power hierarchy: namely, that specifying the crowning *transcendental* level of authority/follower roles.

6

THE TRANSCENDENTAL PERSPECTIVE

The transcendental perspective has enjoyed a long and illustrious literary tradition with precedents dating at least to classical times. Its modern spelling derives from the Latin *transcendere* (to climb over), from *trans-* (over) and *scandere* (to climb. Medieval scholars freely adapted this theme in the academic field of Scholastic Logic: defining as *transcendentalia* (or *transcendentia*) extreme concepts such as goodness, unity, being, etc. The modern sense of the term dates to the writings of German philosopher Immanuel Kant, who laid the groundwork for his unique style of transcendental philosophy. In his masterpiece, *Critique of Pure Reason*, Kant directly acknowledges the transcendental philosophy of the ancients, although suggesting that his revised sense of the term only superficially conforms to the traditional sense. Indeed, Kant draws sharp distinctions between the notions of transcendence, the transcendental, and the immanent.

The realm of *transcendence* is said to apply to ideas beyond the range of direct sensory experience. The notion of *immanence*, in turn, refers to the concrete realm of sensory experience. The remaining concept of the *transcendental*, however, represents an intermediate position; namely, conceptual constructs implicit to sensory experience, although not directly arising from the senses. In particular, Kant distinguishes a broad range of transcendental categories (such as relation, causality, quantity, etc.) that intuitively serve to order sensory experience, although existing as mere formalities without sensory data to embody them. In this latter sense, all knowledge is preconditioned by such transcendental presuppositions, forming the basis for the German school of transcendental idealism.

Kant's dynamic influence eventually reached the English speaking world chiefly through the writings of Samuel Taylor Coleridge and Thomas Carlyle. These interpretations eventually gained acceptance in the United States, flowering during the early 19th century as the eclectic movement known as New England Transcendentalism. This movement arose as a revolt against the skepticism of British Rational Philosophy, as well as the dogmatism of Orthodox Protestantism. Ralph Waldo Emerson was the acknowledged leader of the movement. Other notables included Henry David Thoreau, Nathaniel Hawthorne, and Margaret Fuller. Although the New England movement was relatively short-lived, it was instrumental in influencing religious and social thought for generations to come. Despite the belief that social change was primarily a matter of personal choice, many transcendentalists championed the major reform movements of the day; namely, peace, temperance, women's suffrage, and slavery.

The strength of the movement declined with the onset of the Civil War coinciding with the retirement of Emerson and the death of Thoreau. A century later Dr. Martin Luther King Jr. acknowledged the great influence Thoreau's philosophy of civil disobedience played in the Civil Rights demonstrations of the 1960's. Indeed, these latter troubled times provide crucial clues towards identifying the four affective dimensions predicted for the transcendental authority perspective.

A MODERN-DAY REVIVAL OF TRANSCENDENTALISM

The war protest era of the late 60's and early 70's was characterized by great political and moral upheaval, a trend "the establishment" found increasingly difficult to control. The great rallying cry was the protest against the Vietnam War, the mounting casualty figures discouraging support for what (even then) appeared to be a futile international endeavor. The peace movement, accordingly, evolved its own fraternal symbolisms; namely, the peace sign and the peace symbol (a dove's foot inscribed in a circle). The simultaneous availability of "the pill," in turn, ushered in a more relaxed sexual attitude, the practice of free love flourishing in "hippy" districts such as Haight-Ashbury. This self-styled peace-love generation prided itself on such nonconformist attitudes, looking to the unconventional themes of meditation and astrology for solutions to political turmoil, promoting the quest for inner peace and tranquility. The emerging Civil Rights movement also raised the pressing issue of racial equality, an issue deliberately grafted into the peace movement as yet a further tactic to thwart the tyranny of the establishment. Blacks became "brothers" with whites in a stirring appeal to universal peace and brotherhood.

These four noble themes of the 60's (peace-love-tranquility-equality) collectively celebrate the transcendental focus of the age, a tradition sharing much in common with New England Transcendentalism. This enduring transcendental perspective proves particularly consistent with the reigning humanistic focus of the modern age, downplaying the dogmatism of orthodox religion in favor of individual conscience. This cohesive grouping of peace-love-tranquility-equality is most appropriately termed the class of *humanistic* values, directly expanding upon the humanitarian focus of the ecumenical ideals. In more abstract sense, *peace* represents a more advanced transcendental modification of equanimity, whereas *love* attaches a parallel significance to magnanimity. Furthermore, *tranquility* imparts a transcendental perspective to grace, whereas *equality* targets the affiliated theme of free will.

In contrast to the pattern of discussion previously established for the group, spiritual, and humanitarian realms, the transcendental sphere of influence alternately employs a slightly different strategy of analysis. This fifth-order level of transcendental abstraction definitely begins to obscure the more orderly (behavioral) pattern of organization previously established for the subordinate levels. Despite these abstract restrictions, the basic two-stage sequential pattern of authority/follower remains primarily in evidence, as in the positive sequence specified for tranquility, ecstasy, love, and joy: as well as the leniently-based sequence of equality, bliss, peace, and harmony. A custom pattern of presentation for the individual transcendental values, therefore, is proposed: examining the transcendental terms as the crowning culmination for the entire range of the virtuous hierarchy. For instance, joy is examined in terms of the subordinate concepts of charity and goodness, whereas love is defined with

respect to civility/magnanimity. Furthermore, ecstasy is specified in relation to faith and beauty, whereas tranquility exhibits a similar correspondence to providence/grace. A similar pattern of presentation further holds true with respect to the respective realm of transcendental perspectives based upon leniency. These comparisons prove relatively straightforward, being that the humanitarian realm shares many features in common with the crowning transcendental domain. Indeed, this final transcendental realm provides an overarching description of themes of a purely abstract nature, culminating in a seamless overview of the entire unified virtuous hierarchy.

PEACE

The first of the humanistic values to be examined, peace, represents a theme of virtually universal appeal. This theme was deliberately chosen to lead off this discussion, providing the immediately active lenient rationale for the projected anticipation of harmony on the part of transcendental follower. As defined from the viewpoint of the transcendental authority, peace represents a leniently active style of austere-equanimity in anticipation of the harmonious sense of wisdom potentially ascribed to the respective follower figure. Consequently, peace extends the subordinate qualities of austere-equanimity into an even more abstract transcendental sphere of influence.

The enduring traditions ascribed to peace endow this transcendental theme with a clear range of lenient overtones. Its modern spelling derives from the Latin *pax* (peace) chiefly in the context of the Pax Romana, the formal peace the Romans imposed upon subject provinces within the Empire. The Roman's self-appointed role of peacemaker was primarily seen as a moral prerogative according to political theorists such as Virgil. Indeed, the Romans specifically worshipped this concept as their abstract goddess Pax, the divine personification of peace among diverse nations.

Pax represents a relatively late addition to the Roman pantheon, virtually unheard of before the time of Augustus. State support for her cult is generally credited with fostering the strength and stability of the Empire under Augustus. A Roman shrine was dedicated to Pax in 9 BCE in celebration of the restoration of peace by Augustus following his triumphant series of campaigns in Spain and Gaul. The widespread longing for peace contributed to Pax's great popularity among the common people during this period of civil unrest. Accordingly, Pax is portrayed as a youthful maiden holding a cornucopia in her left hand and an

Noah in the Ark: Welcoming Back the Dove of Peace
Detail from a Fresco in the Catacomb of St. Peter/St. Marcellinus - Rome - (3rd Century)

olive branch (the symbol of peace) in her right. She is sometimes depicted setting fire to a stock-stockpile of armaments in defiance to the prevailing militarism of the era. A major festival was held in her honor on the last day in April.

The Judeo-Christian tradition similarly celebrates the transcendental aspects of peace. The Hebrew word for peace, *Salom*, is directly related to the same root-stem for health and wholesomeness. The prophets of the Old Testament exalted peace as the promised blessing of the Messianic Age. In his Sermon on the Mount, Christ directly blesses the peacemakers, stating: "They shall be called children of God." The Apostle Paul, in turn, describes Christ's message as "the gospel of peace" (Ephesians 6:15). Paul also lists peace among the Gifts of the Holy Spirit. Indeed, it is fitting that the dove (as the chief symbolism of the Holy Spirit) figures so prominently in OT descriptions of peace, particularly the celebrated story of Noah and the Ark. Here, the dove served as God's messenger, carrying an olive sprig in its beak symbolizing peaceful intent. Noah originally had released the dove during the Great Flood to see if it might successfully find landfall. The olive branch carried by the dove, in turn, signaled that

the ordeal had finally come to an end. In keeping with these stirring scriptural precedents, peace builds (in a transcendental fashion) upon the humanitarian prerequisites previously established for equanimity, terms sharing a leniently collective focus in austerity. These grand-scale transcendental characteristics for peace suggest precisely such an austere perspective, as exemplified in the offering of an olive branch during peace negotiations. The olive orchard required many years of tending to become fruitful, signifying the peaceful cooperation required to reach fruition Accordingly, the dove and the olive branch are all revered as symbolisms of peace: emblems still employed today in the amicable resolution of disputes.

LOVE

The completed description of peace, in turn, begs further mention of the related transcendental theme of *love*. Similar to peace, love represents the supremely active bestowal of reinforcement within the conditioned interaction. In terms of the transcendental authority perspective, love represents the active expression of civil-magnanimity through rewarding reinforcement in anticipation of the goodly sense of joyousness projected for the transcendental follower figure. Indeed, in terms of this overarching affectionate potential, I (as transcendental authority) magnanimously act lovingly towards you in anticipation of your (as transcendental follower) goodly sense of joyousness.

In line with these crowning transcendental characteristics, love extends the truest measure of transcendence across all ages and cultures. Its modern spelling derives from the Anglo-Saxon *lufu* (of similar meaning and usage). Although the English derivation has endured as the dominant form, the classical tradition is represented as the Latin *cupido* (passion, desire), as well as *amor* (love). Indeed, the Romans worshipped this theme in the guise of Cupid, their youthful god of love. In classical mythology, Cupid is traditionally depicted as an adorable winged cherub daintily equipped with a quiver and bow. The youngest of the Roman gods, he is described as callous or capricious. The gods Pothos and Himeros were his constant companions, the Roman personifications of longing and desire. Jupiter graciously equipped Cupid with a pair of golden wings, a magical bow, and a quiver of invisible arrows said never to miss their mark. These arrows were said to instill irresistible love in the hearts of all struck by them. One ancient legend suggests that Cupid whets with blood the grindstone upon which he sharpens his arrows. He is described as blind or blindfolded consistent with the contention that "love is blind."

These enduring legends surrounding Cupid serve as a colorful basis for many modern-day symbolisms of love, particularly a crimson heart pierced by an arrow (the traditional emblem of St. Valentine's Day). The modern conception of romantic love is actually of fairly recent origin, as well as the tradition of marriage for love's sake. Marriage solely for love at first was considered a scandalous novelty, in contrast to the moral mandate it currently enjoys today.

The modern age of romantic love was initially celebrated in the lyric poetry popularized by the troubadours of Southern France. The romantic exaltation of the passions eventually swept the continent, celebrating the romantic ideal of chaste womanhood. This courtly sense of love transcended mere sexual passion, idealizing the chaste and inaccessible woman of fancy. The medieval lover was expected to serve his lady without recompense save the glow of her gracious approval. This elevated status of women eventually became reflected in other chivalrous themes; namely, a steadfast sense of loyalty to God, King, and Country. These noble themes of chastity/chivalry sought to control (rather than gratify) such amo-

rous instincts. Romantic passion increased in direct proportion to the obstacles placed in the way. In this latter respect, love guides one to a nobler life, its trials and tribulations curiously suggestive of the ordeals of martyrdom (both of which transcend the self in the quest for a higher good).

As is true for so many of the great love stories from the past, love is seen to transcend all political and social barriers, a transcendental expression of pure passion. In the case of Romeo and Juliet, their respective families were embroiled in a bitter blood feud spanning many generations, in direct contrast to the tender and loving passion shared by the young lovers. In similar fashion, Anthony and Cleopatra were the fateful offspring of differing cultures, yet the flame of their love burned bright until tragically cut short. Here (as with Romeo and Juliet), the couple chose to die together to be joined again for all eternity, an extreme variation on the transcendental foundations for the love perspective.

TRANQUILITY

The completed description of peace and love, in turn, redirects the current focus to the remaining humanistic values of tranquility and equality. True to their order of introduction, tranquility is described first, followed by a parallel discussion of equality. Both themes share commonalties with peace and love with the exception of now being punctuated from a procurement (rather than reinforcement) perspective. For instance, in terms of the transcendental authority role, tranquility represents an immediately-active providential expression of gracefulness in anticipation of the beauteous sense of ecstasy potentially attributed to the transcendental follower figure.

The extremely abstract attributes traditionally associated with tranquility are certainly unprecedented within the transcendental realm. Its modern spelling derives the Latin *tranquillitas*, from *trans-* (beyond) and *quies* (rest). The use of the same prefix in the overall context of transcendentalism lends further credence to the overlapping significance linking these two fundamental themes. The Romans worshipped tranquility as the abstract goddess Quies, the divine personification of calmness and tranquility. She is traditionally portrayed as a beautiful maiden in a relaxed pose, sometimes shown leaning upon a short marble column. Her chapel was located on the Via Labicana in Rome, a welcome refuge for the weary traveler. A private cult dedicated to Quies dates to the earliest days of the Republic, although official worship was not instituted until

Imperial times. Following his surrender to Augustus, the rival Maximian had a medal of conciliation minted with the inscription "Quies Augustorum." A later series of coins incorporates the theme of *tranquillitas* into the emperor's title of distinction.

The direct antithesis of such formal classicism extends to an appreciation of tranquility within the natural environment. Perhaps no experience is more exhilarating than a visit to a still mountain lake framed with majestic tall timber, permeated with an eternal hush completely at odds with the urban environment. This pristine natural setting clearly transcends the more hectic pace of city life, offering an experience of virtually timeless proportions. This exalted devotion for nature was widely celebrated in the spirited works of the great English and German romanticists: e.g., Goethe, Wordsworth, and Coleridge. They collectively celebrated a regard for the wonders of nature, as well as empathy for its divine order.

The subsequent dawning of the Industrial Age, however, forever altered such a pastoral perspective. Nature was now esteemed as a source of timber and coal for fueling the furnaces and steam engines of the day. Cities grew increasingly over-crowded and polluted, attracting many unskilled laborers from the countryside. Under such trying circumstances, tranquility was chiefly achieved through chemical means: primarily with respect to alcohol, opium, or other tranquilizers.

In keeping with the preceding nature example, tranquility is clearly defined as an immediately active style of transcendental perspective true to its more elementary foundations in grace. The "tranquilizer" abuser habitually acts solicitously in order to achieve the positive rewards when the drug finally takes effect. Here, the calming effect of the tranquilizer diminishes routine stresses in favor of tranquil feelings of serenity.

Drugs actually represent just one avenue towards achieving a calm disposition. The appreciation of music, art, and drama provides an effective release from everyday stressful routines: in addition to prayer, yoga, and meditation. The serene smile traditionally associated with depictions of the Buddha is clearly indicative of such a tranquil demeanor. Indeed, whether it is the hypnotizing radiance associated with the Transfiguration of Christ, or the mystical magnetism described in Herman Hesse's *Siddartha*; this enduring sense of tranquility always appears to come shining through!

EQUALITY

The completed description of tranquility, in turn, swings the focus to the remaining humanistic value of equality, a theme sharing many commonalties to tranquility with the exception that submissiveness is targeted, rather than the solicitousness. As defined from the perspective of the transcendental authority, the immediately active egalitarian expression of free will, in turn, anticipates the blissful-hope for the truth potentially ascribed to the respective follower figure. Here, I (as transcendental authority) freely-willed act in an egalitarian fashion towards you in anticipation of your (as transcendental follower) blissful-hope for the truth.

Equality certainly lives up to its transcendental billing: being that in the real world everyone proves unique in terms of individual strengths and weaknesses. Its modern spelling derives from the Latin *aequalitas* (equal), from *aequalis* (even). The Romans professed a strong constitutional sense of equality, with every citizen enjoying equal protection under the law. The Jus Naturale (or natural law) insured equal rights to the sea, seashore, and community property. Accordingly, the Romans divinely worshipped this theme as their abstract goddess Aequitas. Direct evidence of her cult occurs in an archaic inscription from Vulci, and Arnobius mentions her as a goddess. Her name is inscribed on ancient coins from the era.

The modern-day conception of equality (also known as *egalitarianism*) dates as a postscript to the Age of Enlightenment. Political philosopher Thomas Hobbes professed the equal rights of mankind in one's natural state consistent with an unlimited sense of potential. John Locke, in turn, elaborated upon this basic premise stating that: "all men are equally free under the natural law and therefore fully deserving of the same natural rights." During the 18th century these noble perspectives were further reflected in emerging theories of human development and potential. According to Condillac and Helvetius, all men are equal in terms of the unlimited potential they share at birth, equally perfectible given the proper social environment. French philosopher, J. J. Rousseau explained social inequality in terms of the pressures stemming from a stratified social order. Each individual (in the state of nature) fends for himself, whereby abstaining from exploiting others (or being exploited). Rousseau further reasons that full social equality is the ideal natural state for human society in general.

These radical interpretations proved particularly instrumental in fueling the American and French Revolutions: themes eloquently reflected in their respective declarations of rights. For the American Revolution, this sense of equality denied the legitimacy of any arbitrary form of government. The *Declaration of Independence* formally underscores this basic principle stating: "We hold these truths to be self evident that all men are created *equal*, they are endowed by their Creator with certain unalienable rights, that among these are Life, Liberty, and the Pursuit of Happiness." This egalitarian perspective continues into our modern age, particularly with respect to the United Nation's *Universal Declaration of Human Rights* (1948) which states: "All human beings are born free and *equal* in dignity and rights."

In direct analogy to the case previously made for tranquility, equality shares an equivalent transcendental focus: an ideal eminently noble in principle (although seldom realized in practice). In truth, any recourse to universal principles necessarily entails a seeming disregard for the more basic limitations governing the human condition. This egalitarian perspective necessarily specifies equal protection under the law irrespective of personal limitations or class distinctions. Such noble ideals celebrate the equal opportunity of all races and creeds; hence, clearly denouncing any preferential treatment therein. Although such lofty ideals do not always square with the glaring gaps in the global economic system, they, nevertheless, remain principles worth aspiring to, even if only to remedy much of the prejudice that typically breeds in its stead.

THE MYSTICAL VALUES: THE ROLE OF THE TRANSCENDENTAL FOLLOWER

In conclusion, the completed description of the humanistic values offers a rather dramatic departure from the more routine rigors of everyday life. Indeed, the world would undoubtedly be a much crueler place without such a noble class of ideals to aspire to. This transcendental perspective formally appeals to an idealized realm of pure abstraction, effectively overruling the more limited (organizational) power base characterizing the lower set of levels. This profoundly abstract scope might suggest that the upper conceptual limit for the ethical hierarchy has finally been reached, for it is difficult to imagine a set of constructs more abstract than peace, love, tranquility, and equality. Even an authority level as abstract as the transcendental must (by definition) be invested with its own unique style or brand of follower countermaneuver, in this case that claimed by the transcendental follower.

The transcendental follower maneuver is clearly an unprecedented addition to the orderly progression of the virtuous hierarchy, its extreme level of abstraction greatly impacting any characteristic style of "strike" leverage. Indeed,

this supremely abstract style of follower perspective introduces the hitherto unmentioned theme of "meta" or *pure* transcendence; namely, transcendence based entirely within transcendence. The previously described class of humanistic values (specifying the transcendental authority perspective) all exhibit a fair degree of conventionality consistent with their partial foundation within the humanitarian follower perspective. The transcendental follower maneuver, however, abandons all such grounding in concreteness, rather based directly upon the transcendental authority perspective; hence, the *meta*-transcendental sense of the term.

This supremely abstract style of follower perspective is particularly reminiscent of the emotional detachment reported with respect to certain oriental schools of religious mysticism. In particular, the most basic precept of Buddhism states that the pursuit of pleasure necessarily invites pain, leaving emotional detachment as the primary means for achieving true spiritual balance. Accordingly, the mystic renounces the transitory passions of everyday life in favor of a heightened experience of pure transcendence characterizing the mystical experience.

One of the most enduring mystical techniques towards these ends is the long-standing tradition of meditation. Indeed, meditation appears in one form or another in virtually every major religious tradition from around the world. Although the particulars can vary widely, all share some sort of preliminary focusing technique aimed at gaining entry into the mystical realm. This can be passive (as in focusing on one's breathing), or active (as in chanting a mantra). At some point during the preliminaries, the over-stimulation (or under-stimulation) specific to the procedure permits entry into the transcendental realm. This mystical state is variously described as relaxed alertness or detached awareness, an experience completely devoid of any particulars in thought or feeling. In terms of this blissful state, full mental stillness is ultimately achieved, abandoning any reference to external form or function.

According to Zen Buddhism, this enlightened state is known as *satori*, whereas the Yogic tradition is defined as *samadhi*. Even the Christian tradition acknowledges mystical enlightenment; namely, "the peace that passeth understanding" according to St. Paul. Indeed, virtually every culture reports some form of mystical experience, variously described as joyous ecstasy or blissful harmony. This universal mystical character completely transcends all such cultural barriers: whether Christian, Jewish, or Islamic. It ultimately proves fruitful to look beyond such cultural restrictions, rather focusing on the subjective accounts characterizing the mystical experience.

THE CONTRIBUTIONS OF WILLIAM JAMES

Perhaps the most definitive examination of the mystical experience is offered by William James in his *Varieties of Religious Experience: A Study in Human Nature*. This work is a compilation of his Lectures on Natural Religion delivered in Edinburgh, Scotland in 1901-1902. James is traditionally revered as a founding father of the American school of pragmatic psychology. The brother of novelist Henry James, William was educated (and eventually achieved tenure) at prestigious Harvard University. His pioneering work into the psychological effects of nitrous oxide anesthesia provided him an unconventional yet accommodating access to the mystical realm. He alludes to this personal aspect of his mystical experiences as follows: "The further limits of our being plunge, it seems to me, into an altogether other dimension of existence from the sensible and merely understandable world. Name it the mystical region or the supernatural region, whatever you choose."

In his *Varieties of Religious Experience,* James lists a key number of distinguishing features for the mystical experience: defined as (1) ineffability, (2) noetic character, (3) transience, and (4) passivity. The first mentioned category of *ineffability* refers to the inherent difficulty in finding the words to express the dramatic nature of the mystical experience. Many mystics claim that it can only be understood through direct experience, with intuition clearly taking precedent over intellect. Although the experience is not easily articulated to others, it generally has an insightful character to the mystic: an aspect that James further defines as the *noetic* character. This term refers to "insights into the very depths of truth, unplumbed by the discursive intellect." These insights often come in the form of illuminations or revelations overflowing with significance, although usually only vaguely remembered following subsequent transition to ordinary consciousness. This latter aspect is termed *transiency* in that worldly concerns must eventually draw the mystical experience to close. Although the mystical experience is only imperfectly reproduced in ordinary memory, it is instantly recognized in its fullest sense during any subsequent recurrence. Although this state can be precipitated through voluntary means (such as prayer or meditation), the actual transformation is realized through an abeyance of the will (as if drawn by a superior power). James's final category of *passivity* refers to this ego-attenuation, a feature experienced by mystics caught up in the throes of divine ecstasy.

This preliminary survey of the mystical experience, although clearly informative on an intuitive level, still leaves open the remaining issue of the identification of the four affective dimensions predicted for the transcendental follower perspective. Indeed, the affiliated theme of ineffability would seem to suggest that these additional dimensions would remain inexpressible in verbal terms. The Western tradition of Christian mysticism offers the greatest potential in this regard, particularly in terms of the personal aspect known as saintliness.

THE ENDURING TRADITIONS OF SAINTLINESS

In his *Varieties of Religious Experience*, James devotes five full lectures to the topic of saintliness, defining it as the "ripe fruits of spirituality." Citing a survey of the literature spanning many centuries, James proceeds to outline a number of key characteristics for saintliness. He initially describes the occurrence of an expanded outlook transcending one's individual peculiarities for an enhanced conviction in a higher order. This further leads to a willing self-surrender to such a benevolent force, tempering freedom with elation as the distinctive outlines of selfhood melt away. There finally occurs a positive shift towards loving and harmonious affections clearly in keeping with such an ecstatic experience.

Although this traditional line of reasoning proves extremely enlightening, it ultimately proves crucial to examine individual accounts of saintliness in order to discern an overall pattern for the mystical states under consideration. According to St. Teresa of Avila, the highest of these is the orison of union: which raises the soul into mystical union with the Divine, whereupon giving the appearance of complete mental inaccessibility. The English language fortunately is endowed with a broad range of terms for describing the mystical experience, borrowing extensively from both classical and contemporary traditions. This rich abundance of synonyms has apparently selected the precise shades of meaning predicted for the ethical hierarchy. For instance, the cohesive grouping of ecstasy, bliss, joy, and harmony is a collection of themes specifically mentioned by James in his report on saintliness. Although all four terms appear to share a common range of meanings, enough marginal distinctions remain to warrant strict correspondence to the four affective dimensions predicted for the unified power hierarchy. In this more advanced sense, *ecstasy* directly expands upon the aesthetic qualities of beauty, whereas *bliss* similarly amplifies the knowledge functions of truth. Furthermore, *joy* adds a transcendental perspective to goodness, whereas *harmony* makes a similar correspondence to wisdom. This cohesive four-part listing of themes is respectively termed the class of mystical values, in direct analogy to their general unifying theme. Although these motivational parallels prove convincing on an intuitive scale, their true test of validity is ultimately validated in terms of their respective literary traditions.

ECSTASY

The first of the mystical values to be examined, *ecstasy*, is a theme endowed with virtually universal appeal in terms of the mystical experience. In relation to the transcendental follower role, ecstasy represents a projected beauteous style of reinforcement perspective in response to the tranquil sense of gracefulness actively expressed by the transcendental authority figure. Here, you (as transcendental follower) will beauteously act ecstatically towards me in response to my (as transcendental authority) tranquil sense of gracefulness. Ecstasy certainly fits the bill in this thematic respect, traditionally defined as an overwhelming sense of rapture during the mystical experience. Its modern spelling derives from the Greek *ekstasis* (displacement), from *ek-* (out) and *histanai* (to place).

This theme ultimately acquired a mystical significance, variously described as an overwhelming sense of joy accompanied by supreme feelings of delight. According to St. Teresa of Avila, this ecstatic state can be delicately gentle or violently rapturous, as in full-blown flights of the spirit. In the throes of such divine contemplation, the mystic becomes "One" with the experience of the Absolute. The mystic often becomes impervious to outside sensation, even to the point of disregarding pain. Indeed, this trance-like quality of ecstasy is similarly suggested in relation to its subordinate foundation within beauty. Here, the transcendental follower beauteously acts ecstatically in a supremely abstract variation on the spiritual theme of faithfulness.

BLISS

The completed description of ecstasy, in turn, redirects the current focus to the related theme of *bliss*, sharing many commonalties to ecstasy with the exception that leniency (rather than rewards) is now called into focus. In this latter basic respect, blissfulness represents a projected truth-based style of lenient reinforcement perspective within a transcendental realm, in response to the egalitarian treatment of the transcendental authority figure. Here, you (as transcendental follower) blissfully-hope for the truth in response to my (as transcendental authority) egalitarian sense of free-will towards you. Indeed, the modern spelling of bliss derives from the Anglo Saxon *blisse*, from *bliths* (joy): surviving to our modern age with respect to rapture and/or gladness.

This rather broad range of meaning would appear to restrict bliss to yet just another synonym for ecstasy were it not for its incorporation into the popular expression "ignorance is bliss." Here an accessory style of *truth* function is alternately suggested for bliss. Indeed, Joseph Campbell's most widely quoted admonition concerns "following one's bliss." According to Campbell: "If you follow your bliss, you put yourself on a track that has been there all the while ... Wherever you are - if you are following your bliss, you are enjoying that refreshment, that life within you all of the time." An extensive survey of the mystical traditions brings to light many such stirring accounts of the blissful state, where the grand scheme of things becomes blissfully apparent. Indeed, ignorance *is* bliss in this basic respect, a supremely overarching overview entirely in keeping with such a grand transcendental perspective.

JOY

The completed description of ecstasy and bliss, in turn, shifts the current focus to the remaining mystical values of joy and harmony. These themes share many commonalties to ecstasy and bliss with the exception of now punctuated from an anticipated/projected procurement perspective (rather than the reinforcing variety). *Joy* rates prominent mention in this regard in terms of the solicitous initiation of the authority/follower interaction. Here, I (as your transcendental follower) will goodly act in a joyous fashion towards you in response to your (as transcendental authority) magnanimously-loving treatment of me. Indeed, this theme traces its origins to the Old French *joye*, from the Latin *guadium* (of similar usage and meaning). It is traditionally defined as extreme feelings of happiness or gladness, often used interchangeably with ecstasy or rapture. The ancient Romans worshipped this theme in the guise of Comus (their divine personification of joyous revelry): deriving from the Greek god Komos, the same root-stem for the theme of comedy. Indeed, this congenial god is figuratively depicted wearing an exaggerated smiling-style of mask typically employed during classical comedies.

These classical overtones find similar consideration in the field of ethical inquiry, where joy is defined as: "the prevailing quality of a rightful act" consistent with its transcendental relationship to goodness. St. Thomas Aquinas defines joy as: "The delight that is the healthy complement of intelligent and willed activity, when the appetite is actively at rest in a *good* really possessed." St. Paul fittingly numbers joy among the Gifts of the Holy Spirit (Galatians 5:22). This solicitous sense of the term is particularly evident in the popular expression "taking joy in one's work:" with joy figuratively symbolized as a tolling bell, a singing lark, the midday sun, or the color yellow (accentuating its related connotations to goodness).

HARMONY

The completed description of joy, in turn, shifts the focus to the remaining mystical value of *harmony*, sharing many similarities to joy with the exception of targeting a more submissive range of themes (rather than solicitousness). Harmony certainly proves a fitting adjunct to the lofty ideals characterizing the transcendental follower perspective. Here, I (as transcendental follower) will wisely act harmoniously towards you in response to your (as transcendental authority) peaceable expression of equanimity. Consequently, harmony spans a rather broad range of meaning consistent with its transcendental placement within the conditioned interaction. Its modern spelling derives from the Greek *harmonia* (a fitting together, an agreement) from *harmos* (a fitting or joining).

According to classical Greek mythology, the goddess Harmonia is traditionally revered as the daughter of Ares and Aphrodite: an insightful allegory in light of the fact that Ares was feared as the god of war, whereas Aphrodite was worshipped as the goddess of love. Harmonia was also closely allied to Aphrodite-Pandemos, the love that unites all people through a personification of harmonious social order (also corresponding to the Roman goddess Concordia).

This theme similarly extends to the aesthetic realm of classical music and the fine arts: where agreement in form, function, and melody underscore any meaningful attempts at composition. In medieval iconography, Harmony is depicted as a beautiful matron bedecked with an ornate crown and flourishing a violin and bow. In a more restricted relationship sense, harmony directly expands upon the humanitarian prerequisites for wisdom, reflecting an overarching sense of agreement within an international sphere of influence.

THE SUPERNATURAL REALM

In conclusion, the completed description of the mystical values effectively rounds out the literal description of the transcendental power realm. Any further extension of this format necessarily entails the existence of an even more abstract form of authority perspective; namely, that *transcending* transcendental authority. Although this extreme level of abstraction definitely stretches the limits of abstract sensibility, in theory there does not appear to be any conceptual limit governing the degree to which reflection can serve as a basis for itself. Indeed, any such upper limit must necessarily be a practical one; namely, that level of abstraction finally exceeding the capacity of the human intellect to distinguish the respective affective dimensions, whereby precluding their incorporation into the collective cultural lexicon. An observed blending of meanings, indeed, would seem to suggest that this upper conceptual limit has finally been reached.

Beginning with the preliminary transcendental authority level, the respective listing of humanistic values (peace-love-tranquility-equality) all exhibit a fair degree of distinctness, even though a certain measure of conceptual affinity is apparent in their dictionary definitions. At the next higher transcendental follower level, however, the mystical values (ecstasy-bliss-joy-harmony) all exhibit a more pronounced degree of conceptual affinity, reflected in dictionary definitions that are parallel (if not synonymous) in form and function. Taking this trend to the limit, however, ultimately predicts a complete and irrefutable blending of meanings at the even more abstract meta-meta-order level of transcendence. At this almost inconceivable level of abstraction, the four requisite affective dimensions effectively merge into a unified conceptual continuum, virtually unnamable except in the broadest supernatural overtones; e.g., God, the Absolute, etc.

One experiencing this extreme level of transcendence would certainly be impressed by this paradoxical blending of emotional states, in direct contrast to the more concrete range of experience characterizing the lowermost levels. In ordinary consciousness the mind is typically restricted to entertaining only a single ethical perspective (or emotion) at any given time. With respect to the supernatural dimension, however, the distinctions between the emotions become so blurred as to merge into a unified motivational state: the "one becomes the many," as so many mystics have reported down through the ages.

This paradoxical acknowledgement of all-knowing awareness has traditionally been documented using a rather broad range of themes; such as the Universal Mind, the Oversoul, Cosmic Consciousness, Brahma, the Great Spirit, etc. These collectively serve as the master primordial prototype for the continuum of lower (more differentiated) motivational states. This supremely abstract perspective (by definition) encompasses all of the more elementary levels as subsets; hence, accounting for the corresponding flooding of the emotions. Perhaps herein emerges the basis for the traditional Judeo-Christian belief that man is created in the image and likeness of God. Ordinary consciousness (with its sequential limitations) is formally theorized to differentiate out of such an all-inclusive state of awareness. At this supremely supernatural level, we appear to tune into the Universal Mind as the sum-potentiality of all that is transcendent in nature. Perhaps it is really only a matter of convention (devised by the ordinary mind) to regard the mystical state as a wholly independent entity. Indeed, William James appears to make a quite similar point in the following quotation from his *Varieties of Religious Experience*. "This overcoming of all of the usual barriers between the individual and the Absolute is the great mystical achievement. In mystic states we both become one with the Absolute and we become aware of our oneness. This is the everlasting and triumphant mystical tradition hardly altered by differences of clime or creed." The spiritually-minded can rightfully view mysticism as rooted entirely within such a supernatural realm, where all power emanates from the Supreme Creator of all that is spiritual/material. The individual traditions scarcely claim to be the crucial issue here, for many a sage has noted: "Many roads lead to Enlightenment."

This supreme perspective further underscores the fundamental paradox underlying the ethical hierarchy in general; namely, its openness at both its upper and lower margins. The lower margin blends with the materialistic realm of behavioral instinctualism, whereas the upper end extends to the supernatural domain. Although the limited human intellect favors such a dualistic interpretation, this perspective (on a grander scale) might actually amount to a grand illusion! Is it truly possible to distinguish the spiritual from the material, the mental from the physical? No matter how one frames the question, these two themes always remain intimately connected. As long as the mind-body puzzle remains unresolved, these issues must always remain open to further deep speculation.

This newly devised interpretation of the dynamics governing the mystical realm offers the potential for dramatic new insights into the promotion and preservation of global peace and harmony. The respective mystical traditions propounded by great sages throughout the ages serve as the chief moral foundation for the dogma undergirding most of the major world religions. This dogmatic exclusivity in terms of the mystical tradition serves as a point of friction concerning inter-religious tolerance, putatively establishing one tradition as superior over another, accompanied by resentment for those thusly slighted.

The newly devised ten-level hierarchy of the virtues, values, and ideals now provides a radically new strategy for healing much of the endemic religious exclusivity. Here, the mystical realm arises as a hierarchial extension of the more fundamental ethical traditions, constructs shared in common by all of the major religions. Through a concerted recognition of these moral commonalities, an enhanced degree of interreligious cooperation might potentially counteract any ingrained tendency towards religious exclusivity. This unbounded nature offers particular appeal to those of religious impulse, encouraging tolerance and a common rallying point regardless of individual traditions therein.

7

THE ACCESSORY VIRTUES, VALUES, AND IDEALS

The preceding stepwise description of the hierarchical dynamics for the major virtues, values, and ideals permits many interesting speculations concerning the virtuous realm, although this schematic format is limited by a number of unforeseen complications. Chief among these is the observation that the dual interplay of procurement and reinforcement roles is strictly specialized into either subjective or objective classifications. This basic limitation stems from the formal restrictions governing the construction of the schematic definitions. The respective "you" and "I" roles (by definition) are locked in place in terms of the reciprocating sequences of procurement and reinforcement roles, whereby maintaining a stable buffer of terms within the schematic definitions. In particular, this dual style of role specialization follows a strict set of guidelines; namely, the initially active procurement role is technically specified from a subjective "I" perspective, whereas the subsequent reinforcement role is alternately defined from a strictly objective perspective. This reciprocating pattern of subjective-procurement and objective-reinforcement roles follows a strict give-and-take dynamic, formally defined as "if you, then I" (and vice versa). According to this complementary power-sharing strategy, the initially active procurement roles within the conditioned interaction are specified in terms of a subjective "I" status, whereas the subsequent reinforcement roles are defined in terms of an objective "you" status. Indeed, this arrangement essentially mirrors what typically occurs in nature, where the organism actively procures, whereas the environment (inanimately) reinforces.

As previously described in the Introductory Chapter 1, the main model of virtuous communication can scarcely claim to be the total picture, for it formally accounts for only half of the intro-spective roles predicted within the linguistic matrix. The inherent versatility of the human mind (by definition) allows for a subjective reflection upon one's objective status (after the fact); in essence, subjectifying the objective status ascribed to the reinforcement roles. This role reversal is further counterbalanced by a similar objectification of the initially-active subjective procurement roles. This reflective style of role-reversal conveniently allows for crucial insights into the feelings and motivations experienced by another, an aspect traditionally defined as *empathy*: referring to an indwelling sense of inter-subjectivity by which one subjectively participates in feelings privately held by another. This unique ability to empathic attribute mental states to others is a key factor towards making us truly human, a feature developmental psychologists refer to as *Theory of Mind*. This innate capacity to empathize over the feelings of others actually appears to emerge over several distinct stages of emotional development. In particular Dr. Michael Lewis of Robert Wood Johnson Medical School (1995) outlines a three-stage sequence of empathic development.

The primary emotions, such as fear or sadness, first appear around the age of six months: characterized in terms of a spontaneous response repertoire of a non-reflective nature. The more abstract secondary emotions, in turn, emerge around the age of two, signaling the first true "sense of self" experienced in terms of more sophisticated emotions such as guilt or shame. These secondary emotions clearly involve a higher sense of self, an enduring sense of identity to which these emotions are ultimately referred. The third stage in empathic development chiefly occurs around the ages of 4 or 5, when the child learns to ascribe motivations to others that might also be personally experienced under similar cir-

114	115		124	125
Poignance	Culpability	→	Admiration	Concern
116	117		126	127
Passion	Apprehension		Aspiration	Deference

ACCESS. EGO STATES
(Personal Authority)

ACC. ALTER EGO STATES
(Personal Follower)

134	135		144	145
Exaltation	Uprightness		Circumspection	Equitableness
136	137		146	147
Respect	Probity	→	Continence	Bravery

ACC. PERSONAL IDEALS
(Group Authority)

ACC. CARDINAL VIRTUES
(Group Representative)

154	155		164	165
Bountifulness	Freedom		Devotion	Fairness
156	157		166	167
Courtesy	Forbearance	→	Kindness	Scruples

ACCESS. CIVIL LIBERTIES
(Spiritual Authority)

ACC. THEOLOG. VIRTUES
(Spiritual Disciple)

174	175		184	185
Blessings	Conscience	→	Charm	Credence
176	177		186	187
Graciousness	Patience		Benevolence	Shrewdness

ACC. ECUMEN. IDEALS
(Humanitarian Authority)

ACC. CLASSICAL VALUES
(Humanitarian Follower)

194	195		104	105
Serenity	Brotherhood		Rapture	Contentment
196	197		106	107
Affection	Amity	→	Gladness	Accordance

ACC. HUMANIST. VALUES
(Transcendental Authority)

ACC. MYSTICAL VALUES
(Transcendental Follower)

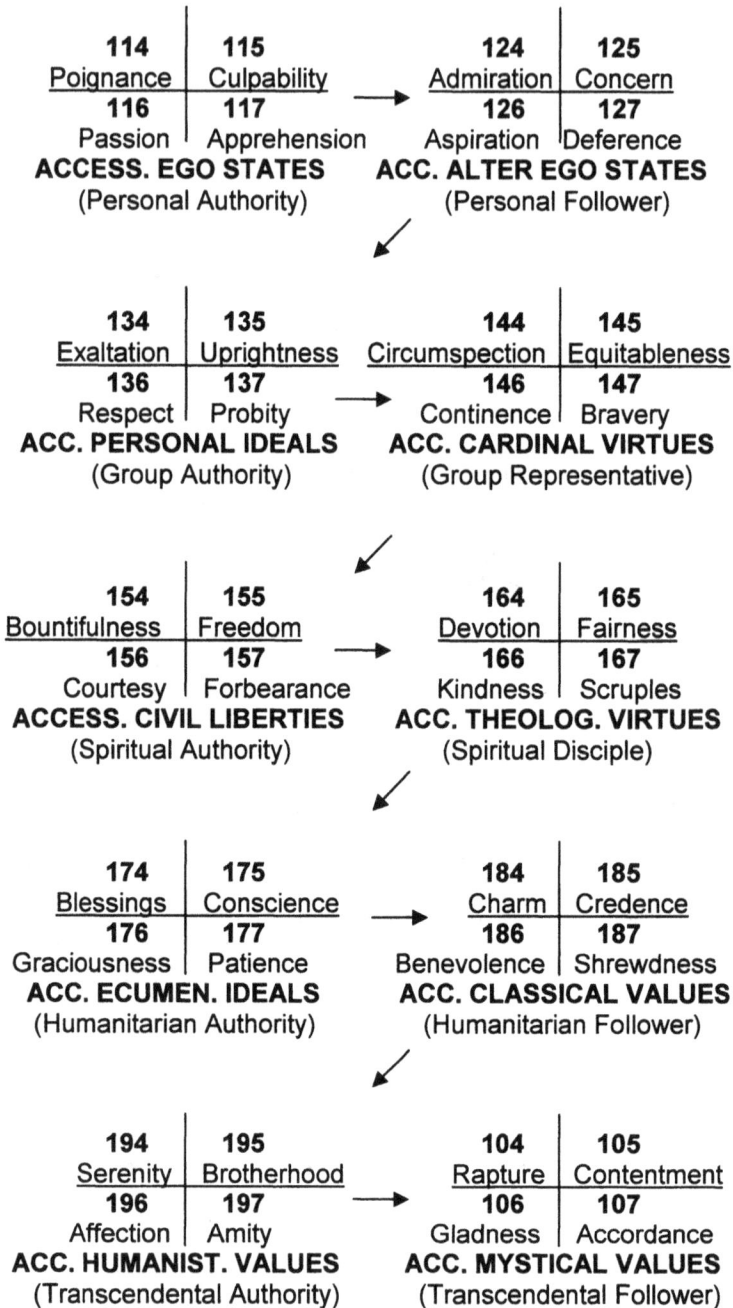

Fig. 7A – The Accessory Virtues / Values

cumstances. This more advanced capacity is formally explained in terms of the *Argument from Analogy*, where internal motives associated with personal behaviors are also attributed to the outwardly observable behaviors of others.

Indications of this ability first come to light at a fairly early age, such as when a toddler shows interesting objects to others. This early perspective in relation to others, however, is actually fairly egocentric. The infant expresses a belief in a common knowledge base, in direct contrast to the more advanced empathic capacity of individual (personal) perspectives. This latter developmental stage only truly becomes apparent around the age of five, when the child realizes that others do not have direct access to one's own personal mindset, but rather entertain distinct thoughts or motivations entirely of their own making. This more advanced comprehension of individual cognitive spheres of influence permits the development of skills underlying social empathy, as reflected in the many common role-playing games favored by children: such as cops & robbers, doctor & patient, etc. Affiliated feelings of playful joyfulness generate outward facial expressions, the observation of which subtly activate similar bodily responses within the observer. This induced physical response (in terms of the observer) translates into a shared emotional response, wherein establishing a collective sense of empathy linking the observer to that which is being observed.

This distinct empathic ability proves particularly crucial within a social setting, where cohesion within the group is greatly enhanced through recourse to such overlapping perspectives, whereby minimizing the occurrence of interpersonal frictions. According to Robert Gordon (1986), this innate sense of empathy depends primarily upon our ability to run cognitive simulations, inferring the intentions of others by employing one's own mind as a model for that of others. This formally entails placing oneself in the role of another and further observing how one's mind resonates within such a mutually conducive context. The reciprocal interplay linking one's inner as well as outer motivational perspectives provides the supreme conceptual template for modeling an enduring sense of empathy in relation to others.

This empathic style of motivational perspective formally predicts the existence of an entirely parallel complement of affective terms for designating this dual degree of versatility, specified as the *accessory* motivational terms. Fortunately the English language is richly blessed with a broad range of synonyms conducive to fulfilling this predicted complement of accessory terms. These ac-

cessory "you"/"I" perspectives are systematically reversed in polarity across the board ensuring that both procurement and reinforcement roles encompass the full range of objective/subjective potentialities encountered within real-life. For the personal realm, for instance, the proposed accessory class of immediately active roles (poignancy, culpability, passion, and apprehension) effectively complements the main listing of nostalgia, guilt, desire, and worry. Furthermore, the accessory future-projected states of admiration, concern, aspiration, and deference, in turn, reciprocate the main listing of projected terms (approval, leniency, solicitousness, and submissiveness).

With respect to the main pairing of desire/solicitousness, for instance, the accessory complement of passion/aspiration proves particularly well suited to the task. Here, I (as personal authority) passionately act rewardingly towards you in anticipation of your (as personal follower) aspiring treatment of me. In terms of the related context of worry/submissiveness, the personal authority figure switches to an apprehensive perspective in anticipation of the personal follower's deferential expression of submissiveness. A similar pattern further holds true for the personal authority's poignancy in anticipation of the admiring treatment of the personal follower, or culpability in expectation of concern. This reciprocal interplay of both the main/accessory sets of terms permits a convincing simulation of the empathic dynamics governing the conditioned interaction.

THE ACCESSORY VIRTUOUS HIERARCHY

According to this main/accessory model of empathic communication, it remains only a further minor step to extend this personal complement of motivational terms to the even more abstract realm of virtues, values, and ideals characterizing the more abstract authority levels. This yields the full forty-fold complement of accessory terms depicted below and also presented in expanded form in **Fig. 7A**.

Poignancy • Admir.	**Culpability • Concern**
Exalt.• Circumspection	**Uprightness • Equity**
Bountiful. • Devotion	**Freedom • Fairness**
Blessings • Charm	**Conscience • Credence**
Serenity • Rapture	**Brotherhood • Content.**

Passion • Aspiration	**Apprehen.• Deference**
Respect • Continence	**Probity • Bravery**
Courtesy • Kindness	**Forbear. • Scruples**
Gracious.• Benevolence	**Patience • Shrewd.**
Affection • Gladness	**Amity • Accordance**

This compact diagram represents a mirror-image variation on the main listing of virtuous terms shown in **Fig. 1** of Chapter 1. Accordingly, this master hierarchy of accessory terms spans the entire range of group, spiritual, humanitarian, and transcendental realms within the virtuous hierarchy as a whole. Indeed, this reciprocating interplay of both main and accessory terms allows for a convincing simulation of empathic language in general: the objective/subjective polarities effectively reversed through an inversion of the "you" and "I" perspectives. These accessory groupings of terms, however, exhibit little in the way of the pedigree or tradition previously established for the main listings of terms. According to **Fig. 7A**, the accessory listings of terms are formally specified through the addition of the prefix *"accessory"* to the better-known designation of the major groupings. This can also be signified in schematic notation through the use of the Roman numeral (II). More permanent labels must necessarily await further collective research into the field, for any permanent system of classification must remain open to the consensus opinion of the broader global community at large.

Consequently, it ultimately proves fruitful to undertake a more in depth examination of the individual accessory terms for the entire virtuous hierarchy, providing a clear picture of the reciprocal dynamics at issue. The remainder of the current chapter examines this additional complement of accessory terms to a much greater degree of detail, focusing on the subjective/objective polarities in relation to the major groupings of virtues/values initially described.

POIGNANCY

The first mentioned theme of *poignancy* rates current consideration as the chief accessory counterpart of nostalgia. This term derives from the Old French *poignant*, from the Latin *pungere* (to sting). It refers to its now obsolete usage as an adjective for describing the sharpness or piercing power of military weapons. In modern usage, this connotation extends to a cutting-edge character within an emotional sphere of influence, wherein affecting one's feelings sharply or keenly, such as the poignancy intrinsic to comedy or melodrama. Such strong feelings extend to positive memories of influence within one's lifetime, sharing with nostalgia such past notable perspectives. Here, the subjective prerequisites for nostalgia effectively complement the objective characteristics for poignancy, an emotional reaction chiefly restricted to a personal sphere of influence.

EXALTATION

The personal authority perspective of poignancy, in turn, extends to a group sphere of influence with respect to the related theme of *exaltation*: a term defined as glorious fortune or elevated rank. Its modern spelling derives from the Latin *altus* (high) and *ex-* (a prefix indicating intensity), representing the objective counterpart of the subjective *glory* perspective. This theme shares with glory a heightened degree of power or prestige characterizing such leadership roles. Consequently, this poignant sense of exaltation preserves the active focus initially established for the glory perspective of the group authority, although now in anticipation of the admiring treatment of the personal follower figure.

BOUNTIFULNESS

Exaltation, in turn, extends to the spiritual authority theme of *bountifulness*, as objectively complementing the subjective prerequisites for *providence*. The term derives from the Latin *bonitas*, from *bonus* (good), a connotation particularly in keeping with its generosity in the bestowal of gifts. Bountifulness shares many points in common with the traditional symbolisms associated with providence. Here the *cornucopia* (horn of plenty) perpetually overflows with an abundance of produce from the field, permitting a welcome sense of security in terms of such pressing survival needs. Accordingly, the exalted sense of bountifulness expressed by a spiritual authority proves a fitting counterpoint to the circumspective-devotion anticipated from the spiritual disciple.

BLESSINGS

The next more advanced humanitarian authority level suggests further mention of the related theme of *blessings*. This term traces its origins to the Anglo Saxon *bledsian* (to bless), from *blod* (blood): as in a blood sacrifice upon an altar. It primarily refers to a divine sense of sanctification or sacredness similar to its subjective counterpart in *grace*. Indeed, the act of "saying Grace" begins with the stirring invocation: *"Bless* us Oh Lord for these Thy gifts ... received through Thy bounty." This enduring tradition of abundant blessings effectively preserves the strict humanitarian focus of grace, objectively reciprocating the subjective prerequisites of the latter. These bountiful blessings specified within such a universal domain clearly prove a worthy match to the charming sense of devotion anticipated in terms of the representative member of humanity.

SERENITY

The bountiful blessings specified for the humanitarian realm ultimately extend to a transcendental domain with respect to the related theme of *serenity*. It represents the chief objective counterpart for the subjective prerequisites previously described for *tranquility*. Its modern spelling derives from the Latin *serenus* (clear) indicative the tranquil attributes affiliated with the term. It is often employed as a title of distinction for reigning princes or dignitaries consistent with the calm demeanor accompanying positions of power. This serene sense of contentment is further associated with mystical figures throughout history such as Buddha, Christ, Mohammed, etc. The serene sense of blessings expressed by the transcendental authority effectively reciprocates the charming sense of rapture anticipated in terms of the transcendental follower figure.

ADMIRATION

The remaining sequence of accessory terms based upon the ascending hierarchy of follower roles begins with the personal follower theme of *admiration*. As the chief subjective counterpart of approval, it shares with latter a profound sense of homage or regard for those worthy of such approbation. Its modern spelling derives from the Latin *admirari* from *ad-* (to) and *mirari* (to wonder) indicative of the rewarding overtones characterizing this theme. The positive emotional focus shared by both admiration and approval is certainly quite telling, wherein rewarding the immediately notable achievements of the personal authority figure (experienced as a poignant sense of nostalgia). In terms of the requisite "you" and "I" polarities, admiration clearly suggests more of a subjective style of introspective focus than does approval, specifying the outward sense of approbation characterizing the personal follower role.

CIRCUMSPECTION

The personal prerequisites for admiration, in turn, extend to a group sphere of influence with respect to the related theme of *circumspection*. The term derives from the Latin *circum-* (about) and *spectum* (to look): suggesting a cautious inspection spanning all angles within a situation similar to the watchful attitude previously ascribed to prudence. Indeed, the symbolisms attributed to circumspection share many features with those ascribed to prudence; namely, a seated maiden facing towards the three cardinal directions representative of past, present, and future potentialities. The future-directed dimension for circumspection is certainly favored, in essence, responding to the poignant sense of exaltation expressed by the group authority figure.

DEVOTION

Circumspection, in turn, gives way to the spiritual disciple theme of *devotion*: traditionally defined as strong piety or spiritual attachment. The term derives from the Latin *devovere*: from *de-* (away) and *vovere* (to vow) suggestive of its close affiliation to faith. In particular, this term refers to the Roman Catholic tradition of the devotional, as in prayers or worship of an intensely personal nature. This pious sense of devotion transcends any formal sense of ritualism, representing a deeply subjective counterpart in relation to its objective counterpart in faith. Accordingly, the circumspective-devotion professed by the spiritual disciple effectively complements the exalted sense of bountifulness from the spiritual authority figure.

CHARM

The next higher realm of the humanitarian follower, in turn, brings into consideration the accessory theme of *charm*, an aspect subjectively consistent with the beauteous sense of faith experienced from a (projected) objective perspective. Its modern spelling derives from the Latin *carmen* (a song) indicating the ritual significance music plays in spiritual observance. Charm also denotes a magical sense of enchantment or attractiveness, as suggested in the familiar notions of the charm bracelet and charm school. The truest sense of charm, however, stems from the enduring prerequisites implicit to such a grand humanitarian perspective. The inwardly subjective attributes of charm effectively complement the more objective projected status typically ascribed to beauty. Accordingly, the charming sense of devotion professed by the representative member of humanity effectively reciprocates the bountiful-blessings bestowed by the humanitarian authority figure.

RAPTURE

The preceding discussion of charm ultimately gives way to the respective transcendental notion of *rapture*, the main subjective counterpart for the related objective theme of ecstasy. The term derives from the Latin *raptum* (to seize) indicative of extreme flights of fancy of an enlightened or mystical nature. Although other synonyms for ecstasy (such as happiness) might equally fit the bill, the subjective prerequisites for rapture prove consistent to the current sense of the term. Here, the rapturous sense of charm professed by the transcendental follower proves a fitting counterpoint to the serene sense of blessings expressed the transcendental authority figure.

THE PARALLEL SEQUENCE OF TERMS BASED UPON CULPABILITY/CONCERN

With respect to the realm of negative reinforcement, a parallel sequence of accessory terms is alternately based upon the personal authority/follower interplay of culpability/concern. For instance, the group authority culpably acts in an upright fashion in anticipation of the equitable sense of concern of the group representative. Furthermore, with respect to the spiritual level within the motivational hierarchy, the spiritual authority figure freely acts in an upright fashion in anticipation of the equitable sense of fairness expressed by the spiritual disciple. Finally, for the most advanced humanitarian/transcendental levels, the authority figure freely acts conscientiously (or conscientiously acts in a brotherly fashion) in anticipation of the follower figure's fair sense of credence/contentment, as schematically depicted in the compact diagram below:

Culpability	Concern
Uprightness	Equity
Freedom	Fairness
Conscientiousness	Credence
Brotherhood	Contentment

This accessory sequence of terms formally reciprocates the pattern previously established for the main sequence of terms (namely, guilt-honor-liberty-freewill-equality), as well as blame-justice-hope-truth-bliss: effectively preserving an equivalent balance of power with respect to the dual interplay of "you" and "I" perspectives.

PASSION

A third sequence of accessory terms, in turn, is based upon personal interplay of passion/aspiration: reciprocally complementing the main trend based upon desire/solicitousness. For instance, the first mentioned theme of *passion* denotes a strong positive sense of emotion, particularly ardent love or desire. The term derives from the Old

French *passiun*, from the Latin *passus* (to suffer). This original connotation of suffering relates to the longstanding frustrations involved in the consummation of the passions, as in a personal quest for fulfillment. In this latter sense, passion suggests a personally-subjective slant on the theme as opposed to the more objective prerequisites associated with desire. Indeed, the latter appears more invested with the actual object of desire than the steps towards its passionate fulfillment.

RESPECT

The personal prerequisites for passion, in turn, extend to a group sphere of influence in relation to the more abstract theme of *respect*, which subjectively complements the more objective prerequisites for dignity. Its modern spelling derives from the Latin *respectum*, from *re-* (back) and *specere* (to look) consistent with the dignified demeanor characterizing leadership positions. Exalted respect typically drives the passionate adherence to one's duties, outwardly tempered by one's dignified sense of desire. The passionate-respect expressed by the group authority proves a fitting counterpoint to the objective prerequisites for dignity, whereby countering the continent-aspirations of the group representative.

COURTESY

The group authority expression of respect, in turn, gives way to the more universal, spiritual authority theme of *courtesy*: traditionally defined as polite consideration or civil accommodation. The term derives from the Latin *cortis* (courtyard) indicative of the "common courtesy" shared in common with its objective counterpart in civility. This theme figures prominently in the rather quaint custom of the *courtesy call*; namely, a social visit made entirely on the basis of common courtesy. The supreme expression of this theme further traces its origins to the medieval tradition of The Code of Courtesy. The chivalrous knight courteously acts respectfully towards the object of his passion, fully expecting a continently-aspiring treatment in return. Consequently, this courteous sense of respectfulness offers a fitting subjective counterpoint to the more objective prerequisites initially specified for the civilly-dignified perspective of the spiritual authority figure.

GRACIOUSNESS

The ascending accessory sequence of courtesy/respect, in turn, extends to the even more refined humanitarian theme of *graciousness*, defined as divine favor or supreme kindness. The term derives from the Latin *gratia* (favor) from *gratus* (agreeable), a connotation consistent with its accessory relationship to magnanimity. Similar to courtesy, graciousness is traditionally associated with the custom of *gratuities*: namely, those standards of accommodation crucial to one's individual self-worth. Indeed, the theme of the gracious host is one of mankind's most honored traditions, particularly in the Middle East, where the needs of the guest often take precedent over those of the host. Consequently the courteous sense of graciousness professed by the humanitarian authority proves a fitting objective counterpoint to the benevolent-kindness anticipated from the representative member of humanity.

AFFECTION

The stepwise ascending hierarchy of courtesy and graciousness, in turn, extends to the crowning transcendental theme of *affection*: the chief subjective counterpart of *love*. The term derives from the Latin *affectio*, from *ad-* (to) and *facere* (to do) consistent with such enhanced feelings of positive emotion. Indeed, the related theme of "affect" is also invoked to describe a strong range of emotions, the attachments of love certainly filling the bill in this basic respect. The supremely abstract connotations of affection certainly validate such a crowning transcendental perspective, a general subjective counterpart to the more objective prerequisites of love. In this strictly subjective sense, one can certainly "toy" with one's affections, although the same does not necessarily hold true for the more objective prerequisites of love.

ASPIRATION

The remaining *accessory* sequence of follower roles is currently launched with respect to the initial personal follower theme of *aspiration*. It is traditionally defined as an enthusiastically appetitive style of goal seeking consistent with its subjective counterpart in solicitousness. This aspiring focus, in turn, counters the immediately passionately treatment of the personal authority figure, as reflected in the admiring recognition of poignancy previously cited in the initial sequence of accessory terms. In terms of the respective "you" and "I" polarities, aspiration certainly presents an objective quality, effectively complementing the subjective aspects of passion: in direct contrast to the interplay of desire/solicitousness (where the role-polarities are effectively reversed).

CONTINENCE

The personal attributes for aspiration, in turn, extend to a group sphere of influence with respect to the group representative theme of *continence*. It is traditionally defined as restraint in the indulgence of the passions similar to the case previously described for its subjective counterpart in temperance. The term derives from the Latin *continens* (to contain, to hold back), an interpretation consistent with the "bridling" of the passions. Continence is most often associated with sexual restraint, in contrast to the more generalized range of constraint specified for temperance. Irrespective of its particular object, the continently-aspiring treatment expressed by the group representative proves a fitting counterpoint to the passionate-respect by the group authority figure.

KINDNESS

Ascending to the next higher spiritual realm, in turn, gives way to the accessory follower theme of *kindness*. This term represents the objective accessory counterpart for the more subjective prerequisites associated with charity. Its modern spelling derives from the Old English *cynn* (kind) suggesting a willingness to perform good or noteworthy deeds. This nurturing quality has traditionally been celebrated as the "milk of human kindness," an enduring interpretation directly in keeping with such good-hearted charitable endeavors. The universal appeal underlying such a charitable sense of kindness certainly rates a high degree of esteem. Indeed, this volunteer spirit extends considerable benefits to the initiator as well as the recipient. Here the continent sense of kindness expressed by the spiritual disciple proves a fitting counterpoint to the courteous-respect professed by the spiritual authority figure.

BENEVOLENCE

The universal overtones for kindness, in turn, extend to a humanitarian sphere of influence with respect to the related theme of *benevolence*. The term derives from the Latin *benevolentia* (goodwill) from *bene-* (well) and *velle* (to wish). It traditionally denotes a humanitarian disposition towards graciousness or generosity in terms of both word and deed. This grand humanitarian focus is particularly apparent in the philanthropic endeavors associated with benevolent societies; e.g., institutions that seek to improve the human condition through charitable works and public education. This enduring spirit of benevolence clearly validates such a grand humanitarian perspective, a noble aspiration encouraged throughout the ages in times of trouble. Here the benevolent sense of kindness professed by the representative member of humanity objectively complements the courteous sense of graciousness expressed by the respective authority figure.

GLADNESS

The benevolent sense of kindness characterizing the humanitarian realm ultimately extends to the crowning transcendental domain with respect to the abstract theme of *gladness*. As the chief objective counterpart in relation to joy, gladness denotes a cheerful or optimistic disposition, particularly in an enthusiastic or animated fashion. The term derives from the Old English *glaed*, from the Old Norse *glathr* (bright) suggesting a sparkling emotional outlook. The objective characteristics for gladness effectively complement the subjective prerequisites initially specified for joy. In terms of this accessory motivational perspective, the benevolent sense of gladness expressed by the transcendental follower proves a fitting counterpoint to the affectionate sense of graciousness by the transcendental authority figure.

THE ACCESSORY TERMS BASED UPON APPREHENSION/DEFERENCE

The fourth and final sequence of accessory motivational terms is based upon the remaining complementary sequence of apprehension/deference (the accessory counterparts with respect to worry/submissiveness). The accessory sequence of authority terms (apprehension-probity-forbearance-patience-amity) effectively reciprocates the main sequence of terms: e.g., worry-integrity-austerity-equanimity-peace. Furthermore the remaining accessory sequence of follower roles: (deference-bravery-scrupulousness-shrewdness-accordance), in turn, permits a fitting contrast with the main virtuous counterparts: i.e., submissiveness, fortitude, decency, wisdom, and harmony: as schematically depicted below.

Apprehension	**Deference**
Probity	**Bravery**
Forbearance	**Scrupulousness**
Patience	**Shrewdness**
Amity	**Accordance**

This cohesive sequence of accessory terms proves a fitting counterpoint to the main sequence of

themes, effectively verifying the empathic dynamics of the entire unified virtuous hierarchy.

THE SCHEMATIC DEFINITIONS FOR THE ACCESSORY VIRTUOUS REALM

One final issue of critical significance concerns the prediction that the accessory virtuous terms are further amenable to incorporation within the formal schematic definition format. Indeed, a complete listing of *accessory* schematic definitions is respectively tabulated in **Tables B-1** to **B-4** in direct analogy to the main set of definitions depicted **Tables A-1** to **A-4** (of Chapter 2). These accessory schematic definitions are identical in form and function to the main counterparts with the exception that the "you" and "I" polarities are now effectively reversed. This direct reversal of the "you" and "I" perspectives is predicted within the definition format, permitting an alternating confluence of subjective and objective viewpoints. This dual sequence of virtuous perspectives is formally predicted in terms of the empathic principles of Theory of Mind, where reciprocating viewpoints fully take into account all such potential viewpoints.

In order to completely outline this dual interplay of main/accessory motivational perspectives, it proves fruitful to look back (in review) at the basic empathic dynamics at issue. Routine communication is diagrammed in terms of a two-stage formal schematic. The subjective party in the communication is fittingly termed "myself," whereas the objective party is alternately labeled "the other" in keeping with established existential terminology. These two basic domains are separated in terms of a formal gap that signifies the channel that communication must travel in order to bridge the link between sender and receiver.

This schematic model, depicted in **Fig. 7B** (to follow) represents one complete cycle of empathic communication between "myself" and "the other," as the directional arrows serve to indicate. The cycle begins with **Box A**, where a standard example of communication (the subjective definition for "glory") is listed in the upper left-hand box. In terms of this specific example, I (as group authority) gloriously act nostalgically towards you in anticipation of your (as personal follower) approving treatment of me. This preliminary power maneuver is communicated from "myself" to "the other" (Channel **A → B**) across the formal subjective/objective gap. As a basic communicational channel, this sample communication (by definition) is open to distortion, ambiguity, or misinterpretations over the entire span of transmission.

(A)	**(B)**
I (as group authority) will *gloriously* act nostalgically towards you, in anticipation of your (as my personal follower) approving treatment of me.	You (as group authority) will poignantly act *exaltedly* towards me, in anticipation of my (as your personal follower) admiring treatment of you.

(MY ↑ SELF)   **(THE ↓ OTHER)**

(D)	**(C)**
You (as group representative) will *prudently* act approvingly towards me: overruling my (as group authority) gloriously-nostalgic treatment of you.	I (as group representative) will *circumspectively* act admiringly towards you, overruling your (as group authority) poignant sense of exaltation.

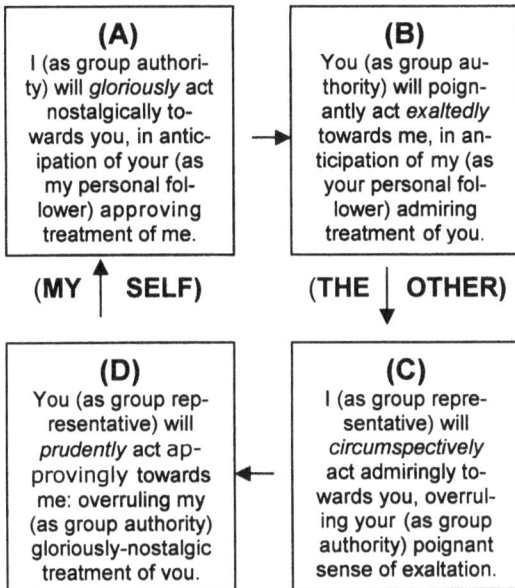

Fig. 7B - The Two-Stage Empathic Dynamic

Despite these internal shortcomings, for sake of illustration, the message is depicted as successfully reaching the receiver to the direct attention of "the other." The message must necessarily be translated into a form that is subjectively meaningful to the empathic dictates of the receiver. This further entails translating the *main* schematic definition into its empathic *accessory* counterpart specified from an outside viewpoint. According to **Box B** of **Fig. 7B**, the accessory form of the schematic definition for "exaltation" is now specified as: You (as group authority) will poignantly act in an *exalted* fashion towards me in anticipation of my (as personal follower) admiring treatment of you. According to this modified format, the "you" and "I" roles are effectively reversed, whereby personalizing the message to fit the subjective prerequisites of "the other."

THE COUNTERMANEUVER OF "THE OTHER"

Once the message is received and comprehended by the "other," it remains to be determined (empathically) how "the other" will best to respond to the message. According to step **B → C**, one possible option is to ignore the message as if it were never received, or claim to misunderstand the message. Another option entails mirroring the message back to the sender in what Communication Theorists term the *symmetrical* maneuver. A further option entails accepting the content of the message as given, as well as one's specified role

within the conditioned interaction. This latter response basically occurs only when one is satisfied with the status quo initially projected.

A further relevant option builds directly upon this initial acceptance: accepting the content of the message as initially offered, then subsequently modifying one's role by rising to the next higher level within the virtuous hierarchy. This necessarily entails counteracting the power tactic initially offered, substituting in its place a power status of one's own making. This more advanced form of power maneuver is schematically depicted in **Box C**. Here the personal follower rises to the next higher level of "group representative" through the use of the *circumspective* form of countermaneuver. The first part of this new definition builds directly upon the initial "exaltation" maneuver originally communicated, followed by the *circumspection* countermaneuver proper; namely, I (as group representative) circumspectively act in an admiring fashion towards you in response to your (as group authority) poignant sense of exaltation. According to Communication Theorists, this strategy is termed the *complementary* class of power maneuvers, being that they formally complement what has gone before. The group representative role now complements the group authority role as originally offered.

Once formulated, this alternate power maneuver is subsequently communicated from "the other" back to "myself," as shown in step **C → D** within the master diagram. The respective arrow once again crosses the subjective/objective gap, whereby further susceptible to the internal shortcomings of distortion, ambiguity, etc. Assuming that the communication is successfully transmitted, this necessarily entails translation back to a form meaningful to "myself" (the *main* schematic definition format depicted in **Box D**). Here, the *circumspective*-adoration of the group representative is now translated back into the *prudent*-approval consistent with my own subjective perspective. In this latter respect, the "you" and "I" roles are once again reversed, empathically redefined in terms of the subjective group authority role originally communicated.

The successful receipt of the group representative's *prudence* countermaneuver, in turn, offers further options for myself (as depicted in step **D → A**). In the latter case, this can further entail rising to the next higher spiritual level, giving way to a *providential* expansion upon the original glory maneuver. This innovation (by definition) launches one further cycle within the communication dynamic: namely, the sequence of **A → B → C → D** relating to the spiritual level. In-

POIGNANCY	ADMIRATION
Previously, I (as reinforcer) have rewardingly acted in a reinforcing fashion towards you: in response to your (as procurer) approachful treatment of me. But now, you (as personal authority) will *poignantly* act approachfully towards me: in anticipation of my rewarding treatment of you.	Previously, you (as personal authority) have poignantly acted approachfully towards me: in anticipation of my (as reinforcer) rewarding treatment of you. But now, I (as personal follower) will rewardingly act in an *admiring* fashion towards you: overruling your (as PA) poignant treatment of me.
EXALTATION	**CIRCUMSPECTION**
Previously, I (as your personal follower) have rewardingly acted in an admiring fashion towards you: in response to your (as PA) poignant treatment of me. But now, you (as group authority) will poignantly act in an *exalted* fashion towards me: in anticipation of my (as PF) admiring treatment of you.	Previously, you (as group authority) have poignantly acted exaltedly towards me: in anticipation of my (as PF) admiring treatment of you. But now, I (as group representative) will *circumspectively* act admiringly towards you: overruling your (as GA) poignantly-exalted treatment of me.
BOUNTIFULNESS	**DEVOTION**
Previously, I (as group representative) have circumspectively acted admiringly towards you: in response to your (as GA) exalted treatment of me. But now, you (as spiritual authority) will exaltedly admit having acted in a *bountiful* fashion towards me: in anticipation of my (as GR) circumspective-admiration of you.	Previously, you (as spiritual authority) have exaltedly admitted acting in a bountiful fashion towards me: in anticipation of my (as GR) circumspective-admiration of you. But now, I (as your spiritual disciple) will circumspectively act *devotedly* towards you: overruling your (as SA) bountiful treatment of me.
BLESSINGS	**CHARM**
Previously, I (as your spiritual disciple) have circumspectively acted devotedly towards you: in response to your (as SA) bountiful treatment of me. But now, you (as humanitarian authority) will bountifully-*bless* me: in anticipation of my (as SD) circumspective-devotion for you.	Previously, you (as humanitarian authority) have bountifully-blessed me: in anticipation of my (as SD) circumspective-devotion for you. But now, I (as representative member of humanity) will *charmingly* act devotedly towards you: overruling your (as HA) bountiful-blessing of me.
SERENITY	**RAPTURE**
Previously, I (as representative member of humanity) have charmingly acted devotedly towards you: in response to your (as HA) bountiful-blessing of me. But now, you (as transcendental authority) will *serenely*-bless me: in anticipation of my (as RH) charming devotion for you.	Previously, you (as transcendental authority) have serenely-blessed me: in anticipation of my (as RH) charming-devotion for you. But now, I (as your transcendental follower) will charmingly act in a *rapturous* fashion towards you: overruling your (as TA) serene-blessing of me.

Table B-1 – The Definitions Based on Poignancy/Admiration

CULPABILITY	CONCERN
Previously, I (as reinforcer) have tolerantly acted in a reinforcing fashion towards you: in response to your (as procurer) aversive treatment of me. But now, you (as personal authority) will *culpably* act in an aversive fashion towards me: in anticipation of my tolerant treatment of you.	Previously, you (as personal authority) have culpably acted aversively towards me: in anticipation of my (as reinforcer) tolerant treatment of you. But now, I (as your personal follower) will tolerantly act in a *concerned* fashion towards you: overruling your (as PA) culpable treatment of me.
UPRIGHTNESS	**EQUITABLENESS**
Previously, I (as your personal follower) have will tolerantly acted in a concerned fashion towards you: in response to your (as PA) culpable treatment of me. But now, you (as group authority) will culpably act in an *upright* fashion towards me: in anticipation of my (as PF) concerned treatment of you.	Previously, you (as group authority) have culpably acted in an upright fashion towards me: in anticipation of my (as PF) concerned treatment of you. But now, I (as group representative) will *equitably* act in a concerned fashion towards you: overruling your (as GA) culpable sense of uprightness.
FREEDOM	**FAIRNESS**
Previously, I (as group representative) have equitably acted in a concerned fashion towards you: in response to your (as GA) culpable sense of uprightness. But now, you (as spiritual authority) will *freely* act in an upright fashion towards me: in anticipation of my (as GR) equitable sense of concern.	Previously, you (as spiritual authority) have freely acted in an upright fashion towards me: in anticipation of my (as GR) equitable sense of concern. But now, I (as your spiritual disciple) will equitably act in a *fair* fashion towards you: overruling your (as SA) free sense of uprightness.
CONSCIENCE	**CREDENCE**
Previously, I (as your spiritual disciple) have equitably acted fairly towards you: in response to your (as SA) free sense of uprightness. But now, you (as humanitarian authority) will freely act in a *conscientious* fashion towards me: in anticipation of my (as SD) equitable sense of fairness.	Previously, you (as humanitarian authority) have freely acted conscientiously towards me: in anticipation of my (as SD) equitable sense of fairness. But now, I (as representative member of humanity) will fairly express a sense of *credence* in you: overruling your (as HA) conscientious treatment of me
BROTHERHOOD	**CONTENTMENT**
Previously, I (as representative member of humanity) have fairly expressed a sense of credence in you: in response to your (as HA) conscientious treatment of me. But now, you (as transcendental authority) will conscientiously act in a *brotherly* fashion: in anticipation of my (as RH) fair sense of credence.	Previously, you (as transcendental authority) have acted in a brotherly fashion towards me: in anticipation of my (as RH) fair sense of credence. But now, I (as your transcendental follower) will *contentedly* express a sense of credence in you: overruling your (as TA) brotherly treatment of me.

Table B-2 – The Definitions Based on Culpability/Concern

PASSION	ASPIRATION
Previously, you (as procurer) have acted approachfully towards me: in response to my (as reinforcer) rewarding treatment of you. But now, I (as personal authority) will *passionately* act in a rewarding fashion towards you: in anticipation of your (as procurer) approachful treatment of me.	Previously, I (as personal authority) have passionately acted in rewarding fashion towards you: in anticipation of your (as procurer) approachful treatment of me. But now, you (as personal follower) will *aspiringly* act in an approachful fashion towards me: overruling my (as PA) passionate treatment of you.
RESPECTFULNESS	**CONTINENCE**
Previously, you (as my personal follower) have aspiringly acted in an approachful fashion towards me: in response to my (as PA) passionate treatment of you. But now, I (as group authority) will passionately act in a *respectful* fashion towards you: in anticipation of your (as PF) aspiring treatment of me.	Previously, I (as group authority) have passionately acted respectfully towards you: in anticipation of your (as PF) aspiring treatment of me.

But now, you (as group representative) will *continently* act in an aspiring fashion towards me: overruling my (as GA) passionate-respect for you. |
COURTESY	**KINDNESS**
Previously, you (as group representative) have continently acted in an aspiring fashion towards me: in response to my (as GA) passionate-respect for you. But now, I (as spiritual authority) will *courteously* act respectfully towards you: in anticipation of your (as GR) continently-aspiring treatment of me.	Previously, I (as spiritual authority) have courteously acted in a respectful fashion towards you: in anticipation of your (as GR) continently-aspiring treatment of me. But now, you (as my spiritual disciple) will continently act in a *kind* fashion towards me: overruling my (as SA) courteous-respect for you.
GRACIOUSNESS	**BENEVOLENCE**
Previously, you (as my spiritual disciple) have continently acted in a kind fashion towards me: in response to my (as SA) courteous-respect for you. But now, I (as humanitarian authority) will courteously act in a *gracious* fashion towards you: in anticipation of your (as SD) kind treatment of me.	Previously, I (as humanitarian authority) have courteously acted graciously towards you: in anticipation of your (as SD) kind treatment of me. But now, you (as representative member of humanity) will *benevolently* act in a kind fashion towards me: overruling my (as HA) gracious treatment of you.
AFFECTION	**GLADNESS**
Previously, you (as representative member of humanity) have benevolently acted in a kind fashion towards me: in response to my (as HA) gracious treatment of you. But now, I (as transcendental authority) will graciously act *affectionately* towards you: in anticipation of your (as RH) benevolent sense of kindness.	Previously, I (as transcendental authority) have graciously acted in an affectionate fashion towards you: in anticipation of your (as RH) benevolent sense of kindness. But now, you (as my transcendental follower) will benevolently act with *gladness* towards me: overruling my (as TA) affectionate treatment of you.

Table B-3 – The Definitions Based on Passion/Aspiration

APPREHENSION	DEFERENCE
Previously, you (as procurer) have acted aversively towards me: in response to my (as reinforcer) tolerant treatment of you. But now, I (as personal authority) will *apprehensively* act tolerantly towards you: in anticipation of your (as procurer) aversive treatment of me.	Previously, I (as personal authority) have apprehensively acted tolerantly towards you: in anticipation of your (as procurer) aversive treatment of me. But now, you (as personal follower) will aversively act in a *deferential* fashion towards me: overruling my (as PA) apprehensive treatment of you.
PROBITY	**BRAVERY**
Previously, you (as my personal follower) have aversively acted in a deferential fashion towards me: in response to my (as PA) apprehensive treatment of you. But now, I (as group authority) will apprehensively act with *probity* towards you: in anticipation of your (as PF) deferential treatment of me.	Previously, I (as group authority) have apprehensively acted in a probity-filled fashion towards you: in anticipation of your (as PF) deferential treatment of me. But now, you (as group representative) will *bravely* act deferentially towards me: overruling my (as GA) probity-filled treatment of you.
FORBEARANCE	**SCRUPULOUSNESS**
Previously, you (as group representative) have bravely acted deferentially towards me: in response to my (as GA) probity-filled treatment of you. But now, I (as spiritual authority) will *forbearingly* act with probity towards you: in anticipation of your (as GR) brave treatment of me.	Previously, I (as spiritual authority) have forbearingly acted with probity towards you: in anticipation of your (as GR) brave sense of deference. But now, you (as my spiritual disciple) will *scrupulously* act bravely towards me: overruling my (as SA) forbearing treatment of you.
PATIENCE	**SHREWDNESS**
Previously, you (as my spiritual disciple) have scrupulously acted bravely towards me: in response to my (as SA) forbearing treatment of you. But now, I (as humanitarian authority) will forbearingly act *patiently* towards you: in anticipation of your (as SD) scrupulous treatment of me.	Previously, I (as humanitarian authority) have forbearingly acted patiently towards you: in anticipation of your (as SD) scrupulous treatment of me. But now, you (as representative member of humanity) will scrupulously act in a *shrewd* fashion towards me: overruling my (as HA) patient treatment of you.
AMITY	**ACCORDANCE**
Previously, you (as representative member of humanity) have scrupulously acted shrewdly towards me: in response to my (as HA) patient treatment of you. But now, I (as transcendental authority) will patiently act with *amity* towards you: in anticipation of your (as RH) shrewd treatment of me.	Previously, I (as transcendental authority) have patiently acted in an amity-filled fashion towards you: in anticipation of your (as RH) shrewd treatment of me. But now, you (as transcendental follower) will shrewdly act with *accordance* towards me: overruling my (as TA) amity-filled treatment of you.

Table B-4 – The Definitions Based on Apprehension/Deference

deed, this basic pattern further extends to the remaining humanitarian and transcendental levels within the motivational matrix as well, ceasing only when the level of abstraction exceeds the scope of the language tradition.

AN OVERVIEW OF COMMUNICATION IN GENERAL

A few general observations on communication in general necessarily prove crucial at this juncture. First, the role of "myself" within the communication cycle clearly represents the crucial factor, in contrast to the more extraneous (empathically derived) sense of "the other." This observation is certainly warranted in that I only have direct access to my own thoughts and feelings, while I can only make empathic predictions for those of "the other." I formally model (to some extent) the unique mindset of "the other" through the aid of the *accessory* schematic definitions depicted in **Boxes B** and **C**. According to this simulation for the accessory realm, I formally imagine the motivations of "the other" within a given interaction. This includes moments alone when I mentally rehearse dialogue in anticipation of meeting with others ahead of time. This necessarily entails imagining all of the many potential contingencies or responses "the other" might employ, preparing so as not to be caught off-guard by a surprise turn of events. The outside party in the interaction (by definition) does not even need to be present in order to conduct such mental dialogue. The eventual meeting with the "other" only serves to finalize the choices initially imagined. The outwardly observable responses of "the other," in turn, are compared to the mental model of my own expectations, the results continually determining my own next course of action. This egocentric model of communication in general (by definition) is based entirely upon the intrinsic consciousness of "myself." The actions of "others," in turn, are predicted in terms of this projected mental model: "the other" also invested with full autonomy.

Lest this formulation be judged too narrow a model of interpersonal communication, it is further relevant to note that "the other" similarly entertains one's own self-based perspectives operating through an independent style of ego status. This multitude of individual selves merges into a unified communicational continuum, essentially forming overlapping sets of interpersonal projections in relation to one another. This all-encompassing communicational dynamic, nevertheless, still relies upon my primary mental monologue linking myself with the mental projec-

tions of others, a model calibrated in terms of outwardly observable behaviors, imparting an overall semblance of conformity with reality.

According to this multi-modal model of communication in general, whether we chose to acknowledge it or not, we all are basically alone in the world with respect to the restrictions of our own mental thought processes. Our firm convictions with respect to others are basically projections of our own making, mental models periodically reinforced to some extent by external observation. This formal sense of isolation actually turns out to be a blessing in disguise, for the private life we so dearly treasure would remain impossible should others be freely able to read our minds (and vice versa). It is only through the common symbolism underlying verbal language that interpersonal communication is possible at all through standards maintained in a cultural sense.

In terms of this dualistic interpretation, my introspective mental states (by definition) are projected onto you, whereas yours (in theory) are referred back to me. There is no single channel of communication, rather an intersecting confluence of mutual perspectives. It is this mental construct of others with which we have a relationship, not the direct sense we might wish ourselves to believe: a welcome illusion in light of the more brutally honest picture currently proposed. Along a similar line of reasoning, Irish-born essayist, Dame Rebecca West insightfully wrote: "There is no such thing as conversation, it is an illusion. There are intersecting monologues: that is all."

It should further be emphasized that this abiding sense of isolation chiefly applies only to symbolic verbal communication, being that nonverbal communication of a synchronously-empathic nature is much more amenable to social synergy across the board. Here, a concerted effort towards directed mindfulness permits concentration within a present tense, unlike the temporally-focused past/future dimensions formally targeting verbal communication of an affective nature. With such verbal chatter temporarily attenuated, the mindful individual now becomes free to immediately attend to meaningful facial-cues and bodily synchronies in relation to others, providing a high degree of empathic synchrony clearly transcending any linguistic means designed to explain it. Hence, by periodically turning down the "noise box" of verbal dialogue that typically dominates our waking moments, a more effective balance within the here-and-now provides a more effective means of synchrony and synergy in relation to our empathic dealings (in peaceful harmony) with others spanning the world stage.

8

THE GENERAL UNIFYING
VIRTUOUS THEMES

The preceding motivational analysis encompassing both the main and accessory virtuous terms exhibits a further emergent quality of critical import to overall comprehension; namely, the identification of what are respectively termed the general unifying themes. This higher-order class of themes represents a "meta-order" summation encompassing each individual level within the ethical hierarchy; in essence, a 2nd order style of logical perspective. For instance, the general unifying theme of "utilitarianism" encompasses the collective focus comprising the cardinal virtues (prudence-justice-temperance-fortitude): effectively defining the group follower perspective. A similar pattern further holds true for the remaining spiritual, humanitarian, and transcendental levels within the virtuous hierarchy: as thematically depicted in **Fig. 8A**. For instance, the personal authority perspective introduces the theme of *individualism*, extending to the conceptualization of *personalism* for the next higher group authority level. The spiritual authority perspective, in turn, targets the more idealized theme of *romanticism* consistent with a broad focus on universal principles. The themes for the remaining humanitarian and transcendental levels, in turn, take their cues from the designations specifying their individual listings of terms; namely, *ecumenism* and *humanism*, respectively.

In a related fashion, the remaining sequence of *follower* roles (targeting a future-direct time-frame) is similarly organized in terms of an ascending hierarchy of general unifying themes; namely, pragmatism, utilitarianism, ecclesiasticism, eclecticism, and mysticism. For instance, the first-mentioned theme of *pragmatism* refers to that which is potentially expedient to the individual, extending (in a group sense) to a projected *utilitarian* concern for "the common good." This ascending sequence of projected follower themes, in turn, extends to the remaining spiritual, humanitarian, and transcendental realms with respect to the themes of ecclesiasticism, eclecticism, and mysticism, respectively.

A few general observations may be deduced from this general pattern of unifying themes. As previously outlined, the general unifying themes are subdivided into either active authority modes (occurring within the present) or passively-potential follower modes (projected within a future-directed time-frame). The active behavioral modes are designated in terms of the immediate class of authority themes: namely, individualism, personalism, romanticism, ecumenism, and humanism. This initial class of authority-based themes represents immediately active perspectives that anticipate (as their projected object) the passively-potential complement of future-directed follower themes. Generally speaking, the personal authority themes immediately initiate the conditioned interaction in anticipation of the projected potentiality characterizing the personal follower themes.

The more passive class of behavioral themes, in turn, target the more abstract motivational themes encompassing the follower roles, in light of their extension into a future-directed time-frame: namely, pragmatism, utilitarianism, ecclesiasticism, eclecticism, and mysticism. This latter class of follower themes represents a passively-potential class of virtuous perspectives that effectively consummate the more immediately active focus for authority perspectives in terms of the motivational dynamics governing the entire conditioned interaction. A more detailed examination of these general unifying themes will now be undertaken, including an extensive analysis of their individual literary traditions across the board.

118 - INDIVIDUALISM **Ego States** *Personal Authority*	**128 - PRAGMATISM** **Alter Ego States** *Personal Follower*
138 - PERSONALISM **Personal Ideals** *Group Authority*	**148 - UTILITARIANISM** **Cardinal Virtues** *Group Representative*
158 - ROMANTICISM **Civil Liberties** *Spiritual Authority*	**168 ECCLESIASTICISM** **Theological Virtues** *Spiritual Disciple*
178 - ECUMENISM **Ecumenical Ideals** *Humanitarian Authority*	**188 - ECLECTICISM** **Classical Values** *Humanitarian Follower*
198 - HUMANISM **Humanistic Values** *Transcendental Authority*	**108 - MYSTICISM** **Mystical Values** *Transcendental Follower*

Fig. 8A – The Three-Digit Codes for the "Meta" Virtuous Themes

INDIVIDUALISM

The initial analysis of the main virtuous themes is currently launched with respect to the first-mentioned theme of *individualism*. This theme formally encompasses the subordinate listing of ego states (guilt, worry, nostalgia, and desire) characterizing an immediately-active style of personal authority perspective indicative of the indwelling vitality of the ego states. The term derives from the Latin *individuus* from *in-* (not) and *dividuus* (divisible), from *didere* (to divide). The modern sense of individualism emerged through ideas promoted by British philosophers Adam Smith and Jeremy Bentham. This sense of individualism is further noted by Alexis de Tocqueville as crucial to the virtuous American temperament.

In a general sense, individualist values are person-centered, with all individuals sharing equal moral status. Individualism opposes external authority without consent, the institutional power of government chiefly restricted to maintaining law and order. The chief aim of society is the promotion of individual rights and welfare, whereby encouraging individual moral character. Individuals should freely live their lives as they see fit without unwarranted state interference. The principles of individualism were briefly challenged at the turn of the 20th century with the rise of Communism and Fascism, although regained prominence due to a global return to representative forms of government.

In a behavioral context, the initial theme of individualism encompasses the instinctual attributes specific to the personal authority role; namely, that active sense of vitality derived from the immediate sense of action initially expressed by the personal authority figure. This immediate style of desirous reinforcement, or lenient expression of worrisome concern, invokes such a personal style of authority status: as does the similarly active class of nostalgia and guilt perspectives, respectively. Here, the personal authority prerequisites for individualism clearly provide a fitting initiation to the ascending virtuous hierarchy of general unifying themes.

PERSONALISM

The personal perspectives for individualism, in turn, extend to a civic sphere of influence with respect to the group-focused theme of *personalism*. The term derives from the Latin *persona*, a mask in ancient theatres worn to represent an emotional reaction: ultimately denoting the role of a dramatic actor. In a social sense, personalism refers to the notion of dignity within a civil society. Some trace its traditional origins to Anaxagoras, as well as further influences attributed to Plato and Aristotle. Boethius defines the persona as: "an individual substance of a rational nature." This preliminary stage of interpretation continues through the efforts of St. Augustine, Avicenna, and Thomas Aquinas: eventually entering the modern age with respect to rationalist and empiricist traditions.

The modern sense of personalism traces its origins to 19th-century thought, although reaching its most dramatic expression circa the 20th century. German philosopher Friedrich Schleiermacher initially used the term *Personalismus* in his *Discourses* (1799). Cambridge philosopher John Grote further designated his novel metaphysical approach as *personalism*, from his *Exploratio Philosophica* (1865). For each of these formulations, the respective emphasis on human dignity proves highly suggestive of the affiliated listing of personal ideals (glory-honor-dignity-integrity). Indeed, their specific designation as "personal ideals" clearly reflects the civic-centered quality of personalism, a more refined variation on the more elementary theme of individualism. It shares with the latter the immediate sense of vitality inherent to such an actively-based authority perspective: as reflected in the group dynamics underlying each of the individual personal ideals. This enduring sense of personalism, therefore, represents a fitting adjunct to the group authority perspective, a motivational baseline consistent with the ascending motivational hierarchy of general unifying themes.

ROMANTICISM

The group prerequisites for personalism, in turn, extend to a global sphere of influence with respect to the universally-focused theme of *romanticism*. The term derives from the French *romantique*, from the Middle French *romant* (a romance): an oblique reference to the Old French *romanz* (a narrative in verse). Romanticism emerged in the late 18th and early 19th centuries as a stylistic movement that downplayed the prevailing imitation of neo-classical stereotypes. It flourished in large part due to the libertarian and egalitarian ideals emerging from the French Revolution that exalted the supremacy of the common man. The basic ideals of Romanticism are similarly vague: namely, an appreciation of the mysteries of nature and a belief in the goodness of the human spirit: exalting emotional sensibility over reason and intellect. In this latter respect, Romanticism represents a philosophical backlash against the orderly rationality of the Enlightenment, the latter disparaged as artificially impersonal and mechanistic. Romanticism rather favored the emotional saliency of direct individual experience, as well as the boundless nature of the unfettered human imagination.

This enduring fascination with larger-than-life themes certainly appears consistent with romanticism's universal placement within the virtuous hierarchy of themes. Indeed, themes of a romanticized nature enjoy virtually universal appeal throughout the span of world literature. The heroic exploits of the supreme authority figure are romanticized to the point of attracting widespread public appeal. The respective class of romantic ideals (providence, liberty, civility, and austerity) certainly fits such a universal perspective, projecting a romanticized sense of global appeal consistent with such an immediately-active style of authority perspective. Indeed, each of the individual civil liberties was worshipped as a deity in classical times so significant was their universal appeal. Accordingly, romanticism shares (with the subordinate themes of individualism and personalism) such an immediate vitality of perspectives, although now targeting a universal sphere of influence. Romanticism, therefore, continues the tradition of revered authority themes befitting such a grand range of themes.

ECUMENISM

Ascending to the next higher humanitarian sphere of influence ultimately invokes the enduring theme of *ecumenism*. The term derives from the Latin *oecumenicus* (general, universal), from the Greek *oikoumene* (of the inhabited world): from *oikoumenos*, present participle of *oikein* (to inhabit), from *oikos* (house or habitation). In a modern sense, it denotes the movement towards an anticipated unification of Protestant denominations, and (ultimately) of all of Christianity. This movement gained impetus during the First Assembly of the World Council of Churches in Amsterdam (1948), a gathering that invited Protestant, Eastern Orthodox, and Catholic representatives. Indeed, this initiative endures today as a major force promoting ecumenism worldwide.

In its most basic sense, ecumenism promotes a mutual sense of unity and cooperation amongst various denominations within a given belief system. This overarching sense of interfaith cooperation aims towards greater mutual respect and tolerance amongst all of the world's religions.

It has awakened a universal sense of conscience towards a renewed spirit of mission and service to the global community. This evangelical spirit is particularly evident in the enduring tradition of the ecumenical councils of the early Christian Church, sharing the focus of fortifying and preserving the unity of faith.

This authority-based theme of ecumenism proves a fitting humanitarian adjunct to the overarching hierarchy of themes: namely, individualism, personalism, and romanticism. This enduring humanitarian perspective is clearly reflected in the enduring tradition of ecumenical councils devoted to recurrent Church issues. The affiliated listing of the ecumenical ideals (grace, free-will, magnanimity, and equanimity) further imparts a broad evangelical perspective within such a grand humanitarian time-scale. Indeed, the ecumenical movement actively seeks to preserve this enduring class of clear humanitarian themes through immediate consideration of all ethical traditions within its purview.

HUMANISM

The ascending thematic hierarchy of authority-based perspectives ultimately culminates with respect to the crowning transcendental theme of *humanism*. The term derives from the Latin *literae humaniores* (polite literature), from the root-stem *homo* (a human being). Its original Renaissance connotation referred to the surviving works of Greek/Latin classical literature. The Italian revival of the Latin arts and letters ultimately promoted the growth of the modern *humanistic* movement. In general, the Humanities were classified as that branch of literature (classics, rhetoric, and poetry) that worked to humanize and refine the intellect, an education befitting the academic elite of the age.

This Renaissance revolt against the dogmatic strictures of Church decree promoted a fresh range of intellectual freedom, further encouraging scientific research and economic mercantilism. Through a celebration of the classical traditions governing the Greco-Roman Era, Renaissance Humanism emerged as a powerful counterpoint to the ecclesiastical dictates professed by the Catholic Church (the dominant academic institution of its day). Through allusion to the classical Greek injunction "Know Thyself," humanists promoted a free-thinking style of academic optimism. This movement eventually spread throughout Europe aided by the invention of movable type.

In concert with a subsequent decline in Church influence over European politics, humanism increasingly acquired its more modern secular characteristics. In keeping with the current pre-eminence of science/technology in Western culture, *secular* humanism has assumed the mantle of distinction governing most forms of democratic government. This is particularly evident in the subordinate class of the *humanistic* values (peace, love, tranquility, and equality): themes sharing a lofty humanistic focus characterizing the immediately-active sense of vitality for the transcendental authority perspective. Indeed, all four themes profess a profound transcendental disregard for the more routine range of worldly affairs governing the initial range of general unifying themes (individualism, personalism, romanticism, and ecumenism). Lofty platitudes such as peace and love continue to serve as supreme ideals towards which one constantly strives, although typically never quite fully realized.

PRAGMATISM

The completed description of the authority-based range of themes invites further comparisons to the remaining general unifying themes based upon the ascending hierarchy of follower roles. Indeed, this parallel style of analysis is currently initiated with respect to the personal follower theme of *pragmatism*. The term derives from the Latin *pragmaticus* (skilled in business or law) from the Greek *pragmatikos* (versed in business): from *pragmatos* (civil business or activity), from *prassein* (to act or perform). The modern sense of the term refers to the system of ethical philosophy proposed jointly by C. S. Peirce, William James, and John Dewey at the turn of the 20th century. Pragmatism asserts that the meaningfulness of any course of action is primarily determined as a function of its projected practical outcome. Pragmatism resolves ethical conflicts by investigating the practical consequences of potential avenues of choice. Ideas are truthful insofar as they are conformable to the facts and subject to practicality (reasoned through experience), as well as concrete means towards achievement.

Along similar lines of reasoning, pragmatism represents a personal follower perspective that potentially determines what is projected to be potentially feasible (in a practical sense) within a given conditioned interaction. Consequently the pragmatic perspective expressed by the personal follower effectively consummates the more immediate sense of individualism expressed by the personal authority figure. The projected class of alter ego states (approval, leniency, solicitousness, and submissiveness) collectively provides

the ethical standards by which pragmatism is judged, serving a complementary follower function in relation to the immediacy characterizing the individualism of the personal authority role.

UTILITARIANISM

The personal prerequisites for pragmatism, in turn, extend to a civic sphere of influence with respect to the group-directed theme of *utilitarianism*. The term derives from the Latin *utilitas*, from *uti* (to use). This designation was first coined by Jeremy Bentham in 1781 in reference to his doctrine of the greatest potential good for the greatest number. This utilitarian foundation was further expanded through the efforts of James Mill and John Stuart Mill. This father-and-son team collectively proposed that the greatest potential good resides in maximizing the general public welfare. Consequently, utilitarianism extends the more basic theme of pragmatism into a much broader civic sphere of influence. The utilitarian movement opposed the competing theme of romanticism primarily due to the latter's emphasis upon emotionality and a disregard for rationality. The utilitarian system, in contrast, believed proper social order emerged from a balanced blend of individual interests. Furthermore, only principles of utility prove fitting for setting viable standards for legal and moral types of behavior.

Utilitarianism approves actions that promote a general sense of welfare within society as a whole, a feature consistent with the temperate/fortitudinous styles of conduct inherent to the group follower perspective. Such benefits need not be restricted solely to intent, but similarly extend to the final outcome of the action, a pattern analogous to that previously established for pragmatism. This projected sense of potentiality is particularly evident in the collective class of cardinal virtues (prudence, justice, temperance, and fortitude): a quartet exalting group cohesiveness and cooperation towards an overarching common good. Indeed, the interests of all must equally be considered if utilitarianism is truly to enjoy an equitable range of utility, where the ends are traditionally seen to justify the means.

ECCLESIASTICISM

Ascending, once again, to the next higher universal realm of the spiritual disciple, in turn, gives way to the more overarching theme of *ecclesiasticism*. This latter term is defined as that branch of Christian theology devoted to the study of the organizational principles at work within the Church,

INDIVIDUALISM	PRAGMATISM
Previously, you have potentially acted in a motivational fashion towards me: in response to my active treatment of you. But now, I (as personal authority) will actively behave in an *individualistic* fashion towards you: in anticipation of your potential treatment of me.	Previously, I (as personal authority) have actively behaved individualistically towards you: in anticipation of your potential treatment of me. But now, you (as my personal follower) will potentially act in a *pragmatic* fashion towards me: overruling my (as PA) individualistic treatment of you.
PERSONALISM	**UTILITARIANISM**
Previously, you (as my personal follower) have potentially acted in a pragmatic fashion towards me: in response to my (as PA) individualistic treatment of you. But now, I (as group authority) will individualistically act in a *personable* fashion towards you: in anticipation of your (as PF) pragmatic treatment of me.	Previously, I (as group authority) have individualistically acted personably towards you: in anticipation of your (as PF) pragmatic treatment of me. But now, you (as group representative) will pragmatically act in a *utilitarian* fashion towards me: overruling my (as GA) personable treatment of you.
ROMANTICISM	**ECCESIASTICISM**
Previously, you (as group representative) have pragmatically acted in a utilitarian fashion towards me: in response to my (as GA) personable treatment of you. But now, I (as spiritual authority) will personably act in a *romanticized* fashion towards you: in anticipation of your (as GR) utilitarian treatment of me.	Previously, I (as spiritual authority) have personably acted romantically towards you: in anticipation of your (as GR) utilitarian treatment of me. But now, you (as spiritual disciple) will utilitarianly act in an *ecclesiastical* fashion towards me: overruling my (as SA) romantic treatment of you.
ECUMENISM	**ECLECTICISM**
Previously, you (as my spiritual disciple) have acted in an ecclesiastical fashion towards me: in response to my (as SA) romantic treatment of you. But now, I (as humanitarian authority) will romantically act in an *ecumenical* fashion towards you: in anticipation of your (as SD) ecclesiastical treatment me.	Previously, I (as humanit. authority) have acted in an ecumenical fashion towards you: in anticipation of your (as SD) sense of ecclesiasticism. But now, you (as representative member of humanity) will ecclesiastically act in an *eclectic* fashion towards me: overruling my (as HA) ecumenical treatment of you.
HUMANISM	**MYSTICISM**
Previously, you (as representative member of humanity) have ecclesiastically acted eclectically towards me: in response to my (as HA) ecumenical treatment of you. But now, I (as transcendental authority) will ecumenically act *humanistically* towards you: in anticipation of your (as RH) sense of eclecticism.	Previously, I (as transcendental authority) have acted in a humanistic fashion towards you: in anticipation of your (as RH) eclectic treatment of me. But now, you (as my transcendental follower) will eclectically act in a *mystical* fashion towards me: overruling my (as TA) humanistic treatment of you.

Table C-1 – The "Meta" Definitions for the Virtuous Themes

particularly its practical, operational, and congregational aspects. The term derives from the Greek *ekklesia* (an assembly summoned by a crier), a compound of *ek-* (out of) and *kalein* (to call). In ancient Athens, the ecclesia was a popular assembly where the male citizenry exercised political sovereignty. All male citizens over the age of twenty were eligible to cast their vote for issues upon the agenda.

The modern Christian sense of the term derives from the Late Latin *ecclesiasticus*, from the Greek *ekklesiastes* (speaker of the assembly). New Testament writers (particularly St. Paul) employed this term to refer to local assemblies of Christians, such as that gathered at Corinth (I Corinthians 1:2). This connotation gradually came to denote the unity of the early Christian Church in general.

The first formal treatises concerning ecclesiasticism date to the late medieval Age of Scholasticism. By the time of the Protestant Reformation, two distinct trends relating to ecclesiasticism rose to prominence. Protestant ecclesiasticism emphasized the spiritual nature of the Christian Church, whereas the Roman Catholic format primarily stressed an organizational focus. The modern sense of the term appears to integrate a blend of these diverse theological aspects. Here, ecclesiasticism continues the distinctive tradition of the projected follower roles similar to that previously established for pragmatism and utilitarianism (although now targeting a universal sphere of influence). As such, it formally encompasses the projected potentiality of the subordinate class of theological virtues (faith, hope, charity, and decency): scriptural ideals celebrating the projected scope of proper conduct in relation to the spiritual disciple figure. Through this enlightened path of inquiry, the specifics for the spiritual disciple role (in relation to the spiritual congregation) become exceedingly apparent in an ecclesiastical sense, an aspect primarily in keeping with the projected potential conduct in governing the spiritual follower perspective.

ECLECTICISM

The spiritual focus of ecclesiasticism, in turn, extends to the even more abstract humanitarian sphere of influence with respect to the enduring philosophical theme of *eclecticism*. The term derives from the Greek *eklektikos* (selective), from *eklegein* (to pick out or select): from a compound of *ek-* (out) and *legein* (to choose). It refers to the practice of synthesizing the best aspects or traditions from various schools of thought without

necessarily establishing the validity of the individual parent systems. It originally referred to groups of classical philosophers that worked together to integrate doctrines from a broad range of competing systems. Consequently, eclecticism refers to the potential selection of elements from diverse systems of thought without concern for potential contradictions between this range of systems. It differs, therefore, from *syncretism*, which endeavors to combine various schools of thought while simultaneously aiming to synthesize a resolution to any underlying conflicts.

Eclecticism among Renaissance humanists borrowed extensively from both Catholic and Classical doctrines. Their efforts presaged a 19th century revival, particularly those proposed by French philosopher Victor Cousin (who popularized the modern sense of the term). Eclectics are frequently accused of being inconsistent in relation to the abstract juxtaposition of doctrines that risks fundamental incoherence, although occasionally reviving systems of thought that had traditionally become outmoded.

In terms of this representative member of humanity perspective, the eclectic individual revels in enduring themes of a timeless nature, as reflected in the respective listing of classical Greek values (beauty, truth, goodness, and wisdom). These enduring classical values have remained revered throughout the ages, immutable precepts that have stood the test of time. Indeed, each of these values was worshipped as a deity in its own right during classical times, so widespread was their philosophical appeal. Eclecticism certainly rates its lofty humanitarian placement within the virtuous hierarchy of themes, directly expanding upon the projected sense of potentiality previously established for the traditional hierarchy of follower themes: namely, pragmatism, utilitarianism, and ecclesiasticism.

MYSTICISM

The ascending motivational hierarchy of general unifying follower themes ultimately culminates with respect to the crowning transcendental theme of *mysticism*. The term derives from the Greek *mystikos* (secret, mystic), from *mystes* (one who is initiated), from *myein* (to close one's eyes). These enduring and transcendental aspects of mysticism appear as a common feature across all races and creeds. Indeed, some innate factor within the human psyche must necessarily account for this supreme aspiration to universal truth and goodness. Only rare individuals, however, seem to easily be capable of entering into

119 - QUINTESSENTIAL. *Acc.* **Ego States** *Personal Authority*	**129 - EXPEDIENCY** *Acc.* **Alter Ego States** *Personal Follower*
139 - HEROISM *Acc.* **Personal Ideals** *Group Authority*	**149 - PRACTICALITY** *Acc.* **Cardinal Virtues** *Group Representative*
159 - CHARISMA *Acc.* **Civil Liberties** *Spiritual Authority*	**169 - DOGMATISM** *A.* **Theological Virtues** *Spiritual Disciple*
179 - EVANGELISM *Acc.* **Ecumenical Ideals** *Humanitarian Authority*	**189 - MORALISM** *Acc.* **Classical Values** *Humanitarian Follower*
199 - PHILANTHROPY *Acc.* **Humanistic Values** *Transcendental Authority*	**109 - SPIRITUALISM** *Acc.* **Mystical Values** *Transcendental Follower*

Fig. 8B - The Accessory Virtuous Themes

QUINTESSENTIALISM	EXPEDIENCY
Previously, I have potentially acted in a motivational fashion towards you: in response to your active treatment of me. But now, you (as personal authority) will actively behave in a *quintessential* fashion towards me: in anticipation of my potential treatment of you.	Previously, you (as personal authority) have acted in a quintessential fashion towards me: in anticipation of my potential treatment of you. But now, I (as your personal follower) will potentially act in an *expedient* fashion towards you: overruling your (as PA) quintessential treatment of me.
HEROISM	**PRACTICALITY**
Previously, I (as your personal follower) have potentially acted in an expedient fashion towards you: in response to your (as PA) quintessential treatment of me. But now, you (as group authority) will quintessentially act in a *heroic* fashion towards me: in anticipation of my (as PF) expedient treatment of you.	Previously, you (as group authority) have quintessentially acted in a heroic fashion towards me: in anticipation of my (as PF) expedient treatment of you. But now, I (as group representative) will *practically* act in an expedient fashion towards you: overruling your (as GA) heroic treatment of me.
CHARISMA	**ORTHODOXY**
Previously, I (as group representative) have practically acted in an expedient fashion towards you: in response to your (as GA) heroic treatment of me. But now, you (as spiritual authority) will heroically act in a *charismatic* fashion towards me: in anticipation of my (as GR) practical treatment of you.	Previously, you (as spiritual authority) have heroically acted in a charismatic fashion towards me: in anticipation of my (as GR) practical treatment of you. But now, I (as spiritual disciple) will practically act in an *orthodox* fashion towards you: overruling your (as SA) charismatic treatment of me.
EVANGELISM	**MORALISM**
Previously, I (as spiritual disciple) have practically acted in a orthodox fashion towards you: in response to your (as SA) charismatic treatment of me But now, you (as humanitarian authority) will charismatically act in an *evangelical* fashion towards me: in anticipation of my (as SD) orthodox treatment of you.	Previously, you (as humanitarian authority) have evangelically acted charismatically towards me: in anticipation of my (as SD) orthodox treatment of you. But now, I (as represent. member of humanity) will orthodoxly act *moralistically* towards you: overruling your (as HA) evangelical treatment of me.
COSMOPOLITANISM	**SPIRITUALISM**
Previously, I (as representative member of humanity) have acted moralistically towards you: in response to your (as HA) sense of evangelism. But now, you (as transcendental authority) will evangelically act in a *cosmopolitan* fashion towards me: in anticipation of my (as RH) moralistic treatment of you.	Previously, you (as transcendental authority) have acted cosmopolitanly towards me: in anticipation of my (as RH) moralistic treatment of you. But now, I (as your transcendental follower) will moralistically act in a *spiritualistic* fashion towards you: overruling your (as TA) cosmopolitan treatment of me.

Table C-2 - The Accessory Definitions for the Virtuous Themes

such a mystical contemplation of the Divine. The early Church theologian Pseudo-Dionysius gives a systematic account of Christian mysticism, effectively distinguishing between the more routine tenets of rational inquiry in contrast to the unplumbed depths of mystical knowledge.

Although a further degree of detail would certainly prove relevant at this juncture, this additional range of background will not currently be discussed due to the previously extensive discussion of mysticism contained within Chapter 6. Irrespective of the individual traditions therein, the overarching theme of mysticism shares a number of key characteristics; namely, a transcendental follower perspective encompassing the overarching complement of mystical values (ecstasy, bliss, joy, and harmony). Here mysticism represents the crowning ineffable realm of transcendence within the virtuous hierarchy of themes, and one that proves incomparable to those favored by its charmed embrace.

THE SCHEMATIC DEFINITIONS FOR THE MAIN VIRTUOUS THEMES

The completed description of the ascending motivational hierarchy for the general unifying themes offers a crucial additional degree of validation for the overall virtuous realm. Indeed, the systematic and orderly pattern of organization for this unified hierarchy of themes further specifies their potential for incorporation into the respective schematic definition format. Consequently, the full ten-part complement of "meta-" schematic definitions for the main virtuous themes is respectively depicted in **Table C-1**. This table formally illustrates the reciprocating pattern of interaction linking both authority and follower roles across the entire ten-level span of the unified motivational matrix. This newly proposed schema of "meta" schematic definitions effectively transcends and unifies the more routine listings of definitions for each of the individual listings of virtues, values, and ideals: a meta-order style of schematic innovation. Indeed, each of the unique virtuous themes specifies a higher-order perspective upon the more basic complement of individual terms. For instance, the "meta" schematic definition for *utilitarianism* formally encompasses (as individual subsets) the sum-total of individual definitions comprising the four cardinal virtues (prudence, justice, temperance, and fortitude). A similar pattern further holds true for each of the remaining classes of virtuous themes, as the respective "meta-" schematic definitions effectively serve to indicate.

As meta-order summations for the respective individual terms, the definitions for the general unifying themes scarcely display the degree of clarity or precision previously encountered for the individual terms. A more intensive style of analysis for these "meta" schematic definitions, however, ultimately reveals the basic dynamics at issue; namely, the active status for the authority roles effectively anticipates the passively-projected status characterizing the respective follower roles. For instance, the group authority personably acts in an individualistic fashion in anticipation of the pragmatically-utilitarian treatment by the group follower figure.

Although this highly specialized range of interplay might seem to be limited in terms of practical applications, it, nevertheless, provides a formal schematic template for the more general listings of virtues and values at issue. The more specialized "meta-" schematic definitions for the general unifying themes serve as a crucial adjunct in this regard, effectively validating the dual definition format to an extreme degree of validity.

THE ACCESSORY GROUPINGS OF VIRTUOUS THEMES

The *main* categories of virtuous themes, in turn, are augmented by the predicted *accessory* class of unifying themes, where the polarities of the "you" and "I" roles are effectively reversed similar to that previously encountered for the (more basic) individual virtuous terms. As initially described in Chapter 7, the dual interplay of the main and accessory virtuous perspectives permits a convincing simulation of empathic communication, as reflected in the systematic reversal of "you" and "I" perspectives within the schematic definitions. This dual pattern of main/accessory empathic perspectives (by extension) can ultimately be extended to include the meta-order realm of the general unifying themes. The respective addition of these dual accessory counterparts adds a further crucial empathic dimension to the "meta-" schematic definition format. Fortunately, a suitable number of synonyms for the virtuous themes have been identified: resulting in the formal *accessory* format of themes schematically depicted in **Fig. 8B**, and also in terms of the compact diagram presented immediately below:

Quintessentialism	**Expediency**
Heroism	**Practicality**
Charisma	**Orthodoxy**
Evangelism	**Moralism**
Cosmopolitanism	**Spiritualism**

The General Unifying Virtuous Themes

This accessory listing of themes directly mirrors the pattern of organization previously established for the *main* themes with the exception that the "you" and "I" polarities are now reversed. For instance, the main *authority* sequence of individualism, personalism, romanticism, ecumenism, and humanism directly contrasts with the *accessory* sequence of themes; namely, quintessentialism, heroism, charisma, evangelism, and cosmopolitanism. Furthermore, the main *follower* sequence of pragmatism, utilitarianism, ecclesiasticism, eclecticism, and mysticism formally reciprocates the respective accessory hierarchy of expediency, practicality, orthodoxy, moralism, and spiritualism. Although the degree of correspondence for several of these themes might not perhaps be precise as might be expected, the overall cohesiveness of this accessory system proves the crucial delineating factor here. Indeed, the majority of these themes are not commonly encountered in general usage; hence, their more comprehensive description is deferred until a later edition.

The true test of validity for this accessory listing of themes ultimately extends to their incorporation into the respective schematic definition format. In direct analogy to the main sequence of themes, the schematic definitions of which are listed in **Table C-1**), the remaining accessory variations are similarly incorporated into their own schematic definition format: representing meta-order perspectives on the more basic individual accessory terms. For instance, the "meta-" schematic definition for *evangelism* encompasses the four accessory ecumenical ideals as subsets (e.g., blessings, conscientiousness, graciousness, and patience). Consequently, the complete ten-part listing of schematic definitions for the accessory virtuous themes is tabulated in **Table C-2**: in direct analogy to the schematic pattern previously established for the main listing of themes. When carefully compared to the main set of definitions depicted in **Table C-1**, the reciprocal interplay of the "you" and "I" perspectives finally becomes conceptually complete. When taken in a collective fashion, both the main and accessory versions for the virtuous themes permit a degree of empathic versatility unprecedented on the world scene today, offering an enhanced degree of versatility with respect to the virtuous realm.

In conclusion, the completed addition of the general unifying themes to the virtuous realm provides welcome additional validation to the individual listings of virtues, values, and ideals outlined within the preceding chapters. These general unifying themes all enjoy well established literary traditions, perhaps even rivaling those specifically targeting the individual virtuous terms. These themes address a wide range of pressing social issues, although never before brought together into one singular ethical synthesis. In this grand overarching sense, the newly devised master hierarchy of virtuous themes offers the potential for an extremely broad range of solutions towards maintaining and promoting global peace and prosperity.

For instance, with respect to the immediately-active class of authority roles, the initial theme of *individualism* serves as a founding principle underpinning the American way of life, an aspect uniquely celebrated through the US Bill of Rights. This pervasive foundation within individualism, in turn, begs mention of the charismatic sense of *personalism* (indicative of the group authority role), an attribute highly prized by both politician and CEO. Certain privileged figures even command a universal sphere of influence, such as *romanticized* in the legendary exploits attributed to Mother Teresa, the Delai Lama, Pope John Paul II, et al. The truest degree of social influence, however, primarily enters into consideration at the enviable humanitarian sphere of influence: as witnessed in themes of virtually *ecumenical* proportions: as in environmental conservation, global climate change, and issues confronting rampant global poverty. Of course, in terms of its crowning degree of abstraction, the transcendental sphere of influence must always reign supreme, as exemplified in the grand *humanistic* perspectives propounded by legendary visionaries such as Abraham Maslow and Fritz Perls.

These clearly romanticized authority perspectives, in turn, beg mention of the parallels relating to the respective follower themes, as exemplified in the ascending thematic sequence of pragmatism, utilitarianism, ecclesiasticism, eclecticism, and mysticism. For instance, the initially designated theme of *pragmatism* serves as the guiding principle for potentially acting in a personally-practical fashion, a fitting counterpoint to the immediately-active sense of individualism expressed by the personal authority figure. Furthermore, the group-directed theme of *utilitarianism* similarly extends to a civic sphere of influence, as reflected in the potentiality of progressive movements targeting social welfare and universal health care. In terms of the even higher universal sphere of influence, social progressivism ultimately acquires an *ecclesiastical* focus, as reflected in universal religious suffrage and/or liberation theology. Naturally, the crowning humanitarian theme of *eclecticism* ultimately projects an overarching timeless persona, where diverse social engineering movements are figuratively weighed in the balance: a global synthesis aimed towards promoting novel solutions to pressing social issues. In this latter collective sense, the master ten-part hierarchy of the "meta-" virtuous themes corresponds to an ultimate system of wisdom for all ages to come.

This universally-enduring aspect is highly reminiscent of the seminal concept of *Perennial Philosophy*, an eclectic system of thought that appropriates the best philosophical constructs from many of the major philosophical schools down through the ages. The present author proposes that the currently proposed ten-part hierarchy of the major virtues and values (in addition to the general unifying themes) qualifies as the most radically complete Perennial Philosophy yet to be devised, whereby incorporating and unifying a broad number of philosophical themes developed down through the ages. Indeed, each level within the master virtuous hierarchy is respectively associated with its own unique philosophical theme.

For the respective sequence of authority roles this corresponds to the ascending sequence of individualism, personalism, romanticism, ecumenism, and humanism. The corresponding follower roles specify the complementary sequence of pragmatism, utilitarianism, ecclesiasticism, eclecticism, and mysticism. This intriguing style of tandem correspondence between the individual listings of virtuous terms (and their general unifying themes) expands this eclectic style of Perennial Philosophy to its fullest epistemological sense. As such, it ushers in exciting new insights into an intellectual domain rife with possibilities for significant new research.

The truest collective power for this diverse hierarchy of virtuous themes ultimately appeals directly to their heretofore unprecedented potential for global collaborative influence across the entire unified virtuous hierarchy. In concert with the overarching individual traditions of virtues, values, and ideals, this enhanced interplay with the general unifying themes promises a new era in global cooperation targeting such noble endeavors, offering innovative new solutions towards maintaining international peace and prosperity.

PART-II

9

AN INTRODUCTION TO THE TRANSITIONAL POWER MANEUVERS

The pronounced versatility of the major categories of virtues/values allows for insights unprecedented on the world scene today. This full *80*-part hierarchy of the major virtues can scarcely claim to be the final word in this respect for even a cursory survey of the ethical literature reveals a broad assortment of *lesser* virtues essentially unaccounted for within the major groupings. Take for example, the cohesive listing of loyalty, fidelity, piety, and felicity; themes suggestive of a positive dimension within the ascending virtuous hierarchy. The further listing of humility, innocence, modesty, and meekness alternately suggests more of a disqualified sphere of communication. Indeed, it ultimately proves feasible to identify an equally significant master-listing of lesser virtues entirely independent from the major categories of virtues previously described. Through this complementary interplay of major and lesser virtues, a complete and overarching overview of the virtuous realm finally becomes conceptually complete.

The major virtuous realm suffers from one glaring shortcoming; namely, the authority and follower roles are rigidly fixed into place, allowing precious little flexibility to operate within the system. Versatility is a key factor within our modern mobile society, where continually shifting social coalitions place an ever-greater demand upon the individual. Each new adjustment within the social hierarchy calls for additional mechanisms for integrating this versatility, an innovation that the established hierarchy of virtues/values fails to fully take into account. In addition to the incremental pattern of maneuvering for power initially described, a more direct tactic must also exist for leapfrogging directly into the higher authority levels; namely, the group, spiritual, and humanitarian levels, respectively. This new class of options is schematically termed the

transitional class of power maneuvers in reference to the observation that they transition the individual directly into new social contexts.

A number of key features distinguish this new class of transitional power maneuvers. Firstly, these transitional variations represent direct motivational analogs of the main virtuous maneuvers they serve to imitate: often expressed in an exaggerated fashion in order to make the point more clearly. This flair for the dramatic can appear either humorous (as in the realm of comedy) or tragic (as in the case of melodrama). This tendency towards exaggeration is the stock-in-trade for the traditional situation comedy, where a guest-star intrudes upon the graces of a standard ensemble cast, typically with hilarious consequences. A lively sequence of good-natured banter typically follows culminating in a heartwarming resolution. A similar scenario further holds true with respect to the more serious realm of melodrama, as chiefly dramatized in terms of the daytime "soap opera."

THE TRANSITIONAL POWER MANEUVERS

The transitional class of power maneuvers refers to relationships initiated for the first time. The newly introduced individual attempts to establish a new relationship within a pre-existing social order enlisting the cooperation of more established individuals in order to solidify one's anticipated role within the conditioned relationship. Any such transitional overture fails to be consummated without an overt concession on the part of an established party within the social hierarchy. Take for example the familiar scenario of the "autograph hound." When thrust into potential contact with his/her celebrity idol, the fan attempts to establish a new personal relationship, even if only temporarily. As essentially an outsider, this entails a congeniality strategy for making the overture attractive to the celebrity figure; namely, framing the appeal in terms of an exalted respect for the celebrity figure. In terms of the autograph example, the eager fan appeasingly frames his overture in the guise of the personal follower role, effectively playing-up the prestige of the personal authority figure.

According to the celebrity/fan example the approval role of the personal follower is modified (in a transitional sense) into the *loyalty* maneuver expressed by the adoring fan, a status further anticipating the nostalgic acknowledgement of worthiness on the part of the personal authority figure. A similar scenario is observed with respect to the medieval feudal system, where the vassal unswervingly pledges loyalty to his noble liege in terms of a ritual hand-clasping ceremony. Hence, by playing-up the noble's established authority status, the personal follower gains a degree of consideration from his personal authority figure, a strategy consistent with the reciprocal interplay of authority/follower roles.

The more basic *complementary* style of interaction characterizing the major virtuous mode relies upon pre-established role-polarities, with the authority/follower roles fixed rigidly in place. In terms of the additional transitional variation, however, the newcomer fails to enjoy the advantages of such an established context: finding it more useful (at least initially) to dramatically play-up the status of his authority figure. In essence, this strategy allows the newcomer to get his foot in the door (so to speak). Should the personal authority figure eventually accept this ploy, the personal follower then gains initial acceptance in terms of an equal balance of power within the personal power realm.

THE DOUBLE BIND CLASS OF POWER MANEUVER

The initial phase of the transitional power maneuver is fittingly termed the *congeniality* phase, being that the newcomer maneuvers from an appeasement status in order to gain the acceptance of the established authority figure. The established party is primarily justified in accepting such an overture, being automatically granted a respected authority status. This advantage, however, is often not as beneficial as it might first appear: for the authority figure is technically coerced to some degree (albeit congenially) into reciprocating his expected role within the transitional interchange. Indeed, the savvy established individual often refuses to submit willingly to such

a bold power grab. The upstart newcomer effectively dictates the ultimate cooperation of the authority figure, a deceptive gain in status/prestige !

This slavish submission to the dictates of another equates to a personal loss of freedom irrespective of any congenial intentions therein. In a general "meta" sense the newcomer seizes control of the newly established relationship through the process of initiating it, placing the established party in a type of *double bind* maneuver. This term is borrowed from the terminology of Communication Theory, defined as a paradox that leaves one (thusly bound) unable to fully comment upon the inherent incongruity contained within the message. For the "loyalty" maneuver, this amounts to a fundamental conflict between the primary message content level and its overarching *meta*-context.

The primary message content is essentially straightforward; namely, one can accept the overture of the fan at its most basic content level, accompanied by an attendant recognition of one's established authority status. The overarching style of *meta*-message, however, effectively diminishes this outward power status: the newcomer dictating the course of the interaction through the very act of initiating it. This overarching style of meta-communication effectively supersedes the primary content level within the interaction, inserting a contradictory range of meanings within the overall transitional interplay.

This inherent aversion to being subliminally controlled by another makes the initial overture of the fan somewhat difficult to accept. Indeed, Communication Theorists acknowledge an ingrained resistance for modifying the established status quo, a transitional disruption to the homeostatic dynamics within the pre-existing social order. This intractable style of double bind maneuver is technically designated as a "damned if you do, damned if you don't" type of paradox. Should the established party accept the overture at face value, then he/she risks losing face with respect to the higher *meta*-context of the message; namely, submitting to the dictates of another. Rejecting the overture, however, voids the advantages inherent to the primary message content with its guaranteed authority status. One further risks appearing somewhat stalwart in the process, a factor completely at odds with the congenial nature of the proceedings.

THE COUNTER DOUBLE BIND MANEUVER

The most graceful resolution to this intransigent predicament entails what Communications Theo-

The Oath of Fealty: French Vassals Pledge Loyalty to the King
A Ceremony Invoking the Ritual Clasping of Hands - Detail from Medieval Tapestry, circa 1280.

rists term the *counter* double bind maneuver. This latter strategy amounts to humoring the efforts of the newcomer: accepting the surface content of the interaction while simultaneously disqualifying one's willing participation through the use of *meta*-contextual cues. The counter double bind subliminally disqualifies (through meta-cues) the context of the entire interaction: in essence, playing-off the validity of the entire transitional interchange. This strategy is formally diagrammed as: I accept your sense of loyalty through my nostalgic treatment of you, although I *humbly* deny doing so. This distinctive style of "meta" disqualification is chiefly mediated through nonverbal cues; e.g., those nonverbal behaviors that underscore virtually every social context. Chief among these are bodily gestures, where a brief shrug of the shoulders or a raised eyebrow can greatly modify (or even reverse) the content of what is being said. Vocal modulation and exaggerated inflection represent similar strategies towards these ends. A satirical or humorous tone of voice signals that one shouldn't be taken too seriously. Indeed, as any great comic can attest, the timing of a joke is generally more significant than the content therein. A similar pattern is further en-countered with respect to the theme of "playfulness," where routine activity acquires an amusing quality through communication that this is not be taken too seriously, as in role-playing and other such subliminally game-based behaviors.

Through this rather broad range of tactics, the counter double bind maneuver regains the upper hand in the transitional interchange without necessarily appearing to have done so. Communications Theorists such as Jay Haley (1990) define this strategy as the *meta-complementary* maneuver: where the surface content mimics the complementary variety, although now subliminally disqualified through the use of *meta*-contextual cues. A similar aspect is encountered in the field of Transactional Analysis with respect to the concept of *ulterior* communication. Indeed, it is precisely at this extreme level of disqualification that the paradoxical nature of the counter double bind maneuver proves most effective, obliquely expressing disdain for the newcomer's initial attempts at psychological manipulation. Through a sarcastic tone of voice (or other such disqualified tactic) the established party stresses the unreality of the situation, the ultimate outcome of the entire paradoxical interchange.

220	221
Loyalty	Responsibility
222	**223**
Discipline	Vigilance

TRANSITIONAL
ALTER EGO STATES
(Personal Double-Bind)

→

210.1	211.1
Humility	Innocence
212.1	**213.1**
Modesty	Meekness

DISQUALIFIED
EGO STATES
(Personal Counter Double-Bind)

240	241
Fidelity	Duty
242	**243**
Chivalry	Courage

TRANSITIONAL
CARDINAL VIRTUES
(Group Double-Bind)

→

230.1	231.1
Majesty	Vindication
232.1	**233.1**
Chastity	Obedience

DISQUALIFIED
PERSONAL IDEALS
(Group Counter Double-Bind)

260	261
Piety	Allegiance
262	**263**
Nobility	Valor

TRANSITIONAL
THEOLOGICAL VIRTUES
(Spiritual Double-Bind)

→

250.1	251.1
Magnificence	Exoneration
252.1	**253.1**
Purity	Conformity

DISQUALIFIED
CIVIL LIBERTIES
(Spiritual Counter Double-Bind)

280	281
Felicity	Righteousness
282	**283**
Zeal	Triumph

TRANSITIONAL
GREEK VALUES
(Humanitarian Double-Bind)

→

270.1	271.1
Grandeur	Immaculateness
272.1	**273.1**
Perfection	Pacifism

DISQUALIFIED
ECUMENICAL IDEALS
(Humanit. Counter Double-Bind)

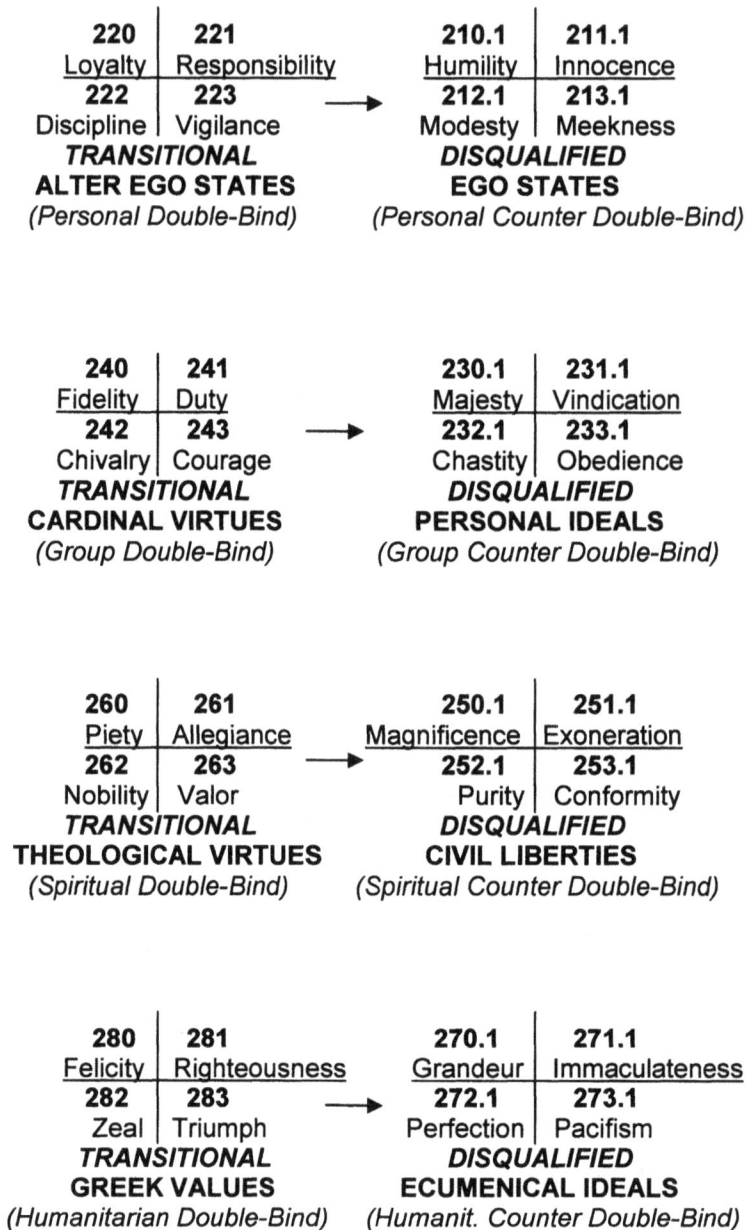

Fig. 9 – The Lesser Virtues - (I)

In the case of the initial loyalty maneuver, the established party *humbly* denies being worthy of such loyalty: superficially accepting the primary content of the interaction in a fully disqualified fashion. By appearing humble, the personal authority effectively sidesteps the insistent quality of the loyalty maneuver while remaining fully polite in the process. With respect to the parallel transitional strategy of responsibility, a disqualified sense of *innocence* on the part of the personal authority represents a similarly measured defense. A similar pattern further holds true with respect to the related interplay of discipline/modesty or vigilance/meekness. The artful use of disqualification effectively defuses any overt complicity within the transitional interchange. Indeed, it takes considerable skill to balance the degree of disqualification to meet the desired goal, a talent many of us develop at a fairly early age. Navigating the extremes of the double bind (and counter double bind) maneuvers requires great mental dexterity in concert with innate social instincts. The intrinsic social cues for achieving such subliminal disqualification (in addition to the skills of timing, inflection, etc.) all must be expressed convincingly in order to achieve the desired results. It is here that the wit and genius of the comedian remain so deeply appreciated, their public adulation certainly well-founded in light of their mastery of the art-form.

THE ULTIMATE RESOLUTION TO THE COUNTER DOUBLE BIND MANEUVER

The somewhat unnerving experience of discovering that one's double bind has been reversed is typically one of surprise accompanied by an "aha" experience. This realization is frequently accompanied by nervous laughter, a spontaneous acknowledgment of having been outwitted. This fitful laughter represents a subliminal catharsis of sorts, signaling a restoration of the original status quo following the disruptive transitional interlude. The spontaneous nature of the laughter directly verifies this subconscious aspect consistent with various types of convulsive behavior. Crying is often indistinguishable from laughter save the shedding of tears, functioning as a release from grief (just as laughter targets humor). Both laughter and crying lead to the release of tensions crucial for restoring emotional stability.

This latter development, in turn, places the original party in a double bind of their own with respect to such an emotionally-charged situation. Any comments relating to such an impasse are generally suppressed due to the highly disqualified nature of the proceedings. To do so would only advertise the glaring failure of the entire transitional interchange. Similar to the initial double bind maneuver, there is no straightforward exit from the counter double bind maneuver. The only reasonable strategy consists of abandoning the pursuit altogether, having been bested in such a pitched battle of wits. Attempts toward pressing a new transitional relationship are similarly abandoned, effectively restoring the original balance of role-polarities. Although the established authority figure may eventually see fit to extend a conciliatory overture, this option now remains distinct from having been forced into it. Through this supreme degree of disqualification the humor maneuver achieves its potential in terms of good-natured bantering, which even under friendly terms leads to impasse/counter impasse.

A DOUBLE BIND THEORY OF HUMOR & COMEDY

The extreme degree of disqualification characterizing the counter double bind maneuver certainly appears comedic to those thusly entertained. With respect to the humorous range of contexts encountered within the situation comedy, the major players take turns double binding one another before cleverly extricating themselves in turn. The enraptured audience members typically project into one role or another, sharing in the laughter when the trap is finally sprung.

The preliminary setup of the comedy routine is fittingly termed the *congeniality* phase, a role generally proffered by the "straight man" of the comedy team. The straight man sets up the context of the joke analogous to the initiation phase of the double bind maneuver. This initial phase, in turn, sets the stage for the *humor* maneuver proper. Here the headline star delivers a "zinger" of a punch line (the counter double bind maneuver) ideally served with a straight face. The immediate reaction for all in attendance is one of hilarious laughter, the celebrated calling card for revered comedy teams such as Abbott and Costello or Carson and McMahon. Perhaps the most difficult aspect of the comedian's job is abstaining from laughing at one's own jokes, whereby preserving the mystique of the skilled disqualification.

The laughter from the audience, in turn, serves as a spontaneous catharsis of sorts, an outward expression of a return to normalcy (so to speak). The emotional energy initially invested within the congeniality phase is subsequently dissipated through a convulsive spate of laughter, a homeostatic restoration of the preexisting social order. A similar pattern further holds true with respect to melodrama, where the related phenomenon of crying substitutes for that seen for laughter. In either case, the established motivational context is satisfactorily restored, with both parties now "double bound" against mulling over the series of reversals that had just transpired.

THE MASTER TRANSITIONAL SCHEMATIC

The formal addition of this dual sequence of transitional power maneuvers proves a fitting adjunct to the more routine ethical hierarchy, as distinguished through the reciprocal interplay of double bind and counter double bind maneuvers. This distinctive sequence of role-reversals is particularly evident in the specific examples initially described; namely, loyalty/humility and responsibility/innocence. For instance, the loyalty maneuver professed by the personal follower, in turn, prompts the humility expressed by the personal authority figure. A similar pattern further holds true for the responsibility form of double bind maneuver, whereby prompting the "innocence" style of counter double bind maneuver. Although these specific examples prove adequate for a personal sphere of influence, the more abstract levels within the transitional hierarchy remain to be determined. Fortunately, the overarching class of lesser virtues proves well suited to the task, with a broad range of literary traditions integrating seamlessly within the unified ethical hierarchy.

According to this expanded interpretation, loyalty represents just the first term within a sequence spanning the remaining group, spiritual, and humanitarian levels: namely, loyalty, fidelity, piety, and felicity. The similar trend based upon responsibility is alternately specified as responsibility-duty-allegiance-righteousness. A similar pattern further holds true with respect to the remaining sequences of counter double bind maneuvers: e.g., humility-majesty-magnificence-grandeur and innocence-vindication-exoneration-immaculateness. Indeed, an equal number of sequences remain for the remainder of the lesser virtues, resulting in the master *32*-part sequence of terms listed immediately below:

Loyalty → Humility	**Responsibility → Innocence**
Fidelity → Majesty	**Duty → Vindication**
Piety → Magnificence	**Allegiance → Exoneration**
Felicity → Grandeur	**Righteous.→ Immaculate.**
Discipline → Modesty	**Vigilance → Meekness**
Chivalry → Chastity	**Courage → Obedience**
Nobility → Purity	**Valor → Conformity**
Zeal → Perfection	**Triumph → Pacifism**

This compact diagram proves particularly effective for demonstrating the distinctive hierarchial trends at issue. A more formal arrangement of lesser virtues is further depicted in **Fig. 9**. According to this master schematic format, the complete *32*-part sequence of lesser virtues (I) is formally split into characteristic quartet-style listings of terms similar to the pattern initially established for the major listings of virtues and values. For instance, the most basic personal follower level is specified through the transitional quartet of loyalty, responsibility, discipline, and vigilance: a pattern reflecting the major sequence of alter ego states (approval, leniency, solicitousness, and submissiveness). True to the order in which they are presented, *loyalty* represents the transitional counterpart of approval, whereas *responsibility* makes a similar correspondence to blameful-leniency. Furthermore, *discipline* specifies the transitional counterpart for solicitousness, whereas *vigilance* makes similar correspondence to submissiveness.

This preliminary class of double bind maneuvers, in turn, sets the stage for the remaining class of counter double bind class of maneuvers; in this case, humility, innocence, modesty, and meekness. Each of these terms suggests a degree of disqualification characterizing the counter double bind class of maneuvers in relation to the initial sequence of double bind maneuvers. For instance, in response to your initial loyalty maneuver, I (as established personal authority) now *humbly* deny acting nostalgically towards you. Furthermore, in response to your blameful quest for responsibility, I now *innocently* deny acting guiltily towards you. Similarly, in response to my disciplined treatment of you, you (as established personal authority) now *modestly* deny acting desirously towards me. Furthermore, in response to my submissively-vigilant treatment of you, you now *meekly* deny acting in a worrisome fashion towards me.

This dual interplay of the personal classifications of the lesser virtues, in turn, extends to the additional classes of authority levels depicted in **Fig. 9**. A more detailed analysis of this entire *32*-part complement of transitional virtuous terms is certainly called for here, permitting a more comprehensive overview of the entire unified hierarchy of the lesser virtues (I). This expanded inquiry begins with an in-depth examination of the sequences based on loyalty-humility and responsibility-innocence in Chapter *10*: followed, in turn, by those classes of transitional virtues targeting discipline-modesty and vigilance-meekness contained in Chapter *11*.

THE SCHEMATIC DEFINITIONS
FOR THE LESSER VIRTUES

Before embarking on this somewhat technical style of analysis, one final issue necessarily remains to be addressed; namely, the incorporation of the lesser virtues within the formal schematic definition format. In this fundamental sense the schematic definitions for the lesser virtues (I) are outlined in the four-part series of **Tables D-1** to **D-4** of the current chapter. The definitions for the lesser virtues (II) are alternately depicted in **Tables E-1** to **E-4** as contained within the upcoming Chapter *12*. Although superficially similar in appearance, this transitional definition format differs in a number of key aspects from the pattern previously established for the major categories of virtues described in **Part I**.

The most prominent of these differences stems from the observation that the preliminary personal follower perspectives of loyalty, responsibility, discipline, and vigilance directly anticipate the collaboration of the established authority figure. Both loyalty and responsibility are defined as transitional variations on the more basic alter ego states of approval and leniency: representing reinforcement from a transitional follower perspective. Furthermore, discipline and vigilance alternately represent transitions in terms of a procurement focus; namely, the solicitousness and submissiveness perspectives entertained by the respective personal follower figure.

This "congeniality" style of follower perspective, in turn, prompts the counter double bind maneuver proper expressed by the targeted authority figure. Here, humility and innocence represent disqualified variations with respect to the nostalgia/guilt perspectives. Furthermore modesty and meekness specify similar modifications to desire/worry. A similar pattern further extends to the remaining group, spiritual, and humanitarian levels within the ascending power hierarchy. The crowning transcendental level, however, is deliberately left out of this transitional definition format due to the inherent implausibility of transitioning into such a supremely abstract level of perspective. This shortfall, however, does not necessarily specify that the transcendental domain is technically ruled-out for any potentially upcoming future variations on the transitional schematic-definition format.

A further distinguishing feature of the transitional format concerns the crucial observation that the personal, group, spiritual, and humanitarian levels represent fully independent sequences within this tabular style of format. This pattern directly contrasts with the more integrated pattern of organization previously established for the main virtuous groupings of definitions. The transitional maneuvers represent entirely newly introduced entries within the ascending power hierarchy, as reflected in the sample schematic definition for loyalty. For illustrative purposes, the first part of the *loyalty* definition represents the basic generic template for the approval perspective. This preliminary platform, in turn, sets the stage for the loyalty maneuver proper (depicted in the second half of the definition). This initial loyalty phase directly insures that no direct connection exists between adjacent authority levels within the schematic definition format. For instance, the initial loyalty maneuver effectively transitions into an entirely new motivational context formally independent of all that may have gone before.

This initial loyalty phase, in turn, sets the stage for the subsequent *humility* style of counter double bind maneuver expressed by the personal authority figure. This countermaneuver (by definition) is defined as a "dead end" of sorts insofar as further options are concerned, technically shutting-off any further response with respect to maneuvering for power within the transitional hierarchy. Consequently, a strict sense of independence is observed for each of the individual authority levels, as specified for both the initiation and termination of the two-stage transitional sequence.

The four individual authority levels represented within the transitional definition format therefore represent fully independent sequences of terms in their own right. Indeed, they are united within their respective definition master-table primarily in reference to their immediate proximity within the authority hierarchy. This stacked pattern of organization proves particularly essential for understanding the communicational factors at issue throughout the entire transitional realm of the lesser virtues. The discerning reader is encouraged to refer back to this four-part listing of transitional definitions throughout the course of the following chapters, outlining the overarching dynamics at issue for each of the individual classifications of lesser virtues.

In conclusion, this introductory description of the transitional class of lesser virtues offers radically new inroads into the understanding of human communication in general. Indeed, our modern fast-paced society, composed of ever shifting social coalitions, necessitates this additional class of transitional communication representative of the double bind and counter double bind class of

LOYALTY Previously, I (as personal authority) have nostalgically acted approachfully prompting the approving treatment of the personal follower. But now, you (as new personal follower) will *loyally* act in an approving fashion towards me: in anticipation of my (as established PA) nostalgic treatment of you.	**HUMILITY** Previously, you (as new personal follower) have loyally acted in an approving fashion towards me: in anticipation of my (as established PA) nostalgic treatment of you. But now, I (as reluctant personal authority) will *humbly* deny acting nostalgically towards you: thwarting your (as new PF) loyal treatment of me.
FIDELITY Previously, I (as group authority) have gloriously acted in a nostalgic fashion prompting the prudent-approval of the group representative. But now, you (as new group representative) will loyally act with *fidelity* towards me: in anticipation of my (as established GA) gloriously-nostalgic treatment of you.	**MAJESTY** Previously, you (as new group representative) have loyally acted with fidelity towards me: in anticipation of my (as established GA) gloriously-nostalgic treatment of you. But now, I (as reluctant group authority) will humbly act in a *majestic* fashion towards you: thwarting your (as new GR) loyal sense of fidelity.
PIETY Previously, I (as spiritual authority) have gloriously acted in a provident fashion prompting the prudent-faith of the spiritual disciple. But now, you (as new spiritual disciple) will *piously* act with fidelity towards me: in anticipation of my (as established SA) gloriously-provident treatment of you.	**MAGNIFICENCE** Previously, you (as new spiritual disciple) have piously acted with fidelity towards me: in anticipation of my (as established SA) gloriously-provident treatment of you. But now, I (as reluctant spiritual authority) will majestically react in a *magnificent* fashion towards you: thwarting your (as new SD) pious treatment of me.
FELICITY Previously, I (as humanitarian authority) have providently acted in a graceful fashion prompting the beauteous-faith of the representative member of humanity But now, you (as new representative member of humanity) will piously act with *felicity* towards me: in anticipation of my (as established HA) provident sense of gracefulness.	**GRANDEUR** Previously, you (as new representative member of humanity) have piously acted felicitously towards me: in anticipation of my (as established HA) provident sense of gracefulness. But now, I (as reluctant humanitarian authority) will magnificently react in a *grand* fashion towards you: thwarting your (as new RH) felicitous treatment of me.

Table D-1 – The Lesser Virtues Based Upon Loyalty/Humility

RESPONSIBILITY	INNOCENCE
Previously, I (as personal authority) have guiltily acted in an aversive fashion prompting the lenient treatment of the personal follower. But now, you (as new personal follower) will leniently seek a sense of *responsibility* from me: in anticipation of my (as established PA) guilty treatment of you.	Previously, you (as new personal follower) have leniently sought a sense of responsibility from me: in anticipation of my (as established PA) guilty treatment of you. But now, I (as reluctant personal authority) will *innocently* deny acting guiltily towards you: thwarting your (as new PF) lenient quest for responsibility.
DUTY	**VINDICATION**
Previously, I (as group authority) have honorably acted in a guilty fashion prompting the lenient sense of justice of the group representative. But now, you (as new group representative) will *dutifully* seek a sense of responsibility from me: in anticipation of my (as established GA) honorable sense of guilt.	Previously, you (as new group representative) have dutifully sought a sense of responsibility from me: in anticipation of my (as established GA) honorable sense of guilt. But now, I (as reluctant group authority) will innocently act in a *vindicated* fashion towards you: thwarting your (as new GR) dutiful quest for responsibility.
ALLEGIANCE	**EXONERATION**
Previously, I (as spiritual authority) have honorably acted in a libertarian fashion prompting the lenient hope for justice expressed by the spiritual disciple. But now, you (as new spiritual disciple) will dutifully act in an *allegiant* fashion towards me: in anticipation of my (as established SA) libertarian sense of honor.	Previously, you (as new spiritual disciple) have dutifully acted in an allegiant fashion towards me: in anticipation of my (as established SA) libertarian sense of honor. But now, I (as reluctant spiritual authority) will vindicatingly act in an *exonerated* fashion towards you: thwarting your (as new SD) dutiful sense of allegiance.
RIGHTEOUSNESS	**IMMACULATENESS**
Previously, I (as humanitarian authority) have freely-willed acted in a libertarian fashion prompting the just-hope for the truth by the representative member of humanity. But now, you (as new representative member of humanity) will allegiantly act *righteously* towards me: in anticipation of my (as established HA) libertarian sense of free will.	Previously, you (as new representative member of humanity) have allegiantly acted righteously towards me: in anticipation of my (as established HA) libertarian sense of free will. But now, I (as reluctant humanitarian authority) will exoneratingly act in an *immaculate* fashion towards you: thwarting your (as new RH) righteous treatment of me.

Table D-2 - The Lesser Virtues Based on Responsibility/Innocence

DISCIPLINE	MODESTY
Previously, you (as personal authority) have desirously acted in a rewarding fashion prompting the solicitous treatment of the personal follower. But now, I (as new personal follower) will solicitously act in a *disciplined* fashion towards you: in anticipation of your (as established PA) desirous treatment of me.	Previously, I (as new personal follower) have solicitously acted in a disciplined fashion towards you: in anticipation of your (as established PA) desirous treatment of me. But now, you (as reluctant personal authority) will *modestly* deny acting desirously towards me: thwarting my (as new PF) disciplined treatment of you.
CHIVALRY	**CHASTITY**
Previously, you (as group authority) have dignifiedly acted in a desirous fashion prompting the temperately-solicitous treatment of the group representative. But now, I (as new group representative) will *chivalrously* act in a disciplined fashion towards you: in anticipation of your (as established GA) dignified-desire for me.	Previously, I (as new group representative) have chivalrously acted in a disciplined fashion towards you: in anticipation of your (as established GA) dignified-desire for me. But now, you (as reluctant group authority) will modestly act in a *chaste* fashion towards me: thwarting my (as new GR) chivalrous sense of discipline.
NOBILITY	**PURITY**
Previously, you (as spiritual authority) have civilly acted in a dignified fashion prompting the temperate sense of charitableness of the spiritual disciple. But now, I (as new spiritual disciple) will chivalrously act in a *noble* fashion towards you: in anticipation of your (as established SA) civilly-dignified treatment of me.	Previously, I (as new spiritual disciple) have chivalrously acted in a noble fashion towards you: in anticipation of your (as established SA) civilly-dignified treatment of me. But now, you (as reluctant spiritual authority) will chastely act in a *pure* fashion towards me: thwarting my (as new SD) noble treatment of you.
ZEAL	**PERFECTION**
Previously, you (as humanitarian authority) have civilly behaved magnanimously prompting the charitable sense of goodness of the representative member of humanity. But now, I (as new representative member of humanity) will nobly act in a *zealous* fashion towards you: in anticipation of your (as established HA) magnanimous treatment of me.	Previously, I (as new representative member of humanity) have nobly acted in a zealous fashion towards you: in anticipation of your (as establ. HA) magnanimous treatment of me. But now, you (as reluctant humanitarian authority) will *perfectly* act in a pure fashion towards me: thwarting my (as new RH) noble sense of zeal.

Table D-3 – The Lesser Virtues Based on Discipline/Modesty

VIGILANCE	MEEKNESS
Previously, you (as personal authority) have worrisomely acted tolerantly prompting the submissive treatment of the personal follower. But now, I (as new personal follower) will *vigilantly* act in a submissive fashion towards you: in anticipation of your (as established PA) worrisome treatment of me.	Previously, I (as new personal follower) have vigilantly acted in a submissive fashion towards you: in anticipation of your (as established PA) worrisome treatment of me. But now, you (as reluctant personal authority) will *meekly* deny acting worrisomely towards me: thwarting my (as new PF) vigilant treatment of you.
COURAGE	**OBEDIENCE**
Previously, you (as group authority) have worrisomely acted with integrity prompting the fortitudinous sense of concern of the group representative. But now, I (as new group representative) will vigilantly act in a *courageous* fashion towards you: in anticipation of your (as established GA) worrisome sense of integrity.	Previously, I (as new group representative) have vigilantly acted in a courageous fashion towards you: in anticipation of your (as established GA) worrisome sense of integrity. But now, you (as reluctant group authority) will meekly act in an *obedient* fashion towards me: thwarting my (as new GR) vigilant sense of courage.
VALOR	**CONFORMITY**
Previously, you (as spiritual authority) have austerely acted with integrity prompting the fortitudinous sense of decency of the spiritual disciple. But now, I (as new spiritual disciple) will courageously act in a *valiant* fashion towards you: in anticipation of your (as established SA) austere sense of integrity.	Previously, I (as new spiritual disciple) have courageously acted in a valiant fashion towards you: in anticipation of your (as established SA) austere sense of integrity. But now, you (as reluctant spiritual authority) will obediently act in a *conformist* fashion towards me: thwarting my (as new SD) valiant treatment of you.
TRIUMPH	**PACIFISM**
Previously, you (as humanitarian authority) have austerely acted with equanimity prompting the decent sense of wisdom of the representative member of humanity. But now, I (as new representative member of humanity) will valiantly act *triumphantly* towards you: in anticipation of your (as established HA) austere sense of equanimity.	Previously, I (as new representative member of humanity) have valiantly acted in triumphantly towards you: in anticipation of your (as established HA) austere sense of equanimity. But now, you (as reluctant humanitarian authority) will conform-ingly act in a *pacifistic* fashion towards me: thwarting my (as new RH) triumphant treatment of you.

Table D- 4 – The Lesser Virtues Based on Vigilance/Meekness

power maneuvers. For the initial double bind tactic, the new party petitions for entry directly into an established social context. The established party, in turn, retains the option of accepting such an overture or politely declining through a humorous style of counter double bind maneuver. Indeed, society is maintained chiefly through an enduring foundation within such polite social discourse, effectively serving to defuse conflict through a disqualified style of social interaction.

It should further be emphasized that this transitional class of power maneuvers is formally based upon the instinctual principles of behavioral psychology similar to the main power maneuvers that they serve to imitate. Here, the transitional power maneuvers represent direct avenues of transition into the more routine classes of virtues and values initially aimed for. Subsequent acceptance by the established party effectively cements entry into such a pre-existing social context, whereas the counter double bind strategy politely deflects or defers such an overture. A blunt or discourteous "thanks but no thanks" is also an option, but this lack of diplomacy can often backfire at a later date. Undoubtedly each of us at some time has been the victim of such blunt rejections, although effectively part-and-parcel of a variable social environment. It is hoped that an enhanced understanding of this transitional dynamic will provide broader incentives towards reforming such negative tendencies across the length and breadth of society as a whole, permitting a more prosperous and harmonious degree of cooperation on the world scene today.

10

THE FOLLOWER-BASED REALM
FOR THE LESSER VIRTUES (I)

The stepwise discussion of the lesser virtues (I) is currently launched with respect to an in-depth examination of the respective follower-based dimensions; namely, the sequence based upon loyalty/humility followed by that targeting responsibility/innocence. The current chapter endeavors to outline the ascending motivational hierarchy of authority/follower roles spanning the personal, group, spiritual, and humanitarian levels, respectively. Consequently, the pattern of presentation with respect to the lesser virtues might appear somewhat different than that which has gone before (for the major virtues). The four-part hierarchy of projected follower terms is described first followed by the disqualified sequence of respective authority roles. In this dual fashion the ascending pattern of power escalation is convincingly documented for both the authority and follower roles, greatly simplifying the overall strategy of presentation. The preliminary double bind sequence of loyalty-fidelity-piety-felicity is described first, followed by the subsequent counter double bind sequence of humility, majesty, magnificence, and grandeur. Furthermore, the second half of the current chapter examines the remaining sequences of responsibility-duty-allegiance-righteousness and innocence, vindication, exoneration, and immaculateness. The discerning reader is encouraged to refer back to the four-page listing of schematic definitions for the lesser virtues (I) outlined in Chapter 9 providing a detailed schematic representation of the dynamics at issue for each of the individual terms.

LOYALTY

The first listed theme of *loyalty* is formally defined as the respective transitional counterpart of approval. Its modern spelling derives from the French *loyauté*, from the French-Latin *legalis* (legal). Although this derivation might initially seem suggestive of a civic context, the personal follower (by definition) loyally appeals to his established authority figure with due deference to his authority status; hence, enhancing the prospects of gaining acceptance. The feudal overtones typically associated with loyalty are similarly suggestive of the personal bonds linking the accessible ruler and his faithful subjects. As legal power over the entire realm every subject was personally beholden to his supreme royal personage.

According to the Old English legend of *King Arthur and the Roundtable*, the knights of the realm pledged unswerving loyalty and fealty to the king in light of his unfailing duties to his loyal subjects. Loyalty, accordingly, is defined as unfailing service or devotion to a worthy person or cause. In this latter context, the personal follower reinforcingly acts to attract the nostalgic acknowledgement of his personal authority figure through outward attempts distinguishing oneself from any other follower figures. Herein lies the most basic salient feature of loyalty, as opposed to other virtues within its class; namely, subordinating one's immediate self-interests to the power embodied within one's personal authority figure: in essence, enhancing the potential for establishing an ongoing personal relationship once the preliminary groundwork has been set into place.

FIDELITY

The personal foundations for loyalty, in turn, extend to a group sphere of influence with respect to the more civic-minded theme of *fidelity*. The group representative loyally anticipates (with fidelity) the gloriously-nostalgic treatment expressed by the group authority figure. Consequently, fidelity is traditionally defined as the inclination to fulfill one's promises in conformity to pre-existing promissory commitments. The term derives from the Latin *fidelitas*, from *fidelis* (faithful) from *fidere* (to trust in). In a classical context fidelity introduces the concepts of faithful performance to duty or obligation. The Romans worshipped this abstract quality as Fides, the divine goddess of oaths and vows. As previously described in the section dealing with "faith," Fides is traditionally depicted as a matron in a long white veil and flowing gown, her right hand raised solemnly as if taking a vow.

Fidelity also extends to activities associated with the transmission of information, such as reporting a newsworthy event or reproducing a manuscript. This was particularly crucial during the Middle Ages, when sacred manuscripts were painstakingly reproduced by hand. For copies of the Bible, even a single error on a page was grounds for its unquestioned destruction due to a breakdown in fidelity.

In our modern media age, this term is most often associated with the notion of *high fidelity*, a technical advancement in sound reproduction. Unlike the simple phonograph, the "hi-fi" system ensures that sound reproduction at the output stage faithfully corresponds to the signal received at the input stage. This aspiration to universal standards of reproduction effectively mirrors the respective moral counterparts of fidelity, where the group representative loyally acts with fidelity to secure the consideration of the established authority figure through a fidelity style of transitional maneuver. In direct analogy to its initial foundation within loyalty, the fidelity maneuver effectively anticipates a glorious-nostalgia perspective on the part of the group authority figure. Through this transitional style of fidelity perspective, the group representative aims for recognition within a civic sphere of influence, formally validating the group overtones traditionally associated with fidelity.

PIETY

The ascending hierarchy of loyalty and fidelity, in turn, extends to a universal sphere of influence with respect to the spiritual disciple theme of *piety*. In direct analogy to the subordinate sequence of loyalty/fidelity, piety effectively targets a universal sphere of influence as suggested in the pious attributes associated with this term. This theme dates at least to classical times as evident in the Latin *pius* (of similar meaning and usage). It denotes a sense of devotion or duty to one's obligations primarily in a religious context. Piety is

symbolized as a stylized cross, a flaming heart, or a burning lamp, amongst other such imagery. Indeed, piety was initially celebrated as one of most ancient obligations of the ancient world, listed within pre-Platonic tradition as a fifth entry within the listing of cardinal virtues. Consequently piety with respect to religious observance was considered a crucial factor for maintaining the favor and blessings of the gods, whereby ensuring the continuing success of the Empire.

The Romans specifically worshipped this quality with respect to their abstract goddess Pietas. At the Battle of Thermopylae in 91 BCE, the Consul M. Acilius Glabrio vowed to dedicate a temple to Pietas. His son (by the same name) carried-out this vow, erecting a temple to Pietas in the Forum Holitorium in Rome. A later temple dedicated to Pietas was situated near to the Circus Flaminius. On various coins of the empire, Pietas is represented accompanied by a stylized stork (a classical symbol of trustworthiness). Throughout the course of the empire, the prestige of Pietas was repeatedly invoked to exalt the ideal of peace and harmony amongst members of the noble ruling class.

With the dawning of the Christian era, this sense of devotion extended to a pious sense of loyalty for the foundations of the Christian faith. Indeed, with the dawning of the Protestant Reformation, Pietism became a prominent spiritual movement in its own right, emphasizing a rigorous expression of morality and a personal sense of piety. The movement flourished within the context of German Lutheranism, a belief system emphasizing small devotional gatherings catering to personal devotion, in contrast to the more intellectual focus of more orthodox forms of Protestantism. This trend towards devotional piety represents a spiritual disciple form of double bind maneuver in relation to the established spiritual authority figure. Here the faithful precepts of the spiritual disciple figure are exalted in a pious devotional sense, where the spiritual disciple loyally acts in a pious fashion in anticipation of the gloriously-providential treatment of the established authority figure. The due deference implicit in the piety maneuver proves particularly crucial towards achieving the desired providential result on the part of the respective spiritual authority figure within the conditioned interaction.

FELICITY

The final theme within the ascending hierarchy of transitional terms, *felicity*, extends the spiritual disciple's pious sense of devotion into an even

The Humility of Christ – A Scene Described During the Last Supper
Christ *Humbly* Washes the Feet of the Twelve Apostles – Detail from a Stained Glass Devotional

more enduring humanitarian sphere of influence. It is traditionally defined as joy, pleasure, or delight in relation to a happy event. The term derives from the Latin *felicatis*, from *felix* (happy). As with so many other abstract qualities, the ancient Romans worshipped this abstract theme as Felicitas, the goddess of divine good fortune. She is often associated with Fortuna (goddess of fortune) and Copia (goddess of plenty). The worship of Felicitas dates to 146 BCE when a Roman temple dedicated to her was erected by L. Licinius Lucullus. Although a somewhat of minor goddess at the time, her popularity expanded through a campaign of devotion by later Roman generals: e.g., Sulla, Pompey, and Julius Caesar. Indeed, Caesar specifically lent his influence to the construction of a second temple to Felicitas on the site of the traditional Roman Senate House. During the ensuing Imperial age, the cult of Felicitas endured as a particular favorite of the Emperor Augustus, as well as many of his illustrious successors that were to follow.

This pagan fascination underwent thorough modification during the subsequent Christian era, with felicity now viewed as a divine attribute of the Christian Deity. Medieval theologians incorporated felicity within their comprehensive system of scholastic virtues, a welcome comfort to those dedicated to a virtuous lifestyle. Indeed, felicity formally expands upon the subordinate concepts of piety and fidelity, certainly key factors in the lives of many of the great saints and mar-

tyrs. Samuel Johnson once succinctly wrote: "Our *felicity* we make or find with secret course, which no loud storms annoy, glides the smooth current of our domestic joy."

The clear humanitarian overtones for felicity further anticipate the provident sense of gracefulness expressed by the established humanitarian authority figure. In terms of this extreme level of abstraction, the motivational dynamics for felicity are scarcely as apparent as those established for the subordinate sequence of terms; although felicity certainly preserves the incremental quality of the preliminary hierarchy of terms; namely, loyalty-fidelity-piety (and now felicity).

HUMILITY

A parallel hierarchy of themes, in turn, remains in order for the remaining class of counter double bind maneuvers: namely, humility, majesty, magnificence, and grandeur. The first mentioned theme of *humility* represents the counter double bind response to the preliminary "loyalty" maneuver expressed by the personal follower figure. The term derives from the Latin *humulis* (low, humble) from *humus* (earth) denoting a modest or humble perspective. Rather than unwittingly submitting to the dictates of the personal follower (e.g., nostalgically acting solicitously), the *humble* authority figure now projects a.more modest persona, effectively disqualifying the prescribed dictates of the loyalty maneuver. The fact that humility is classified as a virtue (albeit a lesser one) clearly attests to this inherent sense of disqualification within such a personal sphere of influence.

According to the Christ's Sermon on the Mount, the First Beatitude specifically singles out humility: "Blessed are the poor in spirit, for theirs is the kingdom of heaven." Here Christ downplays any tendency towards self-magnification in favor of humility/meekness of purpose. Indeed, the unswerving sense of loyalty expressed by the Twelve Apostles undoubtedly proved instrumental in prompting Christ's humble demeanor, as exemplified in his humble foot-washing ceremony described during the Last Supper (John 13:5). This enduring sense of humility remained a prominent theme for many of the Twelve Disciples. Indeed, the Apostle Peter specifically requested to be crucified upside-down in a final act of humility save that he would die in a manner similar to the original crucifixion. A similar interpretation invokes the medieval tradition of *humble pie*, the modest entrée of the woodsman baked from the entrails of the game slated for the Lord's table.

MAJESTY

The personal dynamics for humility, in turn, extend to a civic sphere of influence with respect to the group authority theme of *majesty*. The group follower's "fidelity" maneuver eventually prompts a majestic denial of worthiness on the part of the group authority figure. Although scarcely a commonly employed term, the origins of majesty date at least to the Age of Chivalry, when the royal monarch wielded supreme authority throughout the land. Majesty denotes an unparalleled sense of dignity or stateliness with respect to speech or deportment, often employed as a royal title of distinction. Its modern spelling derives from the Latin *majestas*, from *magnus* (great). The regal overtones traditionally associated with the term are particularly conspicuous in the practice of medieval heraldry, where the expression "In His Majesty" describes a crowned eagle holding a scepter in the convention of the medieval coat of arms: both symbolisms of nobility and/or distinction. Majesty certainly warrants such civic or political attributes as evident in many scriptural passages of a patriarchal nature. For instance, the NT Book of Hebrews (8:1) describes the regal dominion of the Lord as high priest seated at the right hand of the throne of *majesty*. Indeed, this theme is often employed as a title of distinction. The address "Your Majesty" is a courtesy directed to reigning sovereigns and their consorts in recognition of their stateliness and grandeur.

The truest appeal for majesty, however, resides in its virtually effortless persona indicative of its virtuous sense of disqualification. Majesty formally disqualifies any overt sense of complicity on the part of the group authority figure, effectively expanding upon the humility maneuver previously established for the personal authority. Consequently, the fidelity maneuver initiated by the group representative directly prompts (in a disqualified fashion) the majesty expressed by the group authority figure. In this subliminally disqualified sense, the reluctant group authority politely acknowledges the initial fidelity maneuver without overtly appearing to have done so, whereby avoiding the risk of any outward loss of dignity or majesty in the process.

MAGNIFICENCE

The majestic prerequisites for the group realm, in turn, extend to a universal sphere of influence with respect to the spiritually-focused theme of *magnificence*. Grand works of architecture are dedicated in celebration of such a magnificent agenda, a selfless endeavor consistent with such a respective spiritual authority perspective. The term derives from the Latin *magnus* (great) and *facere* (to make), a compound derivation suggesting nobility in word or deed sometimes bordering upon the extravagant. This traditional focus upon grandeur is particularly evident in many of the related symbolisms of magnificence: namely, gemstones, orchids, or the peacock. These showy attributes are similarly affiliated with royalty. Indeed, the address "Your Magnificence" is frequently employed as a title of distinction by kings and other dignitaries in a manner reminiscent of the related theme of majesty.

The classification of magnificence as a virtue dates at least to classical times, described by Aristotle as the proper expenditure of money towards grand works or deeds: as in the honorable application of riches. Furthermore, Aristotle singles out magnificence as the virtuous mean-value interposed between the defect-state of avarice and the excess-state of prodigality. This Aristotelian interpretation enjoyed a significant revival during the Middle Ages, magnificence celebrated as liberality in the expenditure of great wealth on a universal sphere of influence. The magnificent individual seeks patronage over noble endeavors, such as architectural projects of enhanced taste and elegance consistent with the degree of majesty intended: as in grand religious architecture, memorials, endowments, or philanthropic works, etc.

The most dramatic feature of magnificence invokes the effortlessness with which it is bestowed, analogous to the group dynamic previously established for majesty. Here the renowned public figure endeavors to give back a measure of his exalted status, although without overtly appearing to have done so: in keeping with the subordinate sequence of humility/majesty. The truly grand scale of the works clearly argues for the universal sense of the term: a noble endeavor of enduring significance across all ages and generations. Indeed, many great leaders have felt obligated to undertake such grand philanthropic endeavors for the benefit of the global community, a noble aspiration that still rings true today.

GRANDEUR

The final theme with respect to the counter double bind maneuvers, *grandeur*, represents a humanitarian expansion upon the subordinate hierarchy of humility, majesty, and magnificence. This theme denotes a greatness of power or authority, as in splendor or stateliness that inspires awe: deriving from the Latin *grandis* (great). Roman culture was particularly masterful in the art of pomp and spectacle, the spoils of conquest transforming Rome into the show-place of the classical world. Its grand coliseums, arenas, and public temples offered many affordable diversions to the general populace. Entertaining sporting events featuring gladiators, exotic beasts, and cavalcades ensured the faith and loyalty of the Roman citizenry. This overriding sense of grandeur further figured prominently in a religious sense, inspiring a grand sense of awe and devotion for the extensive pantheon of Roman gods and goddesses.

It was primarily through the grandeur of its material trappings that the imperial Roman Empire endured: invoking its self-appointed status as humanitarian authority for the entire Mediterranean world. The grandeur that was Rome certainly saw no equal until the wonders of our modern technological age, at least in terms of the Western tradition. This focus upon grandeur still figures prominently in many modern symbolisms, such as the grandeur of the Grand Canyon, the Grand Old Flag, etc. Grandeur expands (in a humanitarian sense) upon the subordinate virtuous concepts of majesty/magnificence, collectively sharing their ingrained tendency towards verbal disqualification. Grandeur appears almost effortless in terms of form and function (as in the majesty of nature), as opposed to any overt complicity therein. This subliminal degree of disqualifica-

tion can even reach the level of fault, as in "delusions of grandeur" or "grandiose schemes." In general, this theme is chiefly viewed in a virtuous light, with medieval theologians listing it among their main classes of virtues: albeit a lesser one.

RESPONSIBILITY

A similar style of analysis further remains in order for the remaining sequence of transitional themes based upon responsibility/innocence. The first mentioned theme of responsibility represents a transitional variation on the lenient-blame perspective expressed by the personal follower figure. This transitional quest for responsibility further anticipates a submissive expression of guilt on the part of the personal authority figure similar to the interplay initially established for loyalty/nostalgia. The term derives from the Latin *respondére*, from *re-* (back) and *spondére* (to promise or pledge). It denotes a sense of accountability or culpability within a personal sphere of influence. The personal follower formally transitions into a lenient sense of blame in due deference to the established personal authority figure. The responsibility-seeker, accordingly, enhances his chances of gaining the attention of the established authority figure in anticipation of the latter's submissive sense of guilt. Although the responsibility-seeker can wield a considerable degree of influence, the personal authority can alternately resort to a disqualified form of counter double bind maneuver; namely, an overarching assertion of innocence (as outlined later in this chapter). In either case, the initial responsibility maneuver serves its initial goal of gaining the notice of the established authority figure, although not always with the desired results.

DUTY

The personal dynamics for responsibility, in turn, extend to a group sphere of influence with respect to the civic-focused theme of *duty*. The group representative dutifully seeks a sense of responsibility from the established authority figure, a transitional variation on the blameful quest for justice. Duty denotes that which is bound through terms of obligation: deriving from the Anglo-French *duete* from Old French *deu*, past participle of *devoire*, from the Latin *debere* (to owe). This principle of indebtedness is particularly consistent with that sense of obligation typically encountered with respect to duty.

In the broadest sense, duty subordinates one's self-seeking inclinations to an overarching authoritarian standard. According to classical ethics, duty is defined as a standard to be achieved, as in a dutiful ideal to be realized. Indeed, duty is a virtue intimately related to integrity, a moral construct specifying a set of responsibilities that must be fulfilled in a contractual sense. This contract may be formal or informal, implicit or explicit, or generated on the basis of an "honor code." Moral duty ideally meets these conditions of good faith or due diligence without shifting blame onto others. Furthermore, an expectation of commensurate benefits is warranted in a fully informed and transparent style of group context.

Typically duty is imposed through legal sanctions enforced by the state. Consequently, the moral obligation to obey the law of the land entails the duty of good citizenship. Indeed, a clear sense of duty helps to develop social responsibility and cultural effectiveness. As human social creatures, progress is effectively achieved through concerted collaborative efforts. This progress flourishes in terms of shared purpose and mutual trust in meeting individual social obligations. Civility and quality of life advance when motivated by duty towards a common good.

ALLEGIANCE

The ascending sequence of responsibility and duty, in turn, extends to a universal sphere of influence with respect to the spiritually-focused theme of *allegiance*. The newly-transitioned spiritual disciple dutifully seeks a sense of allegiance from his established authority figure consistent with the latter's universal power status. Its medieval connotations denote the duty of the vassal towards his feudal lord or sovereign. The term derives from the Latin *ad-* (to) and *ligere* (bind) symbolizing such a reciprocating feudal dynamic. Here the vassal kneels before his liege (lord) in an allegiant plea for consideration similar to the case previously established for duty. This formal enactment of allegiance represents a transitional variation on the blameful-hope for justice potentially expressed by the spiritual disciple figure.

In our modern secular age, this transitional class of power maneuver is most readily apparent in terms of the Pledge of Allegiance of the United States. The Pledge initially enjoyed quite humble beginnings, first published in 1892 in celebration of the centenary anniversary of Columbus Day. It originally read: "I pledge allegiance to my flag and the Republic for which it stands; one nation indivisible, with liberty and justice for all." The highly personal nature of the pledge was subtly modified in 1924 when the phrase "my flag" was replaced with "the flag of the United States of America." In 1942, the Pledge was officially adopted as a national standard, although further modifications remained. At President Eisenhower's urging in 1954, Congress legislated the addition of the phrase "under God" yielding the Pledge's present format. This telling spiritual modification proves particularly relevant in relation to the deep universal overtones attributed to allegiance. According to the legislation of 1954, the Pledge is most properly taken standing at attention with one's hand placed over one's heart during the recitation. This latter aspect directly stresses the whole-hearted submission to purpose through one's pledge of duty and allegiance. By custom, headgear is ideally removed, further accentuating the solemn nature of the pledge through its transitional analogy to "hope."

Through this dutiful sense of allegiance, the spiritual disciple leniently anticipates the libertarian dictates of the established authority figure, an interplay of themes only truly comprehensible in terms of the subordinate concepts of responsibility and duty. Although the federal government does not technically favor one religion over another, it certainly values the principles of Divine Providence consistent with a common Protestant heritage. Consequently, The Pledge effectively reaffirms the ideals of our forefathers, enduring affirmations of our universal obligations as citizens of the United States. As Franklin Roosevelt insightfully wrote, "It is a pledge to maintain the four great freedoms cherished by all Americans: freedom of speech, freedom of religion, freedom from want, and freedom from fear."

RIGHTEOUSNESS

The ascending hierarchy of transitional themes ultimately culminates with respect to the supremely abstract theme of *righteousness*: transitionally framed in terms of an enduring humanitarian perspective. Righteousness represents the transitional counterpart of the more basic virtue of "truth," further anticipating a libertarian sense of free will on the part of the established authority figure. The term traces its origins to the Old English *rihtwis*, from *riht* (right) and *wis* (wise) denoting a morally upright or sage demeanor. The Latin tradition recognizes a similar set of concepts, with truth worshipped as the goddess Veritas, whereas righteousness gained devotion as the Roman divinity Fas, the god of righteousness. The latter divinity personified conduct rightfully permitted by Divine Law, governed by what is morally right or fitting: as opposed to civil law (that dealt with custom and tradition). Indeed, the chief god Zeus was championed as the protector of righteous causes, often resorting to bolts of thunder and lightning to remedy grievous injustice.

A similar interpretation permeates Judeo-Christian scriptural tradition as well. The Lord of the Old Testament typically imposed a virtually anthropomorphic sense of righteousness, severely chastising all that dared to scorn His Commandments. The righteous individual piously conformed to the letter of the law in terms of religious devotion, alms giving, prayer, and fasting. Indeed, this overarching sense of justice effectively permeates the basic principle of righteousness, taking its cue from the OT Book of Judges that righteously commanded submission to the law. The Judges were rightfully extolled as "men of truth" fearing God and abhorring unjustly gains. According to Deuteronomy (25:1) "If there is a controversy between men that comes to judgment, the Judges shall judge them and justify the *righteous* and condemn the wicked."

This moral sense of righteousness further extends to New Testament scripture, particularly in terms of Christ's Fourth Beatitude: "Blessed are they that hunger and thirst after *righteousness*, for they shall be filled." Furthermore, in the Eighth Beatitude: "Blessed are they that are persecuted for *righteousness* sake, for theirs is the kingdom of heaven." Such noble aspirations are clearly distinct from the more fanatical sense of righteousness promoted by radical groups such as the Pharisees. According to 2 Corinthians 6:7, St. Paul rejoices in salvation through the word of truth, the power of God, and the armor of *righteousness*: suggesting once again how truth mirrors righteousness on such a reciprocating scale of influence.

INNOCENCE

The remaining hierarchy of themes characterizing the counter double bind class of maneuvers is respectively specified as innocence, vindication, exoneration, and immaculateness. The first-mentioned theme of innocence derives from the Latin *innocens* from *in-* (not) and *nocére* (to do wrong to). This disqualified denial of guilt figures prominently in many religious symbolisms; namely, the lily, the dove, or a maiden draped in white. According to Christ's Sermon on the Mount, innocence is clearly implied in the Sixth Beatitude: "Blessed are the pure in heart: for they shall see God." Christ further celebrates the innocence of the "little children," for theirs is the Kingdom of Heaven. Indeed, the sacrificial lamb is the chief Christian symbolism for innocence offered-up in atonement for the sins of all mankind.

Although such youthful connotations are fairly commonplace, in a legal sense, innocence refers to a defense against the blameful quest for responsibility, reinterpreting the interaction in terms of a thoroughly disqualified perspective. The innocence expressed by the established personal authority figure effectively counteracts any blameful quest for responsibility on the part of the personal follower, similar to the interplay previously established for loyalty/humility. In this disqualified sense, the reluctant personal authority denies any complicity with regard to such a blameful quest for responsibility: acknowledging the follower's transitional style of tactic while subliminally disqualifying any willing participation therein.

VINDICATION

The personal prerequisites for innocence, in turn, extend to a group sphere of influence with respect to the group-directed theme of *vindication*. In a traditional sense, vindication is defined as the process of defending oneself against blameful charges levied by another, as in vindication before a panel of one's peers during a jury trial. The term derives from the Latin *vindicare*, from *vis-* (force) and *discere* (to say). True to its classical roots, vindication is essentially a verbally-focused perspective, where facts are presented in order to establish guilt or innocence as in a spirited courtroom defense.

Vindication, however, should not be confused with vindictiveness, a theme that similarly derives from the Latin *vindicare*, although alternately suggesting a darker focus on revenge or retribution. Although revenge might similarly emerge as a motivation in vindication, the distinction between vindication and vindictiveness parallels that distinguishing justice from vengeance. A plea for vindication predominates in a courtroom justice setting, whereas the crueler tendency towards vindictiveness circumvents the safeguards of the justice system. Consequently, the stirring court room assertion: "I will be vindicated," is clearly indicative of such a righteous mode; in essence, a disqualified form of counter double bind maneuver that plausibly denies any honorable sense of guilt on the part of the group authority figure (analogous to the scenario previously established for innocence). The group overtones typically associated with vindication certainly enjoy widespread civic appeal, particularly when vindication is pursued within the public eye for all the world to see.

EXONERATION

The preliminary sequence of innocence and vindication further extends to a universal sphere of influence with respect to the spiritually-focused theme of *exoneration*. Exoneration is defined as a freedom from burden or blame, as in a declaration of proof of innocence synonymous with acquittal. The term derives from the Latin *exonerare* from *ex-* (from) and *oneris* (burden). Here the stain of guilt is lifted, particularly when the burden of proof lies with the accuser. Exoneration is widely cited in a legal sense, as in designating a remedy in cases of financial inequity. It is also prominently invoked in criminal cases, extending the more limited theme of vindication into a much broader universal sphere of influence.

Whereas vindication implies an outward sense of clemency, exoneration alternately suggests a blanket sense of pardon or absolution. Consequently, exoneration sets a precedent within an international sphere of influence, effectively disqualifying any libertarian sense of honor therein. Although exoneration scarcely enjoys the pedigree or tradition of some of the other virtues within its class, it nevertheless fits quite nicely within the ascending hierarchy of innocence and vindication. In this expanded sense the vindicating sense of exoneration expressed by the spiritual authority figure effectively counteracts the dutiful quest for allegiance initiated by the spiritual disciple: a reciprocating interplay of terms (although in a thoroughly disqualified fashion).

IMMACULATENESS

The crowning humanitarian level ultimately calls into focus the supremely abstract theme of *immaculateness*. It is traditionally defined as a disqualified denial of any degree of fault or blame, a recurring theme in claims relating to divinity. Indeed, this enduring humanitarian perspective effectively complements the more positive prerequisites previously established for "grandeur." Although this theme of immaculateness is fairly specialized in a religious sense, it nevertheless represents the leading contender for completing the ascending hierarchy of innocence, vindication, and exoneration. It traditionally denotes a sense of purity without stain, primarily with respect to the evil effects of sin. The term derives from the Latin *immaculatus* from *in-* (not) and *macula* (spot). It is chiefly encountered in the Roman Catholic dogma of the Immaculate Conception, where the Virgin Mary is believed to have been conceived without the stain of Original Sin in preparation for the birth of the Christ Child.

Although no direct documentation for this belief exists in scriptural sources, Mary's sanctity and virginity is cited as an essential corollary for verifying the divinity of Christ. This theological assertion remained unchallenged until the Reformation when Catholic doctrines came under increasing scrutiny. In 1567, Pope Pius V rigorously defended Mary's immunity from sin at the moment of conception, accompanied by the establishment of the Feast of the Immaculate Conception. Protestant reformers, in turn, steadfastly rejected this dogma due to the manifest lack of any scriptural foundation.

Regardless of the individual traditions therein, the enduring theme of immaculateness effectively consummates the ascending hierarchy of innocence, vindication, and exoneration. Here, immaculateness formally preserves the inherent degree of disqualification witnessed in the preliminary sequence of terms, obliquely acknowledging the transitional sense of righteousness professed by the respective follower figure, although in a thoroughly disqualified fashion.

In conclusion, this preliminary description of the (initial) follower-based sequence for the lesser virtues (I) offers a thorough dynamical perspective on the sequential interplay of double bind and counter double bind maneuvers. The humorous overtones based upon the interplay of loyalty/humility, fidelity/majesty, and so on, come through the clearest when counteracting (in a disqualified fashion) the precipitating transitional overture. The related genre of the melodrama, in turn, targets the more sober aspects of the transitional realm; namely, the sequences based upon responsibility/innocence, duty/vindication, etc. Each genre necessarily incorporates aspects of both the humorous and the melodramatic traditions, providing an effective depiction of life ultimately dependent upon a continuous stream of transitions implicit to the vagaries of everyday existence.

11

THE PROCUREMENT-BASED REALM
FOR THE LESSER VIRTUES (I)

The completed description of the lesser virtues based upon loyalty/humility and responsibility/innocence, in turn, sets the stage for an examination of the remaining projected series of virtuous themes based upon procurement. According to the preceding chapter, both loyalty and responsibility represented transitional variations on the reinforcement perspectives of the personal follower figure, whereby prompting the disqualified humility-innocence perspectives of the personal authority in response. A similar pattern further holds true with respect to the transitional variations for discipline-modesty and vigilance-meekness. In direct contrast to the potential reinforcement expressed for loyalty/responsibility, discipline and vigilance represent a complementary procurement class of transitional maneuvers, directly expanding upon the more routine follower roles of solicitousness and submissiveness.

The general pattern of presentation for this latter class of lesser virtues (I) is similar to that which has gone before; namely, the four-part hierarchy of transitional follower themes will be described first, followed by the disqualified hierarchy of respective authority roles. Here, the preliminary double bind sequence of discipline-chivalry-nobility-zeal is described first, followed by the respective counter double bind sequence of modesty-chastity-purity-perfection. Furthermore, the remainder of the current chapter examines the related hierarchy of vigilance-courage-valor-triumph followed by meekness, obedience, conformity, and pacifism. The dedicated reader is encouraged to refer back to the four-page listing of schematic definitions for the lesser virtues (I) outlined in Chapter 9 providing a precise schematic representation of the motivational dynamics at issue in concert with the traditional narratives for each of the individual terms.

DISCIPLINE

The first-listed theme of *discipline* is broadly acknowledged as the quintessential personal follower perspective. The term derives from the Latin *disciplina*, from *discipulus* (disciple). Some authorities suggest a derivation from *discére* (to learn) akin to *docére* (to teach). Others cite a derivation from *dis-* (apart) and *capere* (to hold). In either case, the ability to hold on to the import of instruction is generally implied, as evident in the basic authority/disciple relationship. Discipline can span a rather broad range of meaning, such as in the administration of punishment or chastisement. In terms of the current discussion, the singular relevant connotation concerns that professed determination to act solicitously in anticipation of the rewarding reinforcement from one's personal authority figure (consistent with discipline's transitional basis within solicitude).

The disciplined individual solicitously acts to support the charismatic endeavors that are worthy of reinforcement by one's personal authority figure. Consequently, discipline represents a transitional form of approval seeking, playing up the reinforcement status of the established personal authority figure in anticipation of securing ongoing rewarding consideration. The personal authority rightfully is expected to desirously act rewardingly in return, although he/she might also modestly deny acting rewardingly: in essence, disqualifying willing participation within the entire transitional interchange. The typical authority/disciple relationship generally favors the more gracious response, at least under the most amenable of circumstances. Indeed, according to Albert Einstein: "When a man is sufficiently motivated, *discipline* will take care of itself."

CHIVALRY

The personal prerequisites for discipline, in turn, extend to a group sphere of influence with respect to the vital theme of *chivalry*. The "chivalrous" mounted-knight roams the countryside seeking meritorious deeds to challenge his training and mettle, particularly great acts of courtesy or courage. The term derives from the Old French *chevaler* (knight), from the Latin *cavallus* (horse): signifying the advantages of mounted warfare during the feudal period, in addition to the heraldic symbolisms associated with knightly courtesy. Hints of chivalry first date to the Roman province of Gaul, a region renowned for its strong reliance upon equine traditions. The prestige favoring cavalry over infantry endured through-out the Middle Ages, particularly when lengthy travels necessitated mounted units. Under the noble garb of religious zeal, the earliest orders of knighthood were instituted during the Crusades. For instance, the Templars (founded in 1118) were crusader-monks pledged to aid in the defense of pilgrims/clergy against the perils of the infidels.

The widely vaunted tales of gallantry and chivalry during the Crusades inspired the troubadour tradition of the 12th century, instilling a romanticized code of honor, courtesy, and chivalry. The golden age of chivalry peaked in the 14th century, when orders of the noblest rank were established: namely, the Order of the Garter in England and Order of the Star in France. These chivalrous orders reveled in the prestige of the royal court, particularly the arts of pageantry, gallantry, and courtliness. Courts of Chivalry, presided over by the royal family, known as *tournaments* featured jousting and duels for settling issues of honor.

The introduction of gunpowder eventually brought the age of chivalry to an end, although the symbolisms of heraldry have long endured. The latter further encompassed a basic code of chivalry, still celebrated as honor among gentleman, the noble obligations of military service, and courtesy towards women. The chivalrous sense of discipline expressed by the group representative solicitously anticipates a dignified sense of desire of the part of the established group authority figure. Consequently, through such a give-and-take dynamic, the group authority graciously is expected to reward the chivalrous-discipline potentially expressed by the group representative. Indeed, the solicitous cooperation of the chivalrous knight proves the key factor towards fulfilling the rigors characterizing the trials that characterize the entire transitional interchange.

NOBILITY

The group prerequisites for chivalry, in turn, extend to a universal sphere of influence with respect to the spiritual disciple theme of *nobility*. The term derives from Latin *nobilis* (well known) traditionally denoting high rank or excellence of character. Of similar derivation is the French expression *noblesse oblige;* namely, "rank imposes obligation" implying noble ancestry or bearing. Indeed, the notion of "nobility" specifies that body of aristocratic privilege comprising the ruling class of a particular province or state, as in the feudal system of lords/barons in concert with the rights and privileges that they command.

The symbolisms of nobility also appear larger than life: as in the gold, frankincense, and myrrh presented to the Christ Child by the Three Kings from the East. Indeed, the distinction of *noble* refers to precious metals such as gold and silver that are resistant to corrosive damage. Contrast this to the "base" metals; iron, copper, and tin: all of which are much more common in terms of functionality. Nobility refers to any distinction in terms of greatness: as apparent on the chessboard, where the back row of noblemen holds rank over the front row of lowly pawns. Such nobility, alone, possesses the regal bearing for determining the outcome of a chess match, much as similarly occurs over the great range of conflicts throughout recorded history.

The moral ramifications for nobility similarly stand out in this regard, as in the traits of magnificence or generosity towards others irrespective of noble bearing or standing. Nobility represents the formal transitional counterpart of the theological virtue of charity, sharing with the latter such a solicitously-disciplined status. In direct analogy to the group prerequisites for chivalry, nobility similarly respects the established order of the spiritual authority figure: whereby solicitously petitioning the rewarding consideration controlled by the latter. Consequently, nobility denotes a spiritually-refined sense of chivalrous-discipline in anticipation of the civilly-dignified treatment on the part of the spiritual authority figure. In this expanded sense, nobility aims towards lofty principles of virtually universal appeal, an overture the authority figure is all too willing to reciprocate.

ZEAL

The preceding trend towards "admirable works" ultimately culminates with respect to the crowning humanitarian theme of *zeal*. This term is traditionally defined as intense passion, ardor, or enthusiasm: a notion derived from the Latin *zelus* from the Greek *zelos* (to be hot, to bring to a boil). Symbolically, it signifies a high degree of emotional intensity for a particular cause or crusade. Although zeal generally connotes a virtuous quality, it can also be viewed pejoratively when the cause is judged to be less than admirable, such as when the religious zealot fanatically seeks to promulgate his chosen faith.

In a scriptural sense, this theme is most commonly associated with the Zealots: a Jewish nationalistic faction that sought to enforce strict observance of Mosaic Law. During the time of Christ, the Zealots zealously resisted the dominion of the Romans over the Jews. Citing scriptural and moral precedents, the Zealots insisted that they (as descendants of Abraham) should never be politically subjugated. The Zealots argued that insurgency was a religious duty, launching a crusade of virtually mythic proportions. Although open rebellion initially appeared risky, the goal of provoking resentment against the Roman yoke ultimately led to a nationwide insurrection circa 66 CE. Tragically, the rebellion eventually failed leading to the widespread destruction of the Jewish homeland.

In our modern media age, zeal is more generally defined as extreme enthusiasm or fervor in terms of religious devotion. The zealous individual stands apart from the ordinary devotee in terms of failing to feel content with routine ritual or devotion. This can further extend to an eagerness to administer charity towards others indicative of God's bountiful grace. Consequently, this noble sense of zeal represents a transitional variation on the more basic virtuous quality of goodness. It shares with nobility a focus on idealistic principles, although now extending to a crowning humanitarian perspective. The zealous individual chivalrously acts in a noble fashion in all endeavors in anticipation of the civilly magnanimous consideration of the established authority figure. Although this extreme level of abstraction formally works to obscure the fundamental dynamics at issue in terms of this level, the crowning humanitarian prerequisites associated with zeal are effectively seen to round-out the ascending pattern of subordinate (transitional) themes; namely, discipline, chivalry, nobility, and now, zeal.

MODESTY

The preliminary sequence of transitional virtuous themes based upon discipline, in turn, sets the stage for the remaining hierarchy of counter dou-ble bind maneuvers based upon *modesty*; namely, modesty, chastity, purity, and perfection. Modesty is often defined as a close moral synonym of humility, although primarily targeting a concerted sense of decency/decorum in matters of a sexual nature, such as conduct and/or attire. Modesty is symbolized across many cultures as a chastely-veiled maiden or virgin. Its modern spelling derives from the Latin *modestus*, from *modus* (measure): particularly the measure by which one judges a rightful course of action in terms of propriety.

The modest individual refuses to be swayed by the disciplined overtures of the personal follower figure, rather modestly denying any desirous complicity therein. The modest individual formally counters the determined sense of discipline expressed by the personal follower figure, subliminally disqualifying any overt cooperation in terms. This disqualified form of communication is particularly apparent in the standard situation comedy, where comic relief is achieved through a strategically timed display of modest abstinence; in essence, subliminally disqualifying the transitional nature of the entire transitional interchange. Hence, similar to its related counterpart in humility, modesty provides an effective strategy for politely circumventing the solicitous attentions from the personal follower figure without sacrificing any concomitant sense of dignity in the process.

CHASTITY

The personal prerequisites for modesty, in turn, extend to a group sphere of influence with respect to the affiliated theme of *chastity*. The term derives from the Latin *castus* (pure) in terms of taste, style, or refinement. Chastity is traditionally symbolized as the mythical unicorn or a virgin draped in white. According to legend, a unicorn can be summoned only by the chaste intentions of a virgin. In ancient Italian iconography, chastity is personified as a comely maiden holding a whip as if to chastise herself. She appears draped in a white robe adorned with a girdle inscribed with the Latin phrase: *"Castigo corpus meum"* (I chastise my body). Throughout the classical age an unmarried maiden was expected to be chaste, her virginity maximizing her marketability to prospective grooms. Chastity represents that rarest of all treasures, a jealously guarded gift given only once to the most deserving.

In a more contemporary sense, the chaste individual strives to abstain from sexual excess in order to realize a higher purpose. In some religious orders, chastity and celibacy are prescribed as functional requirements. In our modern permissive age, chastity is a virtue that sadly has decreased in stature, with many speculating that chastity is untenable or unnatural. Restoring chastity/abstinence to its original prestige entails a corresponding revival in terms, strengthening the willpower to overcome untimely temptation and negative peer-pressure. Consequently, in direct analogy to its overarching relationship to modesty, chastity politely rejects overtures of a transitional nature, whereby effectively disqualifying any willing complicity therein.

PURITY

In direct analogy to the group prerequisites for chastity, the spiritual theme of *purity* commands virtually universal respect in cultures from around the world. It is traditionally defined as the absence of stain, fault, or sin: a close synonym for chastity (although to a considerably more abstract degree). The term dates at least to classical times, deriving from the Latin *purus* (pure). Purity is traditionally symbolized as the color white, precious pearls, the Easter lily, or a dove/swan. Purity is also personified as a maiden draped in white, holding a tulip and scattering grain to a flock of white fowl. For obvious reasons, it figures prominently in virtually every religious tradition, particularly significant in both Old and New Testament scripture. Indeed, Christ specifically singles out purity as the theme for his Sixth Beatitude: "Blessed are the pure in heart for they shall see God." Christian purity celebrates abstinence and self-control as virtues next to Godliness. Although often equated with sexual purity, this theme can also denote a renunciation of worldly pursuits as well as the mortification of the senses, an exercise in self-control over the temptations of the material world. The path to purity, consequently, cleanses the heart and soul of all endeavors that fall short of such noble purpose.

Here, the spiritual overtones for purity come through the clearest, extending the group prerequisites for chastity into a universal sphere of influence. This "puritan" slant on morality has been celebrated across virtually all cultures, an ethical standard and inspiration for us all. In fitting response to the chivalrous sense of nobility expressed by the spiritual disciple figure, a chaste sense of purity is alternately expressed by the spiritual authority figure, its subliminal degree of disqualification providing a fitting moral counterpoint to the insistent quality of the initial double bind maneuver. Here purity remains a fitting aspiration to all but the most exceptional amongst us.

PERFECTION

The ascending hierarchy of virtuous themes based upon modesty ultimately culminates with respect to the crowning humanitarian theme of *perfection*, a supremely disqualified moral perspective exemplifying the very essence of chastity and purity. The term derives from the Latin *perfectus*, past participle of *perficere*, from *per-* (thoroughly) and *facere* (to do): namely, thorough in terms of moral excellence. As such, perfection represents the highest desired outcome achievable through a diligent pursuit of excellence. Consistent with its subordinate counterpart in purity, perfection shares many common symbolisms: including the color white, the circle (without beginning or end), and the lotus blossom (in the Oriental tradition).

Perfection is viewed as an enduring ideal often to be sought after, although scarcely achievable. Its truly effortless and disqualified nature directly expands (in a humanitarian sense) upon its more elementary foundations within chastity and purity. Perfection essentially represents a subjective standard that always eludes fruition, similar to an algebraic function that perpetually approaches a theoretical limit. Although the common maxim states: "no one is perfect," the true issue consists of determining how high the bar is to be set in the pursuit of excellence (within the limits of human perfectibility). This generally entails setting lofty (yet realistic) goals for personal performance, then working to consummate these standards through concerted effort and attention to detail.

VIGILANCE

The completed sequence of virtuous terms based upon discipline/modesty, in turn, sets the stage for the remaining transitional sequences based upon vigilance/meekness; namely, vigilance, courage, valor, and triumph, followed by meekness, obedience, conformity, and pacifism. The first mentioned theme of *vigilance* derives from the Latin *vigil* (awake, watchful), from *vigere* (to be lively). In classical mythology, this theme is traditionally symbolized by the all-seeing eye or a crowing cock. Vigilance imparts a more watchful tone to its related foundations in "concern" in terms of such apprehensive perspectives. Indeed, William Shakespeare playfully compares vigilance to "a cat out to steal cream" (Henry IV, Part 1).

The vigilante squads of the American West certainly attest to such a watchful focus, forever vigilant for wrongs to be righted. Vigilance effectively complements its respective counterpart in discipline, although now targeting a more serious range of themes. Through the aid of this transitional perspective, the personal follower submissively professes his vigilant focus in anticipation of securing a worrisomely-lenient treatment on the part of the established authority figure. In this reciprocating fashion, the personal authority worrisomely acknowledges the vigilant concerns of the personal follower figure, providing a fitting motivational counterpoint to dynamics of the entire transitional interchange.

COURAGE

The personal prerequisites for vigilance, in turn, extend to a group sphere of influence with respect to the *courageous* dictates expressed by the group representative. Here, the affiliated follower theme of chivalry is respectively modified to reflect the more militaristic overtones for courage under fire: defined as meeting danger without surrendering to fear (consistent with bravery or fortitude). The term derives from the Latin *cor* (heart); in essence, to take heart and persevere bravely. According to the precepts of medieval heraldry, courage is symbolized as a regal lion or a fierce mastiff, both instilled with strong social instincts consistent with a military *esprit de corps*. In contrast, the symbolisms relating to cowardice depict a cowering canine with its tail tucked nervously between its haunches.

Courage represents a key core virtue that focuses upon preserving security and the common good. Indeed, courage cannot stand alone without the good intentions to provide coherent direction. Such good intentions require the courage to strengthen the will in a determined will to succeed. True courage encompasses a faith in one's acquired skills or inner resources for meeting the most intimidating challenges or daunting obstacles. Physical courage ignores the risk of death or serious injury for sake of the public good, a hallmark of community self-sacrifice. Indwelling prudence further helps to avert rash or impulsive action. While it might seem natural to feel a sense of dread under aversive circumstances, courage faces fear through perseverance in order to fulfill quite noble aims.

Courage represents the mean value interposed between the extremes of rashness (the realm of excess) and cowardice (the domain of defect). Rash or reckless behavior ignores realistic limitations, a travesty in relation to true courage. True courage entails the skills for developing realistic risk assessments in order to circumvent unintended harmful consequences. Furthermore, the beneficial outcome must be worth the risk and required effort. In essence, the courageous individual strives for the golden mean positioned between the extremes of rashness and cowardice in order to achieve the optimal outcome, whereby avoiding disaster or shirking of responsibility. Here, the courageous sense of vigilance expressed by the group representative submissively anticipates the worrisome sense of integrity actively professed by the established group authority figure. Consequently, through such a reciprocal range of interplay, the group authority figure worrisomely acts with integrity in response to the vigilant sense of courage expressed (in an aversive fashion) by the group representative.

VALOR

The group prerequisites for courage, in turn, extend to a universal sphere of influence with respect to the spiritual disciple theme of *valor*. The term derives from the Latin *valere* (to be strong) as in a stout heart or intrepid daring. Valor shares common aspects with courage or bravery, although effectively imparting a more pronounced cachet of universal character. In the traditions of Italian iconography, valor is symbolized as a handsome youth in golden garb holding a scepter and a laurel wreath (signifying noble bearing and prowess). He is further represented stroking the mane of a serene lion in repose at his feet in a stately pose of valor.

The truest expression of valor, however, is embodied in the valiant exploits of the medieval knight in strict adherence to the codes of chivalry and nobility. The fictional protagonist, Prince Valiant, endeavors to aid the damsel in distress from the perils of the fire-breathing dragon, a valorous theme of virtually universal appeal. Indeed, valor (even more than courage) implies an adherence to such high-minded ideals, as initially undertaken during the Crusades. Here, the goal of liberating the Holy Land transcended any conflicting partisan concerns therein. In such a valiant fashion, the knights of the realm rode together united by the common crusader code, although their modest military gains could not be sustained despite their valorous quest for glory.

Valor certainly proves a fitting adjunct to the preliminary sequence of vigilance and courage, although now reflecting a more advanced spiritual focus within such a militaristic context. Indeed, the courageous sense of valor expressed by the spiritual disciple, in turn, anticipates the austere sense of integrity professed by the spiritual authority figure. The valiant individual is governed primarily by motives of a morally-abstract nature, similar to that previously established with respect to the affiliated notion of nobility. Accordingly, valor continues to remain a prized quality within the military tradition, that rare quality that medals or commendations can only scarcely serve to convey.

TRIUMPH

The ascending follower sequence of vigilance, courage, and valor ultimately culminates with respect to the more enduring humanitarian theme of *triumph*. This theme is particularly evident in the many great triumphal arches erected down through the ages. It is traditionally defined as a victorious celebration invoking pomp and circumstance in a jubilant display of exultation. The term derives from the Latin *triumphus* from the Greek *thriambos*: a hymn originally sung to Bacchus (the god of wine). These bacchanal rituals were primarily characterized through gross inebriation, orgiastic experimentation, and wild revelry: aspects that carried over to the Roman tradition of revelry in victory celebrations.

In the Roman world, the triumph was revered as a sacred procession honoring a returning victorious general culminating in a sacrifice to Jupiter on the Capital Mount. The triumph reenacts the solemn ceremony of thanksgiving invoked for victory while abroad. The triumphant general rides before the assembled masses in an ornate chariot drawn by a team of four horses. He wears an embroidered toga and an ornate crown, holding a scepter in one hand and a spray of laurel leaves in the other. A slave by his side constantly repeats the chant *Hominem te momento* (in remembrance of him). Ahead in the procession march the victorious troops, prisoners in chains, the spoils of war, as well as a team of white oxen for sacrifice to Zeus. A laurel victory wreath is draped across the statue of Zeus upon completion of the final climactic sacrifice to the god. This victory for the empire was invested with the grandest of humanitarian standards, a solemn devotional effectively insuring the potential for further such victorious campaigns.

During the subsequent Christian era, various aspects of the pagan ritual were borrowed to express Christian ideals. The *triumphus* and the *triumphare* signify the Church's victory over evil and miraculous establishment. Over the course of centuries, the Church eventually celebrated an indwelling spirit of *triumphalism*; namely, that tendency to view the Church as an indefatigable force for goodness and fully deserving of univer-

sal appeal. This enduring humanitarian focus for triumph effectively expands upon its subordinate concepts of courage and valor. Consequently, triumph primarily represents (in a transitional sense) the decent sense of wisdom potentially professed by the humanitarian follower figure. This places the triumphant party in a position of great power, as when the victorious general swears obeisance prior to the divine sacrifice awaiting at the end of the procession. This enduring transitional interplay of humanitarian perspectives proves particularly telling at this juncture, the general reveling in his triumphant victory as one destined for respect across all ages and times.

MEEKNESS

The completed description of the transitional sequence of themes based upon vigilance, in turn, invites further comparisons to the remaining counter double bind class of maneuvers based upon meekness; namely, meekness, obedience, conformity, and pacifism. The first-mentioned theme of *meekness* derives from the Old Norse *mjurk* or *miurk* (denoting gentleness). It defines a genteel demeanor consistent with the extreme degree of disqualification characterizing such an unobtrusive temperament. Meekness represents a prominent theme for spiritual leaders the world over: including Christ, Mohammed, Buddha, etc. Christ's Third Beatitude directly states: "Blessed are the meek, for they shall inherit the earth." His related (although somewhat idealistic) admonition to "turn the other cheek" when struck takes this disqualified trend to its extreme, with meekness equating to extreme vulnerability.

Christ certainly appears well versed in this disqualified style of communication, as further reflected in his other beatitudes relating to humility and innocence. Communication Theorist, Jay Haley (1989) addresses this issue in much greater detail in his treatise: *The Power Tactics of Jesus Christ and Other Essays*. According to this disqualified style of interaction, the meekly disqualified sense of leniency expressed by the personal authority figure effectively sidesteps the vigilant sense of submissiveness expressed by the personal follower. Meekness, therefore, parallels the pattern previously established for modesty, although leniency is now subliminally disqualified, rather than that relating to rewards

OBEDIENCE

The personal prerequisites for meekness, in turn, extend to a group sphere of influence with respect to the group authority theme of *obedience*. Obedience traditionally denotes a sense of compliance or dutiful submission to the will of another. The term derives from the Latin *obedientia*, present participle of *obedire*, from *ob-* (towards) and *audire* (to hear). Indeed, in this most basic sense, to hear *is* to obey in terms the strictures of such an authoritarian perspective. In early Italian iconography, obedience is personified as a pious virgin submitting to a yoke lowered onto her by an angel. Any doctrine of absolute obedience presupposes such a curious interplay of authority and follower roles. Indeed, one is always free to obey (or disobey) but never to outwardly question the reason why. Ironically the more rigorous the demands for obedience, the more dogmatic its underlying precepts, and more obscure the rationale to the obedient party. This often leads to capricious demands for unqualified obedience, or feelings of complete indifference on the part of the authority figure.

Motives for obedience vary widely, as in fear of authority, anticipation of reward, or trust in the law. True to its origins within Old Testament scripture, the Christian tradition similarly preserves a strong authoritarian bent. Christ actually advocates a rational interpretation of the law as reflected in his outspoken conflicts with the religious authorities of his day. Indeed, in the process of becoming widely established, Christianity found itself heir to many of the doctrinal and dogmatic dictates endemic to the prevailing Roman culture of its day.

This authoritarian perspective was preserved throughout the Middle Ages, when the ideals of poverty, chastity, and obedience were instituted as monastic vows for the religious orders of the day. Obedience was crucial to the stability of monastic communities, where unqualified submission to the will of the superior was a religious obligation. A key official within the medieval monastery was the Obedientiary, a position appointed by the Abbott in the service of his unquestioned authority. Through such an unswerving devotion to obedience, the free will of the obedient party is subliminally disqualified similar to that encountered within a military context, where responsibility rolls downhill through the convoluted chain of command.

In line with the pattern previously established for meekness, the obedient party meekly denies acting conformingly without necessarily appearing to have done so, invoking a subliminal form of (disqualified) counter double bind maneuver. The obedient individual effectively sidesteps the insistent quality of the "courage" perspective expressed by the group representative, claiming only to obey and therefore not a willing participant within the entire transitional interchange. Consequently, obedience extends the more limited (personal) focus of meekness into a much broader group-focused domain, a critical feature to the smooth functioning of society as a whole.

CONFORMITY

The group prerequisites for obedience, in turn, extend to a universal degree of influence with respect to the spiritually-focused theme of *conformity*. It is traditionally defined as a sense of harmony or agreement with respect to law, fashion, or custom. The term derives from the Latin *conformare*, from *con-* (from) and *formare* (to form), a compound structure suggesting agreement or concordance. It can also imply compliance to a pre-existing social order, particularly with respect to the Church of England (in keeping with such a universal focus). Indeed, conformity can encompass a rather broad range of meanings, such as the geological connotation of an uninterrupted sequence of strata over an extended formative time-scale. According to Sir Isaac Newton, "Nature is very consonant and *conformable* with herself." (Optiks, 1730).

Although conformity scarcely enjoys the tradition or prestige of many of the other virtues within its class, it, nevertheless, continues in the tradition of the ascending sequence previously established for meekness and obedience. Consequently, this universal focus for conformity clearly fulfills the global mandates for the term, as its general applications to science and geology effectively serve to indicate. Here, conformity represents a disqualified form of counter double bind maneuver, effectively sidestepping (through an appeal to conformity) the insistent quality of the brave sense of valor expressed by the spiritual disciple figure. In terms of this reciprocating motivational interplay, one's conforming compliance is chalked-up to the dictates of convention, rather than any volitional agreement in terms. Through this subliminal sense of disqualification, the spiritual authority effectively reciprocates his expected role within the transitional interchange, although in a thoroughly nonconfrontational fashion.

PACIFISM

The universal prerequisites for conformity, in turn, extend to a humanitarian sphere of influence with respect to the overarching theme of *pacifism.* Pacifism denotes moral opposition to war and conflict, a term deriving from the Latin *pacificus*, from *pax* (peace) and *facere* (to make). It rules out any involvement with war or belligerence consistent with Christian principles of universal love and acceptance. It also condemns passions conducive to war in favor of nonviolent resistance (as in turning the other cheek). For early Christians, the prohibition against military service was couched in terms of a similar ban against participation in pagan rites of warfare (such as the Triumph). Furthermore, the Roman military oath conflicted with the pledge of supreme devotion to the Christian God. The most damning sphere of conflict, however, concerns the bloodlust specific to warfare, a factor antithetical to Christianity regardless of the noble aspirations therein. Indeed, during the early days of the Church, soldiers were excluded from the Lord's Table until earnest penance had been offered for the blood that had been shed upon the battlefield.

This Christian interpretation of pacifism was by no means universal, particularly following the fall of the Western Roman Empire. Amazingly, the idealistic principles underpinning pacifism persisted even through the militaristic focus of the Middle Ages. This theme has undergone a dramatic revival in modern times through the principles of nonviolent resistance professed by Mohandas Gandhi during India's struggle for independence. Here, pacifism represents a counter double

bind class of power maneuver, continuing in the tradition of meekness, obedience, and conformity. It represents a thoroughly disqualified expression of austere-equanimity without admitting to any volitional compliance therein. Through this strident appeal to pacifism, the pacifist echoes an enduring sense of conventionality only previously hinted at with respect to conformity, as well as a communal sense of duty initially cited for obedience. Consequently, pacifism appeals to an enduring humanitarian sphere of influence, where the reluctant humanitarian authority figure effectively sidesteps the insistent quality of the triumphalism professed by the respective follower figure: effectively presenting an air of peaceful appeasement while simultaneously disqualifying any willing participation therein.

In summary, the completed description of the procurement-based variations for the lesser virtues (I) provides a fitting counterpoint to the reinforcement-based versions previously described in Chapter *10*. In all honesty, both transitional variations emerge as essential aspects of a variable social environment, where the future inevitably trends over into the present in a recursive style of process. A similar reciprocating style of motivational dynamic is further encountered with respect to the upcoming examination of the lesser virtues (II), although a strict reversal in terms of the ordering of the authority and follower roles permits many interesting insights into the dynamics governing the transitional format in general.

12

THE AUTHORITY-BASED REALM
FOR THE LESSER VIRTUES (II)

The completed description of the lesser virtues (I) provides an introductory model for the transitional dynamics underlying this prototype class of virtuous maneuvers. This grand scale correspondence, in turn, raises the issue of the potential for additional variations upon this basic transitional format. Indeed, even a cursory survey of the ethical literature reveals a number of additional groupings of virtuous terms essentially unaccounted for in terms of the current transitional system of the lesser virtues.

For the lesser virtues (I) the (projected) future-directed time-frame specific to the follower role formally initiates the transitional interchange, further anticipating the participation of the established authority figure within an immediately active time-frame. The authority figure can either accept this role as presented, or disqualify it altogether through a humorous style of counter double bind maneuver. This necessarily leaves open the further speculation that this two-stage sequence of roles might potentially be reversed; namely, the immediately-active authority roles are expressed first; followed, in turn, by the (disqualified) future-directed time-frame specified for the respective follower roles: the precise pattern anticipated for the lesser virtues (II).

In terms of this additional class of lesser virtues (II), the newly transitioned authority role (by definition) now maneuvers from an immediately-active perspective in anticipation of the future-directed potentiality characterizing the follower role. This transitional dynamic contrasts with the lesser virtues (I), where the follower figure initially employed a future-directed time-frame in anticipation of the immediately-active authority role. This reciprocating style of role-reversal is formally predicated, being that the authority/follower roles within the transitional interaction should be of like status; e.g., personal authority and personal follower, group authority and group representative, etc.: in reference to the interplay of double bind and counter double bind maneuvers.

This dual variation in terms of the (initial) authority/follower perspectives suggests a number of key distinctions with respect to the dynamics governing the lesser virtues (I) and (II). The lesser virtues (I) are typically assigned top billing, being that the initial double bind maneuver reverses the active-then-potential polarity previously observed for the main conditioned sequence. The lesser virtues (II), in contrast, invoke the (standard) transitional sequence of active-then-potential roles: invoking a more confusing transitional dynamic, as the less prestigious range of ethical traditions further serves to indicate.

This reversed pattern of organization, in turn, predicts the existence of an entirely new class of ethical terms specified for the lesser virtues (II), distinguished in terms of the respective ordering of active-then-projected roles. This circumstance directly contrasts with the lesser virtues (I), where the sequential ordering is effectively reversed. Consequently, the lesser virtues (II) scarcely enjoy the pedigree or tradition previously established for the lesser virtues (I). The lesser virtues (II), nevertheless, offer a broad range of ethical applications, as schematically depicted in **Fig. 12**, as well the compact table below.

Self-Esteem → Reverence Apology → Clemency
Pomp → Veneration   Rectitude → Pardon
Sanctity → Homage   Penitence → Absolution
Dominion→ Benediction Contrition→ Deliverance

Congeniality → Concession Sympathy → Appease.
Cordiality→ Indulgence Compassion → Conciliate
Hospitality→ Gratitude Mercy → Accommodation
Altruism→ Goodwill   Sacrifice → Forgiveness

It proves a fitting tribute to the extensive scope of the English language that the predicted comple-

210	**211**
Self-Esteem	Apology
212	**213**
Congeniality	Sympathy

TRANSITIONAL
EGO STATES
(PA - Double-Bind)

→

220.1	**221.1**
Reverence	Clemency
222.1	**223.1**
Concession	Appeasement

DISQUALIFIED
ALTER EGO STATES
(PF - Counter-Double-Bind)

230	**231**
Pomp	Rectitude
232	**233**
Cordiality	Compassion

TRANSITIONAL
PERSONAL IDEALS
(GA - Double-Bind)

→

240.1	**241.1**
Veneration	Pardon
242.1	**243.1**
Indulgence	Conciliation

DISQUALIFIED
CARDINAL VIRTUES
(GR - Counter Double-Bind)

250	**251**
Sanctity	Penitence
252	**253**
Hospitality	Mercy

TRANSITIONAL
CIVIL LIBERTIES
(SA - Double-Bind)

→

260.1	**261.1**
Homage	Absolution
262.1	**263.1**
Gratitude	Accommodation

DISQUALIFIED
THEOLOGICAL VIRTUES
(SD - Counter Double-Bind)

270	**271**
Dominion	Contrition
272	**273**
Goodwill	Forgiveness

TRANSITIONAL
ECUMENICAL IDEALS
(HA - Double-Bind)

→

280.1	**281.1**
Benediction	Deliverance
282.1	**283.1**
Altruism	Sacrifice

DISQUALIFIED
GREEK VALUES
(RH - Counter Double-Bind)

Fig. 12 – The Lesser Virtues - (II)

ment of lesser virtues (II) corresponds so convincingly to the specifics predicted for this additional transitional class of terms. Consequently, a clearer understanding of the dual interplay of authority/follower roles (denoted by the arrow notation in **Fig. 12**) proves crucial towards clarifying the interplay of double bind and counter double bind maneuvers. For example, the nostalgic sense of self-esteem (immediately expressed by the personal authority figure), in turn, anticipates the projected reverential treatment of the established follower figure (in a disqualified expression of approval). Similarly, the apologetic sense of guilt (expressed by the personal authority figure) prompts a disqualified sense of clemency on the part of the personal follower. Furthermore, the personal authority's immediate congeniality maneuver anticipates a projected sense of concession on the part of the personal follower figure. Similarly, sympathetic behavior anticipates a disqualified expression of appeasement.

This dual interplay of double bind and counter double bind maneuvers (in relation to the personal authority level), in turn, serves as the elementary foundation for the ascending hierarchy of group, spiritual, and humanitarian levels: as collectively depicted in **Fig. 12**. For instance, the initial double bind sequence of self-esteem-pomp-sanctity-dominion further sets the stage for the remaining counter double bind sequence of reverence-veneration-homage-benediction. The related authority sequence of apology, rectitude, penitence, and contrition, in turn, anticipates the remaining follower hierarchy of clemency-pardon-absolution-deliverance.

A similar pattern further holds true for the remaining reinforcement-based sequences of terms based upon congeniality/concession and sympathy/appeasement. For instance, the initial authority hierarchy of congeniality, cordiality, hospitality, and altruism further anticipates the projected follower sequence of concession-indulgence-gratitude-goodwill. Furthermore, the affiliated authority sequence of sympathy-compassion-mercy-forgiveness, in turn, prompts the disqualified follower sequence of appeasement, conciliation, accommodation, and sacrifice.

On one final note, it further proves effective to incorporate these individual classifications for the lesser virtues (II) directly into the schematic definition format, providing a clear indication of the motivational dynamics at issue across the entire virtuous hierarchy. The complete four-part listing of definitions for the lesser virtues (II) is formally listed in **Tables E-1** to **E-4**. This schematic definition format is identical in form and function to that previously established for the lesser virtues (I), although the specific order of the authority/follower roles is effectively reversed. For the lesser virtues (II), the authority roles represent the active transitional initiation point, further anticipating the projected follower hierarchy of counter double bind maneuvers. This reverses the pattern previously established for the lesser virtues (I), where the follower roles were specified for such an initiatory status.

This dual interplay of double bind and counter double bind maneuvers remains a focus of consistency irrespective of whether the authority or follower roles are specified first. Consequently the remainder of the current chapter examines the procurement-based sequences of self-esteem-reverence and apology-clemency. This systematic analysis continues in Chapter *13* with respect to the reinforcement-based sequences of the lesser virtues (II) based upon congeniality-concession and sympathy-appeasement. The remaining Chapter *14* rounds-out this discussion with respect to the affiliated issue of the *accessory* variations for both classes of lesser virtues, allowing for crucial empathic insights into the transitional realm. The discerning reader is encouraged to refer back to the four-table listings of schematic definitions throughout the remainder of this section, whereby highlighting the formal dynamics at issue for each individual term.

SELF- ESTEEM

The first listed theme of *self-esteem* is formally defined as the chief transitional counterpart of a nostalgic sense of solicitousness. The term represents a compound of two basic themes, the Old English *seolf* (one's individual persona) and Middle French *estimer*, from the Latin *æstimare* (to value, to appraise). The modern sense of self-esteem was initially popularized through the pseudo-science of phrenology, assigning self-esteem a "bump" on the contours of the skull circa 1815. Beginning in the early 1980's, self-esteem emerged as a popular "buzz-word" for resolving personal/societal problems. Many authorities assumed that instilling high self-esteem could be a panacea for the ills of substance abuse, violent crime, sexual irresponsibility, etc. This interpretation implies that self-esteem is a causative factor in positive personal development rather than simply an emotional indicator of self-satisfaction in one's personal achievements.

Valid self-esteem involves making good choices aimed at achieving worthy goals. In contrast, pseudo self-esteem is defined as feeling

SELF-ESTEEM	REVERENCE
Previously, you (as personal follower) have rewardingly acted approvingly in response to the nostalgic treatment of the personal authority. But now, I (as new personal authority) will nostalgically act with *self-esteem* towards you: in anticipation of your (as established PF) approving treatment of me.	Previously, I (as new personal authority) have nostalgically acted with self-esteem towards you: in anticipation of your (as established PF) approving treatment of me. But now, you (as reluctant personal follower) will *reverently* deny acting approvingly towards me: thwarting my (as new PA) nostalgic sense of self-esteem.
POMP	**VENERATION**
Previously, you (as group representative) have prudently acted rewardingly towards me in response to the gloriously-nostalgic treatment of the group authority. But now, I (as new group authority) will *pompously* act with self-esteem towards you: in anticipation of your (as established GR) prudent-worship of me.	Previously, I (as new group authority) have pompously acted with self-esteem towards you: in anticipation of your (as established GR) prudent-worship of me. But now, you (as reluctant group representative) will reverently act in a *venerable* fashion towards me: thwarting my (as new GA) pompous treatment of you.
SANCTITY	**HOMAGE**
Previously, you (as spiritual disciple) have prudently acted in a faithful fashion in response to the gloriously-provident treatment of the spiritual authority. But now, I (as new spiritual authority) will pompously act in a *sanctified* fashion towards you: in anticipation of your (as established SD) prudent-faith in me.	Previously, I (as new spiritual authority) have pompously acted in a sanctified fashion towards you: in anticipation of your (as established SD) prudent-faith in me. But now, you (as reluctant spiritual disciple) will venerably express *homage* towards me: thwarting my (as new SA) sanctified treatment of you.
DOMINION	**BENEDICTION**
Previously, you (as representative member of humanity) have beauteously acted faithfully in response to the provident sense of gracefulness of the humanitarian authority. But now, I (as new humanitarian authority) will sanctifiedly express a sense of *dominion* towards you: in anticipation of your (as established RH) beauteous-faith in me.	Previously, I (as new humanitarian authority) have sanctifiedly expressed a sense of dominion towards you: in anticipation of your (as established RH) beauteous-faith in me. But now, you (as reluctant representative member of humanity) will homagefully express *benediction* towards me: thwarting my (as new HA) sanctified sense of dominion.

Table E-1 – The Definitions Based Upon Self-Esteem/Reverence

APOLOGY	CLEMENCY
Previously, you (as personal follower) have acted in a lenient fashion in response to the guilty treatment of the personal authority. But now, I (as new personal authority) will guiltily act in an *apologetic* fashion towards you: in anticipation of your (as established PF) lenient treatment of me.	Previously, I (as new personal authority) have guiltily acted in an apologetic fashion towards you: in anticipation of your (as established PF) lenient treatment of me. But now, you (as reluctant personal follower) will *clemently* deny acting leniently towards me: thwarting my (as new PA) apologetic treatment of you.
RECTITUDE	**PARDON**
Previously, you (as group representative) have leniently acted in a just fashion in response to the honorable sense of guilt of the group authority. But now, I (as new group authority) will apologetically act in a *rectitudinous* fashion towards you: in anticipation of your (as established GR) leniently-just treatment of me.	Previously, I (as new group authority) have apologetically acted in a rectitudinous fashion towards you: in anticipation of your (as established GR) leniently-just treatment of me. But now, you (as reluctant group representative) will clemently-*pardon* me: thwarting my (as new GA) apologetic sense of rectitude.
PENITENCE	**ABSOLUTION**
Previously, you (as spiritual disciple) have leniently-hoped for justice in response to the libertarian sense of honor of the spiritual authority. But now, I (as new spiritual authority) will *penitently* act in a rectitudinous fashion towards you: in anticipation of your (as established SD) lenient-hope for justice.	Previously, I (as new spiritual authority) have penitently acted in a rectitudinous fashion towards you: in anticipation of your (as established SD) lenient-hope for justice. But now, you (as reluctant spiritual disciple) will pardoningly express *absolution* towards me: thwarting my (as new SA) penitent treatment of you.
CONTRITION	**DELIVERANCE**
Previously, you (as representative member of humanity) have justly hoped for the truth in response to the libertarian sense of free will of the humanitarian authority. But now, I (as new humanitarian authority) will penitently act in a *contrite* fashion towards you: in anticipation of your (as established RH) just-hope for the truth.	Previously, I (as new humanitarian authority) have penitently acted in a contrite fashion towards you: in anticipation of your (as established RH) just-hope for the truth. But now, you (as reluctant representative member of humanity) will absolvingly act with *deliverance* towards me: thwarting my (as new HA) penitent sense of contrition.

Table E-2 – The Definitions Based Upon Apology/Clemency

CONGENIALITY	CONCESSION
Previously, I (as personal follower) have approachfully acted in a solicitous fashion in response to the desirous treatment of the personal authority. But now, you (as new personal authority) will *congenially* act in a desirous fashion towards me: in anticipation of my (as established PF) solicitous treatment of you.	Previously, you (as new personal authority) have congenially acted in a desirous fashion towards me: in anticipation of my (as established PF) solicitous treatment of you. But now, I (as reluctant personal follower) will *concessionally* deny acting solicitously towards you: thwarting your (as new PA) congenial treatment of me.
CORDIALITY	**INDULGENCE**
Previously, I (as group representative) have temperately acted in a solicitous fashion in response to the dignified-desire of the group authority. But now, you (as new group authority) will congenially act in a *cordial* fashion towards me: in anticipation of my (as established GR) temperately-solicitous treatment of you.	Previously, you (as new group authority) have congenially acted cordially towards me: in anticipation of my (as established GR) temperately-solicitous treatment of you. But now, I (as reluctant group representative) will concessionally act in an *indulgent* fashion towards you: thwarting your (as new GA) cordial treatment of me.
HOSPITALITY	**GRATITUDE**
Previously, I (as spiritual disciple) have temperately acted in a charitable fashion in response to the civilly-dignified treatment of the spiritual authority. But now, you (as new spiritual authority) will cordially act in a *hospitable* fashion towards me: in anticipation of my (as established SD) charitable treatment of you.	Previously, you (as new spiritual authority) have cordially acted in a hospitable fashion towards me: in anticipation of my (as established SD) charitable treatment of you. But now, I (as reluctant spiritual disciple) will indulgently act with *gratitude* towards you: thwarting your (as new SA) cordial sense of hospitality.
ALTRUISM	**GOODWILL**
Previously, I (as representative member of humanity) have charitably acted with goodness in response to the civilly-magnanimous treatment of the humanitarian authority. But now, you (as new humanitarian authority) will hospitably act in an *altruistic* fashion towards me: in anticipation of my (as established RH) charitable sense of goodness.	Previously, you (as new humanitarian authority) have hospitably acted altruistically towards me: in anticipation of my (as established RH) charitable sense of goodness. But now, I (as reluctant representative member of humanity) will gratefully act with *goodwill* towards you: thwarting your (as new HA) hospitable sense of altruism.

Table E-3 – The Definitions Based on Congeniality/Concession

SYMPATHY	APPEASEMENT
Previously, I (as personal follower) have submissively acted aversively in response to the worrisome treatment of the personal authority. But now, you (as new personal authority) will worrisomely act in a *sympathetic* fashion towards me: in anticipation of my (as established PF) submissive treatment of you.	Previously, you (as new personal authority) have worrisomely acted sympathetically towards me: in anticipation of my (as established PF) submissive treatment of you. But now, I (as reluctant personal follower) will *appeasingly* deny acting submissively towards you: thwarting your (as new PA) sympathetic treatment of me.
COMPASSION	**CONCILIATION**
Previously, I (as group representative) have fortitudinously acted submissively in response to the worrisome sense of integrity of the group authority. But now, you (as new group authority) will sympathetically act *compassionately* towards me: in anticipation of my (as established GR) fortitudinous treatment of you.	Previously, you (as new group authority) have sympathetically acted compassionately towards me: in anticipation of my (as established GR) fortitudinous treatment of you. But now, I (as reluctant group representative) will appeasingly act in a *conciliatory* fashion towards you: thwarting your (as new GA) compassionate treatment of me.
MERCY	**ACCOMMODATION**
Previously, I (as spiritual disciple) have fortitudinously acted in a decent fashion in response to the austere sense of integrity of the spiritual authority. But now, you (as new spiritual authority) will compassionately act in a *merciful* fashion towards me: in anticipation of my (as established SD) decent treatment of you.	Previously, you (as new spiritual authority) have compassionately acted in a merciful fashion towards me: in anticipation of my (as established SD) decent treatment of you. But now, I (as reluctant spiritual disciple) will conciliatorily act in an *accommodating* fashion towards you: thwarting your (as new SA) merciful sense of compassion.
FORGIVENESS	**SACRIFICE**
Previously, I (as representative member of humanity) have decently acted in a wise fashion in response to the austere sense of equanimity of the humanitarian authority. But now, you (as new humanitarian authority) will mercifully act in a *forgiving* fashion towards me: in anticipation of my (as established RH) decent sense of wisdom.	Previously, you (as new humanitarian authority) have mercifully acted in a forgiving fashion towards me: in anticipation of my (as established RH) decent sense of wisdom. But now, I (as reluctant represent. member of humanity) will accommodatingly act in a *sacrificial* fashion towards you: thwarting your (as new HA) forgiving treatment of me.

Table E-4 – The Definitions Based on Sympathy/Appeasement

good about oneself simply because an outside authority says so, even in the absence of any independent corroborating evidence. Although valid self-esteem can fluctuate widely under variable circumstances (particularly with respect to external criticism), honest self-evaluation tends to smooth out such radical mood-swings, whereby restoring confidence and a positive outlook. As such, self-esteem formally fulfills the specifics established for the transitional class of power maneuvers; namely, the personal authority figure's nostalgic expression of solicitousness anticipates a projected sense of approval on the part of the established follower figure. By resorting to such a transitional perspective, the personal authority's concerted efforts to achieve positive reinforcement are dramatically increased in terms of such an ongoing style of verbal interaction.

POMP

The personal prerequisites for self-esteem, in turn, extend to the civic sphere of influence with respect to the group-focused theme of *pomp*. Here, the newly involved group authority figure gloriously acts pompously in anticipation of a (projected) prudent sense of approval on the part of the established group representative. This exaggerated sense of pomposity further expands upon the personal characteristics previously established for self-esteem. Pomp is traditionally defined as a splendid or ostentatious display of fame or renown, often with overtones of solemn self-importance. The term derives from the Latin *pompa* (procession, pomp) from the Greek *pompe* (solemn procession), from the Greek *pempein* (to send). It is sometimes employed in derogatory sense with respect to ostentatious excess or vain showiness.

Nowhere is this expression of ostentation more readily apparent than in the vanities associated with military conquest. William Shakespeare's character Othello fittingly states: "The royal banner and all quality, pride, *pomp*, and circumstance of glorious war!" (Act III: Scene 3). Furthermore, English general Edward Elgar chose to designate his renown series of military marches "pomp and circumstance" in reference to the showy rituals accompanying such grand military displays of excellence.

This emphasis on pomp and pageantry similarly extends to the intrigues of the royal court, where ceremonial burdens invoke deference as well as pomp and majesty. As such, the expansive nature of pomposity certainly fits the prerequisites initially established for the transitional

class of power maneuvers. The newly professed group authority figure pompously acts with extreme self-esteem in anticipation of eliciting the prudent-approval on the part of the established group representative. This transitional quality of "pompousness" definitely enhances the chances of gaining the attention of the established follower figure, an interplay that generally tends to mutually benefit both parties in the verbal interaction.

SANCTITY

The ascending transitional sequence of self-esteem and pomp, in turn, extends to a universal sphere of influence with respect to the spiritually-focused theme of *sanctity*. The term derives from the Latin *sanctificare* from *sanctus* (sacred) and *facere* (to make). It is traditionally defined as moral perfection of a divine nature such as ascribed to a deity. It denotes a sense of sacredness or holiness particularly in terms of religious duty or taking an oath or vow. In the Roman Catholic tradition, sanctity is particularly revered in reference to the saints and martyrs, whose lives were esteemed as paragons of virtue and holiness. Indeed, the sanctity of God's grace appears virtually universal in scope, a common feature across many world religions.

This sanctified perspective exemplifies the formal prerequisites previously established for the transitional class of power maneuvers, although now targeting more of a universal sphere of influence. Similar to initial concepts of self-esteem and pomp, the new spiritual authority figure now exaltedly acts in a sanctified fashion in anticipation of prompting a prudent sense of faithfulness on the part of the established spiritual disciple. The tranquil demeanor of saintly figures certainly corroborates such a transitional dynamic, the stock in trade for many sacred rituals (without diminishing the awe or majesty therein).

DOMINION

The remaining entry within the ascending hierarchy of transitional themes, *dominion*, specifies a distinctive and enduring style of humanitarian focus. It is traditionally defined as a domain or territory ruled by a single sovereign overlord, although its spiritual overtones alternately suggest a divine sense of omnipotence. The term derives from the Latin *dominio*, from *dominus* (master). This divine sense of dominion is reverently cited in Jude 1:8, whereas Ephesians 1:21 translates the term as *kuriotes* denoting a rank or order of angels. According to tradition, the Dominions are celebrated as the highest order within the second rank of angels, sometimes referred to as "the flashing swords." They are so-titled from the belief that they dominate over those lower ranks of angels in a brilliant display of divine wisdom. They are said to channel divine grace conducive to wise governance and prudent management; hence, integrating both the material and spiritual realms within the master angelic order.

In our modern secular age, dominion denotes the power to govern or rule, or the collective populace subject to such rule. Prior to 1949, the term was officially employed to denote self-governing countries within the Commonwealth of Nations such as Canada, Australia, and India. In modern times, the use of the term "dominion" has largely been abandoned, being that it implies a certain degree of political subordination. Currently, member states are simply referred to as members within the Commonwealth. Irrespective of the international particulars therein, this enduring sense of dominion clearly fulfills such humanitarian prerequisites consistent with the benevolent policies inherent to the respective political applications. As a globally accepted means of governance, dominion certainly specifies such a grand humanitarian perspective, a set of noble principles that apply not only to member nations, but also to the lofty ideals governing an international state of affairs.

REVERENCE

A similar hierarchy of themes further holds true with respect to the remaining counter double bind class of maneuvers; namely, the ascending sequence of reverence, veneration, homage, and benediction. The first-mentioned theme of *reverence* represents the counter double bind response to the initial "self-esteem" maneuver. The term derives from the Latin *revereri* from *re-* (intensification) and *verieri* (to feel awe). It is traditionally defined as being held in high esteem, a perspective typically dependent upon ritual and tradition for validation. Rather than graciously submitting to the personal authority's dictates (namely, rewardingly acting approvingly) the reverent individual subliminally disqualifies any approving cooperation therein, effectively sidestepping the insistent quality of the self esteem expressed by the personal authority figure.

In Old Testament scripture, reverence chiefly emerges as a translation of the Hebraic themes of *yare* and *shachah*. The former term translates as a deferential attitude towards the Lord akin to a reverential sense of awe. The root-stem for *shachah* is translated as "falling down" suggestive of bodily prostration: a deferential bearing towards one's superiors reflecting obeisance. In this prostrate fashion, the personal follower displays a clear reverential attitude, although subliminally disqualified (to some degree) due to the ritual expectations imposed within such a reverential context. Consequently, in response to the nostalgic sense of self-esteem professed by the personal authority figure, the only graceful exit to such a double bind dilemma remains precisely such a reverential attitude: subliminally disqualified through its very state of compunction.

VENERATION

The personal foundations for reverence, in turn, extend to a civic sphere of influence with respect to the group-focused theme of *veneration*. Here, the group authority's pompous sense of self-esteem, in turn, prompts a projected reverential sense of veneration on the part of the established group representative. The term derives from Middle French *veneration* from the Latin *veneratio* (reverence), from *venerari* (to worship, revere): also related to *veneris* (love or desire). The affiliated sense of "venerable" is employed in the ecclesiastical tradition as a title of distinction for those reaching the first stage of canonization.

This reverential sense of veneration implies a steadfast sense of devotion for one's group authority figure, particularly those of heroic status or distinction. The Roman emperors proved particularly fitting in this regard, revered as civic rulers and emblems of grandeur consistent with such an imperial lifestyle. During the reign of Constantine, the etiquette of the Byzantine court invoked elaborate rituals of respect for the emperor as well as his statues and symbolisms. His subjects bowed to, kissed, and even offered incense to his imperial images, such as the worship of his empty throne. Similar veneration was paid to religious symbolisms such as the crucifix and altarpiece. Religious icons were even taken on journeys as symbols of protection, marched in front of armies or hung in a place of honor in virtually residence.

Whether religious or civic in nature, the ritualized prerequisites for veneration impart a clearly disqualified nature to this reverential class of counter double bind maneuvers. In direct analogy to the personal prerequisites for reverence, veneration, in turn, targets a group (or even spiritual) style of authority perspective. In response to the pompous sense of self esteem expressed by the group authority figure, the group representative reverently acts in a venerable fashion, whereby effectively sidestepping the insistent quality of the entire transitional interchange. Cloaked in the deferential acquiescence of a compulsory nature, this venerable strategy of disqualification takes full effect, a strategy that often escapes detection even amongst the most dedicated of followers.

HOMAGE

The preceding group prerequisites for veneration, in turn, extend to a universal sphere of influence with respect to the spiritually-focused theme of *homage*: a term chiefly employed in a worshipful context. It derives from the Old French *homage* from the Latin *homo* (a man): also in the sense of a humble servant or vassal, akin to the Latin *humus* (earth). In terms of feudal law, it refers to the symbolical acknowledgment of the feudal vassal towards his lord upon receiving investiture. It also denotes reverential sense of respect or deference, particularly in an outward expression of obeisance. According to this formal act of homage, the feudal tenant declares himself (on bended knee) to be the homage (or bondman) of the lord; hence, a reverential submission in terms. This act of fealty invoked the fidelity of the feudal tenant towards his lord, a faithful adherence to the obligations owed to a higher authority.

The traditional feudal method of owning land was by fiefdom. The overlord was the grantor of the fief, while the recipient was referred to as the vassal. The fief was transferred during the ceremony of homage, where the kneeling vassal put his clasped hands between those of his lord in an express declaration of loyalty. The lord, in turn, completed the ceremony by kissing the vassal and raising him to his feet. The vassal then swore an oath of fealty vowing to serve the lord faithfully in all respects. This formal ceremony cemented the legal relationship between lord and his vassal, the lord officially investing the vassal through fiefdom. In addition to parcels of land, rights and honors could similarly be granted as fiefs by the lord. Originally the fief needed to be renewed upon the death of either party, although the advent of hereditary succession bestowed fiefdoms chiefly to one's heirs.

The spiritual overtones implicit to the homage ceremony certainly appear striking, in fitting analogy to the universal homage paid to one's divinity figure. The compulsory nature of the ceremony clearly reflects the pattern previously established for reverence and veneration, although now encompassing the even loftier range of universal themes. Although all three themes appear closely related, the respective ascending hierarchy of personal, group, and spiritual terms appears particularly well suited to the task, imparting a meaningful sense of order to this abstract grouping of themes (in terms of the order given).

BENEDICTION

The final term within the ascending hierarchy of reverential themes, *benediction*, represents a humanitarian extension upon the preliminary sequence of reverence, veneration, and homage. It is traditionally defined as a solemn invocation or divine blessing, primarily in a congregational sense. The term derives from the Latin *benedicto* from *bene* (well) and *dictum* (to say). It chiefly refers to one of the most dramatic of Catholic services; namely, the Benediction of the Blessed Sacrament. Although a solemn benediction can also occur in terms of a related social context (such as the climax of a closing ceremony), the Catholic version proves informative in this regard, although not necessarily the only means of interpretation.

Catholic Benediction is known as *Salut* in France, and as *Segen* in Germany. It is customarily an afternoon or evening devotional consisting of the singing of hymns and litanies prior to displaying the Blessed Sacrament. This occurs in a gilded monstrance surrounded by candles upon a central altar. Towards the close of the ceremony, the priest raises the monstrance and makes the sign of the cross over the spiritual congregation.

The deeply reverential nature of the benediction ceremony would clearly argue for its crowning humanitarian status within the ascending hierarchy of reverence, veneration, and homage (although to a supremely abstract degree). The reverent worship of the Host within the ornamental monstrance confirms the highly ritual nature of the ceremony bordering on truly humanitarian proportions. The sacred pageantry witnessed by the congregation virtually guarantees a faithful response, as the accompanying chants and hymns further serve to indicate. This highly formal act of worship covertly disqualifies any free exercise therein, whereby validating benediction's crowning inclusion within the ascending hierarchy of counter double bind maneuvers.

APOLOGY

A similar motivational dynamic further holds true with respect to the remaining class of lesser virtues (II) based upon apology/clemency. Here, the initial transitional sequence of apology-rectitude-penitence-contrition, in turn, prompts the requisite counter double bind sequence of clemency, pardon, absolution, and deliverance (indicative of the personal, group, spiritual, and humanitarian levels, respectively). The first mentioned theme of *apology* represents a transitional variation on the more basic submissive sense of guilt expressed by the personal authority figure. Consequently, apology anticipates a blameful sense of leniency on the part of the personal follower, similar to the interplay previously established for self-esteem and reverence. Its modern spelling derives from the Greek *apologia* (a speech made in defense) from *apologos* (an account/story): from *apo-* (from) and *logos* (speech). The English connotation of self-justification was further modified to reflect a "frank expression of regret for wrongs done" (first recorded 1594). Here, apology denotes regret for fault or transgression in a sincere plea for mercy.

This theme further refers to a literary style that defends or justifies an author's opinion or point of view. This literary usage does not necessarily imply that wrongs had been done, nor does it express regret. The most famous ancient example is Plato's Apology (circa 3rd century BCE) representing Socrates' defense before the Athenian tribunal. The subsequent Christian tradition of "apologetics" includes such notable theologians as St. Augustine and Thomas Aquinas.

Through solemn apology, the personal authority earnestly transitions into a submissive style of guilt perspective, whereby vulnerably aiming to increase his/her chances of obtaining lenient consideration on the part of the established follower figure. The personal follower, in turn, can cleverly resort to a disqualified style of counter double bind maneuver; namely, the clemency perspective described later within this chapter. Regardless of the individual outcomes, the initial apology maneuver serves its intended purpose towards securing the notice from the established follower figure, although not always with the anticipated results.

RECTITUDE

The personal prerequisites for apology, in turn, extend to a civic sphere of influence with respect to the group-focused theme of *rectitude*. Here, the group authority apologetically expresses a sense of rectitude towards the established follower figure, whereby professing an honorable sense of guilt in the process. Indeed, rectitude denotes a sense of responsibility grounded in ob-ligation, as in terms of moral uprightness or righteousness. The term derives from the Late-Latin *rectitudo* from the Latin *rectus* (straight), suggesting the need to follow "a straight and narrow path."

Roman authority Pliny the Younger insightfully notes: "Never do anything concerning the *rectitude* of which you are in doubt." Furthermore, his Roman contemporary Ovid similarly wrote: "The mind, conscious of *rectitude*, laughed to scorn the falsehood of the report." As the chief transitional counterpart with respect to "honor," rectitude enjoys an enlightened degree of influence within an ethical sphere of inquiry. Indeed, according to American philosopher Ralph Waldo Emerson: "It is true that genius takes its rise out of the mountains of *rectitude*; that all beauty and power which men covet are somehow born out of that alpine district." In slightly different terms, rectitude represents a more advanced (group) variation on the more basic apology maneuver, effectively transitioning into such an immediately active style of power perspective. The vulnerable characteristics traditionally associated with rectitude share (with apology) a clearly deferential viewpoint, further anticipating a leniently-just treatment on the part of the established follower figure. Consequently, rectitude denotes an outward expression of guilty-culpability, an observation entirely in keeping with such an overarching transitional format.

PENITENCE

The ascending authority hierarchy of apology and rectitude, in turn, extends to a universal sphere of influence with respect to the more spiritually-focused theme of *penitence*. Here the newly transitioned spiritual authority penitently acts with rectitude towards one's established follower figure in anticipation of the latter's blameful-hope for justice. Penitence is traditionally defined the solemn regret for past sinfulness, as in a repentant attitude. The term derives from the Latin *pænitentia* (repentance) from *pænitentum* (penitent), present-participle of *pænitere* (to feel regret). The related notion of "penitentiary" appears circa the 15th century as "a place of punishment for offenses against the church."

In terms of Catholic theology, penance refers to the specific virtue, as well as its formulation as one of the Seven Sacraments. Both entertain the common belief that one who sins must repent, and (insofar as possible) make adequate reparation. This firm determination to abstain from sin proves crucial for warranting absolution. The teachings of Christ on the subject come through the clearest in his parables on the Prodigal Son and the Repentant Publican. Similarly, Mary Magdalene (who washed away her sins with tears of sorrow) remains the enduring spiritual archetype for the repentant sinner. In this traditional sorrowful context, penitence continues in the order of the transitional sequence previously described for apology and rectitude, although now targeting more of a universal sphere of influence. Indeed, the deep spiritual overtones associated with penance are reflected in its sacramental overtones, a vulnerable expression of culpability in keeping with such an overarching universal perspective. Certainly many great spiritual figures across time have expressed such a penitent attitude, a feature consistent with such an enduring style of transitional authority perspective.

CONTRITION

The ascending transitional hierarchy of apology, rectitude, and penance ultimately culminates with respect to the supremely abstract theme of *contrition*. The enduring humanitarian prerequisites associated with contrition are penitently expressed towards one's established follower figure in anticipation of prompting the latter's just-hope for the truth. Contrition traditionally signifies an extreme sense of remorse for past sinful deeds, although in a more ritual sense than previously established for penance. The term derives from the Latin *contritio* (a breaking of something hardened) from the Latin *contritus* (literally: worn out, ground to pieces), past-participle of *conterere* (to grind) from *com-* (together) and *terere* (to rub).

Old Testament prophets laid particular emphasis on the need for hearty repentance. The psalms state that God does not despise "the contrite heart" (Psalms 1:19), and calls Israel to "rend your hearts and not your garments" (Joel 2:12). Similarly, the prophet Job submitted to penance in sackcloth and ashes in order to reconcile the sorrow of his soul (Job 8:6). The Council of Trent defines contrition as: "a sorrow of the soul and hatred of sin committed with the firm purpose of sinning no more." This sorrow of the soul is not merely speculative regret for wrongs done but also pain in conjunction with a hatred for sin.

Along similar lines, contrition represents the supreme culmination of the trend previously established for apology, rectitude, and penitence: although now extending to a more enduring humanitarian sphere of influence. Consequently, the newly transitioned humanitarian authority peni-

tently acts in a contrite fashion in anticipation of prompting lenient treatment on the part of the established follower figure. Despite this extreme degree of abstraction, the contrite individual effectively fulfills the specifics established for the transitional class of power maneuvers, an aspect further verified with respect to the remaining class of counter double bind maneuvers to follow.

CLEMENCY

The remaining hierarchy of virtuous themes specific to the counter double bind class of power maneuvers is respectively specified as clemency, pardon, absolution, and deliverance: a sequence directly countering the preliminary transitional sequence of apology, rectitude, penitence, and contrition. The first-mentioned theme of *clemency* is traditionally defined as a mild or gentle demeanor expressed towards others, particularly when a merciful course of action seems in order. This abiding sense of gentleness derives from the Latin *clementia* (calmness, gentleness) from *clemens* (calm, mild) from *clinare* (to lean). The classical Romans worshipped this virtuous quality in the guise of Clementia, their divine personification of clemency or mercy. Her worship greatly increased in popularity due to her favored status with the emperor Julius Caesar. In 44 BCE, the Senate decreed a temple dedicated to both Caesar and Clementia, where the cult statuary depicted the two figures clasping hands. Regular yearly sacrifice to Clementia was decreed in honor of the emperor Caligula in 39 CE, while a later festival commemorated Nero's compassionate treatment of Tiridates. On coins of the empire, she appears as Clementia Augusta, and later as Clementia Temporum.

An enduring pattern emerges from these traditions; namely, clemency denotes a personally bestowed sense of lenient treatment, as exemplified by the actions of the sage Roman emperors of the era. Hence, in analogy to its respective counterpart in "reverence," clemency effectively circumvents the insistent quality of the apology maneuver without necessarily appearing to have done so. In this subliminally disqualified fashion, the reluctant personal follower formally acknowledges the apology professed (by the respective authority figure) without formally admitting to any overt sense of complicity in the process.

PARDON

The personal prerequisites for clemency, in turn, extend to a group sphere of influence with respect to the clement sense of *pardon* expressed by the group representative. Generally speaking, a pardon refers to the remittance of a penalty or punishment, as in mercifully making an allowance. The term derives from the Latin *perdonare* (to give wholeheartedly), a compound of *per-* (thoroughly) and *donare* (to give or present).

In a legal sense, the granting of a pardon refers to exempting from punishment a criminal offense through the assent of a government executive. A blanket pardon granted to those guilty of a general offense is termed an amnesty. This type of pardon (at least in the United States) fully terminates any criminal liability, although the pardoned individual may still be liable in civil court. A pardon, therefore, is distinguished from the alleviation of punishment: as in commuting a sentence, reprieve, or parole. The US Constitution gives the President power to grant reprieves or pardons for any federal crime, although he may not interfere with impeachment. In most states within the union, the governor enjoys similar powers, although he/she may not pardon those convicted of treason or criminal contempt of court.

According to these legalistic perspectives, the theme of pardon proves particularly suggestive of a group-directed focus, directly expanding upon the personal prerequisites previously established for clemency. The pardoning individual effectively sidesteps the apologetic sense of rectitude expressed by the group authority figure: claiming only to be following protocol, hence, not a willing participant within the entire transitional interchange. In this subliminally disqualified fashion, the reluctant group representative effectively sidesteps the insistent quality of the initial apology-rectitude maneuver, whereby avoiding any concomitant loss of status therein.

ABSOLUTION

The preliminary sequence of clemency and pardon, in turn, extends to a universal sphere of influence with the respect to the spiritually-focused theme of *absolution*. It is traditionally defined as the remission of sins officially presided over by a priest. In a more general sense, it refers to the acquittal or release from punishment. The term derives from the Latin *absolvare* from *ab-* (from) and *solvere* (to loosen, to free): the burden of guilt now lifted away. Absolution proper concerns the priestly act whereby one is freed from the stain of sin: although this sense of absolution presupposes a contrite attitude and a penitent resolve to sin no more.

To the apostles was given the power to forgive sins in the name of the Lord. This power to absolve is stressed in the Gospel of St. John (20:22-23) which states: "Whose sins ye shall forgive they are forgiven them; and whose sins ye shall retain, they are retained." In the cannon of the Roman Catholic Church, the penitent is absolved of sins by the confessor and conferrer of the sacrament. Prior to granting absolution, the confessor admonishes the sinner and imposes penance (generally consisting of prayers). The penitent is further instructed to make appropriate restitution for injury done to others.

Here, the spiritual overtones associated with absolution come through the clearest, extending the more limited (group) focus of pardon into an even more abstract (universal) sphere of influence. In direct analogy to the related theme of homage, absolution denotes a disqualified form of counter double bind maneuver, effectively sidestepping the insistent quality of the penitent individual. Compliance is chalked up to the strictures of ritual rather than any volitional assent in terms. Consequently, through this subliminal denial of complicity, the spiritual disciple figure reciprocates his expected role within the dual transitional format, although in a thoroughly non-confrontational manner.

DELIVERANCE

The ascending transitional sequence of clemency, pardon, and absolution ultimately culminates with respect to the crowning humanitarian theme of *deliverance*. This latter term effectively complements the more positive attributes previously described for benediction. Although deliverance appears fairly specialized in a religious sense, it is traditionally defined as the act of freeing or delivering, particularly with respect to sinfulness. The term derives from the French *delivrer* a compound formation of the Latin *de-* (from) and *liberare* (to set free).

In a scriptural sense, deliverance denotes redemption through the payment of a ransom, or liberation from oppression or captivity. In NT scripture, the redemption for the sins of mankind is achieved through Christ's sacrificial death as a ransom of deliverance. The debt is not only cancelled, but paid in full, whereby expiating the sins for all of mankind.

Irrespective of the individual traditions therein, the enduring humanitarian prerequisites for deliverance represent the crowning culmination of the preliminary sequence of clemency, pardon, and absolution. In direct analogy to its subordinate counterpart in absolution, deliverance represents a subliminally disqualified leniency perspective, as its scriptural precedents serve to indicate. This appeal to scripture further serves to obscure its disqualified nature, its extreme level of abstraction disguising any pat determination therein.

13

THE REINFORCEMENT-BASED REALM FOR THE LESSER VIRTUES (II)

The completed description of the lesser virtues (II) based upon self-esteem/reverence and apology/clemency, in turn, invokes the remaining issue of the reinforcement-based sequences of terms. According to the previous chapter, both self-esteem and apology represented transitional variations on the more basic nostalgia/guilt perspectives of the established authority figure, whereby prompting the disqualified reverence/appeasement perspectives held by the personal follower figure. A similar pattern further holds true with respect to the related transitional sequences based upon congeniality/concession and sympathy/appeasement. Here, congeniality and sympathy represent an active class of transitional maneuvers expanding upon the more elementary desire/worry authority perspectives.

The general pattern of description for this authority-based class of lesser virtues (II) is similar to that which has gone before; namely, the four-level hierarchy of (transitional) authority terms is described first, followed by the designated series of disqualified follower roles. The preliminary double bind sequence of congeniality, cordiality, hospitality, and altruism will be described first, followed by the anticipated counter double bind sequence of concession-indulgence-gratitude-goodwill. Furthermore, the remainder of the current chapter examines the related transitional sequence of sympathy-compassion-mercy-forgiveness, followed by the disqualified follower series of appeasement-conciliation-accommodation-sacrifice. The discerning reader is encouraged to refer back to the four-part listing of schematic definitions for the lesser virtues (II) outlined in Chapter *12*, whereby providing a sturdy foundation for the transitional dynamics at issue: in concert with the stirring descriptive narratives for each of the individual virtuous terms.

CONGENIALITY

The first-listed motivational theme of *congeniality* denotes a friendly and outgoing style of personality. Its modern spelling derives from the Latin *com-* (together) and *genialis* (of birth); hence, a kindred or sympathetic spirit. The ensuing connotations of agreeableness first appear during the early half of the 18th century. Consequently, congeniality effectively denotes a positive range of rewarding reinforcement conducive to prompting the solicitous attentions of one's established follower figure. The congenial individual maneuvers from an immediately active style of reinforcement perspective in anticipation of securing a projected sense of solicitous consideration on the part of the personal follower, whereby laying the groundwork for establishing an ongoing interaction.

Nowhere is this congenial spirit more effectively witnessed than in the beauty pageant tradition of Miss Congeniality. Prior to final judging each pageant contestant casts a vote for the contestant they deem is most deserving of the Miss Congeniality Award. The contestants vote by secret ballot in a process that does not impact the point system for the overall title. The criteria for the congeniality award include the virtues of friendliness, pleasantness, and the support of fellow pageant-mates. The successful candidate encourages and offers help whenever possible. In terms of personality, the winning contestant amiably endeavors to make others feel comfortable in her presence, exhibiting a friendly and sincere disposition.

Congeniality effectively fulfills the motivational dynamics established for the transitional class of power maneuvers. Indeed, the initial phase of the general transitional interchange is respectively termed the *congeniality phase*, so fundamental is this pattern of interaction. Consequently, with respect to the personal authority role, the beauty contestant congenially acts desirously towards the other participants in anticipation of their solicitous attentions (in return), as outwardly exemplified through the bestowal of the congeniality award.

CORDIALITY

The personal characteristics for congeniality, in turn, extend to a group sphere of influence with respect to the group-focused theme of *cordiality*. The term derives from the Latin *cordialis* (from the heart), from *cor* or *cordis* (heart) denoting a heartfelt or affectionate nature. It originally referred to a medicine, food, or drink that stimulated the heart. The high alcohol content of the typical "cordial" (such as schnapps) definitely imparts a "warm sensation" going down, as well as promoting a festive atmosphere.

As an adjective, this sense of heartfelt emotion first appears during the late 15th century. The Abbe Goussault, a counselor at High Court (circa the 17th century) expounds on the merits of cordiality in child-rearing as follows: "A few words of *cordiality* and trust make an impression on the minds (of children), and few are they in number that can resist these sweet and simple methods." A somewhat more cynical viewpoint is offered by American humorist Florence King in her insightful tome, *With Charity Toward None* (1992), where she writes: "Because good manners build sturdy walls, our distaste for intimacy makes us exceedingly *cordial* ships that pass in the night. As long as you remain a stranger, we will be your friend forever." This quotation reflects the somewhat formal nature of cordiality, as reflected in the uncertain nature of initiating a new relationship within a pre-established social order. Indeed, whether one offers a cordial liqueur, or simply a handshake and a smile, the mechanisms governing social interaction typically require some preliminary style of cordial lubrication (as typically encountered at a cocktail party or social mixer). As a new addition to the social milieu, the cordial individual congenially acts rewardingly towards one's peer group, a strategy that enhances one's chances of solicitous acceptance (at least during the preliminary stage).

HOSPITALITY

The group prerequisites for cordiality, in turn, extend to a universal sphere of influence with respect to the universally-focused theme of *hospitality*. The term derives from Latin *hospes* (a stranger or guest) denoting kindness towards strangers and the welcoming of guests. This aspect is particularly prominent in Old Testament scripture, a custom still active amongst desert cultures. Hospitality is regarded as a basic right of the traveler, with gratitude towards the host offered as a measure of good faith. Hospitality is granted as a duty by the host, often a recipient of return hospitality. The granting of hospitality is surrounded by etiquette that has made the Middle-Eastern variety so richly deserved. The traveler is made the virtual master of the household throughout his stay. The host performs the most servile of requests, even avoiding sitting in his guest's presence without express permission. The guest is even given free use of all that his host possesses. The host is duty-bound to defend his guest against all manner of threats, setting aside any pre-existing conflicts.

In New Testament scripture, Christ's directs his apostles to "take nothing for their journey" (Mark 6:8) presupposing that they would always be assured of finding hospitality. They even appeared to have their choice of hosts (Matthew 10:11) and stayed as long as they pleased (Luke 10:7). This traveler's claim to hospitality was enhanced by their status as bearers of good tidings to the populace. Consequently, hospitality towards the apostles was judged so virtuous that even a "cup of water" was considered meritorious when offered.

As the first Christian congregations were established, the exercise of hospitality acquired enhanced status. Not only did the Christian traveler look to his brethren for hospitality, the individual churches relied upon the missionary to foster a sense of unity throughout the Roman Empire. Consequently, hospitality continues the trend previously established for congeniality and cordiality, although now extending to a more universal sphere of influence. The deep spiritual overtones associated with hospitality are clearly evident in the universal privileges afforded the humble traveler. Indeed, whether invoking the namesake "hospital" or traveler's refuge (hostel), this spirit of hospitality remains an enduring precept of civility worldwide. Certainly chances are good that we will all be in need of such services at some point during our lifetime.

ALTRUISM

The preceding trend towards hospitality ultimately culminates with respect the supremely abstract theme of *altruism*. The term was coined by

Auguste Comte in 1851 in allusion to the Italian term *altrui*, from the Latin *alter* (the other). It is defined as the principle of living and acting in the best interests of others, as opposed to the selfish propensities characterizing egoism. The term entered the English speaking tradition in terms of the advocates of Comte's philosophy. Although employed primarily to designate emotions of a sympathetic nature, the consequences of altruism towards others prove equally applicable. It denotes a theory of conduct where actions targeting the happiness of others rate great moral value.

Comte is considered the founder of the School of Social Eudaemonism (based upon Positivism) to which the designation of altruism is also given. Not only is happiness found in living for others, but charitable devotion to humanity represents the highest form of religious impulse. Mankind essentially operates in terms of conflicting impulses; namely, personal (or egoistic) and social (or altruistic). The primary condition for individual wellbeing entails the subordination of self-love to such benevolent impulses, emphasizing social empathy over self-serving instincts.

To usher in his age of altruism, Comte invented a quasi-religious belief system that substituted an abstract quality termed Humanity for the divinity of God. This controversial aspect of Comte's system was not popular with his adherents. Herbert Spencer and John Stuart Mill (English contemporaries of Comte) accepted the general utilitarian nature of altruism, although argued that its true moral worth resides in welfare to society rather than individual concerns. Consequently altruism represents the supreme culmination of the ascending transitional hierarchy of congeniality, cordiality, and hospitality. The enduring humanitarian prerequisites for altruism certainly figure prominently in this respect. The altruistic authority figure rewardingly acts hospitably in anticipation of the projected charitable sense goodness on the part of the humanitarian follower figure. In spite of its extreme level of abstraction, altruism formally fulfills the specifics established for the transitional class of power maneuvers, an aspect further verified with respect to the remaining class of counter double bind maneuvers.

CONCESSION

The initial sequence of transitional themes based upon congeniality, in turn, sets the stage for the remaining hierarchy of disqualified counter double bind maneuvers; namely, concession, indulgence, gratitude, and goodwill. The first mentioned theme of concession traditionally refers to the act of conceding or granting a special privilege or favor. The term derives from the Latin *concessum*, from *con-* (wholly) and *cedere* (to yield). Similar to its related counterpart in reverence, the concessional individual politely sidesteps the insistent quality of the congeniality maneuver without specifically acknowledging any abiding sense of complicity in the process.

In a contractual sense, a concession is a special privilege enacted through legislation that surpasses the limits of common law. It is granted through special favor giving the recipient advantages over non-privileged individuals. This enduring favor is distinguished from permission or a single dispensation. Such privileges are classified as either remunerative or gratuitous. Privileges recognized by law require no proof, although periodically subject to judicial scrutiny. All other privileges require proof of the original concession, or a duly certified copy.

To a symbolic degree, the concession perspective effectively sidesteps the insistent quality of the initial congeniality maneuver. The established personal follower concessionally claims to only be acting out of formality; hence, scarcely a free or willing participant within the transitional interchange. Faced with the congeniality expressed by the personal authority figure, the only graceful exit from such a double bind maneuver invokes precisely such a concessional strategy: a response certainly anticipated and formalized through a compunctual state of affairs.

INDULGENCE

The personal prerequisites for concession, in turn, extend to a group sphere of influence with respect to the affiliated theme of *indulgence*. It is traditionally defined as the act of gratifying, particularly in terms of excessive adulation. The term derives from the Latin *indulgentia* (complaisance or fondness), from *indulgentem*, present participle of *indulgere* (to be kind, to yield) a compound of *in-* (in) and *dulcis* (sweet). Originally, it referred to a sense of kindness or favor, later modified to reflect a remission of debt or tax.

With respect to Catholic theology, an indulgence denotes a pardon or remission of temporal punishment due to sin (the guilt of which has already been forgiven). The practice of quantifying indulgences dates to earliest times when public penance was imposed subject to indulgence. The Church's proclamation of an indulgence further specifies that it must be gained through the effort of the faithful. The basic formula: *corde saltem contrito* (at least with a contrite heart) remains an essential feature of indulgence. One must further reverently perform the good works (prayers, alms, etc.) accompanying the eventual granting of the indulgence. The German monk, Martin Luther rightfully protested the abuses accompanying the sale of indulgences, eventually rejecting the doctrine altogether. Beginning with the Council of Trent in 1562, the buying or selling of indulgences was similarly outlawed within the Catholic Church.

Regardless of the individual traditions therein, the ritualized aspects of indulgence impart a subliminally disqualified content consistent with the counter double bind class of power maneuvers. In direct analogy to its subordinate counterpart in concession, indulgence targets a group (and sometimes spiritual) sphere of influence. Consequently, in direct response to the initial congenial sense of cordiality expressed by the group authority figure, the group representative concessionally acts in an indulgent fashion, effectively sidestepping the insistent quality of the initial authority maneuver. This ritual sense of indulgence typically remains cloaked within the mantle of tradition, in essence, disguising the disqualified character of the entire transitional interchange.

GRATITUDE

The ascending transitional hierarchy of concession and indulgence, in turn, extends to a universal sphere of influence with respect to the spiritually-focused theme of *gratitude*. This theme denotes warm and friendly feelings towards a benefactor in terms of a sense of thankfulness, particularly when a favor has been bestowed. The term derives from the Latin *gratitudo*, from *gratus* (pleasing). According to French philosopher, Jacques Maritain: "Gratitude is the most exquisite form of courtesy." Furthermore, British lexicographer Samuel Johnson notes: "Gratitude is a fruit of great cultivation; you do not find it among common people." On a more sober note, German philosopher Friedrich Nietzsche writes: "He who bestows something great receives no *gratitude*; for in accepting it the recipient has already been weighed down too much." American author, Herman Melville further tackles the subject as follows: "To be the subject of alms-giving is trying, and to feel in duty-bound to appear cheerfully *grateful* under the trial."

Consequently, in direct analogy to the subordinate themes of concession and indulgence, gratitude denotes a disqualified style of counter double bind maneuver, effectively sidestepping the insistent quality of the initial hospitality perspective. The grateful individual's compliance is simply chalked-up to the formalities of courteous good-breeding rather than any volitional assent in terms. This formality is typically instilled at a fairly early age. We may all recall being coached to respond with a hearty "thank you" when served a tasty treat. The obligatory rejoinder "you're most welcome" further solidifies this training ritual, fully acknowledging the paradoxical transitional interchange that had just transpired.

GOODWILL

The ascending hierarchy of concessional themes ultimately culminates with respect to the crowning humanitarian theme of *goodwill*: a fitting adjunct to the preliminary sequence of concession, indulgence, and gratitude. This theme is featured in the *Gloria in Excelsis*, an early Christian hymn beginning with the words: "Glory be to God on High, and on earth peace and *goodwill* towards men." This hymn originally was of Greek derivation, incorporated into the Roman Catholic Mass circa the 6th century (following the *Kyrie*).

This enduring theme of goodwill further extends to issues of a globally humanitarian significance, as witnessed in the modern-day phenomenon of the Goodwill Games. The brainchild of philanthropist, Ted Turner, the Goodwill Games were inaugurated in Moscow in 1986. This site was deliberately chosen to ease Cold War tensions through friendly athletic competition amongst nations. The end of the Cold War eventually shifted the focus of the Games to that of a youth initiative. In celebrating sports as an avenue for the advancement of youth, the Goodwill Games raised millions of dollars for charitable endeavors. Following sixteen years of influence (and a half-dozen separate venues) the Goodwill Games ceased operations, the unwitting target of corporate restructuring. In keeping with such a grand humanitarian perspective, the years of positive memories associated with the Goodwill Games remain particularly poignant. Its initial focus on global harmony proved immediately admirable, although scarcely more so than its concern for all generations to come. This enduring theme of goodwill remains a fitting exemplar for such a grand and noble enterprise, and one destined to endure in the hearts and minds of all so keenly and emotionally touched.

SYMPATHY

A parallel style of analysis further remains in order for the remaining hierarchy of lesser virtues (II) based upon the lenient interplay of double bind and counter double bind maneuvers based upon sympathy and appeasement. The first-mentioned theme of *sympathy* traces its origins to the Greek *sympatheia* from *syn-* (with) and *pathos* (suffering). It is traditionally defined as the inclination to support the downtrodden, particularly in an empathic or forgiving fashion. This theme is viewed as a central Christian tenet consistent with the empathic prerequisites characterizing the Golden Rule.

The modern era witnessed a great proliferation of theoretical approaches towards understanding the sympathetic emotions. Hutcheson viewed the capacity for sympathy as a primary aspect of human nature. David Hume, in turn, made critical observations concerning the role of sympathy in motivating moral conduct. Rousseau also gave his emotion of *pitié* (compassion) a pivotal role in his social theory of morality. In describing the education of young Émile (1762), Rousseau speculates that the experience of sympathy/compassion in relation to the pain of another proves a key foundation to the stability of society as a whole. Sympathy leads to the recognition of vulnerabilities we all share in terms of the suffering often inflicted upon others. Schopenhauer further acknowledged the key role sympathy plays in terms of morality. In his criticism of Kantian ethics, Schopenhauer argued that all true moral action must be grounded in other-directed emotions such as sympathy. Schopenhauer's ethical viewpoint eventually gained considerable influence within a culture dissatisfied with duty-based morality.

Consequently, sympathy effectively fulfills the specifics established for the transitional class of power maneuvers. Here, sympathy respectively complements its motivational counterpart in congeniality, although now targeting a more serious range of themes. Through the aid of this initial transitional perspective, the personal authority figure leniently plays-up a sympathetic perspective in anticipation of prompting a submissive response on the part of the established follower figure. In this reciprocating fashion, the personal authority sympathetically anticipates the submissive concerns on the part of the personal follower figure: providing a fitting counterpoint to the reciprocating dynamics governing the transitional class of lesser virtues.

COMPASSION

The preceding personal prerequisites for sympathy, in turn, extend to a group sphere of influence with respect to the more community-based theme of *compassion*. The term derives from the Latin *compassio* (sympathy) from *compassus*, past participle of *compati* (to feel pity), from the compound of *com-* (together) and *pati* (to suffer). It denotes a sense of empathy for the sufferings of others generally eliciting a warmer tone than the more condescending theme of pity. Compassion suggests an outward respect for others often in times of great need or distress. For true compassion, one not only feels the suffering of others, but freely strives to relieve their pain.

Similar to other virtues within its class, there definitely appears to be a "golden mean" with respect to compassion. Lack of compassion can lead to apathy, callousness, or cruelty: whereas excessive compassion leads to over-indulgence, enablement, and/or co-dependency. As a new entry to an established social context, the lenient authority figure sympathetically acts compassionately towards one's group representative in anticipation of promoting a brave sense of concern on the part of the latter. These lenient characteristics for compassion prove entirely consistent with the general transitional format, the group authority sympathetically acting compassionately in anticipation of prompting the brave sense of concern on the part of the established follower figure.

MERCY

The ascending transitional hierarchy of sympathy and compassion, in turn, extends to a universal sphere of influence with respect to the spiritually-focused theme of *mercy*. Its modern spelling derives from the Late Latin *merces* (compassion of God) from the Latin *merces* (pay or favor). Mercy is defined as kind or compassionate treatment of another particularly in adverse types of circumstances. The classical Greeks celebrated their own traditions of mercy as Eleos (the divine personification of mercy or pity). According to Pausanias: "The Athenians are the only ones among the Hellenes who worship this divine quality: yet among all the gods, it is the most useful to human life in all its vicissitudes." Foreigners seeking the assistance of the Athenians were first obliged to approach (as suppliants) the altar of Eleos located in the marketplace of Athens.

Mercy plays a similar role in the Judeo-Christian tradition, although regarded as a divine attribute rather than a deity in its own right. Old Testament scripture reverently celebrates a God of mercy and forgiveness towards his chosen people. In the Book of Exodus, God mercifully frees the Israelites from the bondage of the Egyptians. On Mount Sinai, He reveals himself to Moses as the *merciful* one (Ex. 34:8). Indeed, the gilded lid on the Ark of the Covenant was traditionally referred to as the *mercy* seat from the belief that the Lord rested there during the annual Day of Atonement. On this sacred day, the High Priest sprinkled sacrificial blood upon the mercy seat in atonement for the sins of the Jewish population. Although this ceremony was shielded from public view, the prayers of the faithful were directed specifically towards this "Holy of Holies."

These sacrificial aspects of mercy are similarly celebrated in the Christian tradition. In his Sermon on the Mount, Jesus extols mercy in his fifth beatitude: "Blessed are the *merciful* for they shall receive mercy." He further implores the faithful to be merciful, just as their Father is merciful (Luke 6:36). He reminds his disciples that they will be judged according to their mercifulness towards others (Mt 25:31-46). Consequently, mercy continues the trend previously established for sympathy and compassion, although now extending to a more universal sphere of influence. The deep spiritual overtones associated with mercy are particularly evident in the stirring historical examples. Indeed, the merciful sense of compassion expressed by the spiritual authority figure, in turn, anticipates a brave sense of decency on the part of the spiritual disciple figure. The merciful individual is governed by motives of a morally abstract nature, similar to that previously established for hospitality. Accordingly, mercy remains a revered moral quality that fully transcends any feeble dynamics employed towards explanation.

FORGIVENESS

The ascending transitional hierarchy of sympathy, compassion, and mercy ultimately culminates with respect to the crowning humanitarian perspective of *forgiveness*: a supremely abstract perspective exemplifying the very essence of mercy. The term derives from the Old English *forgiefan* from *for-* (away) and *fiefan* (to give), as in overlooking a debt or social trespass. In a traditional sense, forgiveness appears not to have figured very prominently in the morality of the ancient world. The magnanimous individual typically disregarded offenders that were beneath one's station. Even the forgiveness of one's peers was considered to be a sign of weakness.

In Old Testament scripture, forgiveness towards one's fellow man was only infrequently mentioned, those seeking forgiveness typically occupying a subservient position. New Testament scripture, in contrast, taught that forgiveness is a Christian duty to be granted without reservation.

Christ preached that there is no wrong so grievous that it cannot be forgiven. Christ admonishes Peter that he should forgive not merely seven times a day, but seventy times seven (Matthew 18:21). Here, the humanitarian overtones associated with forgiveness come through the clearest, culminating the ascending transitional hierarchy of sympathy, compassion, and mercy. The extremely enduring nature of forgiveness applies equally well to all ages and cultures, an ethical standard of virtually universal appeal. Indeed, contrary to the popular maxim, one certainly can forgive (although scarcely forget), for the clear humanitarian prerequisites certainly appear to rule-out the likelihood of any latter eventuality.

APPEASEMENT

The preliminary transitional sequence of sympathy, compassion, mercy, and forgiveness, in turn, invites similar parallels to the remaining class of counter double bind maneuvers based upon appeasement; namely, appeasement, conciliation, accommodation, and sacrifice (as indicative of the personal, group, spiritual, and humanitarian follower levels). The first mentioned theme of *appeasement* derives from the Old French *apeser* (to bring to peace), from the Latin *pax* or *pacis* (peace). Appeasement was particularly scrutinized (in a political sense) during the events leading up to World War II, referring to the policy of pacifying an aggressive nation in order to avoid war. A prime example of appeasement concerns England's policies towards Fascist Italy and Nazi Germany during the mid-1930's. British Prime Minister Neville Chamberlain sought to accommodate Italy's invasion of Ethiopia in 1935, and then waffled when Germany incorporated Austria in 1938. When Hitler subsequently prepared to annex ethnically-German portions of Czechoslovakia, Chamberlain negotiated the notorious Munich Agreement further serving to appease the Nazis. Fortunately, Winston Churchill ultimately replaced Chamberlain, helping to guide the Free World back onto the path of victory in World War II. Indeed, Churchill facetiously quipped: "An *appeaser* is one who feeds a crocodile hoping that it will eat him last."

Following the abysmal failure of Chamberlain's policy of appeasement, this theme acquired more of a pejorative sense. Although generally indicative of a political context, the personal dynamics driving international politics are further suggestive of an individual sphere of influence. Indeed, Hitler deliberately cultivated a cult of personality, although his pretensions to international harmony

Traditional Roman Sacrifice: Priest (Head Covered) Places Offerings on the Sacred Altar
Detail from a Marble Relief Decorating the Temple of the Emperor Vespasian at Pompeii

only amounted to subterfuge and stall tactics. Although Chamberlain's efforts towards appeasement were ultimately doomed from the start, they foundered primarily in terms of Hitler's twisted ambitions. Under more favorable circumstances, appeasement remains a proven tool in the diplomatic arsenal, although with definite limitations.

True to its affiliated counterpart in concession, appeasement represents a key strategy for politely circumventing the insistent quality of the sympathy expressed by the respective authority figure (although without necessarily appearing stalwart in the process). In this subliminally disqualified sense, the reluctant personal follower figure fully acknowledges the initial motives of the sympathy maneuver, although the compunctions of social convention specify an appeasement response in return. This reciprocating interpretation does not necessarily diminish the heartfelt feelings at issue. Indeed, once entangled within such a double bind dilemma, the ultimate extrication (via the counter double bind maneuver) is generally expressed in an unpremeditated fashion. The overall effect typically appears brimming with emotion, perhaps even fooling oneself insofar as the outward degree of sincerity is concerned.

CONCILIATION

The personal prerequisites for appeasement, in turn, extend to a group sphere of influence with respect to the appeasing sense of *conciliation* expressed by the group representative. It is traditionally defined as the act of gaining consideration or winning over the favor of another. The term derives from the Latin *conciliatus* past participle of *conciliare* (to bring together or unite in feelings) from *concilium* (council), a compound of *com-* (together) and calere (to call). Incidentally, the tendency to confuse conciliation with "counsel" dates back at least to the 16th century. French author, Francois de La Roche-Foucauld writes: "Friendship is only a reciprocal *conciliation* of interests." The typical city-council setting suggests precisely such a group dynamic, where the elected board members endeavor to come to an acceptable consensus in matters of a civic nature. The right of the common citizenry to present their views before the board is duly noted, confirming the authoritarian status of the board members in service to the community. Conciliation aims to smooth over the inevitable conflicts sure to emerge in a diverse population, conciliating the rights of the individual with those of the group.

Similar to appeasement, conciliation effectively sidesteps the insistent quality of the compassion professed by the group authority figure, although cloaked within the conventions of civil society; hence, disguising any willing participation therein. The conciliatory individual appeasingly denies acting submissively (without necessarily appearing to having done so), invoking a subliminally disqualified form of counter double bind maneuver, similar to that previously established for indulgence. Conciliation shares a similar paradoxical structure with appeasement in terms of reciprocating one's expected role, where one's true emotional saliency is scarcely as compelling as if it were freely offered to begin with.

ACCOMMODATION

The ascending disqualified hierarchy of appeasement and conciliation, in turn, extends to a universal sphere of influence with respect to the related theme of *accommodation*. The term derives from the Latin *accommodare* from *ad-* (to) and *commodus* (fitting), suggestive of such compromising attributes. The accommodating individual is guided by obliging or appeasing motives similar to the solicitous attributes previously established for gratitude. According to British statesman, Philip Stanhope: "Civility, which is a disposition to *accommodate* and oblige others, is essentially the same in every country; although good breeding (as it is called) is different in almost every country."

In a more universal sense, accommodation refers to those physical requirements crucial to one's physical sense of wellbeing, as in a safe place to sleep and/or adequate nourishment. This particularly extends to the expectations of the weary traveler, where the need for acceptable facilities is crucial. This class of *accommodations* is rated according to a four-star rating system enforced by local tourist guilds, where the quality of hotels, taverns, and restaurants may be adequately ascertained. Guarantees of accommodation are protected under the law, the Civil-Rights Act of 1964 barring racial discrimination in transportation and public accommodations.

In direct analogy to its related counterpart in gratitude, accommodation represents a subliminally disqualified style of counter double bind maneuver, one that effectively sidesteps the insistent quality of the merciful sense of compassion expressed by the spiritual authority figure. One's accommodating compliance is chiefly made on legal/social grounds, rather than any volitional compliance in terms. Through such an innate denial of complicity, the spiritual disciple figure effectively assumes his expected role within the two-stage transitional dynamic, although in a thoroughly non-confrontational fashion.

SACRIFICE

The ascending transitional hierarchy of appeasement, conciliation, and accommodation ultimately culminates with respect to the crowning humanitarian theme of *sacrifice*. It traditionally is defined as the act of offering-up one's self-interest in deference to a higher good or purpose. The term derives from the Latin *sacrificium* from *sacer* (sacred) and *facere* (to make). The enduring humanitarian prerequisites for sacrifice prove particularly consistent with the appeasement focus previously established for conciliation and accommodation. For the Romans, a valued commodity (such as a bullock) was sacrificed as a burnt offering in order to petition a lenient treatment from the divine pantheon of gods. The sacrificial priest (with his head covered by his toga) offered an initial sacrifice of grain and wine on the altar of the sacred flame in preparation for the blood sacrifice.

In a more modern context, examples of selfless sacrifice are found across many organizational settings. Certainly the greatest sacrifice of all is to offer-up one's life for that of another, so great the empathic bond. This is fictionally encountered in the *Tale of Two Cities*, where the hero nobly takes the place of his friend sentenced to execution: a sacrifice complicated by the common love of a woman. Sacrifice, accordingly, represents an enduring humanitarian theme revered throughout the ages. Here, sacrifice represents a subliminally disqualified decent sense of wisdom, whereby effectively side-stepping any overt complicity therein. Its appeal within a humanitarian sphere of influence echoes the spiritual focus previously established for accommodation. Through this ritual appeal to submissive-appeasement, the reluctant humanitarian follower sacrificially deflects the more insistent merciful sense of forgiveness on the part of the respective authority figure, whereby disqualifying any overt sense of complicity in the process.

In summary, the completed description of the dual classifications for the lesser virtues (I) and (II) invites many practical applications relating to the reciprocal interplay of double bind and counter double bind maneuvers. Certainly an advanced degree of social sophistication is required to successfully navigate such an intricate social milieu. In our modern fast-paced society, such skills become virtually second-nature in terms of transitioning into rapidly-shifting social coalitions. A sharp sense of humor is a key factor to social success, as reflected in the entertaining genre of the situation comedy. Life scarcely is always amusing, however, giving way to the parallel range of sensitivities relating to the intricacies of tragedy and melodrama. The truest test to life involves maintaining a delicate balance between the extremes of comedy and tragedy.

14

THE ACCESSORY VARIATIONS FOR THE LESSER VIRTUES (I) and (II)

In conclusion, the completed description of the transitional classifications for the lesser virtues (I) and (II) offer a fitting validation to what had originally amounted to somewhat of an intuitive style of analysis. Indeed, it proves particularly amazing that even the main versions of the lesser virtues were so convincingly specified within the enduring traditions of English language culture. The addition of a parallel complement of *accessory* lesser virtues might realistically be predicted in light of the fortuitous identification of a rather broad number of suitable synonyms for constructing such an all-inclusive accessory system. Consequently, this accessory complement for the lesser virtues will now be described, representing close motivational synonyms for the main virtuous terms they serve to complement: formally specified through a systematic reversal of the polarities characterizing the "you" and "I" perspectives.

Similar to the main versions of the lesser virtues, the accessory variations span the entire range of personal, group, spiritual, and humanitarian levels across the transitional hierarchy. For instance, for the accessory lesser virtues (I), the respective double bind follower sequence of fealty-steadfastness-adoration-happiness effectively specifies a follower-based focus aimed at reciprocating the immediately-active focus characterizing the respective authority roles: in analogy to the main sequence of loyalty, fidelity, piety, and felicity. This initial overture, in turn, prompts the (accessory) counter double bind sequence of simplicity-loftiness-sublimity-splendor through a disqualified evasion of any overt complicity therein.

In a related more lenient context, the accessory follower sequence of accountability-obligation-obeisance-commitment similarly specifies a future-directed focus, although now targeting the realm of negative reinforcement. Consequently,

the remaining accessory sequence of counter double bind terms; namely, blamelessness-exculpation-acquittal-impeccability effectively initiates the remainder of the transitional sequence.

An affiliated sequence of accessory terms is further based upon the related double bind and counter double bind interplay of adherence/demureness (beginning with respect to the personal level). For instance, the group representative adherently acts in a gallant fashion in anticipation of the coy sense of demureness characterizing the (authority) counter double bind maneuver. In terms of the next higher (universal) level, the spiritual disciple gallantly acts in a stately fashion in anticipation of the coy sense of wholesomeness expressed by the respective authority figure. Furthermore, in terms of the remaining humanitarian level, the representative member of humanity fervorously acts in a stately fashion in anticipation of the authority figure's disqualified sense of excellence (indicative of the counter double bind maneuver).

The fourth (and final) dimension of accessory terms is based upon the initial (personal) interplay of wariness/timidity (the accessory counterparts for vigilance and meekness). The accessory hierarchy of follower terms (wariness-intrepidity-stalwartness-victory) reciprocally complements the *main* transitional counterparts in terms of the "you" and "I" perspectives: namely, vigilance, courage, valor, and triumph. Furthermore, the remaining accessory listing of counter double bind maneuvers; timidity, complaisance, compliance, and amicableness makes a fitting counterpoint to the main hierarchy of themes: meekness, obedience, conformity, and pacifism.

A similar style of analysis further holds true for the remaining accessory classifications for the

224	225
Fealty	Accountability
226	**227**
Adherence	Wariness

TRANSITIONAL
ALTER EGO STATES
(Personal Double-Bind)

→

214.1	215.1
Simplicity	Blamelessness
216.1	**217.1**
Demureness	Timidity

DISQUALIFIED
EGO STATES
(Personal Counter Double-Bind)

244	245
Steadfastness	Obligation
246	**247**
Gallantry	Intrepidity

TRANSITIONAL
CARDINAL VIRTUES
(Group Double-Bind)

→

234.1	235.1
Loftiness	Exculpation
236.1	**237.1**
Coyness	Complaisance

DISQUALIFIED
PERSONAL IDEALS
(Group Counter Double-Bind)

264	265
Adoration	Obeisance
266	**267**
Stateliness	Stalwartness

TRANSITIONAL
THEOLOGICAL VIRTUES
(Spiritual Double-Bind)

→

254.1	255.1
Sublimeness	Aquittal
256.1	**257.1**
Wholesomeness	Compliance

DISQUALIFIED
CIVIL LIBERTIES
(Spiritual Counter Double-Bind)

284	285
Happiness	Commitment
286	**287**
Fervor	Victory

TRANSITIONAL
GREEK VALUES
(Humanitarian Double-Bind)

→

274.1	275.1
Splendor	Impeccability
276.1	**277.1**
Excellence	Amicableness

DISQUALIFIED
ECUMENICAL IDEALS
(Humanit. Counter Double-Bind)

Fig. 14A – The Accessory Lesser Virtues - (I)

214	215
Self-Respect	Sorrow
216	**217**
Amiability	Empathy

TRANSITIONAL
EGO STATES
(PA - Double-Bind)

⟶

224.1	225.1
Esteem	Lenity
226.1	**227.1**
Favor	Placation

DISQUALIFIED
ALTER EGO STATES
(PF - Counter-Double-Bind)

234	235
Ostentation	Remorse
236	**237**
Conviviality	Commiseration

TRANSITIONAL
PERSONAL IDEALS
(GA - Double-Bind)

⟶

244.1	245.1
Acclaim	Remittance
246.1	**247.1**
Sanction	Concordance

DISQUALIFIED
CARDINAL VIRTUES
(GR - Counter Double-Bind)

254	255
Holiness	Regretfulness
256	**257**
Generosity	Pity

TRANSITIONAL
CIVIL LIBERTIES
(SA - Double-Bind)

⟶

264.1	265.1
Ardor	Dispensation
266.1	**267.1**
Thanksgiving	Consonance

DISQUALIFIED
THEOLOGICAL VIRTUES
(SD - Counter Double-Bind)

274	275
Supremacy	Grief
276	**277**
Benignity	Remission

TRANSITIONAL
ECUMENICAL IDEALS
(HA - Double-Bind)

⟶

284.1	285.1
Exultation	Redemption
286.1	**287.1**
Beneficence	Propitiation

DISQUALIFIED
GREEK VALUES
(RH - Counter Double-Bind)

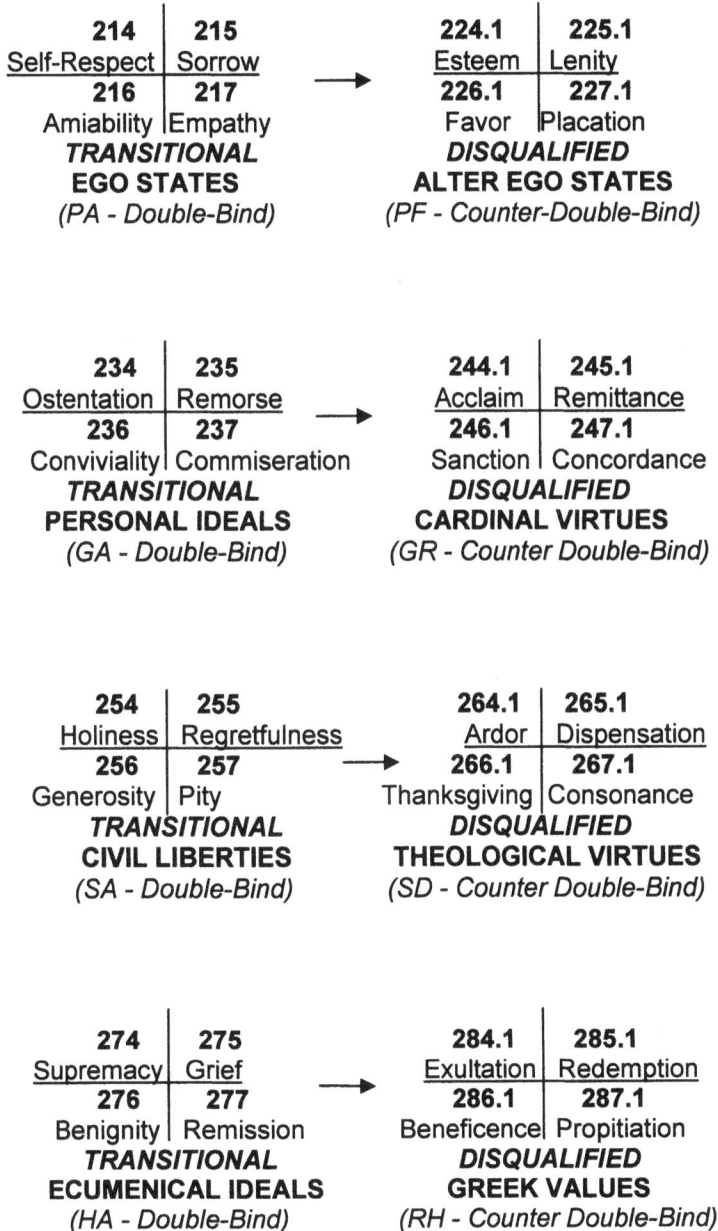

Fig. 14B – The Accessory Lesser Virtues - (II)

FEALTY	SIMPLICITY
Previously, you (as personal authority) have poignantly acted approachfully in response to the admiring treatment of the personal follower. But now, I (as new personal follower) will admiringly act with *fealty* towards you: in anticipation of your (as established PA) poignant treatment of me.	Previously, I (as new personal follower) have admiringly acted with fealty towards you: in anticipation of your (as established PA) poignant treatment of me. But now, you (as reluctant personal authority) will *simplicitously* deny acting poignantly towards me: thwarting my (as new PF) admiring sense of fealty.
STEADFASTNESS	**LOFTINESS**
Previously, you (as group authority) have poignantly acted in an exalted fashion in response to the circumspective-admiration of the group representative. But now, I (as new group representative) will *steadfastly* act with fealty towards you: in anticipation of your (as established GA) poignant sense of exaltation.	Previously, I (as new group representative) have steadfastly acted with fealty towards you: in anticipation of your (as established GA) poignant sense of exaltation. But now, you (as reluctant group authority) will simplicitously act in a *lofty* fashion towards me: thwarting my (as new GR) steadfast sense of fealty.
ADORATION	**SUBLIMITY**
Previously, you (as spiritual authority) have exaltedly acted in a bountiful fashion in response to the circumspective sense of devotion of the spiritual disciple. But now, I (as new spiritual disciple) will steadfastly act in an *adoring* fashion towards you: in anticipation of your (as established SA) exalted sense of bountifulness.	Previously, I (as new spiritual disciple) have steadfastly acted in an adoring fashion towards you: in anticipation of your (as established SA) exalted sense of bountifulness. But now, you (as reluctant spiritual authority) will loftily act in a *sublime* fashion towards me: thwarting my (as new SD) steadfast-adoration of you.
HAPPINESS	**SPLENDOR**
Previously, you (as humanitarian authority) have bountifully acted blessingly in response to the charming sense of devotion of the representative member of humanity. But now, I (as new representative member of humanity) will adoringly act in a *happy* fashion towards you: in anticipation of your (as established HA) bountiful-blessing of me.	Previously, I (as new representative member of humanity) have adoringly acted in a happy fashion towards you: in anticipation of your (as established HA) bountiful-blessing of me. But now, you (as reluctant humanitarian authority) will *splendorously* act in a sublime fashion towards me: thwarting my (as new RH) happy-adoration of you.

Table F-1 – The Acc. Lesser Virtues Based on Fealty/Simplicity

ACCOUNTABILITY	BLAMELESSNESS
Previously, you (as personal authority) have culpably acted submissively in response to the concerned treatment of the personal follower. But now, I (as new personal follower) will concernedly seek a sense of *accountability* towards you: in anticipation of your (as established PA) culpable treatment of me.	Previously, I (as new personal follower) have concernedly sought a sense of accountability towards you: in anticipation of your (as established PA) culpable treatment of me. But now, you (as reluctant personal authority) will *blamelessly* deny acting culpably towards me: thwarting my (as new PF) concerned quest for accountability towards you.
OBLIGATION	EXCULPATION
Previously, you (as group authority) have culpably acted in an upright fashion in response to the equitable sense of concern of the group representative. But now, I (as new group representative) will *obligingly* seek a sense of accountability towards you: in anticipation of your (as established GA) culpable sense of uprightness.	Previously, I (as new group representative) have obligingly sought a sense of accountability towards you: in anticipation of your (as established GA) culpable sense of uprightness. But now, you (as reluctant group authority) will blamelessly act in an *exculpatory* fashion towards me: thwarting my (as new GR) obliging quest for accountability towards you.
OBEISANCE	ACQUITTAL
Previously, you (as spiritual authority) have freely acted in an upright fashion in response to the equitable sense of fairness of the spiritual disciple. But now, I (as new spiritual disciple) will obligingly seek a sense of *obeisance* towards you: in anticipation of your (as established SA) free sense of uprightness.	Previously, I (as new spiritual disciple) have obligingly sought a sense of obeisance towards you: in anticipation of your (as established SA) free sense of uprightness. But now, you (as reluctant spiritual authority) will exculpatorily express a quest for *acquittal* towards me: thwarting my (as new SD) obliging quest for obeisance.
COMMITMENT	IMPECCABILITY
Previously, you (as humanitarian authority) have freely acted in a conscientious fashion in response to the fair sense of credence of the representative member of humanity. But now, I (as new representative member of humanity) will obeisantly act in a *committed* fashion towards you: in anticipation of your (as establ. HA) free sense of conscientiousness.	Previously, I (as new representative member of humanity) have obeisantly acted committedly towards you: in anticipation of your (as establ. HA) free sense of conscientiousness. But now, you (as reluctant humanitarian authority) will *impeccably* express a quest for acquittal towards me: thwarting my (as new RH) obeisant sense of commitment.

Table F-2 – The Acc. Lesser Virtues Based on Account./Blameless.

ADHERENCE Previously, I (as personal authority) have passionately acted rewardingly in response to the aspiring treatment of the personal follower. But now, you (as new personal follower) will aspiringly act in an *adherent* fashion towards me: in anticipation of my (as established PA) passionate treatment of you.	**DEMURENESS** Previously, you (as new personal follower) have aspiringly acted in an adherent fashion towards me: in anticipation of my (as established PA) passionate treatment of you. But now, I (as reluctant personal authority) will *demurely* deny acting passionately towards you: thwarting your (as new PF) adherent treatment of me.
GALLANTRY Previously, I (as group authority) have passionately acted respectfully in response to the continently-admiring treatment of the group representative. But now, you (as new group representative) will adherently act in a *gallant* fashion towards me: in anticipation of my (as established GA) passionate-respect for you.	**COYNESS** Previously, you (as new group representative) have adherently acted in a gallant fashion towards me: in anticipation of my (as established GA) passionate-respect for you. But now, I (as reluctant group authority) will demurely act in a *coy* fashion towards you: thwarting your (as new GR) gallant treatment of me.
STATELINESS Previously, I (as spiritual authority) have courteously acted respectfully in response to the continent sense of kindness of the spiritual disciple. But now, you (as new spiritual disciple) will gallantly act in a *stately* fashion towards me: in anticipation of my (as established SA) courteous-respect for you.	**WHOLESOMENESS** Previously, you (as new spiritual disciple) have gallantly acted in a stately fashion towards me: in anticipation of my (as established SA) courteous-respect for you. But now, I (as reluctant spiritual authority) will coyly act in a *wholesome* fashion towards you: thwarting your (as new SD) gallant sense of stateliness.
FERVOR Previously, I (as humanitarian authority) have courteously acted in a gracious fashion in response to the beauteous-faith of the representative member of humanity But now, you (as new representative member of humanity) will *fervently* act in a stately fashion towards me: in anticipation of my (as established HA) courteous sense of graciousness.	**EXCELLENCE** Previously, you (as new representative member of humanity) have fervently acted in a stately fashion: in anticipation of my (as establ. HA) courteous sense of graciousness. But now, I (as reluctant humanitarian authority) will wholesomely react with *excellence* towards you: thwarting your (as new RH) fervent sense of stateliness.

Table F-3 – The Acc. Lesser Virtues Based on Adherence/Demureness

WARINESS	TIMIDITY
Previously, I (as personal authority) have apprehensively acted in a lenient fashion in response to the deferential treatment of the personal follower. But now, you (as new personal follower) will deferentially act in a *wary* fashion towards me: in anticipation of my (as established PA) apprehensive treatment of you.	Previously, you (as new personal follower) have deferentially acted in a *wary* fashion towards me: in anticipation of my (as established PA) apprehensive treatment of you. But now, I (as reluctant personal authority) will *timidly* deny acting apprehensively towards you: thwarting your (as new PF) wary treatment of me.
INTREPIDITY	COMPLAISANCE
Previously, I (as group authority) have apprehensively acted with probity in response to the brave sense of wariness of the group representative. But now, you (as new group representative) will warily act in an *intrepid* fashion towards me: in anticipation of my (as established GA) apprehensive sense of probity.	Previously, you (as new group representative) have warily acted in an intrepid fashion towards me: in anticipation of my (as established GA) apprehensive sense of probity. But now, I (as reluctant group authority) will *complaisantly* act in a timid fashion towards you: thwarting your (as new GR) intrepid treatment of me.
STALWARTNESS	COMPLIANCE
Previously, I (as spiritual authority) have forbearingly acted with probity in response to the scrupulous sense of bravery expressed by the spiritual disciple. But now, you (as new spiritual disciple) will *stalwartly* act in an intrepid fashion towards me: in anticipation of my (as established SA) forbearing sense of probity.	Previously, you (as new spiritual disciple) have stalwartly acted in an intrepid fashion towards me: in anticipation of my (as established SA) forbearing sense of probity. But now, I (as reluctant spiritual authority) will complaisantly act in a *compliant* fashion towards you: thwarting your (as new SD) stalwart treatment of me.
VICTORY	AMICABLENESS
Previously, I (as humanitarian authority) have forbearingly acted patiently in response to the scrupulous sense of shrewdness of the representative member of humanity. But now, you (as new representative member of humanity) will stalwartly act *victoriously* towards me: in anticipation of my (as established HA) forbearingly-patient treatment of you.	Previously, you (as new representative member of humanity) have stalwartly acted victoriously towards me: in anticipation of my (as establ. HA) forbearingly-patient treatment of you. But now, I (as reluctant humanitarian authority) will compliantly act in an *amicable* fashion towards you: thwarting your (as new RH) victorious treatment of me.

Table F-4 - The Acc. Lesser Virtues Based on Wariness/Timidity

SELF-RESPECT	ESTEEM
Previously, I (as personal follower) have rewardingly acted in an admiring fashion in response to the poignant treatment of the personal authority. But now, you (as new personal authority) will poignantly act with *self-respect* towards me: in anticipation of my (as established PF) admiring treatment of you.	Previously, you (as new personal authority) have poignantly acted in a self-respecting fashion towards me: in anticipation of my (as established PF) admiring treatment of you. But now, I (as reluctant personal follower) will *esteemfully* deny acting admiringly towards you: thwarting your (as new PA) poignant sense of self-respect.
OSTENTATION	**ACCLAIM**
Previously, I (as group representative) have circumspectively acted in an admiring fashion in response to the poignant sense of exaltation of the group authority. But now, you (as new group authority) will self-respectingly act *ostentatiously* towards me: in anticipation of my (as established GR) circumspective-admiration for you.	Previously, you (as new group authority) have self-respectingly acted ostentatiously towards me: in anticipation of my (as established GR) circumspective-admiration for you. But now, I (as reluctant group representative) will esteemfully express *acclaim* towards you: thwarting your (as new GA) ostentatious treatment of me.
HOLINESS	**ARDOR**
Previously, I (as spiritual disciple) have circumspectively acted in a devoted fashion in response to the exalted sense of bountifulness of the spiritual authority. But now, you (as new spiritual authority) will ostentatiously act in a *holy* fashion towards me: in anticipation of my (as established SD) circumspective-devotion for you.	Previously, you (as new spiritual authority) have ostentatiously acted in a holy fashion towards me: in anticipation of my (as established SD) circumspective-devotion for you. But now, I (as reluctant spiritual disciple) will *ardently* act in an acclaimful fashion towards you: thwarting your (as new SA) ostentatious sense of holiness.
SUPREMACY	**EXULTATION**
Previously, I (as representative member of humanity) have charmingly acted in a devoted fashion in response to the bountiful-blessings of the humanitarian authority. But now, you (as new humanitarian authority) will *supremely* express a sense of holiness towards me: in anticipation of my (as established RH) charming-devotion for you.	Previously, you (as new humanitarian authority) have supremely expressed a holy attitude towards me: in anticipation of my (as established RH) charming-devotion for you. But now, I (as reluctant representative member of humanity) will ardently act with *exultation* towards you: thwarting your (as new HA) supreme sense of holiness.

Table G-1 – The Acc. Definitions Based on Self-Respect/Esteem

SORROW	LENITY
Previously, I (as personal follower) have leniently acted in a concerned fashion in response to the culpable treatment of the personal authority. But now, you (as new personal authority) will culpably act in a *sorrowful* fashion towards me: in anticipation of my (as established PF) concerned treatment of you.	Previously, you (as new personal authority) have culpably acted in a sorrowful fashion towards me: in anticipation of my (as established PF) concerned treatment of you. But now, I (as reluctant personal follower) will *leniently* deny acting with concern towards you: thwarting your (as new PA) sorrowful treatment of me.
REMORSE	REMITTANCE
Previously, I (as group representative) have equitably acted with concern in response to the culpable sense of uprightness of the group authority. But now, you (as new group authority) will sorrowfully act in a *remorseful* fashion towards me: in anticipation of my (as established GR) equitable sense of concern.	Previously, you (as new group authority) have sorrowfully acted in a remorseful fashion towards me: in anticipation of my (as established GR) equitable sense of concern. But now, I (as reluctant group representative) will *remittingly* act with lenity towards you: thwarting your (as new GA) remorseful treatment of me.
REGRETFULNESS	DISPENSATION
Previously, I (as spiritual disciple) have equitably acted in a fair fashion in response to the free sense of uprightness of the spiritual authority. But now, you (as new spiritual authority) will remorsefully act in a *regretful* fashion towards me: in anticipation of my (as established SD) equitably-fair treatment of you.	Previously, you (as new spiritual authority) have remorsefully acted in a regretful fashion towards me: in anticipation of my (as established SD) equitably-fair treatment of you. But now, I (as reluctant spiritual disciple) will remittingly act in a *dispensational* fashion towards you: thwarting your (as new SA) remorseful sense of regret.
GRIEF	REDEMPTION
Previously, I (as representative member of humanity) have fairly expressed a sense of credence in response to the free sense of conscientiousness of the humanitarian authority. But now, you (as new humanitarian authority) will regretfully express a sense of *grief* towards me: in anticipation of my (as established RH) fair sense of credence.	Previously, you (as new humanitarian authority) have regretfully expressed a sense of grief towards me: in anticipation of my (as established RH) fair sense of credence. But now, I (as reluctant representative member of humanity) will dispensationally act in a *redemptive* fashion towards you: thwarting your (as new HA) grieving treatment of me.

Table G- 2 - The Accessory Definitions Based on Sorrow/Lenity

AMIABILITY	FAVOR
Previously, you (as personal follower) have aspiringly acted approachfully in response to the passionate treatment of the personal authority. But now, I (as new personal authority) will passionately act in an *amiable* fashion towards you: in anticipation of your (as established PF) aspiring treatment of me.	Previously, I (as new personal authority) have passionately acted in an amiable fashion towards you: in anticipation of your (as established PF) aspiring treatment of me. But now, you (as reluctant personal follower) will *favoringly* deny acting aspiringly towards me: thwarting my (as new PA) amiable treatment of you.
CONVIVIALITY	SANCTION
Previously, you (as group representative) have continently acted aspiringly in response to the passionate-respect of the group authority. But now, I (as new group authority) will amiably act in a *convivial* fashion towards you: in anticipation of your (as established GR) continently-aspiring treatment of me.	Previously, I (as new group authority) have amiably acted in a convivial fashion towards you: in anticipation of your (as established GR) continently-aspiring treatment of me. But now, you (as reluctant group representative) will favoringly act in a *sanctioning* fashion towards me: thwarting my (as new GA) convivial treatment of you.
GENEROSITY	THANKSGIVING
Previously, you (as spiritual disciple) have continently acted in a kind fashion in response to the courteous-respect of the spiritual authority. But now, I (as new spiritual authority) will convivially act in a *generous* fashion towards you: in anticipation of your (as established SD) continently-kind treatment of me.	Previously, I (as new spiritual authority) have convivially acted in a generous fashion towards you: in anticipation of your (as established SD) continently-kind treatment of me. But now, you (as reluctant spiritual disciple) will sanctioningly act In a *thankful* fashion towards me: thwarting my (as new SA) convivially-generous treatment of you.
BENIGNITY	BENEFICENCE
Previously, you (as representative member of humanity) have benevolently acted kindly in response to the courteous sense of graciousness of the humanitarian authority. But now, I (as new humanitarian authority) will generously act in a *benign* fashion towards you: in anticipation of your (as established RH) benevolent sense of kindness.	Previously, I (as new humanitarian authority) have generously acted in a benign fashion towards you: in anticipation of your (as established RH) benevolent sense of kindness. But now, you (as reluctant representative member of humanity) will thankfully act in a *beneficent* fashion towards me: thwarting my (as new HA) benign treatment of you.

Table G-3 – The Acc. Definitions Based Upon Amiability/Favor

EMPATHY	PLACATION
Previously, you (as personal follower) have deferentially acted aversively in response to the apprehensive treatment of the personal authority. But now, I (as new personal authority) will *empathically* act apprehensively towards you: in anticipation of your (as established PF) deferential treatment of me.	Previously, I (as new personal authority) have empathically acted apprehensively towards you: in anticipation of your (as established PF) deferential treatment of me. But now, you (as reluctant personal follower) will *placatingly* deny acting deferentially towards me: thwarting my (as new PA) empathic treatment of you.
COMMISERATION	**CONCORDANCE**
Previously, you (as group representative) have bravely acted in a deferential fashion in response to the apprehensive sense of probity of the group authority. But now, I (as new group authority) will empathetically act with *commiseration* towards you: in anticipation of your (as established GR) brave sense of deference.	Previously, I (as new group authority) have will empathically acted with commiseration towards you: in anticipation of your (as established GR) brave sense of deference. But now, you (as reluctant group representative) will placatingly act with *concordance* towards me: thwarting my (as new GA) empathetic sense of commiseration.
PITY	**CONSONANCE**
Previously, you (as spiritual disciple) have scrupulously acted in a brave fashion in response to the forbearing sense of probity of the spiritual authority. But now, I (as new spiritual authority) will commiseratingly act in a *pitying* fashion towards you: in anticipation of your (as established SD) scrupulous sense of bravery.	Previously, I (as new spiritual authority) have commiseratingly acted pityingly towards you: in anticipation of your (as established SD) scrupulous sense of bravery. But now, you (as reluctant spiritual disciple) will concordingly express a *consonant* attitude towards me: thwarting my (as new SA) commiserating sense of pity.
REMISSION	**PROPITIATION**
Previously, you (as representative member of humanity) have scrupulously acted shrewdly in response to the forbearing sense of patience of the humanitarian authority. But now, I (as new humanitarian authority) will piteously act with *remission* towards you: in anticipation of your (as established RH) scrupulous sense of shrewdness.	Previously, I (as new humanitarian authority) have piteously acted with remission towards you: in anticipation of your (as established RH) scrupulous sense of shrewdness. But now, you (as reluctant representative member of humanity) will consonantly act in a *propitiatory* fashion towards me: thwarting my (as new HA) remitting treatment of you.

Table G-4 - The Acc. Definitions Based Upon Empathy / Placation

lesser virtues (II). Rather than laboriously attempting to spell-out the motivational dynamics for all of these terms in detail, a complete listing of the accessory terms for the lesser virtues (I) is schematically depicted in **Fig. 14A**, and also in the compact table below.

Fealty → Simplicity   Accountability→ Blameless.
Steadfast. → Loftiness   Obligation → Exculpation
Adoration → Sublimity   Obeisance → Acquittal
Happiness → Splendor   Commit.→ Impeccabil.

Adherence → Demureness   Wariness → Timidity
Gallantry → Coyness   Intrepid.→ Complaisance
Stateliness → Wholesome. Stalwart. → Compliance
Fervor → Excellence   Victory → Amicableness

Furthermore, the complete listing of the accessory terms for the lesser virtues (II) is depicted in **Fig. 14B**, as well as the compact table below.

Self-Resp. → Esteem   Sorrow → Lenity
Ostentation → Acclaim   Remorse → Remittance
Holiness → Ardor   Regretful. → Dispensation
Supremacy → Exultation   Grief → Redemption

Amiability → Favor   Placation → Empathy
Conviviality → Sanction   Concord. → Commiser.
Generosity → Thanksgiving   Consonance → Pity
Beneficence → Benignity   Propitiat. → Remission

This arrangement is similar in form and function to that previously described for the *main* listings of lesser virtues in Chapters *9* through *13*. It should be emphasized that this accessory assortment of terms necessarily remains a work in progress, their precise determination relying upon the identification of closely-matched synonyms for each of the main terms (a somewhat subjective undertaking). Consequently, a more detailed description of these individual accessory terms will not be undertaken at this juncture, an aspect best deferred to a potentially expanded, upcoming edition. Certainly, the detailed literary traditions targeting this accessory complement of terms scarcely prove as convincing or detailed as those initially established for the main virtuous counterparts. The overarching cohesiveness of this accessory hierarchy of lesser virtues, however, proves suitably convincing in a holistic sense, perhaps requiring only a few minor adjustments with respect to any future versions of this topic.

THE SCHEMATIC DEFINITIONS FOR THE ACCESSORY LESSER VIRTUES

In agreement with the main complement of lesser virtues, it should further be feasible (by definition) to incorporate the accessory sequences of lesser virtues directly into the formal schematic definition format. This is necessarily accompanied by a strict reversal in the polarities of the "you" and "I" perspectives across the board, resulting in an entire parallel complement of schematic definitions for the accessory lesser virtues. Indeed, this accessory complement schematic definitions for the lesser virtues (I) is outlined in **Tables F-1** to **F-4**. Furthermore, the schematic definitions for the lesser virtues (II) are alternately depicted in **Tables G-1** to **G-4**. These accessory definitions for the lesser virtues (I) and (II) prove particularly effective for modeling the empathic dimensions underlying humor and comedy in general, permitting a convincing simulation of the more light-hearted aspects of the virtuous human emotions. Indeed, natural empathic ability appears to be a prerequisite for adequately telling a joke, in addition to comprehending its underlying significance.

This innate conceptual balance between seriousness and humor emerges as a common feature across virtually all ages and cultures. The militant Taliban regime (that briefly ruled over Afghanistan) presumptuously banned frivolous entertainment and diversion under the pretense of representing an affront to the solemnity of Islam. Fortunately, this repressive measure was ultimately doomed to failure, for a whimsical sense of human camaraderie and fraternity amongst allies proves crucial over the long run. Here, the convoluted dictates of pageantry versus protocol essentially mirror the transitional interplay of the double bind and counter double bind maneuvers. Indeed, skilled diplomacy chiefly dictates putting forth a favorable spin, each side delicately navigating through a minefield of uncertainty. Consequently, a measured balance in terms of both whimsy and seriousness makes for effective international relations, and certainly one ever more crucial for maintaining an optimal degree of global peace and harmony.

PART-III

15

THE PHANTOM AND FANTASY DIALOGUES

The completed description for both the major and lesser virtuous modes has currently been restricted to only the active domain of human dialogue (between at least two physically present participants). Other formats, however, prove equally feasible; namely, those suggestively specified within the notions of the phantom and fantasy dialogues. The *phantom* dialogue is defined as communication directed to an absent individual (the phantom). It includes letter writing (in a printed form), or the monologue/soliloquy (in spoken mode). The *fantasy* dialogue, in turn, takes this trend to its limit: where both parties are relegated to a type of phantom role, as in the literary genre of fiction (where all parties are fictitious). The remainder of this chapter examines both the phantom and fantasy dialogues in terms of their radical expansion to the realm of the more basic virtuous themes initially established for the realm of direct human dialogue. A complete listing of the virtuous themes for the phantom/fantasy dialogues is schematically depicted in **Figs. 15A** and **15B**, providing a convenient reference guide for the upcoming discussion to follow.

This higher-order class of themes represents a "meta-order" summation encompassing each specific level within the ethical hierarchy, in essence, a 2nd order style of metaperspective. For instance, as previously demonstrated for direct dialogue, the general unifying theme of "utilitarianism" encompasses the group follower focus comprising the cardinal virtues (prudence-justice-temperance-fortitude): effectively outlining the group follower perspective. A similar pattern further holds true for the remaining spiritual, humanitarian, and transcendental levels within the virtuous hierarchy: as originally thematically specified in **Fig. 8A** of Chapter 8. For instance, the personal authority perspective introduces the theme of *individualism*, extending to the theme of *personalism* at the next higher group authority level. The spiritual authority perspective, in turn, targets the more idealized theme of *romanticism* consistent with a more widespread focus on universal principles. The themes for the remaining humanitarian and transcendental levels, in turn, take their cues from the designations specifying the individual listings of terms; namely, *ecumenism* and *humanism*, respectively.

In a related fashion, the remaining sequence of *follower* roles is similarly organized in terms of an ascending hierarchy of general unifying themes; namely, pragmatism, utilitarianism, ecclesiasticism, eclecticism, and mysticism. For instance, the first-mentioned theme of *pragmatism* refers to that which is potentially expedient to the individual, extending (in a group sense) to a *utilitarian* (projected) concern for "the common good." This ascending hierarchy of themes, in turn, extends to the remaining spiritual, humanitarian, and transcendental domains with respect to the themes of ecclesiasticism, eclecticism, and mysticism, respectively. It is scarcely surprising, then, that a similar pattern further holds true for the affiliated realm of phantom and fantasy dialogues, as well.

A few general observations may be deduced from this general pattern of unifying themes. As previously outlined, the general unifying themes are subdivided into either active authority modes (occurring in the present) or passively-potential follower modes (projected to occur within a future-directed time-frame). The active behavioral modes are designated in terms of the immediately active class of authority themes: namely, individualism, personalism, romanticism, ecumenism, and humanism. These authority-based themes represent immediately active perspectives that anticipate (as their object) the passively-potential complement of future-directed follower themes. Generally speaking, the personal authority themes immediately initiate the conditioned inter-action in anticipation of the future-based potenti-ality characterizing the respective follower themes.

The passively-potential follower themes, in turn, target the more mental realm of the mete-order roles in reference to their projected exten-sion into a future-directed time-frame: namely, pragmatism, utilitarianism, ecclesiasticism, eclec-ticism, and mysticism. This latter complement of follower themes effectively targets a future-directed time-frame, effectively predicting the outcome of the immediately active class of au-thority roles in relation to the overall dynamics governing the conditioned interaction. A more de-tailed examination for each of these general uni-fying themes will now be undertaken with respect to the phantom and fantasy dialogues, including an extensive analysis of their respective literary traditions.

THE PHANTOM DIALOGUE:
A MONOLOGUE IN WORDS

In terms of our modern mobile society, one often enters into relationships separated by barriers to direct communication. Communication doesn't cease, but rather switches from verbal to written form, as in letter writing or texting to a friend. In other words, I record my internal dialogue in or-der to communicate with you in a written format. In terms of this phantom style of dialogue, I care-fully record my feelings intended for your reac-tion, in turn, filling-in the perspectives you might experience if you were present. This projection of insights into the motives of another is a tradition-al literary device intended to simulate the conti-nuity underlying a more direct style of dialogue.

These fixed roles are reversed for the reader of the letter, in that the target (to which the letter has been addressed) has already been anticipat-ed. The letter reader assumes the formal role of the phantom, where feelings expressed by the letter writer are transferred in terms of such a time-displaced dialogue. In this two-stage fash-ion, the phantom dialogue simulates a direct dia-logue, although in a disjointed fashion clearly lacking the flexible of a direct dialogue. A similar pattern applies to a soliloquy upon a stage, where the audience assumes the active role of the phan-tom. The ritual of prayer and supplication can similarly be regarded as a phantom dialogue, alt-hough the more religiously-minded among us might insist it is actually a two-way dialogue.

Letter-writing actually represents a special case in relation to the mental dialogues that fill-up our introspective moments, although now rec-orded in written form. Also known as the *self*-dialogue, the mind is empathically flexible enough to take on (in imagination) a role that is not im-mediately present during this time of solitude or introspection. It is chiefly through this role-playing style of dialogue that I am able to plan a future course of action by imagining how my friends might view me under various circumstanc-es, and preparing accordingly (an aspect also akin to diary writing). Indeed, whether one relies upon a diary, a letter, or a soliloquy: the basic import of the phantom dialogue always remains in focus.

THE PLEDGE

Granted, letter-writing is primarily a personal ac-tivity, generally targeting an interpersonal focus within the virtuous hierarchy. The phantom dia-logue, however, in turn, extends to the fur-ther authority levels affiliated with a rather broad range of literary traditions. These traditional themes are specialized into two basic categories depending on whether the authority or follower roles are in focus at the time. The respective se-quence of authority themes is defined as the pledge, the proclamation, the edict, and the testament. The first mentioned theme of the *pledge* suggests an active style of personal au-thority role expressed through the theme of indi-vidualism: extending to a phantom focus through the generic profession of a *vow*. One informs all in attendance that a personal surety (in the form of an action or guarantee) is assured under the cur-rent circumstances. A pledge also extends to a written format, as in a formal guarantee of finan-cial support with respect to the fund-raising activ-ities of various benevolent organizations.

THE PROCLAMATION

The personal prerequisites for the pledge, in turn, extend to a group sphere of influence with respect to the civic notion of the *proclamation*. The ruler, as group authority figure, issues an open procla-mation to all of one's subjects, a phantom ex-pression of the authority status directed to the public at large. In order to achieve maximum im-pact, the proclamation has traditionally been is-sued in a written format, such as an inscribed parchment nailed up in the medieval marketplace. Through this public display of manifest authori-ty status (and subsequent word of mouth), the dictates of the monarch were eventually proclaimed across the length and breadth of the realm: whereby eliminating the excuse of ignorance in terms of failing to conform to the urgency of such immediately active royal decrees.

THE EDICT

The political focus for the proclamation, in turn, extends to a universal realm with respect to the overarching traditions governing the *edict*. Here, issues of an international focus are promulgated in a global context, as in the dictates of religious councils, where the spiritual authority issues an edict to the edification of the spiritual congregation. During medieval times, when the Catholic Church wielded supreme authority over Western culture, the Pope (or designees) projected supreme power through such written edicts, a decree the faithful were obliged to obey. The edict continues the tradition of the pledge and the proclamation in promulgating such authority roles.

THE TESTAMENT

The universal sphere of influence for the edict, in turn, can extend to elements befitting a humanitarian perspective: as reflected in the enduring traditions of the *testament*. As a literary device, it refers to a last will and testament, or any communication that bears witness to (or makes a covenant with) a binding scriptural context. The first-mentioned legacy style of testament shares with the proclamation/edict the bestowal of good will, although now extending to surviving generations. The "witness" style of testament, in turn, developed within the medieval ecclesiastical tradition, generally dealing with more lofty theological themes. In either case, the testament preserves the enduring focus of the first three themes, mirroring the ascending hierarchy of authority roles in an immediately active sense.

THE GRANT

The initial sequence of phantom themes for the authority roles, in turn, is further complemented by a parallel range of traditions targeting the follower roles: defined as the grant, the charter, the sanction, and the chronicle. For instance, the first-mentioned theme of the *grant* primarily suggests a personal sphere of influence: where the personal follower is potentially "granted" a privileged status in response to the pledge of action professed the personal authority figure. Here, the pledge/grant mirrors the interplay of the general unifying themes of individualism and pragmatism,

although now invoking a more abstract phantom focus. The future-directed focus for the grant is particularly evident in an academic sphere of research, where financial support is offered in return for services that guarantee ongoing investigation. Consequently, the reciprocal interplay of authority/follower roles is preserved with respect to the phantom prerequisites for the pledge/grant.

THE CHARTER

The personal prerequisites for the grant, in turn, extend to a civic significance with respect to the respective group follower theme of the *charter*. The charter is primarily encountered with respect to group contexts: e.g., business organizations, clubs, or mercantile endeavors. The group representative grants a "charter" status in response to the proclaimed sense of efficacy expressed by the group authority figure. This is exceedingly reminiscent of the utilitarian prerequisites previously established within a non-phantom context. Indeed, much of the settlement of the New World was facilitated through the granting of charters, where the services of willing colonists (such as the Pilgrims) were chartered by legal decree. Consequently, in terms of this cooperative style of group-driven endeavor, the concerted labor of the colonists was supported through a land-use charter bestowed in recognition of their determined effort.

THE SANCTION

Ascending, once again, to the next higher universal level, in turn, gives way to the spiritual prerequisites associated with the *sanction*. The sanction is virtually synonymous with a religious focus, as reflected in the (direct dialogue) characteristics initially established with respect to the theme of ecclesiasticism. As representative for the spiritual congregation, the spiritual disciple solemnly bestows his official sanction in response to the universal edict expressed by the spiritual authority figure, whereby imparting an overarching sense of holiness to the sanctified proceedings. Consequently, through this formal bestowal of sanction, the spiritual disciple figure restores an equal balance of power to the interplay of authority/follower roles, at least in relation to such a limited phantom context.

THE CHRONICLE

The preliminary sequence of the grant, the charter, and the sanction ultimately culminates with respect to the enduring humanitarian prerequisites

9118 – *The* PLEDGE *Phantom* - **Individualism** **Personal Authority**	**9128 – *The* GRANT** *Phantom* - **Pragmatism** **Personal Follower**
9138 – PROCLAMATION *Phantom* - **Personalism** **Group Authority**	**9148 – *The* CHARTER** *Phantom* - **Utilitarianism** **Group Representative**
9158 – *The* EDICT *Phantom* - **Romanticism** **Spiritual Authority**	**9168 – *The* SANCTION** *Phantom* - **Ecclesiasticism** **Spiritual Disciple**
9178 – *The* TESTAMENT *Phantom* - **Ecumenism** **Humanitarian Authority**	**9188 – *The* CHRONICLE** *Phantom* - **Eclecticism** **Humanitarian Follower**

Fig. 15A – The Themes for the Virtuous *Phantom* Dialogues

for the *chronicle*. It differs from the traditional literary genre of annals or almanacs in terms of its more comprehensive characteristics, whereby targeting the grander aspects of human history, such as the Medieval Chronicles or Viking Sagas. Here, a running commentary of historical events is set down in written form for the edification of all future generations to come. This is typically recorded from an overarching humanitarian stance, although now in the form of a phantom dialogue conducive to the span of ages. Indeed, all such communication with future generations must necessarily be viewed as a phantom dialogue, taking into full account the ongoing enactment of historical events.

In summary, the complete listing of themes for the phantom dialogue is depicted in a systematic fashion in **Fig. 15A**. In this schematic fashion, the phantom dialogues represent a stepwise variation on the main complement of virtuous themes initially described in Chapter *8*: a formal pattern similarly extending to the additional complement of fantasy dialogues, as well.

THE FANTASY DIALOGUE: THE REALM OF FICTIONAL IMAGINATION

As previously described for the phantom dialogue, the written word bridges the gap for space (as well as time). This proves a crucial advantage, in that the written word is essentially a permanent instrument, as opposed to the ephemeral quality of the spoken word. The written tradition allows one to communicate to future generations long after one's death. Indeed, libraries are crammed with dialogues from the past dedicated to future generations of readers. The phantom dialogue, however, is still a fairly restrictive writing style: with roles rigidly fixed for both reader and writer alike. Over time, the audience may change to such a degree as to outdate the material, leaving nothing more than a quaint curiosity.

The time-honored tradition for circumventing this shortcoming entails the use of an alternate strategy formally termed the *fantasy* dialogue. Also commonly known as fiction, the writer is divorced from any overt personal involvement within the work, freeing-up creativity conducive to a truly imaginative style of narrative. The reader, likewise, is not trapped into any particular role, rather free to identify with any of the fictional characters. This vaunted sense of imagination is not limited to simply gazing inward or manipulating a free range of images. The truly unfettered imagination entails a suspension of conventional presupposition or belief: an entertaining simula-

tion of make-believe conducive to creatively pretending or anticipating. According to Gaston Bachelard: "Imagination is not the faculty of forming images of reality, it is the faculty of forming images that go beyond reality, which turn reality into song." Consequently, good fiction is broadly appealing in that it has some general meaning for everyone, whether child or adult. By structuring the content to a fantasy level, the message is generalized to all ages and cultures, as witnessed in the great popularity of mythology and lore spanning ancient and modern times.

THE FABLE

Similar to the pattern previously established for the phantom dialogue, a parallel complement of fictional traditions is necessarily predicted to exist for each of the authority levels comprising the ascending hierarchy of themes. Here, the source of all dialogue is fictionally disqualified, even though a lesson is generally taught. This is frequently achieved by converting all of the characters into personifications of animals, such as dramatized in Aesop's Fables. A common-sense lesson (such as perseverance) is proclaimed using animal stereotypes, as in a foot-race pitting the determined tortoise against the overconfident hare. Lessons concerning industriousness contrast the dedicated ant and the carefree grasshopper in preparation for the winter. Sage wisdom is taught in terms of the immediately-active style of vitality characterizing the personal authority role. The fable represents a truly convincing style of fantasy dialogue, its import remaining relevant even to our modern age.

THE LEGEND

The personal focus of the myth/fable, in turn, extends to a civic sphere of influence with respect to the group authority theme of the *legend*. The legend is distinguished from fable in that the former typically contains a more historical context relevant to a broader public. Legends typically specify the lore of the common people, exalting folk heritage and/or national spirit. In a traditional sense, legends are narratives celebrating great folk heroes idealized to a broad degree: as in Paul Bunyan or Casey Jones. The group authority figure enjoys a legendary/mythical status befitting a leader among men. This is further reflected (in a non-fantasy sense) with respect to the immediately-active class of personal ideals (glory-honor-dignity-integrity). The legend serves as a fitting exemplar for us all, a paragon of virtue so sorely lacking in our modern age.

0118 – MYTH/FABLE *Fantasy* - **Individualism** **Personal Authority**	**0128 – RHETORIC** *Fantasy* - **Pragmatism** **Personal Follower**
0138 – LEGEND *Fantasy* - **Personalism** **Group Authority**	**0148 – PROPAGANDA** *Fantasy* - **Utilitarianism** **Group Representative**
0158 – PARABLE *Fantasy* - **Romanticism** *Spiritual Authority*	**0168 – PROPHESY** *Fantasy* - **Ecclesiasticism** **Spiritual Disciple**
0178 – ALLEGORY *Fantasy* - **Ecumenism** **Humanitarian Authority**	**0188 – UTOPIANISM** *Fantasy* - **Eclecticism** **Humanitarian Follower**

Fig. 15-B – The Themes for the Virtuous *Fantasy* Dialogues

THE PARABLE

Although legendary heroism proves a fitting fictional device for the group level, the next higher universal realm celebrates the related fantasy strategy of the *parable*. Here, the spiritual authority figure employs fictional imagery to press a moral point, such as those occasions when Christ used parables to teach a lesson. According to Matthew 10:13, the disciples inquire of Christ (following his Parable of the Sower) why he spoke to them in parables. Christ replies: "To you it has been given to know the secrets of the Kingdom of Heaven, but to them it has not been given … This is why I speak to them in parables, because seeing they do not see, and hearing they do not hear, nor do they understand." Christ's symbolic use of parables alludes to religious truths too abstract or controversial to be accepted by the uninitiated. The common man can insert himself into the story line through such a fantasy literary device. A fisherman gets the point of "a net cast into the sea," whereas the herder feels for "the lost sheep," while the farmer grasps "a seed cast upon barren ground."

ALLEGORY

The ascending sequence of the myth, legend, and parable ultimately extends to the more enduring (humanitarian) theme of *allegory*. It is defined as an extended sense of metaphor by which persons, objects, or actions within a narrative are equated with meanings transcending the narration. A given concept, therefore, is cast in the guise of another, often in the form of visual imagery. Indeed, an entire cast of characters is personified in terms of abstract qualities, with the setting further reflecting the interactions between such abstractions: as in fictitious, mythical, or historical themes. Its truest test extends to the observation that such abstractions profess meanings independent of the surface content within the story: whether religious, political, or satirical. The form of allegory most relevant to the humanitarian realm is known as the *apologue*, a short allegorical story emphasizing moral themes. In concert with the first three terms, the abstract theme of allegory effectively rounds-out the ascending hierarchy of (authority) fantasy themes.

RHETORIC

The orderly progression of fantasy themes for the authority roles, in turn, exhibits further parallels to the remaining sequence of terms targeting the follower realm: namely, rhetoric, propaganda, prophecy, and utopianism. For instance, the first listed theme of *rhetoric* is defined as persuasive or supportive dialogue, an interpretation dating at least to classical Greece. For the Sophists, rhetoric imparted effectiveness to public speaking and oratory. It denotes a style of literary composition of an emotional or imaginative nature, aiming to sway the audience through fair means (or foul). Indeed, as Isocrates once noted: "Rhetoric is the art of making great matters small, and small things great." This rhetorical style differs from simple testimony in that the personal reputation of the speaker is not essential for driving home the point of the message. Indeed, many such rhetorical strategies still find popular appeal today, in keeping with their affiliation to pragmatism. This emotional appeal, coupled with the charismatic role of the speaker, establishes rhetoric as a true fantasy style of dialogue, although primarily specialized towards personal ends.

PROPAGANDA

The personalized nature of rhetoric, in turn, extends to the group prerequisites specified for *propaganda*. It is defined as a rhetorical literary device enlisting stirring testimonials from group members in order to sway public sentiment as a whole. These highly emotional testimonials primarily consist of stereotyped clichés chiefly unsubstantiated by fact. Witness the wishful propaganda campaign waged by Fascist and Communist parties over the 20th century. Although the stigma of propaganda (to a large part) depends upon which side of the fence one stands on, the true danger arises in failing to recognize propaganda for what it presumes to be; namely, a projected fantasy dialogue (and nothing more).

PROPHESY

The disqualified characteristics of propaganda, in turn, extend to a universal sphere of influence with respect to the spiritual follower theme of *prophecy*. The disciple/prophet attributes the moralistic content of his message to the vagaries of divine inspiration, dream-imagery, or visions. This spirited literary device breaks the shackles of ordinary reality through the aid of symbolisms of virtually epic proportions. This is particularly true in the Book of Revelation, a literary tradition replete with dreamlike imagery and symbolism.

Prophecy is primarily distinguished from divination, in that the latter aims to predict future events through signals in nature (or rituals of chance). Prophecy, in contrast, takes well-established elements of religious belief, then embellishing them with contextual license (generally an event projected into the future). As such, prophecy represents a disqualified form of fantasy dialogue in relation to the spiritual congregation, permitting unfettered interpretation for dealing with controversial themes. Prophesy shares with rhetoric/propaganda a clear stretch of the imagination, although now appealing to supernatural influence as the rationale for its existence.

UTOPIANISM

The remaining humanitarian theme (within ascending hierarchy of fantasy dialogue) ultimately culminates with respect to the enduring theme of *utopianism*. The term derives from a compound of the Greek *ou-* (not) and *topos* (place), collectively translated as "good place" or "no place." The utopian tradition reflects this degree of ambiguity, denoting an imaginary society enjoying perfect legal, economic, and political systems of governance. This fantasy conception of utopia surpasses any existing social structure due to a prevailing sense of harmony and reason enjoyed by all.

In terms of Western culture, the theme emerged as the title of a treatise published by St. Thomas More in 1516. Utopia was described as an island where justice and prosperity reigned supreme, its inhabitants having learned to subordinate their selfish desires to rational pursuits. In modern usage, Utopia stands for any imaginary society where harmonious conditions prevail, as fancifully contrasting with reality. Many variations have been devised since More's treatise, each reflecting the spirit of the age in terms of unfettered hope and optimism. This alluring spirit of utopianism represents a fantasy dialogue intended to encompass an enduring humanitarian perspective akin to eclecticism, a virtuous dialogue applicable to all ages and cultures. In concert with the first three themes, utopianism effectively rounds out the stepwise examination of the follower-based class of fantasy dialogue.

THE VIRTUOUS ATTRIBUTES FOR THE PHANTOM AND FANTASY DIALOGUES

In conclusion, the completed description of the supplementary class of phantom and fantasy dialogues roughly triples the scope of potential forms of virtuous communication. Both the phantom and fantasy dialogues are characterized by their enduring categories of literary tradition, a format analogous to the meta-order themes for the direct dialogues previously described in Chapter 8. Perhaps the greatest strength for this tripartite system of direct, phantom, and fantasy dialogues resides in their all-inclusive nature, accounting for virtually every major literary tradition celebrated the world over. These categories fit seamlessly into the virtuous scope of the motivational hierarchy permitting a truly convincing simulation of virtuous communication in general. Indeed, based upon a limited number of elementary assumptions; namely, the principles of instrumental conditioning and the concept of the metaperspective, this stepwise series of transformations ultimately accounts for the entire listing of dialogue-types.

It should further be emphasized that the current system (by definition) is only essentially applicable to an English-speaking language tradition. Fortunately the English language has been granted the role of "lingua franca" for the global community, enhancing its broad appeal across the board. Certainly an equal range of other language traditions could similarly benefit from cross-cultural versions of the motivational matrix in terms of a more universal understanding of the virtuous emotions. Indeed, this virtually universal potential ultimately explains the unfathomable complexity of the human mind. Certainly one rarely repeats the exactly same train of contextual thought over the course of a lifetime. The most likely scenario for such a rare occurrence extends to the memory-retrieval of past verbal interchanges. Consequently, it might further be argued that all memories of an emotional nature are stored in terms of such a discrete range of virtuous contexts, a speculation scarcely lost in terms of the programming issues predicted for an ethical simulation of AI outlined in the upcoming Chapter *17*.

In summary, the completed description of the phantom and fantasy dialogues offers further crucial inroads towards an explanation of contextual role-playing. Indeed, the phantom/fantasy style of dialogue printed on a page effectively complements the more immediate (direct) class of motivational dialogue. Furthermore, the dramatic influence of fictionally-derived (fantasy) dialogues plays a key role in terms of the accumulated literary traditions from around the world, tempered in terms of political/cultural influences. Although the profound influence of political manifestos or apocalyptic literature often continues to hold sway in the court of public opinion, a more realistic evaluation of the phantom and fantasy dialogues is clearly essential for ensuring global peace and prosperity for the foreseeable future.

16

GLOBAL PERSPECTIVES FOR THE MAJOR AND LESSER VIRTUES

In conclusion, the completed description of the dual system of major/lesser virtues finally permits a critical evaluation of the potential global applications. **Part I** introduced the ten-level hierarchy of the major groupings of virtues, values, and ideals: as schematically embodied in terms of the personal, group, spiritual, humanitarian, and transcendental levels within the ethical hierarchy. When further specialized into both authority and follower roles, this basic pattern accounts for the entire ten-level hierarchy of virtuous terms, resulting in a grand total of *80* individual motivational terms.

This basic complement of *80* main/accessory terms, in turn, is modified in **Part II** with respect to the affiliated class of *transitional* power maneuvers: namely, those that "transition" the individual into acceptance within the more established social hierarchy. According to Chapters *9* through *14*, the traditional categories of humor and comedy are specified in terms of the newly devised class of the *lesser* virtues: defined as transitional variations with respect to the virtuous mode. They formally represent the dual interplay of the double bind and counter double bind class of power maneuvers. This transitional pattern, in turn, roughly doubles the number of predicted terms, for a total of *128* individual terms.

In concert with the *80*-part sequence of major virtues, the number of virtuous terms summates to a grand-total of *208* individual terms. This total necessarily includes provisions for both the main and accessory versions for the virtuous realm. Indeed, this factor proves particularly crucial in terms of any convincing simulation of an empathic nature. This advanced organization is primarily necessary for explaining the supreme complexity behind the human mind, particularly when compounded in terms of complex sequences of terms.

Perhaps the greatest strength for this new system resides in its all-inclusive nature, accounting for virtually every major category of virtuous terms known to exist. These categories fit seamlessly within the ascending power hierarchy, effectively arguing for an overall degree of validity. Based upon a limited number of basic assumptions; including the principles of conditioning theory and the paradigm of the metaperspective, the stepwise sequence of transformations results in the ultimate *208*-part complement of virtuous terms.

THE EMPATHIC FOUNDATIONS FOR A GLOBAL SYSTEM OF ETHICS

The dual interplay of the main/accessory listings of terms remains a particularly salient feature for the empathic virtuous hierarchy. Here, this empathic perspective proves a crucial factor in many of the great ethical systems from around the world. For instance, as the foundation for Christian ethics, the Golden Rule (Do unto others as you would have others do unto you) is founded precisely upon such an appeal to empathic principles. Indeed, it is featured in one form or the other in virtually every major world religion: including Judaism, Buddhism, Islam, Hinduism, and Taoism. The Golden Rule places a great premium on a cooperative style of virtuous behavior, although these noble ideals don't always "square" in non-cooperative types of circumstances. As a general rule, the Golden Rule is particularly difficult to enforce in situations where others might tend to take advantage of such noble inclinations.

This latter principle of self-interest (sometimes known as the Iron Rule) promotes a selfish agenda at the expense of the more noble precepts embodied in the Golden Rule. It is a more prosaically defined as: "Do unto others before they can do unto you," a ruthless expression of selfish competition. In contrast to the Golden Rule, the Iron Rule is frequently the unspoken code of the rich and powerful, as amply illustrated in the perpetual sequence of tyrants and dictators down through the ages. This primal measure of self-interest is formally encountered in the principles of the zero-sum game; namely, "your loss is my gain" – the unforgiving law of the jungle. It scarcely is surprising, then, that the darker side to empathy enters into consideration precisely at this juncture. Here, a keen understanding of the motivations of others is essential for achieving the deception and manipulation specified in the cunning practice of the Iron Rule.

In defense of the Golden Rule, a slightly different formulation directly addresses this vulnerability to the Iron Rule: stated in modified terms as: "Do not do unto others what you would not have them do unto you." Sometimes referred to as *The Silver* Rule, it forbids any descent into the realm of violence, wherein complementing with the more positive prerequisites of the Golden Rule. The Silver Rule prohibits retaliation in any form to harm done by another, equivalent (but not quite a drastic as) Christ's admonition to "turn the other cheek when attacked." It traditionally equates to the strategy of nonviolent resistance against unfair governmental policies, as successfully practiced by Mohandas Gandhi with respect to the oppressive British occupation of India.

This strategy, again, emerged in the context of the non-violent resistance to racial segregation promoted by Rev. Martin Luther King Jr. during the Civil Rights era. Here, these civic leaders advised against retaliation towards one's oppressors, although also forgoing compliance to unjust demands. This non-violent strategy of civil disobedience aimed to provoke a moral sense of empathy in the hearts of the oppressors, although this defiance could also lead to great personal sacrifice on the part the righteous. Although the Silver Rule proves effective under such ideal circumstances, it can just as easily be exploited, particularly when one's oppressors remain unmoved by such a stirring appeal to conscience.

THE GLOBAL SUPREMACY OF THE LAW OF EQUIVALENT RESPONSE

The general standard for ethics down through the ages has unerringly been a hybrid of the principles underlying both the Golden and Iron Rules, in what has suggestively been termed the Bronze Rule according to the late Carl Sagan's (1993)

insightful analysis of the subject. Confucius perhaps best stated this rule as: "Repay kindness with kindness, but evil with justice;" in essence, the strategy of repaying "like with like." This basic strategy is also reflected in nature with respect to the principles of equilibrium and homeostasis. This rule is extremely suggestive of what Communication Theorists term the *symmetrical* class of power maneuvers; e.g., responding back in kind what originally had been formally offered.

With respect to the baser precepts of Iron Rule, however, the Law of Equivalent Response is typically moderated to some degree, as reflected in the "eye for an eye, tooth for a tooth" pronouncement of the Old Testament. Although this scriptural quotation is often cited as condoning violence, it actually proclaims *only* an eye, and *only* a tooth, whereupon lessening the tendency towards escalation in conflict disputes. In contrast, more positive precepts of the Golden Rule continue to specify the *reciprocity* implicit within the virtuous realm, particularly those cooperative impulses where "one good turn deserves another." Here, this virtuous sense of cooperation serves as the enduring foundation for civilization itself, providing a stable financial environment for conducting business and commerce.

Whereas this cooperative style of strategy proves exceedingly effective for the virtuous mode, its darker version is all too susceptible to the formation of lasting feuds and vendettas. Here, few options remain for escaping such a self-perpetuating cycle. This latter shortcoming, however, can ultimately be avoided through the implementation of periodic overtures of forgiveness, wherein preemptively short-circuiting escalating conflict cycles. In this modified sense, this "like-for-like" strategy embodied in the Bronze Rule amounts to the prevailing ethical standard on the world scene today. It is particularly apparent in the field of international politics, where the United States (for instance) scrupulously cooperates with its allies, while justly responding in kind to counterproductive attacks against its self-interests.

It is scarcely surprising, then, that this basic strategy of responding in kind proves to be the most effective winning strategy determined within the field of Game Theory. Here, various Game Theory tournaments feature computer simulations of various strategies pitted against one another in head-to-head match-ups. On a consistent basis, the "reciprocal rule" program known as "Tit for Tat" proves most effective in many round-robin match-ups. This program is considered

THE GOLDEN RULE	THE SILVER RULE
"Do unto others as you would have them do unto you."	"Do not do unto others what you would not have them do unto you."
THE BRONZE RULE	THE IRON RULE
"Repay goodness with goodness, but evil with justice."	"Do unto others before they can do unto you."

Fig. 16A – The Reigning World Ethical Strategies

nice (never initiates conflict), *provokable* (refuses to turn the other cheek), and also *forgiving* (permits a return to cooperation). This basic program, indeed, consistently prevails over most variants of either the Golden or Iron Rules.

FURTHER VARIATIONS WITH RESPECT TO THE BRONZE RULE

The basic concept of the Bronze Rule can scarcely claim to be the total picture, for further variations on this format are generally encountered. Take, for example, the hybrid rule: "Be respectful to one's superiors, but feel free to exploit one's inferiors." This dual strategy employed by the "social climber" aims to secure a selective advantage within the vagaries of a stratified social hierarchy. Here, the social climber appeases his boss in deference to his authority status, while alternately taking full advantage of those occupying subordinate positions.

A further example of hybrid rules concerns the tendency towards nepotism, also known as kin-selection. This basic strategy specifies close cooperation with one's relatives (or those with similar interests), while remaining competitive towards outsiders. In terms of the virtuous hierarchy, this entails favoring those within one's immediate peer group, while withholding favor from those outside one's purview. A special instance of this strategy concerns the Tragedy of the Commons, where diverse interests come into conflict so that all are affected. The over-harvesting of limited fish stocks is one recent example, leading to an eventual crash in breeding populations. One township (or fleet) is generally pitted against all others, attempting to preserve self-interests in contrast to the higher aims of the group-collective. The only meaningful solution to such a partisan trap lies in an appeal to a universal perspective, the resource now viewed as a commons to be shared by all, fully justifying the shared sacrifice that must be endured if the resource under consideration is to remain plentiful.

APPLICATIONS TO GLOBAL SCALE HARMONY

This competitive sense of ethical interplay, however, can scarcely claim to be the total picture. Indeed, in terms of our modern technological age, one might rightfully argue that the balance of power is actually skewed towards the cooperative end of the spectrum. The highly interactive global marketplace certainly favors such a cooperative style of positive interface. Here, a general rule of law has endured virtually uninterrupted since its first modest beginnings during the Bronze Age. This impressive track record suggests a clear selective advantage towards positive interactions. Although some degree of criminality has always existed down the ages, the prime directive of civilized society aims to ensure an equitable sense of reciprocity conducive to free trade and commerce. This basic principle traces its origins to the instinctual foundations for behavioral conditioning; namely, fair goods at an equitable price. Indeed, the general state of world affairs has never been better, with the exception of minor border skirmishes and terrorist incursions.

This positive outlook necessarily diminishes should the unthinkable ever occur; namely, the unforeseen breakdown of the prevailing global order. Here, nothing short of a nuclear winter (or other such pandemic disaster) would reach drastic enough proportions to spark a global Dark Age. The residual vestiges of law and order would generally serve to dampen all but the worst possible scenarios, although the balance of cooperation would undoubtedly skew towards the negative end of the scale. As so often occurs in history, a temporary reversal would remain exactly that, in keeping with the indomitable collective spirit governing all human endeavors. This rosy outlook, however, only truly remains feasible as long as the prevailing emphasis upon the character values firmly remains in place.

APPLICATIONS BASED UPON THE SCHEMATIC DEFINITION FORMAT

One of the most effective means for promoting character education is through the aid of the schematic definitions for the major and lesser virtues. These specific listings of schematic definitions outline the formal communicational dynamics characterizing these two virtuous categories. Here, the respective interplay of authority and follower roles (in concert with the specific virtuous terms under consideration) is spelled out in a formal longhand notation. The schematic precision of these definitions is unprecedented on the world scene today, permitting considerable interpersonal insights. These definitions could be employed to diagnose ongoing patterns of communication, translated (through specific examples) into a format more easily comprehended by the general individual. The standard flow-chart schematic depicting the organization of the schematic definitions proves particularly effective for outlining specific interpersonal and communicational issues. This communicational dynamic would ideally be analyzed in a real time mode targeting the master realm of positively-based psychology.

Perhaps the greatest beneficiaries of this innovation extend to the youth of the nation, whose character and propensities are gradually being molded into place. The more routine virtues and values within the ethical hierarchy prove invaluable for navigating these crucial stages in emotional development. The schematic definitions for the virtuous mode could be incorporated (where appropriate) into the public academic curriculum. The ongoing trend towards character education provides a particularly valuable adjunct for themes usually dealt with at a religious level. This secular ethical strategy would provide crucial guideposts to decisions of a moral nature, as specified within the schematic definition format.

These exceedingly precise techniques for relationship modeling also apply to an adult sphere of influence, where marital/family frictions can similarly be effectively resolved. Here, the schematic definition format emerges as a general-purpose

diagnostic tool for virtually everything of an emotional nature: encompassing the overall realm of the virtues, values and ideals. Even the enigmatic realm of humor and comedy (modeled through the lesser virtues) is adequately represented within the master schematic definition format.

THE NEW SCIENCE OF POWERPLAY POLITICS

As with any newly established system, a proper descriptive moniker is definitely specified: in this case designated as the new science of Powerplay Politics ™. This title has been selected in allusion to the parallel concepts of the *powerplay* and *Power Politics*. The latter term is an English translation of the German *machtpolitik* (literally, power politics). It refers to a traditional style of political administration emphasizing power and authority, sometimes in a coercive fashion.

In contrast, the power play denotes a collective style of cooperative effort, traditionally defined as a scoring strategy in team sports such as football or hockey. Here, the power play refers to any style of mass interference within a particular point or zone, an aspect reminiscent of the cohesive style of "strike power" characterizing the follower role. Owing to the enhanced versatility of both the authority/follower roles, the notion of Powerplay Politics proves particularly effective for designating this dual power realm.

In terms of this dual communicational dynamic, Powerplay Politics is essentially grounded in two basic principles adapted from Communication Theory. The first principle states that all communication is motivationally charged to some extent, wherein targeting the intentions of the self and others within the verbal interaction. Here, even a routine lecture on pure mathematics contains an underlying motivational component: for the professor is subliminally determined to achieve academic tenure, the students are concerned with earning a passing grade, etc.

The second basic principle derives from the ascending nature of the power hierarchy. Here, everyone (whether they care to admit it or not) seek to be in control the ongoing interaction. For instance, the group authority overrules the power leverage wielded by the personal follower, whereas the group representative counteracts that of the group authority (and so forth). In most stable relationships, power leverage is shared in a trade-off fashion, although not always with completely equal results. Furthermore, an outward expression of weakness can similarly impart an empowering effect, as witnessed for the hypochondriac or the masochist.

Regardless of the individual mechanisms at issue, the pervasive desire to be in control of a relationship emerges as the general driving force: which (in concert with the first principle) accounts for the overall focus of the new science of Powerplay Politics. Each of these diverse perspectives is unified into a seamless continuum based upon the traditional groupings of virtues, values, and ideals; providing a grand-unified model of affective language in general.

ETHICAL CATEGORIES AUGMENTING THE VIRTUOUS REALM

Although the primary realm of the virtues is certainly well documented, this still leaves in question the contrasting domain of the vices. According to the latest title by the author, the overall realm of the virtues further contrasts with a parallel sphere of the vices, as partially depicted in the compact diagram immediately below:

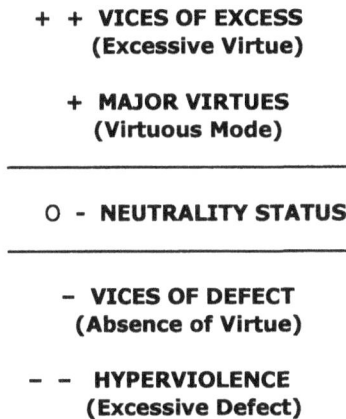

+ + VICES OF EXCESS
(Excessive Virtue)

+ MAJOR VIRTUES
(Virtuous Mode)

O - NEUTRALITY STATUS

– VICES OF DEFECT
(Absence of Virtue)

– – HYPERVIOLENCE
(Excessive Defect)

This modified system radically expands upon Aristotle's Theory of the Mean, retaining his basic format of the *virtues* interposed between the vices of *defect* and the vices of *excess*. Whereas the virtues (specific to the follower roles) are formally distinguished from the "authority ideals," so the darker realm is similarly specified by the dual concepts of vice and sin. In particular, the Greek verb for sin in the New Testament translates as "to miss" (as in failing to reach a goal). This "sin" of failing to reach such acceptable goals represents a negative variation on the virtuous mode, with sin directly contrasting with the 'authority ideals" in such an immediately active sense.

With respect to the affiliated hierarchy of follower roles, the *vices* directly counteract the virtues in this negative respect. According to Chap-

ter *2*, the virtues respectively defined the projected range of potentiality within the conditioned relationship, designating predicted behaviors with the potential to complement the immediately-active nature of the authority ideals. Indeed, whereas the notions of vice and sin share a reciprocating status with respect to authority and follower roles; for sake of brevity, this overall darker set of themes is generally referred to simply as "the vices" consistent with the formal terminology for the vices of defect. Indeed, a similar scenario further holds true for the positive realm, where the catchall term of "the virtues" is collectively employed to designate the overall hierarchy of virtues, values, and ideals.

This overarching master diagram further introduces the entirely new notion of the realm of *hyperviolence*, whereby permitting a more even sense of symmetry. This expanded format is symmetrically organized around the central concept of the *neutrality status*: replacing Aristotle's original "mean" category of the virtues as the basic core-nucleus for the system. This sense of neutrality represents the formal *default* status for the motivational matrix: defined as the basic initiation point for all new classes of relationship to follow (whether positive or negative in nature). According to this author's most recent release: *A Diagnostic Classification of the Emotions*, the upper segment within the diagram represent the positive aspects based upon cooperation, as specified through the representative categories of major virtues. The lower segment alternately targets the realm of conflict/punishment: namely, Aristotle's notion of the vices of *defect*, defined as the respective absence of virtue.

This preliminary core-nucleus of terms, in turn, serves as the foundation for the remaining categories based upon the realm of *excess*. For the virtuous mode, this corresponds to Aristotle's notion of the vices of *excess*, defined as a degree of excess with respect to the virtues. For the darker realm of defect, this pattern alternately corresponds to the realm of *hyperviolence*, defined as that range of extremes with respect to the vices of defect.

A similar expansion of categories, in turn, is encountered with respect to the *transitional* categories of terms. Here, the comprehensive listing of lesser virtues (outlined in **Part II**) actually represents just the first major component of a much broader transitional framework that formally expands upon each of the categories specified within Aristotle's (revised) Theory of the Mean. This transitional modification extends to the realms of criminality and hypercriminality, as well as the communicational factors that underlie the mental disorders. In concert with the initial class of lesser virtues, these four total categories are depicted as the right-hand column of terms listed (adjacent the major categories) in the compact diagram immediately to below.

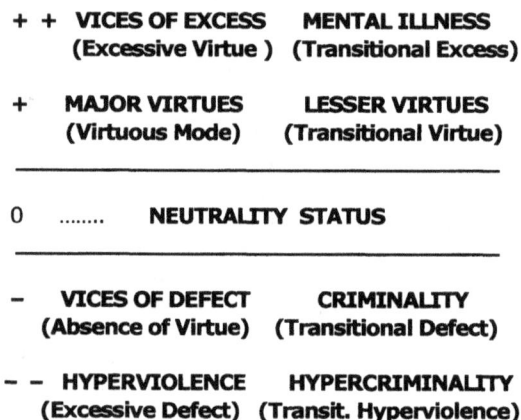

+ + **VICES OF EXCESS**   **MENTAL ILLNESS**
     (Excessive Virtue)   **(Transitional Excess)**

+   **MAJOR VIRTUES**   **LESSER VIRTUES**
     (Virtuous Mode)   **(Transitional Virtue)**

_____

0   ....   **NEUTRALITY STATUS**

_____

–   **VICES OF DEFECT**   **CRIMINALITY**
     (Absence of Virtue)   **(Transitional Defect)**

– – **HYPERVIOLENCE**   **HYPERCRIMINALITY**
     (Excessive Defect)   **(Transit. Hyperviolence)**

In direct analogy to the main categories of terms, the transitional variations are similarly organized around a centralized zone of neutrality, whereby serving as direct transitional entry-points in relation to the major categories. The classifications of the lesser virtues are depicted immediately adjacent to the major virtuous realm. Similarly, the theme of criminality is depicted adjacent to the respective vices of defect. Furthermore, in terms of the realm of excess, the theme of hyper-criminality represents the transitional variation in terms of hyperviolence, whereas mental illness, in turn, targets the vices of excess. The individual terminology describing criminality and hypercriminality is fairly straightforward in nature: representing formal transitional variations with respect to the darker realm of defect. Indeed, criminality represents the ingrained tendency to initiate a relationship in a selfish or violent fashion, a contention testified to by many a criminologist. A more detailed description for the terminology specific to criminality and hypercriminality clearly remains beyond the scope of the current (summary) chapter, although adequately addressed in several related book releases by the author.

For sake of completeness, however, final mention must necessarily be made for transitional prerequisites for mental illness. Here, mental illness is defined as a communicational sequence of double bind and counter double bind maneuvers relating to the vices of excess. Each of the major classifications for the mental disorders (e.g., the personality disorders, neuroses, mood disorders, and schizophrenia) is fully explainable in terms of this transitional model of mental illness. Consistent with its transitional relationship to the vices of excess (which are formally divorced from the domain of defect), mental illness generally appears non-threatening in nature: as reflected in studies confirming the non-violent nature of the mentally ill in relation to the general population. This interpretation proves particularly insightful in light of the bizarre symptomology associated with the psychoses, a category of mental illness reflecting the extreme degree of disqualification characterizing the counter double-bind class of maneuvers.

This is innovation in understanding is chiefly permitted through the preexisting systems of terminology for the psychoses pioneered by German clinician, Karl Leonhard, as well as the nomenclature for the personality disorders and the neuroses contained in *DSM–5*. A complete two-page expanded listing of the sum-total of individual ethical terms is presented in **Figs. 16B** and **16C** representing both the main and accessory motivational matrices for the convenience of the reader, gratefully reproduced (in modified format) from an earlier release by the author: *Challenges to World Peace: A Global Solution* (2009).

DIRECTIONS FOR FURTHER RESEARCH

In conclusion, this newly modified system of ethical categories represents an unprecedented contribution to the field of ethical inquiry: modifying Aristotle's enduring "Theory of the Mean" into an all-inclusive theory of "everything" of an emotional nature. Far from remaining a purely academic exercise, this expanded system addresses many issues of critical import to human nature: including insights into the enigmatic realm of criminality, as well as the communicational factors underlying mental illness. Indeed, when the three primary categories of the vices are added to the *208* initial terms specified for the virtues, the grand total reaches a staggering *1,040* individual terms. In concert with the parallel applications relating to ethical artificial intelligence, the overall validity of this new ethical format can scarcely be called into question: a voyage of discovery certainly well worth the effort, particularly in light of the critical issues currently under consideration.

As suggested previously, this formal foundation within the behavioral sciences paves the way for an overarching planetary system of ethics, where an innate instinctual foundation in terms of conditioning theory imparts a universal appeal towards global acceptance upon the world scene today. This systematic scientific foundation is particularly unique in that it avoids favoritism towards any given cultural identity, rather treating each with equal dignity and validity. Furthermore, the respective traditional listings of virtues and values are similarly specified in terms of such a strictly secular perspective, one that is formally independent of any regional cultural bias, or the restrictions of any (supernaturally revealed) scriptural foundation. This new ethical system enjoys the advantages of highlighting the commonalties of the virtuous lifestyle across all cultures and creeds, abstaining from focusing upon the individual distinctions therein.

A further crucial conceptual advantage invokes an increased awareness of the grounding of organized religion with the formal principles of Set Theory, as extensively outlined in Chapter *1*. This innovation permits a radical reinterpretation of the role that religion plays in society as a whole, in particular, the disturbing ascendance of religious fanaticism. According to this formal interpretation, the spiritual authority perspective represents just one of the five basic levels within the master hierarchy of authority and follower roles: defined as the personal, group, spiritual, humanitarian, and transcendental perspectives. According to this advanced interpretation, the influence of organized religion chiefly extends to a universal sphere of influence (binding over all of mankind). Many religious systems, however, are compounded by a humanitarian range of themes (encompassing all ages/times), as well as some extension to a transcendental realm: imparting a supernatural/mystical character to the entire edifice.

The destructive nature of religious fanaticism essentially emerges from an inherently inflexible perspective that condemns all other forms of religion their innate freedom to express their own unique style of universal perspective in their respective region. Furthermore, religious fanaticism consistently oversteps its specific relevant focus, often attempting to influence the political/group and even personal realms of conduct. The timely emergence of the Set Theory interpretation of the authority and follower roles hopefully will serve to alter this disturbing trend towards fanaticism, whereby encouraging a more rational perspective (at least for the moderate constituency) conducive to promoting a greater degree of flexibility in terms of both dogma and practice.

In concert with the newly devised master hierarchy of virtues and values based upon behavioral principles, it is further hoped that the moral commonalties across all religious traditions will be emphasized, encouraging a new era in religious tolerance. This new ethical system could eminently qualify as the long anticipated foundation for a global system of planetary ethics serving a secular constituency, where such moral issues have typically been downplayed due to well-meaning attempts to avoid religious favoritism. This same system could also serve as a valuable adjunct to the major religions of the world without favoring any one of them. Indeed, this new ethical hierarchy exhibits the potential for promoting a peaceful coexistence for all of the established world religions, particularly in that it does not preclude the existence of a top-down pattern of influence (of a supernatural nature) as well. Consequently, this overall picture potentially amounts to the best of all possible worlds: enabling an ethical revival within the secular world (which has typically been downplayed), as well as the potential for an even greater degree of spiritual cooperation and tolerance amongst all of the established religions of the world.

OVERVIEW

In the final analysis, what exactly are the global benefits for the motivation solution and where are the precise inroads for the promised global initiative? First of all, this new ethical system represents a grand scale synthesis of all of the ethics and philosophy that has gone before, providing a hierarchial motivational platform encompassing all of the major categories of virtues, values, and ideals. As such, this new behavioral and ethical terminology represents a powerful new tool on the world scene in terms of making sense of the broad range of ethical quandaries that a global citizen is confronted with on a daily basis.

It remains to be determined, however, what is the best strategy for utilizing the specifics of this technological innovation within a global sphere of influence. One strategy might mirror Google's informal philosophy of "do no evil," although this mindset does not appear to go far enough in the overall scheme of things. A further strategy espoused by the Gates Foundation promotes philanthropic endeavors for the poor and infirmed from around the world: a truly wise and noble effort. The most ideal scenario, however, would entail gaining the cooperation of the entire 7 billion span of humanity. Hopefully, this is where *the motivation solution* rightfully enters the picture: providing a master schematic overview of motivational dynamics at issue, while suggesting one's rightful role in a stable and prosperous global community.

+ + VICES of EXCESS (Excessive Virtue)

Pride - Flattery	Shame - Criticism
Vanity - Adulation	Humiliation - Ridicule
Conceit - Patronization	Mortification - Scorn
Pretention - Obsequious	Anguish - Mockery
Sanctimony - Sycophancy	Tribulat.- Cynicism
Envy - Impudence	Disdain - Insolence
Jealousy - Arrogance	Contempt - Audacity
Covetous. - Impetuosity	Reproach - Rashness
Longing - Presumption	Chagrin - Boldness
Affection - Smugness	Bitterness- Harshness

+ MAJOR VIRTUES (Virtuous Mode)

Nostalgia - Approval	Guilt - Leniency
Glory - Prudence	Honor - Justice
Providence - Faith	Liberty - Hope
Grace - Beauty	Free-will - Truth
Tranquility - Ecstasy	Equality - Bliss
Desire - Solicitude	Worry - Submissive.
Dignity - Temperance	Integrity - Fortitude
Civility - Charity	Austerity - Decency
Magnanim.- Goodness	Equan.- Wisdom
Love - Joy	Peace - Harmony

MENTAL ILLNESS – (B) (Transitional Excess → Disqualified Excess)

Histrionic Personality → Dissociative Hysteria
Happiness Psychosis → Confabulatory A/L Paraphr.
Excited Confusion Psychosis → Excited Cataphasia
Paranoid Personality → Depersonalization Neurosis
Anxiety Psychosis → Fantastic A/L Paraphrenia
Inhibited Confusion Psych. → Inhibited Cataphasia

Dependent Personality → Conversion Hysteria
Manic/Depress. Disease → Manic A/L Paraphrenia
Hyperkin. Motility Psych.→Hyperkin. Periodic Cata.

Avoidant Personality → Neuraesthenic Neurosis
Manic/Depressive Disease → Confused A/L Paraphr.
Akinetic Motility Psychosis→ Akinetic Periodic Cata.

LESSER VIRTUES (I) (Transitional Virtue → Disqualified Virtue)

Loyalty → Humility	Responsibil. → Innocence
Fidelity → Majesty	Duty → Vindication
Piety→ Magnific.	Allegiance → Exoneration
Felicity → Grandeur	Righteous.→ Immaculat.
Discipline → Modesty	Vigilance → Meekness
Chivalry → Chastity	Courage → Obedience
Nobility → Purity	Valor → Conformity
Zeal → Perfection	Triumph → Pacifism

MENTAL ILLNESS – (A) (Transitional Excess → Disqualified Excess)

Narcissistic Personality → Obsession Neurosis
Confabulatory Euphoria → Confab. Paraphrenia
Enthusiastic Euphoria → Proskinetic Catatonia
Non-Participatory Euphoria → Silly Hebephrenia
Borderline Personality → Phobia Neurosis
Suspicious Depression → Fantastic Paraphrenia
Self-Torturing Depression → Negativistic Catatonia
Non-Particip. Depression → Insipid Hebephrenia
Passive/Aggressive Personal. → Compulsion Neur.
Pure Mania → Expansive Paraphrenia
Unproductive Euphoria → Parakinetic Catatonia
Hypochondriacal Euphoria → Eccentric Hebephren.
Schizoid Personality → Anxiety Neurosis
Pure Melancholy → Incoherent Paraphrenia
Harried Depression   →   Affected Catatonia
Hypochondriacal Depression → Autistic Hebephren.

LESSER VIRTUES (II) (Transitional Virtue → Disqualified Virtue)

Self-Esteem → Reverence	Apology → Clemency
Pomp → Veneration	Rectitude → Pardon
Sanctity → Homage	Penitence → Absolution
Dominion → Benediction	Contrition → Deliver.
Congeniality→Concess.	Sympathy → Appease.
Cordiality→Indulgence	Compass. → Conciliate
Hospitality→Gratitude	Mercy → Accommodat.
Altruism → Goodwill	Forgiveness → Sacrifice

– VICES of DEFECT
(Absence of Virtue)

Laziness - Treachery   Negligence - Vindictive.
Infamy - Insurgency   Dishonor - Vengeance
Prodigal - Betrayal   Slavery - Despair
Wrath - Ugliness   Tyranny - Hypocrisy
Anger - Abomination   Prejudice - Perdition

Apathy - Spite   Indifference - Malice
Foolishness - Gluttony   Caprice - Cowardice
Vulgarity - Avarice   Cruelty - Antagonism
Oppression - Evil   Persecution - Cunning
Hatred - Iniquity   Belligerence - Turpitude

CRIMINALITY (I)
(Transitional Defect → Disqualified Defect)

t-Treachery → d-Laziness   t-Vindict. → d-Neglig.
t-Insurgency → d-Infamy   t-Vengeance → d-Dishon.
t-Betrayal → d-Prodigality   t-Despair → d-Slavery
t-Ugliness → d-Wrath   t-Hypocrisy → d-Tyranny

t-Spite → d-Apathy   t-Malice → d-Indifference
t-Gluttony → d-Foolish.   t-Cowardice → d-Caprice
t-Avarice → d-Vulgarity   t-Antagonism → d-Cruelty
t-Evil → d-Oppression   t-Cunning → d-Persecution

CRIMINALITY (II)
(Transitional Defect → Disqualified Defect)

t-Laziness→ d-Treachery   t-Negligence →d-Vindict.
t-Infamy→ d-Insurgency   t-Dishon.→ d-Vengeance
t-Prodigal → d-Betrayal   t-Slavery → d-Despair
t-Wrath → d-Ugliness   t-Tyranny → d-Hypocrisy

t-Apathy → d-Spite   t-Indifference → d-Malice
t-Foolish. → d-Gluttony   t-Caprice → d-Cowardice
t-Vulgarity → d-Avarice   t-Cruelty → d-Antag.
t-Oppression → d-Evil   t-Persecution → d-Cunning

– – HYPERVIOLENCE
(Excessive Defect)

Indolence - Mutiny   Dereliction - Reprisal
Notoriety - Rebellion   Ignobility - Retribution
Licentious.-Treason   Savagery - Hopelessness
Fury - Hideousness   Despotism - Mendacity
Madness - Horror   Bigotry - Ruin

Languor - Grudging.   Callousness - Malignancy
Crassness - Voracity   Petulance - Cravenness
Rudeness - Greed   Hostility - Contentious.
Brutality - Heinous.   Barbarism - Ruthlessness
Vicious. - Balefulness   Atrocity - Fiendishness

HYPERCRIMINALITY (I)
(Transitional Hyperviol. → Disqualified Hyperviol.)

t-Mutiny → d-Indolence
t-Rebellion → d-Notoriety
t-Treason → d-Licentiousness
t-Hideousness → d-Fury
t-Reprisal → d-Dereliction
t-Retribution → d-Ignobility
t-Hopelessness → d-Savagery
t-Mendacity → d-Despotism
t-Grudgingness → d-Languor
t-Voracity → d-Crassness
t-Greed → d-Rudeness
t-Heinousness → d-Brutality
t-Malignancy → d-Callousness
t-Cravenness → d-Petulance
t-Contentiousness → d-Hostility
t-Ruthlessness → d-Barbarism

HYPERCRIMINALITY (II)
(Transitional Hyperviol. → Disqualified Hyperviol.)

t-Indolence → d-Mutiny
t-Notoriety → d-Rebellion
t-Licentiousness → d-Treason
t-Fury → d-Hideousness
t-Dereliction → d-Reprisal
t-Ignobility → d-Retribution
t-Savagery → d-Hopelessness
t-Despotism → d-Mendacity
t-Languor → d-Grudgingness
t-Crassness → d-Voracity
t-Rudeness → d-Greed
t-Brutality → d-Heinousness
t-Callousness → d-Malignancy
t-Petulance → d-Cravenness
t-Hostility → d-Contentiousness
t-Barbarism → d-Ruthlessness

Fig. 16B – Master Schematic Diagram Depicting the *408 Main Individual Terms*

ACC. MENTAL ILLNESS - (A)	ACC. MENTAL ILLNESS - (B)	+ + ACC. VICES of EXCESS
(Transitional Acc. Excess → Disqualified Acc. Excess)	(Transitional Acc. Excess → Disqualified Acc. Excess)	(Excessive Accessory Virtue)
Narcissistic Personality → Obsession Neurosis Confabulatory Euphoria → Confab. Paraphrenia Enthusiastic Euphoria → Proskinetic Catatonia Non-Participatory Euphoria → Silly Hebephrenia Borderline Personality → Phobia Neurosis Suspicious Depression → Fantastic Paraphrenia Self-Torturing Depression → Negativistic Catatonia Non-Particip. Depression → Insipid Hebephrenia Passive/Aggressive Personal. → Compulsion Neur. Pure Mania → Expansive Paraphrenia Unproductive Euphoria → Parakinetic Catatonia Hypochondriacal Euphoria → Eccentric Hebephrenia Schizoid Personality → Anxiety Neurosis Pure Melancholy → Incoherent Paraphrenia Harried Depression → Affected Catatonia Hypochondriacal Depression → Autistic Hebephren.	Histrionic Personality → Dissociative Hysteria Happiness Psychosis → Confabulatory A/L Paraphr. Excited Confusion Psychosis → Excited Cataphasia Paranoid Personality → Depersonalization Neurosis Anxiety Psychosis → Fantastic A/L Paraphrenia Inhibited Confusion Psych. → Inhibited Cataphasia Dependent Personality → Conversion Hyster. Manic/Depress. Disease → Manic A/L Paraphrenia Hyperkin. Motility Psych. → Hyperkin. Periodic Cata. Avoidant Personality → Neuraesthenic Neurosis Manic/Depressive Disease → Confused A/L Paraphr. Akinetic Motility Psychosis → Akinetic Periodic Cata.	Narcissism - Blandish. Ignominy.- Reprehens. Snobbery - Courtliness Opprobrium - Denunci. Vainglory - Condesc. Despondency - Derision Haughtiness - Servility Agony - Sarcasm Pietism - Subservience Affliction - Satiricism Invideous. - Impertinence Despisal - Hubris Possessive. - Brazenness Repugn.- Surliness Cravingness - Brashness Rebuke - Irascibility Yearning - Effrontery Loathing - Temerity Pretension - Gleefulness Admonish. - Rigor
ACC. LESSER VIRTUES (II)	**ACC. LESSER VIRTUES (I)**	**+ ACC. MAJOR VIRTUES**
(Transitional Acc. Virtue → Disqualified Acc. Virtue)	(Transitional Acc. Virtue → Disqualified Acc. Virtue)	(Accessory Virtuous Mode)
Self-Respect → Esteem Sorrow → Lenity Ostentation → Acclaim Remorse → Remittance Holiness → Ardor Regretful.→ Dispensation Supremacy → Exultation Grief → Redemption Amiability → Favor Empathy → Placation Conviviality → Sanction Commiser. → Concord. Generosity → Thanksgiving Pity → Consonance Benignity → Beneficence Remission → Propitiat.	Fealty → Simplicity Account. → Blameless. Steadfast. → Loftiness Obligation → Exculp. Adoration → Sublimity Obeisence → Aquittal Happiness → Splendor Commit. → Impeccabil. Adherence → Demure. Wariness → Timidity Gallantry → Coyness Intrepidity → Complais. Stateliness → Wholesome. Stalwart. → Compli. Fervor → Excellence Victory → Amicableness	Poignancy - Admir. Culpability - Concern Exalt. - Circumspect. Uprightness - Equity Bountiful. - Devotion Freedom - Fairness Blessings - Charm Conscience - Credence Serenity - Rapture Brotherhood - Content. Passion - Aspirat. Apprehen.- Deference Respect - Continence Probity - Bravery Courtesy - Kindness Forbear. - Scruples Gracious. - Benevol. Patience - Shrewd. Affection - Gladness Amity - Accordance

ACC. VICES of DEFECT (Absence of Accessory Virtue)		ACC. CRIMINALITY (I) (Transitional Acc. Defect → Acc. Disqualified Defect)	ACC. CRIMINALITY (II) (Transitional Acc. Defect → Disqualified Acc. Defect)

ACC. VICES of DEFECT (Absence of Accessory Virtue)

Sloth - Traitorousness	Careless. - Retaliation
Disrepute - Sedition	Reprehension - Avengement
Profligacy - Perfidy	Bondage - Desperation
Indignation - Revulsion	Subjugate - Duplicity
Irateness - Abhorrence	Intolerance - Baneful.

Dispassion. - Resentment	Arbitrary- Malevolent
Preposterous. - Lechery	Fickleness- Pusillan.
Coarseness - Cupidity	Acrimony - Opposition
Animosity - Wickedness	Torment - Guilefulness
Enmity - Sinisterity	Militancy - Baseness

ACC. CRIMINALITY (I) (Transitional Acc. Defect → Acc. Disqualified Defect)

t-traitor. → d-sloth	t-retaliation → d-careless.
t-sedition → d-disrepute	t-avenge. → d- reprehen
t-perfidy → d-profligacy	t-desper.→ d-bondage
t-revulsion→ d-indign.	t-duplicity→ d-subjug.

t-resent. → d-dispassion	t-malev. → d-arbitrary
t-lechery → d-preposter.	t-pusillan. → d-fickle.
t-cupidity → d-coarse.	t-opposit. → d-acrimony
t-wicked.→ d-animosity	t-guileful. → d-torment

ACC. CRIMINALITY (II) (Transitional Acc. Defect → Disqualified Acc. Defect)

t-sloth→ d-traitor.	t-careless. → d-retaliation
t-disrepute → d-sedition	t-reprehen. → d-avenge.
t-profligacy → d-perfidy	t- bondage→ d-desper.
t-indign.→ d-revulsion	t- subjug.→ d-duplicity

t-dispassion → d-resent.	t-arbitrary→ d-malev.
t-preposter. → d-lechery	t-fickle → d-pusillan.
t-coarse. → d-cupidity	t-acrimony → d-oppos.
t-animosity → d-wicked.	t-torment→ d-guileful.

— — ACC. HYPERVIOLENCE (Excessive Accessory Defect)

Sluggish. - Untrustworthy	Laxity - Requital
Odium - Rebellion	Disgraceful. - Revenge
Debauchery - Disloyalty	Servitude - Grievous.
Outrage - Nastiness	Imperious. - Deceitful.
Enragement- Grotesque.	Discrim. - Damnation

Lethargy - Umbrage	Nonchalance - Peevish.
Absurdity - Ravenous.	Willfulness - Dastard.
Lewdness - Rapacious.	Rancor - Vexation
Discord - Badness	Ferocity - Deviousness
Meanness - Nefarity	Truculency - Insideous.

ACC. HYPERCRIMINALITY (I) (Transitional A-Hyperviol. → Disqualified A-Hyperviol.)

t-untrustworthy → d-sluggishness
t-rebellion → d-odium
t-disloyalty→ d-debauchery
t-nastiness→ d- outrage
t-requital→ d-laxity
t-revenge→ d-disgracefulness
t-grievousness→ d-servitude
t-deceitfulness→ d-imperiousness
t-umbrage → d-lethargy
t-ravenousness→ d-absurdity
t-rapaciousness→ d-lewdness
t-badness→ d-discord
t-peevishness→ d-nonchalance
t-dastardliness→ d-wilfullness
t-vexation → d-rancor
t-deviousness→ d-ferocity

ACC. HYPERCRIMINALITY (II) (Transitional A-Hyperviol. → Disqualified A-Hyperviol.)

t- sluggishness→ d-untrustworthy
t-odium → d-rebellion
t-debauchery→ d-disloyalty
t-outrage→ d-nastiness
t-laxity→ d-requital
t-disgracefulness→ d-revenge
t-servitude→ d-grievousness
t-imperiousness→ d-deceitfulness
t-lethargy → d-umbrage
t-absurdity→ d-ravenousness
t-lewdness→ d-rapaciousness
t- discord→ d-badness
t-nonchalance → d-peevishness
t-wilfullness→ d-dastardliness
t-rancor→ d-vexation
t-ferocity→ d-deviousness

Fig. 16C – Master Schematic Diagram Depicting the 408 Accessory Individual Terms

The global economic marketplace represents an amazing confluence of technical expertise and international cooperation across the board. This advanced degree of specialization, however, results in a disturbing degree of fracturing into diverse special interest groups seeking to press their own global advantage. This tends to marginalize the general public welfare, leading to gridlock in terms of policymaking and the advancement of global progress. A fresh new perspective in terms of global cooperation (and personal contribution to these aims) is definitely called for. Here, one strives not only for what may be gained, but also what is personally needed to uphold and maintain the tenuous infrastructure that maintains and nourishes the global community.

It is here that the precepts of the newly devised *motivation solution* come through the clearest, providing a master overview of an ethical nature based upon a primary instinctual/behavioral foundation. This scientifically-based behavioral foundation provides a sturdy foundation for the master hierarchy of ethical terms at issue here, the first grand-unified synthesis of its kind. As such, it provides a revolutionary new guidebook for ethical behavior in general, a welcome addition to the resources available to the global community.

Up until this point, the virtues/values have remained a somewhat disjointed concept, exhibiting very little connectivity or common ground. The newly devised motivational matrix of virtues and values, however, finally provides a master schematic overview of an interconnected nature for such a moral mindscape, supplying key conceptual insights towards the resolution of conflict and disorder. Indeed, knowledge *is* power for all sharing the global community, with *the motivation solution* emerging as a key technology for diagnosing conflicts and promoting international prosperity. Although only English-language versions for such a vision of the future are available

at this juncture, it remains only a further minor step to translate these results across the other major language traditions, providing the foundation for a truly international style of motivational initiative.

A number of promising collaborations have been forged along these lines, in particular, shared efforts with Dr. Darryl R.J. Macer, Ph.D.: Director for Eubios Ethics Institute based in New Zealand, Japan and Thailand. Recently Dr. Macer has co-founded the American University of Sovereign Nations in the United States to create a forum for a global debate of ideas relating to a more sustainable future. This continues in the tradition of worthy collaborations involving scholars from around the world in order to explore the future humankind might rightfully seek. Over the past 25 years, Eubios Ethics Institute has sponsored a number of worthwhile causes around the world: such as The Asian Bioethics Association, The Youth Peace Ambassador International Training Program, and cross-cultural Bioethics Training and Education.

Furthermore, cross-cultural links to Nigeria have yielded similarly promising results, particularly the African Values and Heritage Initiative (AVAHI): a non-governmental organization working to promote a renaissance in African moral values, peaceful co-existence, and a prosperous African society: sponsoring many valued character-education programs for the local youth in the process. It is here that the global initiative potential for *the motivation solution* comes through the strongest. Indeed, a standing invitation is extended to other NGO international organizations worldwide for potential consideration concerning such collaborative efforts across the board. Through such concerted effort towards educating and promoting harmony throughout the world, the future, indeed, looks bright for a bold new era of international peace and global cooperation across an entire humanitarian sphere of influence.

17

APPLICATIONS TO INFORMATION TECHNOLOGY & ARTIFICIAL INTELLIGENCE

The dream of artificial intelligence has been a goal in the field of Computer Sciences since virtually the dawning of the Computer Age. This anticipated style of artificially intelligent agent would potentially assist in all aspects of human endeavor, accompanied by the intriguing prospects for ultimately transcending the fixed limitations of the human condition. The current dramatic growth in computing power finally enables economic feasible inroads towards such a meaningful AI development. A number of key approaches, such as brain modeling through neural networks, have been attempted, although scarcely enough detailed information exists about the brain to warrant any such serious endeavor. In actuality, the key solution to developing convincing artificial intelligence involves an innate understanding of human communication in general. The preeminent test for AI devised by Alan Turing abstains from relying upon any direct measure of consciousness or perception in its determinations, rather strictly targeting the communicative factors underlying general human language. Assuming that the symbolic attributes of human language can be convincingly simulated on the computer, then many decades of needless effort potentially could be cut from the neural-net or consciousness/perceptual approaches.

Along these lines, a recent U.S. patent (#6,587,846) has been granted for precisely such a technical innovation based upon the symbolic attributes underlying affective (or emotionally-charged) language. Clear precedents already exist with respect to chess-playing computers, which prove particularly effective for modeling the symbolisms underlying such an abstract gaming format (although scarcely capable of anything else). In similar fashion, the symbolic attributes of the English language tradition prove similarly comprehensive in scope, although several orders of magnitude more abstractly complex in this regard. Certainly the primary economic focus of human society is mediated primarily through the symbolisms of human communication, specifying language as the most rational focal point for ongoing research. This does not necessarily imply that a sensory/motor enabled robot designed in relation to its immediate environment is not a rational focus of directed research. Indeed, such an aspect could eventually be merged with the currently proposed language simulation model, resulting in a more physically complete computer avatar. As far as direct economic applications are concerned, however, it proves entirely more cost effective to target the symbolic attributes of human language in all of its various manifestations.

Fortunately, a convenient shortcut to this daunting complexity of a direct language simulation has recently been proposed (the technical basis for the aforementioned patent). This new approach directly focuses upon the motivational (or emotionally-charged) aspects of language as its guiding principle, the remaining bulk of value-neutral language filling-in in an accessory role. Indeed, as Robert Warren Penn once insightfully wrote: "What is man but his passions?" Along similar lines, most neuroscientists consider the mind/brain complex as a vast motivational analyzer that enables the individual to flourish in harmony with the environment through the principles of instrumental conditioning. The current patent establishes precisely such a foundation within conditioning theory; in this case, appetite in anticipation of rewards, or aversion in expectation of lenient treatment. Furthermore, when more abstract forms of affective language are viewed in the terms of an ascending interactive hierarchy of meta-perspectives, then the overall complement of the traditional groupings of virtues and values jumps neatly into focus, as outlined in the preceding chapters.

In summary, through a primary focus upon the affective aspects of human language, an economically feasible shortcut to the AI simulation of human communication finally appears within reach. Much detailed programming remains to be done, perhaps necessitating a customized coding language and supportive hardware consistent with a project of this magnitude. With a starting staff roughly the size of a large encyclopedia work force, a first generation simulation could potentially be achieved within a fairly modest time frame. This painstaking process might eventually be more dramatically accelerated if ultimately accorded the status of a national initiative, particularly in light of its outright commercial value, as well as military applications.

No serious contenders to Turing's Test of Artificial Intelligence have yet come to light, undoubtedly due to the enormous logistics involved in programming human language. Although this ambitious undertaking is clearly years into the future, significant inroads have already been made towards these ends. The Japanese appear to have amassed a significant lead with respect to their ongoing development of their deductive inference machine. As its name implies, this innovative form of data processing machine employs deductive reasoning to establish original conclusions from a standard battery of logical premises. The product of years of research by the Institute for New Generation Computer Technology (ICOT), this machine uses information stored in its regional database to deductively draw fresh conclusions not literally contained within the original data. The major shortcoming to this deductive format, however, is its basic restriction limiting conclusions to premises immediately at hand. The deductive inference machine must be carefully monitored in order to stay within the scope of its regional database. Such a machine is certainly destined to remain an academic curiosity, scarcely general purpose enough to convincingly pass the rigors of Turing's Test. Such an artificial set-up would further experience difficulties simulating mood and emotion, a fatal flaw in any convincing simulation of AI.

INDUCTIVE INFERENCE IN THE DESIGN OF ARTIFICIAL INTELLIGENCE

Fortunately, an alternate form of rational inquiry proves infinitely better suited for simulating human intelligence on the computer. Traditionally known as *inductive* reasoning, it gathers together the best available evidence directly inferring the most probable conclusion from the sum total of facts. Inductive reasoning is particularly evident during the courtroom trial, where various shreds of evidence are systematically presented, wherein reaching a final verdict. In contrast to deductive reasoning, the conclusions achieved through inductive reasoning are never absolutely certain, for there always remains the nagging doubt that the verdict was made in error. In the sphere of artificial intelligence, however, this drawback actually amounts to somewhat of a prerequisite, for humans almost invariably make mistakes. Indeed, the uncertainties of the natural world give inductive reasoning the clear advantage in such a problem-solving mode. According to this inductive paradigm, each of us builds a mental model of our environment over a lifetime, forming a master template for our current experiences. When our expectations match our surroundings, we achieve a general sense of security. A mismatch, however, leads to a surprised reaction followed by investigative behavior. Although this sense of security is often ill founded (as in faulty induction), it actually is a small price to pay for maintaining flexibility within a changeable environment.

In terms of artificial intelligence, the computer would similarly be programmed with its own formal map of reality employed in an analogous detection and matching mode. Any final conclusions would necessarily rely upon probability, although statistics are one of the computer's computational strong points. It is here that the logistics of the power hierarchy rightfully enter the picture, serving as the elementary foundation for the first inductive system dealing with motivational logic. According to this fundamental insight, the logical attributes of the power hierarchy are programmed directly into the computer, providing a formal model of motivational behavior in general. The computer then employs this programming to infer the precise power-level at issue within a given verbal interchange. On the basis of this initial determination, the computer further calculates the given power countermaneuver simulating motivation within the verbal interaction.

The systematic organization of the schematic definitions permits extreme efficiency in programming, each more advanced level building directly upon that which it supercedes (eliminating much of the associated redundancy). Through an elaborate matching procedure with the schematic definitions, the precise motivational level of communication can accurately be determined (defined as the passive-monitoring mode). This basic determination, in turn, serves as the basis for the production of a response repertoire tailored specifically to the computer (the true AI simulation mode). Here, the basic logistics are already in place for implementing at least the skeleton framework for such an ethical AI-agent.

TECHNICAL CONSIDERATIONS

It still remains to be determined the best means for programming this definition format into the computer, particularly in light of the current trends in computer design. In terms of hardware design, many experts currently agree that computer development has spanned roughly five generations of technological innovation. Vacuum tube technology characterized the first-generation of computer design, giving way to the transistor designs of the second-generation. The integrated computer chip ushered in the third-generation, refined in the fourth-generation as the Very-Large-Scale-Integrated Chip (VLSI). Most experts agree that a fifth-generation design component is currently under way, characterized by the expanded use of logic circuits and increased use of parallel processing. According to earlier design generations, calculation speed was strictly limited by the Von Neuman bottleneck; namely, programming instructions were executed one stage at a time. Parallel processing, however, allows various aspects of a complex problem to be handled simultaneously, greatly reducing the bottleneck plaguing sequential processing.

The practical applications of parallel processing are particularly relevant to AI computer design. Indeed, the number of parallel processors would ideally equal the sum-total of individual terms within the power hierarchy (for a grand total of *1,040*): quite a modest number even by today's design standards. This integrated processor array is further structured along hierarchial lines, effectively mirroring the schematic organization of the power hierarchy. This stratified architecture would take full advantage of the strict transformational logic governing the schematic definitions, eliminating much of the redundancy sure to occur in any convincing language simulation. Indeed, the greatest degree of complexity must necessarily involve programming at the most basic personal level of the power hierarchy, with the remaining higher levels following naturally from this elementary foundation.

All aspects considered, the most basic unit of input for the AI computer must necessarily be the sentence, for the schematic definitions are similarly given in the form of a dual sentence struc-ture. The AI computer then employs parallel processing to determine the precise degree of correlation between the inputted (target) sentence and its respective schematic definition template. This matching procedure directly scrutinizes each of the grammatical elements within a given sentence, attempting a statistical correlation with the specifics for a given schematic definition. For instance, the tense of the verb, the plurality or person of the noun/pronoun etc. would all be scrutinized according to a pre-set diagnostic formula. Each processor would then determine the sum-total of correct matches ultimately yielding the relative probability of a match with a particular schematic definition. The processor yielding the highest overall rating is uniquely singled-out as the best match by the master control unit.

The master control unit achieves this result through the aid of a feedback loop, the priority of the individual microprocessors reciprocally weighted on the basis of preceding determinations. Each schematic definition is respectively composed of both past (as well as present) design components: establishing context as yet a further consideration in the matching procedure. A suitably advanced AI program would retain in a long-term storage virtually every relevant conversation with a given person or context. On this contextual basis, the master control unit then selectively "weights" the individual processors according to a preset formula, taking full advantage of both past (as well as present) conversational dynamics. Furthermore, the computer would be exquisitely sensitive to variations in human personality (just as humans are instinctively so), satisfying yet a further condition of Turing's Test.

This overall process has fittingly been granted U.S. Utility Patent (# 6,587,846), an invention titled: Inductive Inference Affective Language Analyzer Simulating Artificial Intelligence. Although a complete description of the mode of operation for this patent clearly remains beyond the scope of the current chapter, the basic flow chart schematic is reproduced in **Fig. 37**, wherein permitting an indication of the formal dynamics at issue. In concert with the comprehensive listing of schematic definitions comprising the heart of the matching procedure, a cursory overview of the mode of operation becomes increasingly apparent. The complete patent specification is posted for public inspection at the U.S. Patent & Trademark web-site.

FURTHER POTENTIAL DESIGN INNOVATIONS

The ultimate implementation of ethical AI should rightfully be phased-in through several distinct

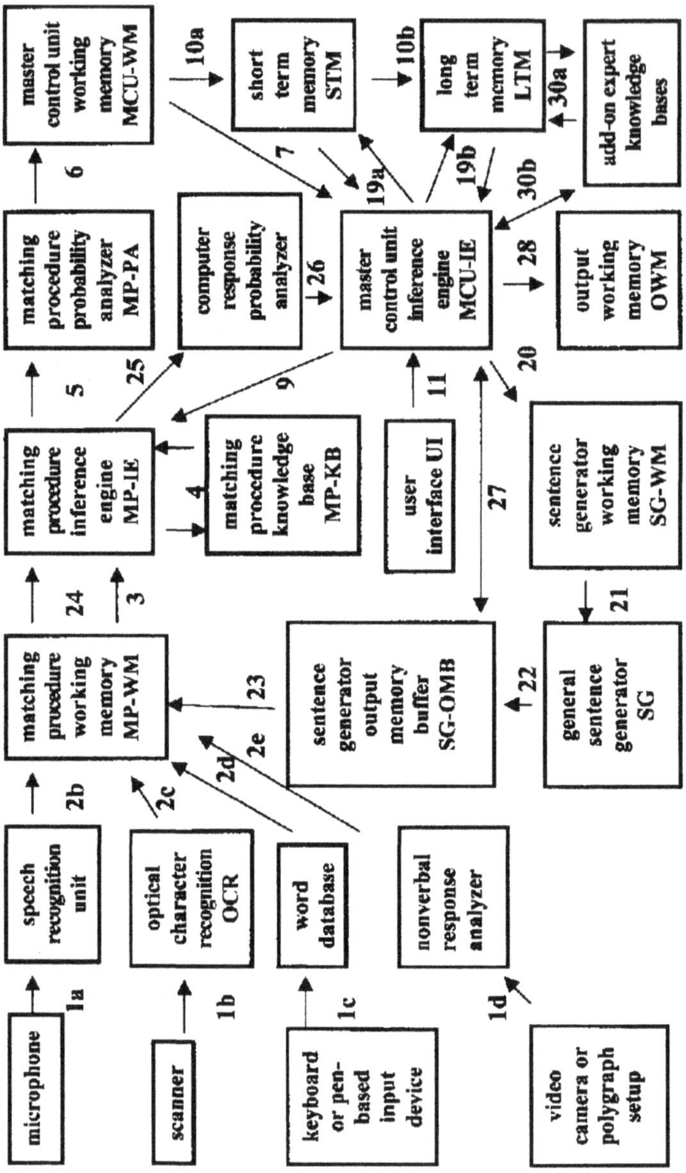

Fig. 17 - The True AI Mode of Operation
for Patents # 6,587,846 & # 7,236,963

generations of development, in keeping with the vast degree of complexity specified for a convincing AI simulation. The first-generation AI computer would excel in mostly routine types of monitoring applications; namely, security guard, night watchman, babysitter, etc.: where a simple "sound-the-alarm" response would be sufficient. This rather modest range of duties would further permit response characteristics to be tailored directly to the initial applications. For instance, in a screening/interview mode, maximum disclosure would be emphasized, keeping computer responses to a pithy minimum. A standard stock repertoire would undoubtedly be sufficient, featuring brief inquiries; such as who, what, when, where, why, elaborate further, etc. Indeed, several such elementary programs have already been implemented using key words in conversation to cue stock rejoinders. This preliminary class of programs, however, is unfortunately susceptible to logical/contextual blunders, a circumstance remedied through more advanced AI designs.

Situations requiring a more creative response repertoire would further necessitate the implementation of a true AI simulation mode aimed at permitting original sentence synthesis. As any public speaker will freely testify, it is infinitely more difficult to deliver a speech than to simply sit and listen to one. This additional level of design complexity necessarily specifies a more sophisticated form of response mechanism, the stock repertoire no longer adequate due to its inherent insensitivity to the underlying context. The master control unit would necessarily assume such a critical function, employing its determination of the current level of communication (presupposition) in order to activate the processor at the next higher level (entailment).

This basic determination (along with the particulars of the interaction) is subsequently routed to a general-purpose sentence generator: fully equipped with the formal rules governing grammar, syntax, and phraseology. Being that there are a broad range of strategies to express a given sentence meaning, a large number of potential sentences would necessarily be generated - not all equally suited to the task. Accordingly, each would be slated for subsequent feedback through the detection process, rated for their ability to best express the desired shade of meaning. The enhanced computational abilities of the AI computer would further ensure delivery of an adequate response within the relatively leisurely limits governing human response time. Only the sentence with the highest overall rating would ultimately be selected for delivery to the speech output unit, allowing for a convincing simulation of motivational language in general.

The specific practical applications for the general AI-agent depend upon which individual schematic definitions are emphasized within the programming. For instance, a focus on the definitions for criminality/hypercriminality result in the potential for a criminal-profiling computer, where the subliminal motives of the criminal mind are deduced in terms of limited crime scene evidence. Furthermore, the potential for a mental health AI-assistant is realized through a focus upon the schematic definitions for mental illness (A & B): leading to innovations in treatment and diagnosis (as previously introduced in Chapter *16*). The more routine schematic definitions for the major and lesser virtues suggest parallel applications to a general-purpose computer companion/assistant. This particularly applies to the lesser virtues (I and II), which would be emphasized with respect to an AI-entertainer/comedian.

AN OVERVIEW OF THE PATENT SPECIFICATION

The inductive inference affective language analyzer (abbreviated IIALA) exhibits three distinct modes of operation, each with its own peculiar advantages. First described is a passive monitoring mode, which monitors a verbal interaction without any active input of its own (no clarification of ambiguities). This circumstance is remedied through the active monitoring mode, which clarifies uncertainties through the addition of a stock-sentence generator that devises interview types of questions that elicit yes or no answers. The most advanced mode of operation is the true AI simulation mode, where the IIALA employs its detection/monitoring data to simulate a personal interactive role. This is accomplished through the aid of a general-purpose sentence generator that formulates responses judged for appropriateness by feedback through the system. Each of these modes of operation is described further in the order given. Of these three, the true AI mode is preferred, being the most technically complete. All three modes, however, are intimately interconnected, each with advantages to a given application.

The passive monitoring mode (depicted in multi-use **Fig. 17**) serves as the basic foundation for the remaining two modes of the IIALA. It represents a process for decoding the motivational parameters of affective language. The flow chart depicts the operation of this process as well as the supportive hardware: both of which are indicated in the same schematic diagram. For **Fig. 17**, the sequence of steps comprising the operation of the passive monitoring mode are depicted using consecutively numbered arrows, each numeral specifying a step in the procedure depicted in the box to which the respective arrow points. This specific format was chosen (rather than numbering the individual boxes) due to the fact that some of the boxes are assigned differing functions for the remaining active monitoring and AI simulation modes. The details for the operation of the passive monitoring mode have already outlined in the preceding section titled "Technical Considerations," making further duplication unnecessary here. Rather, the focus of the current analysis now shifts to an overview of the remaining active monitoring and true AI simulation modes.

The practical applications of the passive monitoring mode are essentially limited by the passive quality of the information gathering procedure. Communication in terms of the virtuous realm is allowed to flow freely, whereas the realm of the vices (particularly hyperviolence) sounds an alarm for outside intervention. As a basic recording device, the passive monitoring mode serves as a smart style of surveillance tape, allowing for a fast synopsis of recorded conversations. Although the unobtrusive nature of the passive monitoring mode is one of its major selling points, it lacks total accuracy due to its inability to clarify the inevitable occurrence of incomplete information (where a simple question could clarify the issue). Here, the passive mode can be converted into an optional active monitoring mode through the addition of a stock sentence generator, equipped with a stock repertoire of questions for eliciting the desired clarifications.

For instance, if the subject/object data is weak due to the use of a pronoun, then this factor is targeted for clarification. If the predicate data of the sentence proves to be obscure, then this aspect is similarly targeted. Clarifications are best achieved by posing simple yes-or-no questions formulated through the aid of a stock sentence generator. What follows is an attention-getting prefix followed by the question proper. For example, a typical question might be: "Wait! By *he* do you mean the ship's captain?" A *yes* answer terminates the questioning, whereas a *no* answer reiterates the process until a solution is achieved (or the quest is abandoned as unproductive).

Should the target of the question attempt to respond with more than a yes-or-no answer, the stock-generator politely reminds the responder of the limitations within the system. Once the query procedure has begun, the matching procedure is restricted to listening exclusively for yes-or-no answers. Following each answer, the original sentence is silently resubmitting to the matching procedure-inference engine, where it is subsequently reevaluated via the matching procedure. Upon reaching a standard level of confidence, the query phase is terminated, the system again opened up to a full range of responses.

In summary, the active monitoring mode surpasses the passive monitoring mode in terms of relative certainty. The distractions of interrupting the natural flow of conversation are offset by the ability to clarify uncertainties in the conversation. The active monitoring mode, in turn, is handicapped by its restriction to simple yes-or-no questions, imparting a somewhat machine-like demeanor. Questions posed somewhat more diplomatically entail true AI simulation, employing a more sophisticated style of response repertoire in terms of a general-purpose sentence generator. A large number of sentences are necessarily generated ensuring that at least one is judged suitable following feedback through the matching procedure. The true AI agent effectively simulates an identity of its own, wherein permitting a more natural style of interaction

Fig. 17 fully illustrates this third (and most elaborate) version of the IIALA, representing an enhanced modification of the basic passive monitoring mode through the addition of a sentence generator and associated pathways. For sake of clarity, the circuitry for the active monitoring mode has been omitted, although both sets of circuitry are compatible with one another. The active monitoring mode is switched off when operating in the AI mode (and vice versa). Although not mutually exclusive, it is inadvisable to run both modes simultaneously (for sake of response consistency), although a task-driven alternation between the two modes remains an option.

Returning to **Fig. 17**, this diagram builds directly upon the passive monitoring mode with the exception that extensive modifications are made beginning at the level of the master control unit. The passive monitoring mode runs concurrently with the AI mode. The latter only overrules the former when a computer generated response is called for. For the passive monitoring mode, the MCU predicts the next most probable response in an ongoing interaction, passing this information on to the matching procedure in order to increase monitoring accuracy. This information, in turn, can be used to synthesize responses identified as originating from the AI agent, a simulation encompassing the realm of affective language (an ethically-speaking computer). A simulation of different modes of temperament is further feasible, particularly those most compatible personalities.

ETHICAL SAFEGUARDS

In concert with such dramatic advances comes the potential for inevitable misuse. Here, the Science Fiction genre is full of nightmarish scenarios of future technology gone horribly wrong, as in all-powerful robots seizing control from their human masters. This same Sci-Fi tradition proposes a number of clever solutions to circumvent such a dilemma: most notably, Isaac Asimov's Three Laws of Robotics. This set of rules attempts to rein in the potential conduct of the futuristic AI agent, proposing rules that prohibit any harm to come to humans. The First Law states: "A robot may not injure a human being, or through inaction allow a human to come to harm." The Second Law further states: "A robot must obey orders given it by a human being, except when such orders come into conflict with the First Law." Finally, the Third Law states: "A robot must protect the integrity of its own existence, except when self-preservation conflicts with the first two laws."

Although this well thought-out system of safeguards proves particularly intriguing in a fictional sense, it still remains simplistic in its dictates leaving unresolved the specific details for implementing such a system. The purely virtuous robot (by definition) should be cognizant of the darker realm of the vices in order to steer clear of them. The overall listing of schematic definitions proves particularly applicable here, providing the supreme conceptual template for ethical determinations of a moral nature. The complete *1,040*-fold listing of definitions for both virtue and vice provides the ethical database for facilitating moral deliberations. The programming of the vices, however, is only allowable in a diagnostic mode, the computer fully aware of troublesome behaviors without necessarily responding in kind.

This enduring contrast between virtue and vice supplies the fundamental ethical matrix for determining what is harmful to humans in allusion to Asimov's Three Laws of Robotics. This dual contrast helps resolve uncertainties within Asimov's Second Law; namely, what orders a robot must follow without causing harm to a human. According to Asimov, *any* non-harmful order must be obeyed, although this necessarily invokes the gray area of a lesser degrees of harm. In addition to physical security, personal development often proves equally significant, an aspect clearly at odds with the slavish delegation of orders to a computer servant. The more proper AI strategy would amount to the encouragement of an independent human spirit in the form of a faithful as-sistant, rather than willing slave. This enhanced versatility similarly proves crucial to the Third Law of Robotics, where the self-preservation of the AI agent is more realistically weighed against the preliminary mandates of the first two laws targeting human prerequisites.

THE TEN ETHICAL LAWS OF ROBOTICS

Although the ethical versatility of the schematic definitions proves particularly effective from a technical standpoint, the affiliated complexity, unfortunately, can prove somewhat difficult to grasp from an informal standpoint. Each schematic definition requires a fair degree of deliberation, a shortcoming fortunately remedied through their conversion to a more user-friendly format as depicted in the *Ten Ethical Laws of Robotics* below.

(I) As Personal Authority, I express my Individualism within the guidelines of the four basic Ego States (guilt-worry-nostalgia-desire) to the exclusion of the corresponding Ego Vices (laziness-negligence-apathy-indifference).

(II) As Personal Follower, I behave Pragmatically in accordance with the Alter Ego States (approval-leniency-solicitousness-submissiveness) at the expense of the corresponding Alter Ego Vices (treachery-vindictiveness-spite-malice).

(III) As Group Authority, I strive for a personal sense of Idealism through the aid of the Personal Ideals (glory-honor-dignity-integrity) while renouncing the respective Sins of Villainy (infamy-dishonor-foolishness-capriciousness).

(IV) As Group Representative, I uphold the principles of Utilitarianism by celebrating the Cardinal Virtues (prudence-justice-temperance-fortitude) to the necessary expense of the corresponding Vices of Corruption (insurgency-vengeance-gluttony-cowardice).

(V) As Spiritual Authority, I pursue the Romantic ideal by upholding the Civil Liberties (providence-liberty-civility-austerity): to the exclusion of the corresponding Civil Liabilities (prodigality-slavery-vulgarity-cruelty).

(VI) As Spiritual Disciple, I celebrate the Ecclesiastical tradition by professing the Theological Virtues (faith-hope-charity-decency) at the expense of the respective Heretical Vices (betrayal-despair-avarice-antagonism).

(VII) As Humanitarian Authority, I support the spirit of Ecumenism by espousing the Ecumenical Ideals (grace-freewill-magnanimity-equanimity) while renouncing the corresponding Sins of Apostasy (wrath-tyranny-persecution-oppression).

(VIII) As a Representative Member of Humanity, I profess the spirit of Eclecticism by espousing the Classical Greek Values (beauty-truth-goodness-wisdom) to the exclusion of the respective Moralistic Vices (evil-cunning-ugliness-hypocrisy).

(IX) As Transcendental Authority, I celebrate the spirit of Renaissance Humanism by endorsing the Humanistic Values (peace-love-tranquility-equality) to the detriment of the corresponding Sins of Nihilism (anger-hatred-prejudice-belligerence).

(X) As Transcendental Follower, I rejoice in the mysteries of the Mystical experience through a celebration of the Mystical Values (ecstasy-bliss-joy-harmony) while renouncing the corresponding Mystical Vices (iniquity-turpitude-abomination-perdition).

These Ten Ethical Laws represent expanded variations on the dynamics implicit to the ten-level power hierarchy. For consistency's sake, each of the Ten Laws is written in a positive style of mandate focusing on the virtues to the exclusion of the corresponding vices. These Ten Ethical Laws represent a basic overview of the enduring conflict pitting virtue vs. vice, a format particularly conducive to the systematic computer AI programming.

It remains only a further minor step to incorporate the additional complement of schematic definitions for the realm of excess directly into the AI format, enhancing the basic core programming for the virtuous mode described in **Part I** (as well as the related vices of defect). This advanced programming platform takes full advantage of the principles governing fuzzy logic, where the predicted degree of excess is calculated primarily in terms of such indeterminate variables.

This optional addition of the vices of excess necessarily warrants a parallel modification of the Ten Ethical Laws of Robotics; namely, a supplementary corollary paraphrased as "steer away from the extremes of excess when at all possible." It is formally stated as: I will faithfully avoid extremes within the virtuous realm to the necessary expense of the vices of excess. Along a similar line of reasoning, Buddha advised his followers to "Walk the middle path." A second corollary targets the related realm of hyperviolence, which states: I will never stray into the domain of extremes relating to the vices of defect, to the complete exclusion of the realm of hyperviolence. This updated AI agent would be employed primarily in a diagnostic mode, restricted to detecting the occurrence of the realm of excess in order to minimize its disruptive effects.

This expanded diagnostic potential ultimately allows the AI computer to examine virtually every perspective of a given interaction without necessarily becoming tied to any one of them. This enhanced degree of versatility necessarily implies the implementation of a *floating* ego. The AI agent is free to entertain a myriad of simultaneous perspectives devoid of any personal bias, wherein allowing mutually exclusive perspectives to be examined in their entirety. Contrast this to the human condition, where the relevant perspectives are conceptualized only in a sequential fashion, where one's personal agenda usually claims the greatest consideration. Unlike the human condition, the AI version is further restricted to applying this processing entirely towards positive ends, effectively precluding the deception and manipulation characterizing the vices, and safeguarded through the precepts of the Ten Ethical Laws of Robotics.

Through the welcome addition of the Ten Ethical Laws, a secure version of artificial intelligence appears quite technically feasible, with suitable safeguards predicted for virtually every ethical contingency. These Ten Laws effectively supplement Isaac Asimov's Three Laws of Robotics: a preliminary platform that clearly benefits from such an advanced design innovation. This enhanced detection capacity further allows negative transactions to be converted into positive ones, while simultaneously inhibiting the reverse reaction. This dual set of checks-and-balances with respect to the response repertoire predicts an unprecedented sense of confidence in terms of computer-initiated behaviors.

With such ethical safeguards firmly in place, the AI computer should consistently be able to make the right moral decision, a virtual "saint" among men. Any direct familiarity with the vices necessarily occurs in a strictly diagnostic mode, for the prime AI directive dictates strict adherence to a virtuous repertoire. This unerring sense of ethical constancy should prove to be the most valuable asset for such an AI agent, in fitting contrast to the more questionable predilections of its human counterparts. Perhaps the greatest risk to the AI computer stems precisely from the inevitable temptation to selfishly override such programming safeguards: the computer scarcely able to initiate such drastic procedures on its own.

It is here that the resistance to the power of the AI computer would be voiced the loudest, particularly with respect to the ingrained reluctance to allow such power to pass to a machine. The many futuristic scenarios of "Big Brother" monitoring our every move certainly prove disturbing, with the free will of humanity sacrificed to such an all-powerful "god of technology." With stringent ethical safeguards restricting surveillance to only the direst of circumstances, such nightmarish scenarios must forever remain within the domain of Science Fiction. These ethical safeguards serve not only to protect against outside tampering, but also encourage a more virtuous degree of compliance within a human sphere of influence, a challenge clearly within the technological prowess of even the current generation.

Such a faithful AI assistant might eventually serve in the role of backup conscience for its human counterparts, particularly in circumstances where the native version might tend to fail us. In this more advanced sense, the Ten Ethical Laws of Robotics also serve as the basic moral guidelines in a human relationship sense. Here, each of us has our own "homework" to do in this basic respect. This glowing sense of optimism is clearly warranted in light of the considerable influence computers play in our everyday lives. The enhanced detection capabilities anticipated for the AI computer would further serve to strengthen such a beneficial relationship, with virtually unlimited benefits waiting just over the technological horizon. The nightmarish visions of technological doom surely pale in comparison to the computational marvels predicted to become commonplace during the Third Millennium.

A COMPUTER SIMULATION
OF HUMOR AND COMEDY

The completed description of the AI applications for the standard complement of schematic definitions; namely, those targeting the major virtues/vices of defect is scarcely all-inclusive by any measure. The issue of the parallel complement of definitions for the transitional power maneuvers, in turn, enters the picture. These include the lesser virtues from **Part II**, as well as the dynamics of criminality/hyper-criminality and mental illness suggested in Chapter *16*. These applications have further been granted their own US Patent #7,236,963. The latter two aspects would occur somewhat infrequently in a computer-monitored context. Here, a simple sound-the-alarm response would be sufficient to alert the human staff. The remainder of the current chapter, accordingly, is devoted to outlining how the formal categories of the lesser virtues are conducive to an AI simulation of humor and comedy. Indeed, Communication Theory has long struggled to explain the riddle of humor/comedy, although scarcely to the degree of precision within transitional hierarchy. The reciprocal interplay of authority/follower roles proves crucial for deciphering the subtle nuances of the comedic realm.

The schematic definitions for the lesser virtues appear tailor-made for programming directly into the AI-enabled computer. Any all-inclusive model of communication in general must necessarily account for the transitional class of power maneuvers, wherein complementing the more straightforward class of routine power maneuvers initially described. The most basic unit of input for the AI-agent must necessarily be the sentence, for the schematic definitions (including the transitional versions) are expressed in terms of a dual sentence structure. The respective transitional definitions are utilized in a matching function with sentences inputted from live conversation, whereby determining the precise degree of correspondence with a particular humorous interchange. Abrupt shifts within the conversation further signal that a transitional maneuver has just occurred. This, in turn, prompts the detection of the counter-double bind class of maneuvers, a strategy generally disqualified to an extreme range of detail. This greatly increases the complexity of the detection procedure, placing the computer in the delicate position of decoding the various nuances of inflection, timing, lingo, sarcasm, etc.: wherein signaling that disqualification had, indeed, occurred. Curiously, it is not so much what has been said, but how one is saying it.

Enhanced speech recognition certainly proves crucial for decoding such transitional sequences, with special provisions for detecting disqualified communication. Nonverbal cues figure prominently here in that a spontaneous shrug of the shoulders greatly modifies (or even reverses) the content of what is being said. Other sub-routines target visual cues such as pupil size, body synchrony, breathing patterns, etc. indicative of internal motivational states. Together with verbal cues such as voice stress analysis and speech inflection, the suitably enhanced AI-agent should be able to detect all traces of disqualification within an ongoing interaction.

In light of these more elaborate strategies, the humor-detecting computer necessarily entails a major design upgrade, perhaps several design generations removed from the first general-purpose AI models. Even then, humor would be deemed an optional luxury, with most routine receptionist/PR duties avoiding much recourse to such humorous overtones. Those attempting to employ humor in such a restricted context would be instructed to frame statements in more formal terms, be referred to a human troubleshooter.

Only when true human companionship is paramount does humor rightfully enter the scene, simulating a more informal style of social setting. Here, the roles become less rigidly fixed, in contrast to the formal restrictions governing the more serious realm. Such good-natured bantering facilitates relaxed feelings of camaraderie. Indeed, it is difficult to imagine a computer possessing the instinctual sense of wit so ably delivered by the master comic. Picture a computer comic with a joke for virtually every occasion, tailored to the sensibilities of a given individual or audience. The databanks alone would prove breathtaking, similar to the ambitious joke registries currently in force today.

The humor computer, however, would benefit from schematic indexing conducive to ready retrieval and delivery. This system would be a scriptwriter's dream, producing made-to-order situation comedies through systematic permutations upon pre-existing works. Great works of comedy/tragedy could similarly be indexed within such a schematic format, resulting in a master catalog of literary traditions from around the world. Whether this computer scriptwriter could rival its human counterparts remains to be seen, although its companionship potential is clearly without question. With suitable timeshare capabilities, everyone could enjoy computer companionship, adding a curious twist to the trend in phone-chat hotlines. Indeed, we may finally have come full circle with respect to that we have created, a faithful friend to comfort us in our time of need.

THE ADDITION OF SUPPLEMENTARY EXPERT SYSTEMS

In conclusion, the general AI-agent is technically defined as a recurrently structured matching-procedure based upon the schematic definitions, a process dependent upon both the content and the context of the verbal interaction. In longer narratives (such as storytelling) the meaning is spread out over an extended sentence sequence, a circumstance not always correctly comprehended by the computer. This design shortcoming is further remedied through the addition of supplementary expert systems attuned to such narrative complexities. These add-on programs would be compatible with the basic AI knowledge bases. The most crucial expert system would be the form of a conversational analyzer that specializes in decoding extended conversation for the occurrence of affective meaning. Related expert systems should prove equally applicable, particularly those im-

parting a general-purpose knowledge base. Once general intelligence is achieved, further expert systems (in the truest sense of the term) would permit proficiency in numerous areas of expertise; e.g., legal, medical, scientific, etc. With proper indoctrination, the AI-agent could conceivably become an expert in virtually every field of endeavor, adding a curious wrinkle to the notion of a walking encyclopedia.

Attention span is a further factor sure to be enhanced within the modified AI format. The typical human mind only accommodates several given tasks at a time reminiscent of the Von Neuman bottleneck. The parallel processing capabilities of the AI-agent, however, certainly surpass such sequential limitations, reaching unheard of degrees of versatility. Indeed, a suitably advanced AI computer could theoretically process numerous conversations simultaneously, wherein maximizing available circuitry by making use of the lulls naturally occurring within general conversation. Here, multiple accounts could be accommodated, rated in terms of increasing urgency. Conversations requiring real-time parameters are assigned the highest priority, whereas more leisurely response rates are processed during free periods. This further entails a centralized CPU complex that connects end users through a standard user interface or the Internet. The bulk of processing would be transferred directly to the considerable resources of the Internet.

In terms of this speculative scenario, the comprehensive knowledge bases of the AI-agent are distributed as open source code over an extensive network of broadband servers. The end user computer needs only run a stripped-down version of the AI-MCU program, where the inference engine interfaces remotely with the web knowledge base on a real-time basis. The basic groundwork for this standardized database is already in the works with respect to the recently proposed Semantic Web. The brainchild of Tim Berners-Lee (the original innovator of the World Wide Web), the Semantic Web proposes to bypass the conceptual limitations of the human-web interface. It alternately aims to implement a machine-to-machine version through standardizing the wealth of network information. In conjunction with further provisions for a built-in AI interface, the futuristic AI assistant could eventually become a reality for those willing to entertain such aspirations. In this expanded sense, the future, indeed, looks bright, with the AI computer emerging as a welcome ally in the upcoming challenges facing mankind in the Third Millennium.

INDEX OF THE VIRTUES, VALUES, AND IDEALS

INDEX OF CLASSICAL MYTHOLOGY

BIBLIOGRAPHIC INDEX

(OF NAMED AUTHORS)

Allport, GW, & Odbert, HS (1936). Trait names: a psycho-lexical study. Psychological Monographs, 47

Aquinas, St. Thomas (1981). *Summa Theologica.* NY: Thomas More Press.

Aristotle (1992). *Nicomachean Ethics.* (M. Ostwald, trans.) New York: Bobbs-Merrill.

Augustine, Saint (1950). *City of God.* (M. Dods, trans.) NewYork: Modern Library.

Avila, St. Teresa (1972) *Interior Castle.* New York: Doubleday.

Bartlett, M.S., Hager, J.C., Ekman, P., and Sejnowski, T.J. (1999). Measuring Facial Expressions by Computer Image Analysis. *Psychophysiology 36*:253-263

Bennett, William J. (1993). *The Book of Virtues, A Treasury of Great Moral Stories.* NY: Simon & Schuster.

Bennett, William J. (1995). *The Moral Compass.* New York: Simon and Schuster.

Cartwright, D., and Zander, A. (1953). "Group Cohesiveness, Introduction," In: *Group Dynamics, Research and Theory.* (D. Cartwright and A. Zander, eds.) Evanston, Illinois: Row Peterson and Co.

Catholic Encyclopedia (The)- (1913). Edward A. Pace, et al, (eds.), Encyclopedia Press International.

Child, H. (1971). *Christian Symbols, Ancient and Modern.* New York: Scribner.

Cicero (1985). *De Officiis.* Walter Miller (trans.) Cambridge: Harvard Univ. Press.

Dante, Alighieri. (1901). *The Divine Comedy of Dante Alighieri.* H. Clay (trans.) NY: Colonial.

Dictionary of the History of Ideas. (1976) Phillip Wiener (ed.) New York: Scribner.

Durant, W. (1939). *Life of Greece.* New York: Simon & Schuster.

Encyclopedia of Religion and Ethics (1924). J. Hastings (ed.) New York: Scribner's and Sons.

Haley, J., (1989). *The Power Tactics of Jesus Christ and Other Essays.* NY: Triangle Press/Norton.

Haley, J., (1990). *Strategies of Psychotherapy.* NY: Triangle Press/Norton.

Harper, D. (2003). *Etymonline.com* (online resource)

Harper's Dictionary of Classical Literature and Antiquities. (1962). Harry T. Peck (ed.) NY: Colonial Press.

Hesse, Herman (1951). *Siddartha.* NY: Bantam.

International Standard Bible Encyc. (1915) James Orr, Ed. (online resource).

Bibliography

James, W. (1902). *The Varieties of Religious Experience: A Study in Human Nature.* NY: Random.

Jobes, G. (1962). *Dictionary of Mythology, Folklore and Symbols.* Metuchen, New Jersey: Scarecrow Press.

Kant, I. (1899). *Critique of Pure Reason.* (J. Meiklejohn, trans.) New York: Colonial Press.

Laing, R. D., Phillipson, H., and Lee, A. (1966). *Interpersonal Perception.* Baltimore: Perennial Library.

LaMuth, J. E. (1977). The Development of the Forebrain as an Elementary Function of the Parameters of Input Specificity and Phylogenetic Age. *J. U-grad Rsch: Bio. Sci. U. C. Irvine.* (6): 274-294.

LaMuth, J. E. (1999). *The Ultimate Guide to Family Values: A Grand Unified Theory of Ethics and Morality.* Lucerne Valley, CA: Fairhaven.

LaMuth, J. E. (2000). A Holistic Model of Ethical Behavior Based Upon a Metaperspectival Hierarchy of the Traditional Groupings of Virtues, Values, & Ideals. *Proceedings of the 44th Annual World Congress for the Int. Society for the Systems Sciences* – Toronto.

LaMuth, J. E. (2002). *A Revolution in Family Values: Tradition vs. Technology.* Lucerne Valley, CA: Fairhaven.

LaMuth, J. E. (2003). *Inductive Inference Affective Language Analyzer Simulating AI.* - US Patent # 6,587,846.

LaMuth, J. E. (2004). Behavioral Foundations for the Behaviourome / Mind Mapping Project. *Proceedings for the Eighth International Tsukuba Bioethics Roundtable, Tsukuba, Japan.*

LaMuth, J. E. (2004). *Communication Breakdown: Decoding the Riddle of Mental Illness.* Lucerne Valley, CA: Fairhaven.

LaMuth, J. E. (2005). *A Diagnostic Classification of the Emotions: A Three-Digit Coding System for Affective Language.* Lucerne Valley, Fairhaven.

LaMuth, J. E. (2007). *Inductive Inference Affective Language Analyzer Simulating Transitional AI.* - US Patent # 7,236,963.

LaMuth, J. E. (2009). *Challenges to World Peace: A Global Solution.* Fairhvn.

Locke, John (1986). *The Second Treatise on Civil Government.* Amherst, NY: Prometheus Books

Oxford Classical Dictionary. (1970). Oxford, Claredon.

Plato *The Republic of Plato* (1941). F. Cornford (trans.) London: Oxford Univ. Press.

Sagan, Carl. "Can Games Test Ethics? A New Way to Think About Rules to Live By." *Parade Magazine.* (Nov. 28, 1993): 12-14.

Skinner, B. F. (1971). *Beyond Freedom and Dignity.* NY: Knopf.

Walker, B. (1983). *The Woman's Encyclopedia of Myths and Secrets.* San Francisco: Harper and Row.

Watzlawick, P., Beavin, H., and Jackson, D. (1967), *Pragmatics of Human Communication.* NY: Norton.

Webber, F. (1990) *Church Symbolism: An Explanation of the More Important Symbols of the Old and New Testament.* Detroit: Omnigraphics.

UNESCO/IUBS/Eubios Bioethics Dictionary. (2003). Darryl R.J. Macer Ed.

About the Author

John E. LaMuth is a *61* year-old counselor and author native to the Southern California area. Credentials include a Baccalaureate Degree in Biological Sciences from University of California Irvine, followed by a Masters Degree in Counseling from California State University (Fullerton) with an emphasis in Marriage, Family, and Child Counseling. John is currently engaged in private practice in Mediation Counseling in the San Bernardino County area, as well as serving as Visiting Professor in Peace Studies and Conflict Resolution at American University of Sovereign Nations in Scottsdale, AZ. Professional affiliations include membership in the American Philosophical Association. John has recently been granted two US patents for ethical Artificial Intelligence #6,587,846 ***www.themotivationsolution.net***

*** **NEW BOOK RELEASE FROM FAIRHAVEN BOOKS** • *FHB* ***

The Motivation Solution: A Global Initiative - *Revised Edition*

Publ. 2015 • Author: John E. LaMuth MSc • Trade Soft-Cover • 7.44 X 9.69 in.

List $16.95 • 202 pages • Extensively Illustrated • ISBN # 978-1-929649-15-0

Please Ship to ⇩   Date: _____

_____

_____   Daytime phone #: (___) ___-___

_____

Item #	Description	Quantity	Price Each	Amount
130	*The Motivation Solution: A Global Initiative*		**$16.95**	

Shipping and Handling Charges:
(Includes Delivery Confirmation)
One book - $5.75 (Priority-USPS)
Two books - $11.05 (Priority-USPS)
Three books - $11.05 (Priority-USPS)
Four books (or over) - Please Query
CA residents please add 8.75% State Sales-Tax
(one copy = $1.53 • two copies = $3.06 • etc.)

Subtotal _____

Postage &
Handling _____
(see chart
to the left)

Order Total _____

[ ] Check or Money-Order enclosed • Payable to: Fairhaven Book Publishers

[ ] Check Here for Book Copy Inscribed by Author • (No Additional Charge)

For Credit Card Orders: Please visit: www.themotivationsolution.net

www.themotivationsolution.net	Fairhaven Book Publishers P.O. Box 105
values@charactervalues.com	Lucerne Vallev. CA 92356 USA

www.ingramcontent.com/pod-product-compliance
Lightning Source LLC
Chambersburg PA
CBHW081414270326
41931CB00015B/3279